RUNNING THE GAUNTLET

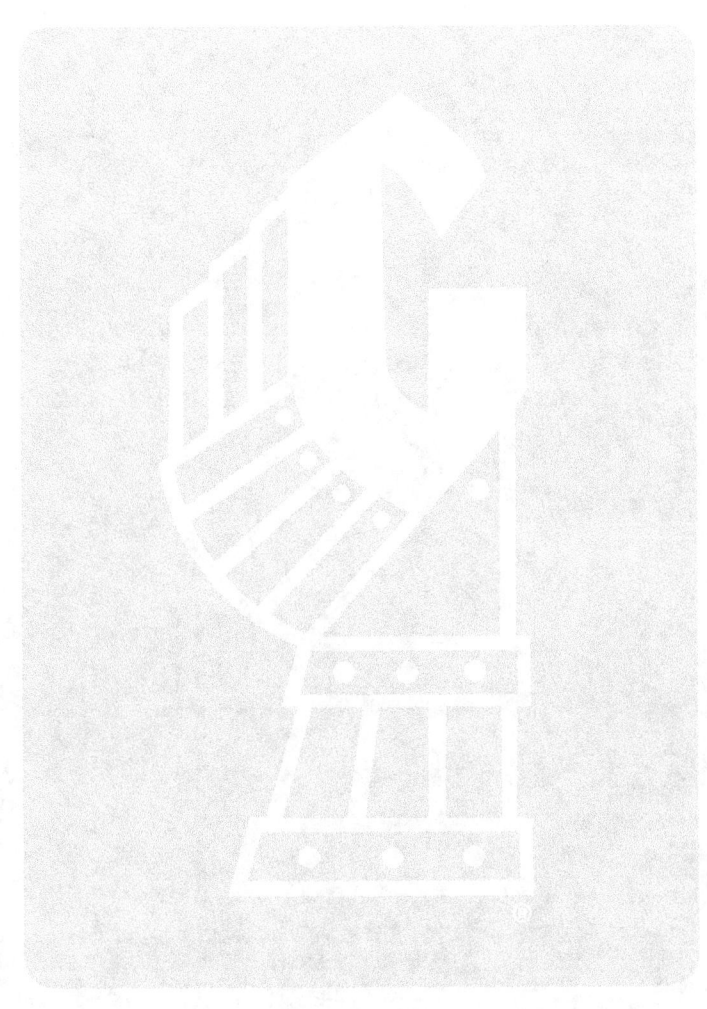

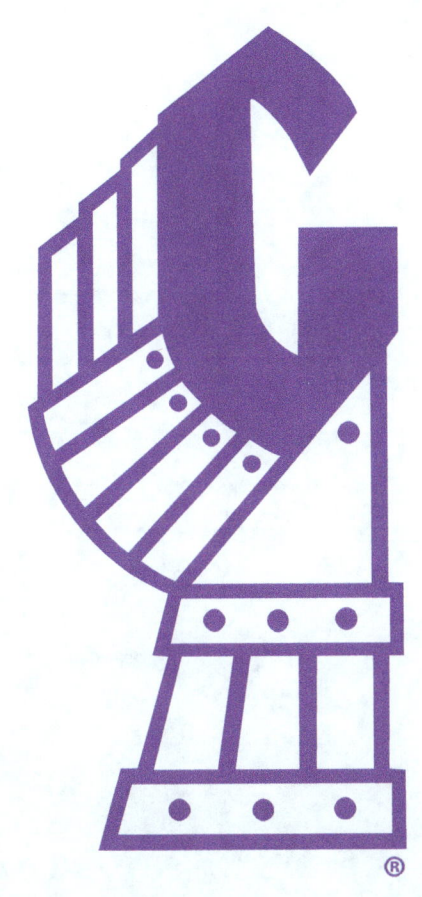

RUNNING THE GAUNTLET

An Intimate History of
the Modern Body Piercing Movement

Jim Ward

"...in the beginning there was Gauntlet."

posted to the rec.arts.bodyart Usenet newsgroup*
June 16, 1998

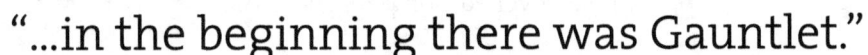

*Created in the early 1990s, rec.arts.bodyart evolved from an online mailing list for tattooing, piercing, and body modification enthusiasts (circa 1989) run by Karl Ëlvis MacRae and originally called "the primitives list" after the book *Modern Primitives*. With input and inspiration from Harry Ugol and Chris Wayne, the usenet group came into being. In due course Lani Teshima-MIller and Anne Greenblatt started collecting and posting FAQ documents. The group has since moved over to Facebook.

ISBN: 978-0-9888516-0-3

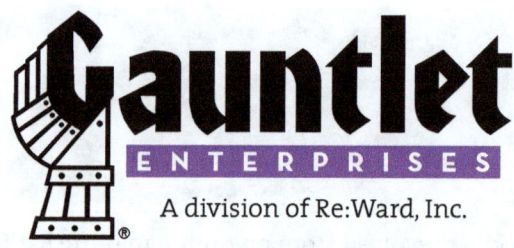

A division of Re:Ward, Inc.

Cover photo: Michael Adrianne

To

Doug Malloy
Fakir Musafar
Elayne Angel
Michaela Grey

and to all the men and women
who helped Gauntlet establish
the standard of excellence
in the body piercing industry ...
I couldn't have done it without you;

And to

Barry Blanchard ...
You made this book possible;

And most of all, to

My beloved partner Drew ...
I wouldn't be here without you.

ACKNOWLEDGEMENTS

Projects like this one don't happen in a vacuum. Though I am responsible for the storytelling, many others have helped bring it to life and hopefully make it a more enjoyable read. I would particularly like to thank Annie Sprinkle, whose constant encouragement and belief in the book have helped keep me moving forward, however slowly, even when I had doubts it would ever see the light of day. I'd also like to thank Elayne Angel, who has helped me refine the content, and to thank Paul King, Michaela Grey, James Weber, Drew Ward, and everyone else who has provided input and feedback. Finally, very special thanks to Lena Strayhorn for copyediting the manuscript and to Michael Osiris Snuffin for doing the same with the finished book.

FOREWORD

In 1981, when I walked for the first time into Gauntlet Enterprises, a small but stylish retail storefront on Santa Monica Boulevard in West Hollywood, I had no idea history was in the making. Modern piercing was being ushered into our contemporary culture then and there. All I knew was that I was thrilled by body piercing and utterly delighted to learn I wasn't alone in what was, at the time, a very obscure pursuit.

I got my nipples pierced that day at the first and only piercing specialty business that existed in the U.S.—and the world. I met a soft-spoken and kindly gentleman there, Jim Ward, Gauntlet's owner and founder. Over the ensuing years, I would see him many times as I brought in countless others to be pierced. Jim and I would become friends, and eventually he would employ me as Manager of the L.A. studio and later Vice President of Gauntlet, Inc.

But back in the early 80s, body piercing wasn't as widely practiced yet. It was still quite underground and many people had never even heard of this way to augment the human body. It was so misunderstood that my former gynecologist broke patient confidentiality (and the law!) to tell my parents that I'd had my nipples pierced. They thought I might need to be institutionalized for harming myself. That may sound absurd now that piercing is so widespread, but it is indicative of how esoteric it was then, and how incredibly differently piercing was perceived just a few decades ago.

By contrast, I describe the current popularity in my book, *The Piercing Bible*:

"In recent times, body piercing has exploded as a form of personal expression nearly anyone may use to enhance their appearance, self-image, and quality of life. The phenomenon is so pervasive that housewives, police officers, and schoolteachers wear tongue, navel, nipple, and other piercings (although you might never know if they don't tell

you). Millions of people are already pierced, and countless more are considering body piercings or have pierced family members, students, or patients...."

Body piercing may not be considered entirely mainstream or accepted in all walks of life, but it is certainly familiar as an option people in today's society may choose for themselves. This massive shift from obscurity to prevalence would likely not have taken place without Jim Ward and Gauntlet. In fact, piercing might never have emerged to become the booming worldwide industry we have today if not for his founding the first legitimate, professional piercing business, and starting the very first piercing publication. His pioneering efforts have literally changed the face (and other body parts) of modern man and woman.

Jim is an enigmatic man; he can be difficult to read. He is reserved, perhaps even reticent, yet he exudes a calm confidence that belies his internal struggles. Even though I have known Jim and been close to him all these years, I was unaware of many of the tribulations he suffered or the fascinating details of his story until he wrote this riveting book. I was stricken by the unflinching honesty of his introspection and the rawness of his revelations.

This volume contains a truly remarkable wealth of historical images. Through them, I was enveloped and transported back to meet all of the characters and experience the key moments of Jim's past.

In the following pages, Jim bares his soul to bring you on the extraordinary journey that led him to establish that first piercing business, expand it to a mighty empire, and tragically, lose it all. Through his efforts, the piercing industry as we know it today was born. This is an up close and personal view of both Jim's own history and the true account of how one man launched a unique business that changed the world.

—Elayne Angel, Author of *The Piercing Bible—The Definitive Guide to Safe Body Piercing* and former Gauntlet Vice President of Southern California Operations

INTRODUCTION

It's late October of 2007. My partner Drew and I are in the local hardware store looking at the Halloween decorations. This is our favorite holiday, and annually our home becomes resplendent with witches, pumpkins, cats, skeletons, and ghouls of every sort and description. On the living room desk we erect a village of porcelain buildings, each one spookier than the last, and every year we enjoy looking for an addition to this burgeoning community.

The offerings this year aren't plentiful, perhaps only half a dozen. But what catches our eye is a box labeled in letters shaped like dripping blood. Inside, it says, is "Blackbeard's Tattoo and Piercing Parlor." I chuckle. This bit of American kitsch produced in China in the thousands if not millions gives testament to the ubiquitous place piercing has taken in popular culture today.

Body piercing has become such a pervasive part of life that many people, especially those born after the early 1980s, don't give it a second thought. Countless ardent devotees take it for granted, never questioning its origins. How many have ever wondered where the most common piercings came from and how they got their names?[1] Where did the piercing techniques and the implements in common usage today originate? Where did so many of those jewelry designs come from? Why is the Brown & Sharpe wire gauge system, originally used for measuring precious metals, now widely used for all body piercing jewelry, even stainless steel which has traditionally been measured by a different system? Who first introduced niobium piercing jewelry? The answers lie in Gauntlet's history.

To put things in perspective, turn back the clock to the mid-1970s, a historic era in the chronicle of piercing, when the world was a very dif-

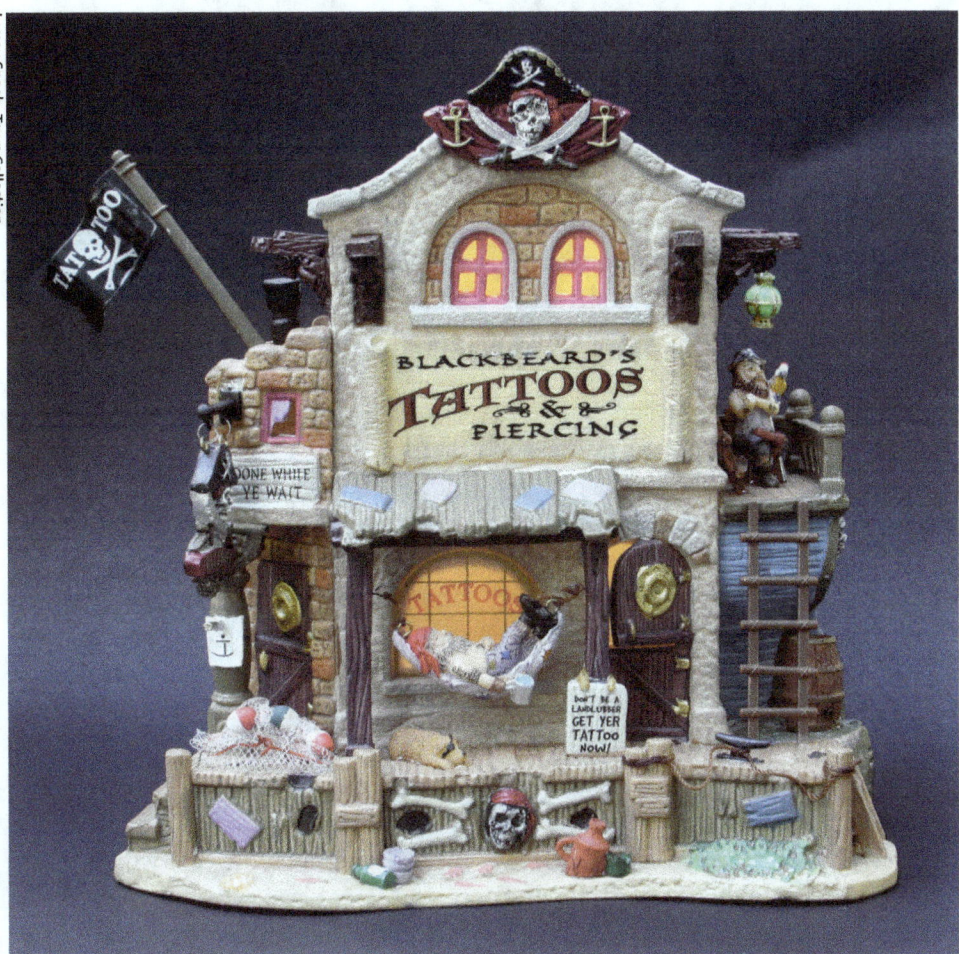

ferent place. In retrospect, life seemed somehow gentler, less complicated and hectic. Ronald Reagan had yet to wrest power from the politically naïve and inept Jimmy Carter. The AIDS epidemic was still some years in the future, and casual sex was commonplace especially in the gay community. Phones were hardwired; there were no personal computers; the Internet was unheard of. People got their news from the newspaper, magazines, television, and radio; research was conducted in libraries. Unless you lived in a large urban area where diverse cultures converged, the only piercings you were likely to see were ear piercings or the rare nostril piercing, and then only on women. Any white male who dared to have his ear pierced might just as well have had the word "GAY" tattooed on his forehead. To the population at large, exotic piercing

was something only seen in the pages of *National Geographic*, something being done by people of color in tribal cultures halfway around the world.

Unknown to them, a handful of individualists were piercing their bodies in places few had ever dreamed of. Only their companions and intimate friends had any idea what lurked beneath the clothes they wore.

Things have changed dramatically in the intervening years. Life moves at a faster pace and, post-9/11, has become more stressful and fear-filled. Several presidents have come and gone. In the face of tragedy, Nero, it is said, fiddled while Rome burned. He was nothing compared to President Ronald Reagan. In the early 1980s, while the conflagration that was AIDS raged unchecked and cut a grisly swath especially through the gay community, Reagan did nothing. Thousands died. Panic and fear and mind-numbing grief brought casual sex and the sexual freedom by which so many gay men had defined themselves to an abrupt end. In time the panic and fear subsided and people became sexually active once again, but safe sex now replaced what once had been so joyous, casual, and carefree.

The cell phone, the personal computer, and the Internet have put the world within reach of nearly everyone, and the phone line is rapidly becoming obsolete. No one is surprised to see pierced tongues, pierced nostrils, multiple ear piercings, or earlobes with holes the size of walnuts on people from every social stratum and walk of life. On a popular sitcom, a 13-year-old son begs his father to let him get his ear pierced so the other boys won't think he's a sissy.

In a 2003 documentary titled *The Social History of Piercing*, MTV called me "the granddaddy of the modern piercing movement." To be honest, I'm not certain where exactly I fall on that family tree, since the movement also has had its godfathers, godmothers, uncles, aunts, and sundry other relatives: people like Fakir Musafar; my European counterpart Alan Oversby, better known as Mr. Sebastian; Sailor Sid Diller; and Tattoo Samy of Frankfurt. It would be more accurate to call me the father of the body piercing industry, making my friend and mentor Doug Malloy its grandfather. All of the early pioneers were, of course, missionaries in their own ways, each extolling the joys of body piercing to receptive people they met, but in my opinion that alone would not have been sufficient to launch a movement. After all, what point is there in creating a market if there is nothing available to service and support it?

Consider tattooing for a moment. It's been around for thousands of years, but it wasn't until the invention of the electric tattoo machine in the late 1800s that tattooing began to spread across cultures and social classes. Something similar had to happen before body piercing could take root and truly flourish. First, there needed to be a universal language, a "menu," if you will, of common piercing placements. Second, there needed to be a system of techniques that could be easily duplicated using readily available standard equipment and suitable jewelry. Gauntlet introduced all of these things.

When I opened Gauntlet in 1975, virtually no one but hardcore fetishists and sadomasochism (S/M) enthusiasts were piercing themselves below the neck. People in the mundane world failed to realize that a little piece of metal strategically inserted in certain locations of the body can significantly amplify erotic sensations in those areas and make sex even more enjoyable. It seemed so clear to me that this was something that could benefit anyone. Why should piercing be limited to a select few? With that in mind, it became my mission to let the world at large in on this amazing secret and to let it know I had the ability to make it a reality.

Gauntlet, the primary subject of this book, was the world's first establishment devoted exclusively to body piercing. It went through several incarnations, beginning as Gauntlet Enterprises, later transitioning into Gauntlet, Inc., and in its final days becoming Gauntlet International.[2] Because I started the business, I was so closely allied with it, especially in the early years, that at times it feels like we were one and the same. Consequently, the story often includes some of my own personal history. If this were a genealogy, it might say: Jim Ward begat Gauntlet (with Doug Malloy's assistance); it fathered the body piercing industry, which in turn gave birth to the movement itself. These are the principal elements that make up this narrative. Of course, I did not do everything alone, and along the way many people have become characters in the story.

I have attempted as much as possible to organize the book chronologically, but as it consists of many different threads, that has not always been possible. Hopefully, as the narrative unfolds, the various pieces will fall into place and a clear picture will emerge.

As I look back on the chain of events that brought that movement into being and propelled it from relative obscurity into the mainstream spotlight, it often seems as if my place in this history was predestined, and I could do nothing other than follow the path that opened before me. So, as a prime player in this drama, allow me to begin with the story of a little boy who grew up to be different, to discover the joys of body piercing, and to realize that maybe he wasn't so different after all.

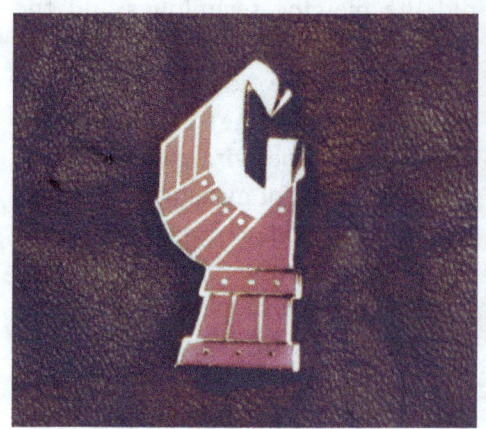

---

[1] It has been brought to my attention that some readers may not be familiar with the common, traditional piercing placements. Brief descriptions with illustrations of these can be found on pages 159 and 160 in the Appendix.

[2] Phoenix-like, Gauntlet Enterprises has re-emerged from the ashes of the bankrupt company. The full account of this rebirth appears in chapter 13.

CHAPTER 1

My partner Drew often says that the only regret he has about leaving Milwaukee is that he didn't do it sooner. I feel that way about Western Oklahoma.

It's not that it isn't possessed of a certain austere beauty. I don't know what things are like today, but in the 1940s fields of wheat stretched to the horizon, bleached blond by a hot summer sun, the landscape dotted with the occasional tree sucking sustenance from the ruddy earth. In the distance skeletal windmills turned lazily, pumping water for thirsty livestock into large round tanks. In winter, trails of wind-driven snow undulated like snakes across the two-lane highway. Tumbleweeds propelled by the same cold wind entangled themselves upon the miles of barbed wire fences. Every so often on those same fences would appear in grisly display the rotting carcasses of coyotes that had been shot or poisoned for the threat they posed to the local farmers' hens.

When the Oklahoma territory was settled in the late 1890s, its primary attraction was not the scenery but the land that the federal government, having driven the indigenous Indians from it, was practically giving away.

For my great-grandfather David Wilson Ward, cheap land was of secondary importance. There was a price on his head, and this desolate country must have seemed like an unlikely place to be discovered. Great-grandfather was a runaway indentured servant. His abuse at the hands of a wealthy Maryland landowner eventually compelled him to flee. We know little about his youth except that he worked as an hostler, caring for the rich man's horses. The man would inspect them by rubbing a white glove over their coat to make sure that it was spotless. If not, great-grandfather's punishment

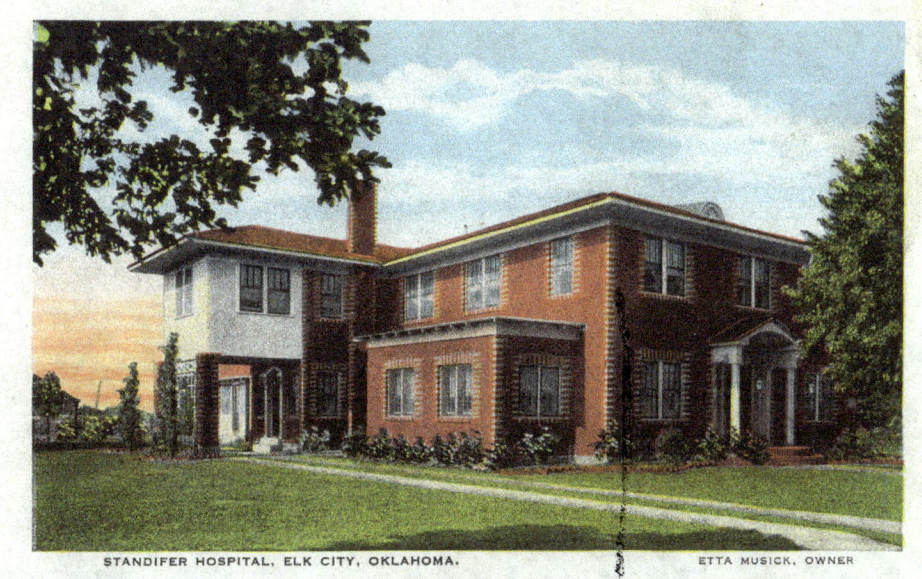

STANDIFER HOSPITAL, ELK CITY, OKLAHOMA.   ETTA MUSICK, OWNER

Postcard of the hospital where I was born

would be severe. The experiences he suffered left deep emotional scars, and he was reluctant to discuss them, even with his family. Till the day he died, he hated rich people.

My mother's side of the family arrived in 1902 under more mundane circumstances. The most colorful was my great-grandfather Marion Ernest McFarland, a traveling salesman of Estey organs and a libertine with a taste for whiskey and women. My grandfather, the eldest son, was named Estey after his father's wares, though his descendents called him Mac.

My maternal grandmother, who we called Mimmie, had been born in Tennessee. She had Cherokee in her bloodline, and it was evident in her features and dark eyes and skin, traits she passed on to most of her children.

Although I'm sure that they loved their family, my Grandma and Granddad Ward were not warm or demonstrative people, and the time I spent with them always seemed like forced confinement. They belonged to a time when the prevailing attitude in child-rearing was that coddling children made them weak, and that offspring would know they were loved, not by overt demonstrations of affection, but

because their parents took care of their physical needs. Like most women of her generation, Grandma Ward was a skilled seamstress and did tatting and crochet work and made beautiful quilts. One year for my birthday, she sewed a shirt for me out of flour sacks with a design of baseballs and bats. Although the food she cooked was pretty basic with an overemphasis on pork, it's her biscuits I particularly remember, perhaps, because she always made tiny ones for the children using her wide gold wedding band as a cutter.

Over the years of my childhood, Granddad and Grandma Ward owned a succession of small grocery stores in places with names like Strong City, Lone Wolf, and Moorewood, which were so small and rural they could hardly be called villages, much less cities. The population of Moorewood was 12.

My parents were childhood sweethearts who eloped and secretly married shortly after they graduated from high school. I was born six months before Pearl Harbor, nine months to the day after my mother's 20th birthday. I once embarrassed her by pointing out that fact and telling her I knew what she got for her birthday that year.

The year I was born both my parents

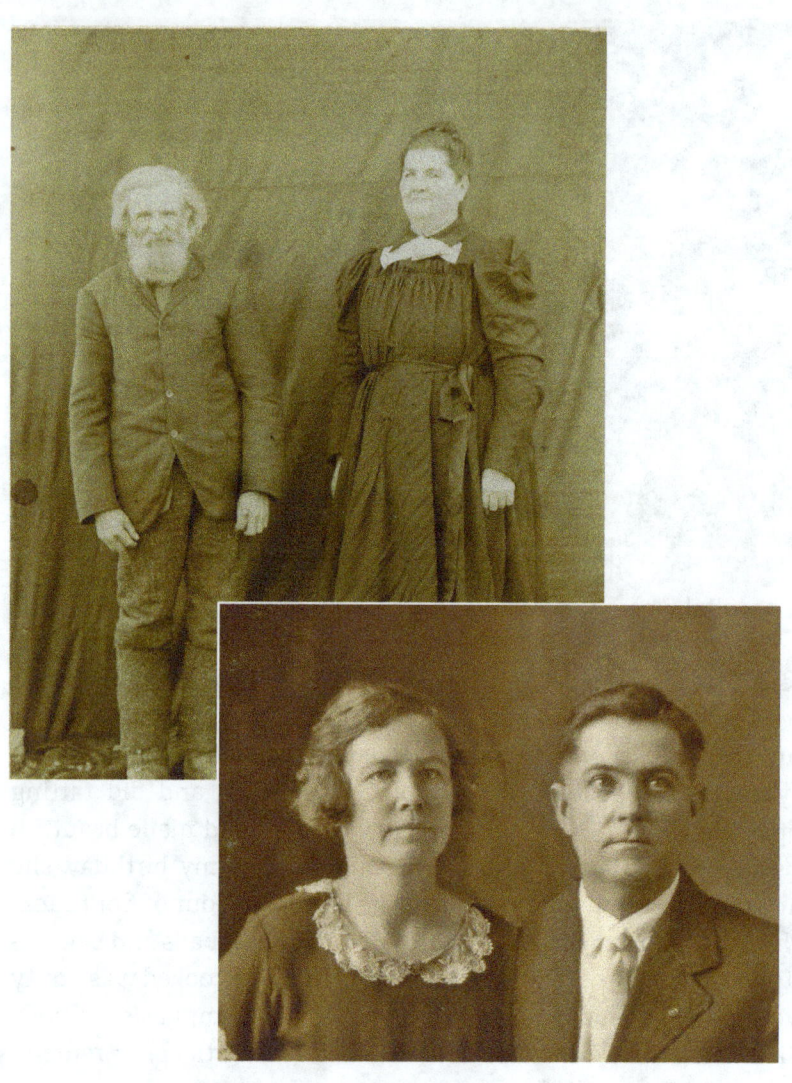

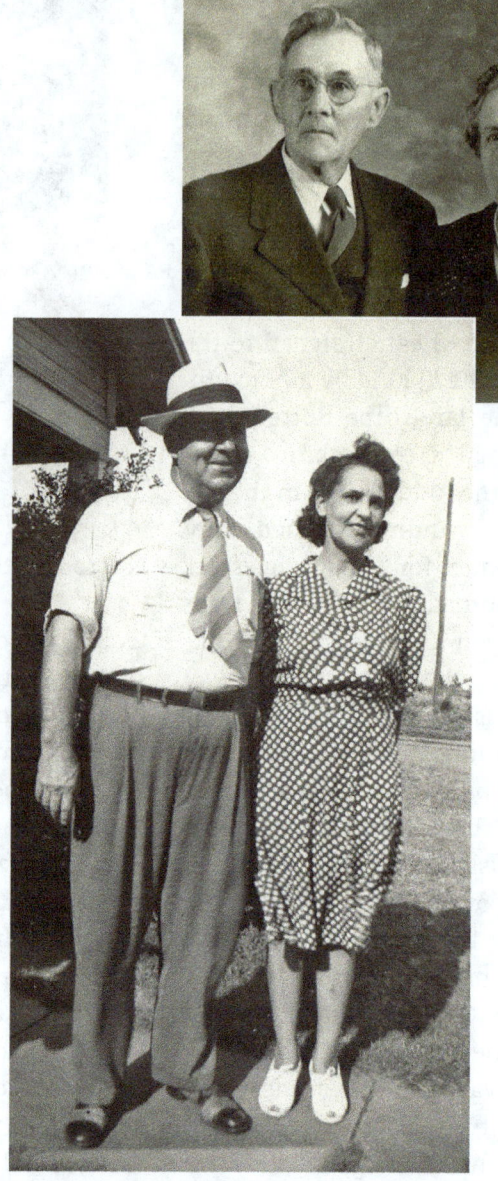

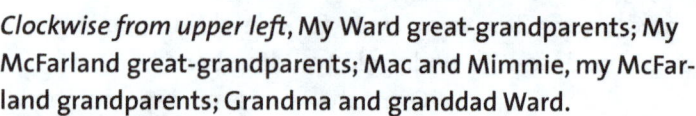

Clockwise from upper left, My Ward great-grandparents; My McFarland great-grandparents; Mac and Mimmie, my McFarland grandparents; Grandma and granddad Ward.

turned 21, perhaps a bit young to undertake the responsibilities of a family. Caring for a baby is not easy, especially when there is a war going on, money is tight, and everything is rationed. Still, my parents always made sure I had at least the physical necessities. We had a roof over our heads. I never went hungry or without clothes. The fact that I needed glasses, dental care, and orthopedic shoes—my feet were flat and narrow—couldn't have made things easier for them.

I was surprised to learn that as early as 1946, Dr. Spock was advising parents on child-rearing. My mother read

and followed his book, which advised, among other things, that giving a male child too much comfort or attention could make him homosexual. Thus, she suppressed her motherly, nurturing instinct, and I grew up to be gay anyway.

For someone whose life has been haunted with feelings of depression, I find it strange that my earliest memory is a happy one. My mother tells me that from my description of the house, I was only about a year and a half old. The memory is of the dining area with small adjacent kitchen. At floor level there were heating vents connected to the furnace in the basement. Through

one of these vents I can hear my father talking to me, but I can't see him. I am filled with delight and wonder.

Following this memory, there is a gap. With the feeling that I have awakened from sleep, I suddenly find myself sitting on the backseat of the family car. Everything is gray: the scratchy upholstery, the sky outside. There are the sounds: rain pelting against the windshield, the slap, slap, slap of the wipers. And when I stand on the seat and look out the back window, I see and hear the gray tarp covering the trailer behind us flapping in the wind. There is a deep feeling of loneliness and sadness. I am about three years old. We are moving back to Oklahoma from Kansas where my father has been working as a welder for Cessna Aircraft, his contribution to the war effort.

Another leap forward: I am sitting on the floor; I know not where. Before me is a brown and white Mounds candy box. Spread out on the floor are family photographs and newspaper clippings. There is one of my father during his time as a welder. I know I'm supposed to feel proud of him, but all I can feel is fear and the pervasive pall of loneliness.

I always assumed that I had been circumcised as a newborn. It came as something of a shock to learn as an adult that I was actually a year and a half old when the procedure was done. At the time the Second World War was in full swing. All able-bodied and qualified medical personnel had been shipped off for the war effort, leaving the old and incompetent behind to tend to the needs of the populace.

My mother took me to an elderly physician for a routine examination. He convinced her that I needed to be circumcised there and then. The procedure was done without anesthetic and, in my mother's words, "He botched it." This resulted in my being taken to the hospital to have the damage repaired as best as possible.

I've seen lots of circumcised penises in my life, and as near as I can tell mine is no more mutilated than these. But I am convinced that the experience itself left deep psychological and psychic scars. I sincerely believe that our sexuality is genetically determined, but how it manifests and is expressed is the result of our upbringing.

Looking back on it, much of my childhood was just as barren and desolate as the Oklahoma landscape. I couldn't wait to escape. In the backyard of one place we lived, there was the beat-up old trailer with wooden slat sides, the

Left, My newly wed parents

Right, My brother and I going native. Our mother made extra money for a while sewing patchwork purses from leather scraps. She made the loincloths from some of the leftovers.

one that we had pulled behind the car when we moved from Kansas. Its tires were flat and had long ceased to be roadworthy. I remember often climbing up to the top and looking southward toward the distant two-lane highway and longing to run away, to follow that road and escape from the desolation of a small, rural town and the harshness of my family life.

My upbringing was strict, and I was deeply indoctrinated in the tenets of my parents' Presbyterian faith. Disciplining a child has to be one of the greatest challenges any parent must face. Without the utmost care it can become abuse and cruelty, especially when "Spare the rod, and spoil the child" is considered essential to the building of his character. In my case, the result was a fearful, timid child, prudish and sanctimonious. Years later in therapy, I remembered being told,

"We punish you because we love you." Translation: punishment equals love. Thus were the seeds of masochism sown deeply, and over the years they were nurtured well.

My early childhood experiences instilled in me a self-loathing that dogs me to this day. No amount of therapy has ever completely uprooted it. As an adult, I realize intellectually that I was dearly loved, but it never felt like that to me as a child growing up. Somehow nothing I did was ever good enough to please my parents. Any spontaneous upwelling of childish joy and playfulness was immediately quashed and frequently ended in punishment.

This was usually meted out by my father. His own upbringing had been hard and had made him into a cold, no-nonsense disciplinarian with a suppressed anger that seethed just below the surface. It took little provocation on my part to unleash it. The most common form of punishment was half a dozen strokes across the butt with a belt. As might be expected, I cried. This seemed to only annoy him further. He would tell me to shut up and stop crying or he'd give me something to cry about. I would stifle my sobs long enough to seek refuge in my bedroom, where I would finish crying, as silently as possible, into my pillow. The logic of making me cry and then forcing me to suppress it was a contradiction that I never understood. It was a form of psychological abuse that left lifelong scars.

It has been my observation that children, lacking intellectual development, take things they are told quite literally. If a parent says, "You're bad," the child

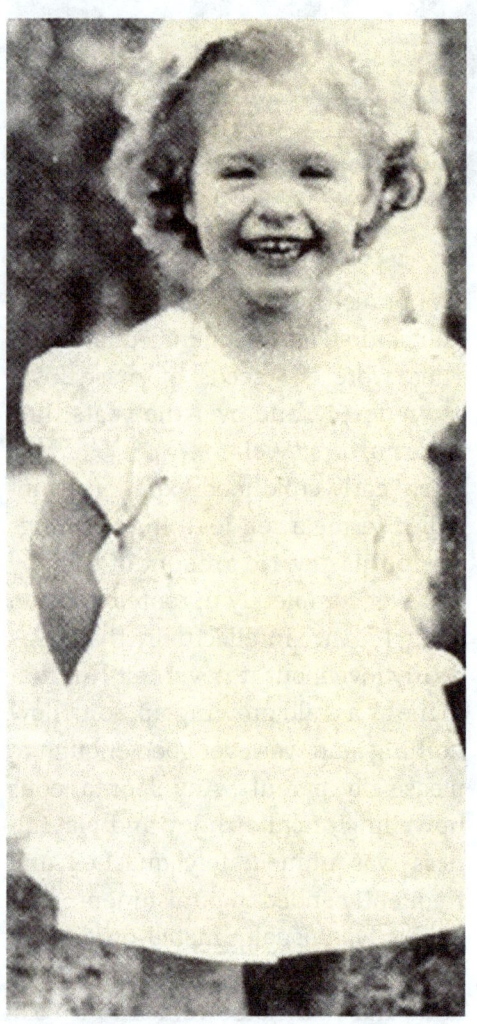

Three-and-a-half-year-old Kathy Fiscus. Her ghost haunted my dreams for months.

doesn't realize that it is their behavior that has elicited the rebuke. They come to believe that there is actually something wrong with them. This can undermine the individual's sense of self-worth and self-esteem. Personally it led me to believe that love was conditional and could be turned off and on like a switch. As long as I was good, my parents—and by inference, other people as well—would love me; if I was bad, they would not. It came as a bit of a shock to realize much later in life that there was such a thing as unconditional love. Even today, if I displease someone I care about, it is difficult for me not to feel it as the end of love.

In 1949, a little girl named Kathy Fiscus fell into an abandoned well near her home in Southern California. The story captured the attention of the media from coast to coast and found its way into our local newspaper. I was almost eight at the time and remember sitting at the kitchen table reading the story in horror. The article included a diagram showing how the well angled at the bottom where the girl had come to rest. Every effort was made to rescue the child, but when workers finally reached her two days after she fell in, she was dead.

This event haunted me for months afterward. I would lie awake at night unable to put it out of my mind, picturing myself in her place, and feeling her terror at being trapped, helpless, and alone. One night I got out of bed and went into the living room, where my parents were reading. Pretending I needed a drink of water or to go to the bathroom, I stopped and sat briefly on the arm of the sofa. I so wanted to tell them how afraid I was and how much I wanted to be held and comforted, but I knew I couldn't. They wouldn't understand and would likely belittle me for showing weakness. I finally went back to bed and forced myself to think about something else. Turning my thoughts to

Santa Claus and Christmas, I was finally able to banish the ghost of Kathy Fiscus. She never kept me awake again, but it was a high price to pay. I had learned how to disconnect from my feelings.

I was the stereotypical sissy kid who grows up gay. I hated sports, and though I never played with dolls, I liked drawing and coloring books and cutting out the paper dolls in *McCall's* magazine. Less stereotypically, I never had any desire to try on my mother's clothes or apply her makeup.

At school I preferred playing jacks or jump rope to baseball or football. Sometimes avoiding these two sports was impossible. The class would select two team captains who would then take turns choosing kids for their side in the ensuing game. Not being good at hitting, catching, or throwing a ball, I was always one of the last to be chosen.

In a feeble attempt to encourage me to be like other boys, my parents bought me a football, and my dad made a half-hearted attempt to teach me—unsuccessfully—how to throw it. I was shamed into joining the Little League football team, something I despised for the one season I was part of it. The game itself never made any sense, and no one bothered to try and explain it to me. The assumption seemed to be that if you were a boy you were born knowing these things or some adult family member had explained it to you. From my perspective, the object of the game was to stand in a line and wait for some bigger kid to knock you down.

The last game of the season, the weather was raw. Somehow I managed to leave home without a coat, wearing only the thin jersey and the rest of my uniform. As always, I spent the entire game warming the bench and freezing in the process. I thought the game would never end. For the benefit of family or friends who might be watching—they weren't—the coach sent me in for one play, long enough to get knocked down once. Finally the game was over. I don't even know—or care—who won. Maybe we did. The coach took us all to the local Dairy Queen for ice cream sundaes. Mine was cherry. Who thought ice cream was a good reward for sitting out in the cold for several hours?

I didn't realize it at the time, but the one big thing that was lacking most during my childhood years in Oklahoma was culture, especially classical music. One Christmas, my parents gave me a toy phonograph. It would play records, but had no mechanism to spin them. To accomplish this required turning the record manually with a wooden disk that slipped over the spindle through the center of the record. With no way to control the speed at which it turned, the pitch would vary widely, and what child could resist exploring the full range of possibilities? It's inconceivable to me that any adult could tolerate this for very long.

With the phonograph I received my first record. It was made of yellow plastic and the music was Bizet's *Farandole*. With this record I tried very hard to turn the handle at a constant speed because the music was so beautiful.

I also loved listening to the Saturday afternoon Metropolitan Opera broadcasts on the radio. The singing transported me, and I was deeply moved by the usually tragic love stories.

Deep in my being was a burning desire to make music myself, but there was no money for an instrument or lessons. Not that it mattered. Aside from some musical toy, the only option was a band instrument, which held no interest for me. An uncle lent me a clarinet he had played in high school and tried to show me how to make it sound. After several unpleasant squawks, I simply gave up.

Sitting in the classroom at school one day, the room was filled with what seemed like heavenly music. Down the hall, someone had brought in an au-

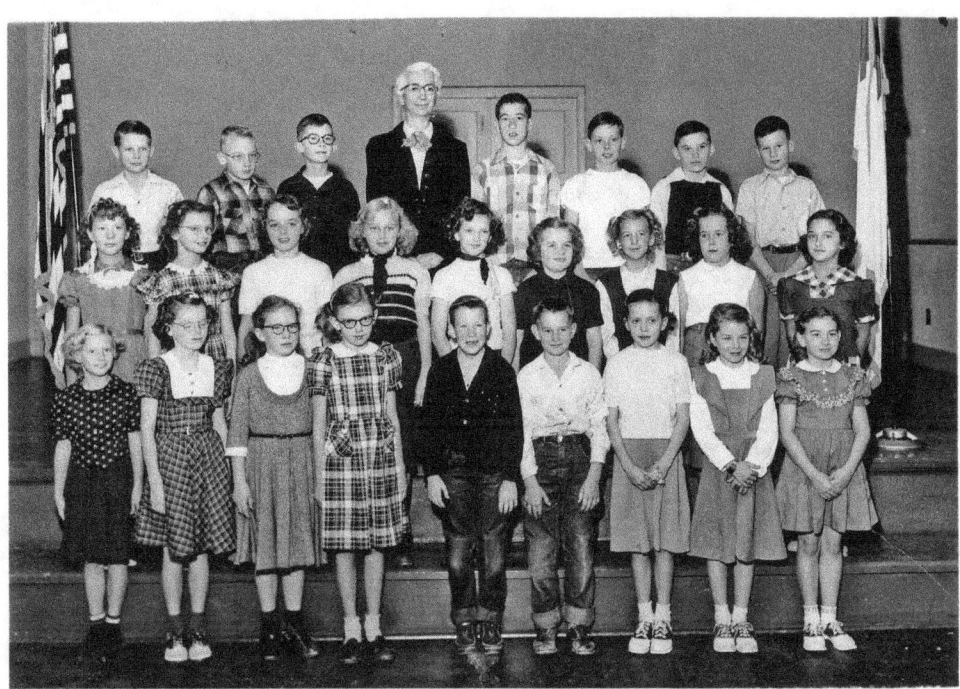

Miss Newman's fifth grade class. I'm the kid with the glasses next to her. James, the boy who showed me how to masturbate, is in the back row on the far right.

toharp and was playing it for the students. I had no idea what the instrument was, but eventually found out and begged my parents to buy me one. It was available through the Sears and Roebuck catalog, and even though the price was relatively low, my parents could not (or would not) indulge me. The only musical outlet we could afford was singing, which I did regularly in school and church.

Fifth grade was my last school year in Oklahoma. My teacher that year was Miss Newman, a horse-faced old biddy so uptight she considered "fanny" a dirty word. Ironically, she threatened to report me to my parents, from whom, of course, I'd learned it in the first place.

What I remember most vividly from that year was an incident involving one of my classmates. His name was James, and he was an impish kid with a knack for getting into mischief. He and several others were in the boys' restroom during recess one day. After finishing at the urinal, he turned and laughingly demonstrated for the rest of us how his penis got bigger and harder when he stroked it. Whether or

not he had any clue what that was all about I've no idea. I was simultaneously appalled and fascinated. Something told me this was naughty and sinful and that I should pray for him.

The year I turned 11, my family moved to Colorado Springs, which had so much more to offer than Oklahoma. The public schools provided free art classes and music lessons that had nothing to do with marching bands. I was in sixth grade when I decided I wanted to learn to play the violin. I started with a rented instrument, but in time my parents obtained a violin from my mother's older brother who owned a music store. As it turned out, I had a natural musical ability, and my teacher was sufficiently impressed with my talent to teach me privately in exchange for odd jobs during the summer months between school years.

Our landlady, a sweet, half-deaf old widow who was a distant relation to my father, had an ancient upright piano that sat unused in her entry hall. One day, on a visit to her home, I sat down, and, with the aid of an elementary piano book, was able to learn and

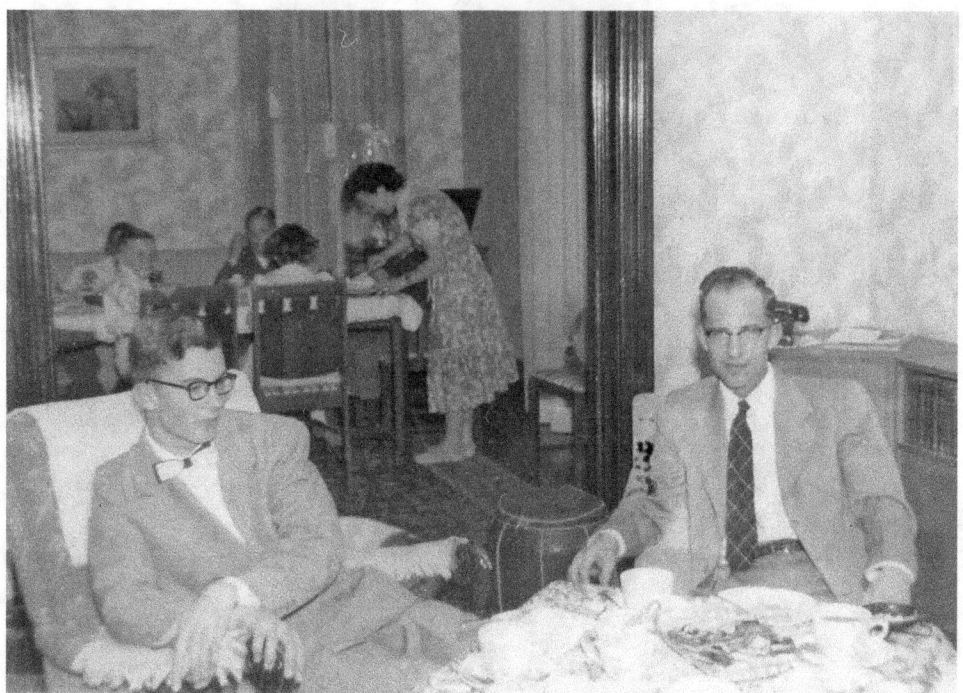

One of those embarassing photos of me as a prissy teenager with my dad. I had yet to discover an identity.

play a few of the simple pieces. Subsequently she offered to sell us the piano for the paltry sum of $25 payable in installments as we could afford it.

The piano gave me many hours of pleasure. I learned to play pieces from the church hymnal and an old collection of music books that belonged to my mother. I also began to write original compositions. The early pieces were romantic rubbish. In high school, I discovered modern music and set out to create something avant-garde. Though I dreamed of someday being a rich and famous composer, it was not destined to be. I simply didn't have sufficient talent, and I was so emotionally screwed up that I didn't have the drive to stick with anything for very long.

Growing up in a very religious household, where the subject of sex was hardly ever discussed, left me totally unprepared for what was happening when my body entered puberty at the age of 11. My mind kept flashing back to that day in the boys' restroom when James had played with himself. Inevitably, I tried it myself. It felt so good I didn't want to stop. Suddenly and unexpectedly, the

most incredible sensation swept over me, and, with an uncontrollable spasm, white fluid shot from my penis. Don't ask me why, but I thought of that white stuff as cultured piss. In retrospect, it seems amazing that the whole experience didn't freak me out more than it did. Perhaps the guilt and shame and the fear of discovery were more powerful, so powerful, in fact, that I couldn't bring myself to tell anyone.

Looking back, I find a certain irony in my choice of an adult profession that celebrates and glorifies the body. I was well past puberty before I was able to shake the shame and self-consciousness I felt about my body and its natural functions. In junior high, I was the first boy in my gym class to develop pubic hair, something that embarrassed me and made me even shier about disrobing and showering with the other boys in my class.

The Boy Scouts, to which I belonged, placed a lot of emphasis on physical fitness, and swimming was an important activity. Every week, I would take the bus downtown to the YMCA for a swim class with a group of fellow

Scouts. It was something I was never very good at.

Across the alley from the Y was an old house that was owned by the Presbyterian Church. It was used as a center for Sunday school and various other youth activities. I will never forget one autumn afternoon there when I was probably 12 or 13 that started with a group of kids my age doing craft projects. Once the class was over and everyone had departed, I realized I really needed to go to the bathroom, but the building was locked and no one was around to let me back in. There was no way I would be able to make it home without peeing my pants. The problem was that I was so inhibited that I couldn't ask a stranger where the nearest restroom was or even to find some secluded spot in the alley and relieve myself. By this time, I was in a panic and kept running back and forth from the church to the center to the Y, trying to figure out what to do. Then the inevitable happened. I could hold it no longer, and stood sobbing with humiliation as the moist warmth spread across the front of my jeans and down my leg. Still weeping, I skulked into the alley. My anguish drew the attention of a passerby who approached me with concern and asked what was wrong. Unable to answer I cried even harder. He took in the situation and stated the obvious, "You pissed your pants." I nodded, to which he replied, "That's nothing to be ashamed of. It can happen to anyone." He continued to reassure and soothe me, making light of my dilemma, and eventually I calmed down and was able to face the bus ride home and the unknown reaction of my parents. Thankfully, they didn't say or do anything to further humiliate me. I've always been grateful for the kind understanding of that stranger who helped me begin to shed some of the inhibitions that had been accumulating over my short lifetime.

Once the intense, guilty pleasure of masturbation had been discovered, nothing, despite my greatest efforts, could stop me from doing it for very long. Prayer didn't help. Memorizing and reciting bible verses didn't help. Not quite understanding why, I began to develop crushes on some of my male classmates as well as the young men who worked as church youth counselors and the newly appointed youth minister. Before his conversion, one of the counselors apparently had been something of a bad boy and had gotten into trouble. He had a tattoo on one forearm, and I found myself particularly attracted to him. I wanted desperately to be close to all these guys, to please them, to be noticed by them, to...? There was an undefined longing for something for which I had no name. It was agony.

Do comic books still contain those ads for Charles Atlas, where the cartoon bully kicks sand in the face of the "90-pound weakling" only to get his comeuppance later when said weakling becomes a buff bodybuilder? The ads often included a large photo of some muscle-bound hunk. In spite of the fact that I lacked any knowledge of the mechanics of sex, I frequently locked myself in the bathroom or the basement and jacked off looking at those photos and fantasizing myself naked and bound and forced in some vague way to please my muscular tormentor.

In time, the guilty burden I was carrying became unbearable, and I finally sought counsel from the church youth minister. The moment was painfully awkward, and I don't recall how I expressed what was troubling me or everything that was said. I do remember Reverend Bill telling me there were three kinds of sexual expression: between a man and woman, between two men (for some reason he didn't think to include lesbians), and masturbation. His mention of male/female

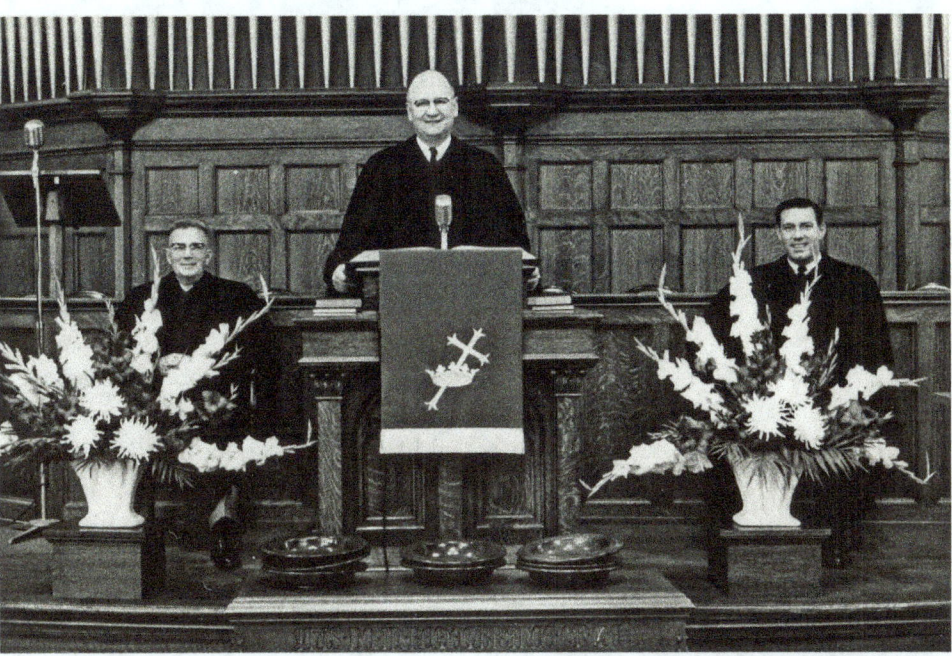

The Presbyterian Church ministers c. late 1950s. Reverend Bill is on the right.

sex elicited no response; mention of the male/male thing probably made me pale or blush; it likely wasn't difficult to see how uncomfortable I was when he got around to masturbation. His counsel was low-key, and he took the time to at least enlighten me on the basics of sexual intercourse.

Soon after this encounter, I had one of my first sexual experiences with another person--Reverend Bill himself. One night we found ourselves sitting in the darkened church talking about something. Reverend Bill put his hand on my leg, and slowly moved to unzip my fly, reach inside my pants, and begin to play with me. I was nervous and found it difficult to get erect, but I didn't want him to stop. It made me feel loved and wanted. I reached over and began to fondle him. This mutual masturbation continued for a little while until he excused himself and said he had to go to the bathroom. A few minutes later he returned, and it was clear that the encounter was over. We had one other such experience the following summer at church camp.

Today this experience would be considered sexual abuse of a minor, but for me at the time it was any-

thing but. I welcomed Reverend Bill's advances and wished they had been more than two furtive and unconsummated interludes.

High school was typical teenage hell. Hating sports and being of an artistic temperament did not make me popular. Academically, I managed to get by and actually garnered enough good grades to be accepted into the National Honor Society. This probably wouldn't have happened if my German teacher, a middle-aged man I now realize was gay, hadn't given me better grades than I deserved. Aside from my music classes, however, everything else seemed dull and uninteresting. Most of my teachers lacked the ability to inspire and motivate their students. In their hands learning was drudgery.

My best friend David was as much a social outcast as I and made no effort to fit in. From his quiet demeanor one would never have guessed that he was extremely intelligent. He was overweight, smoked, and always seemed to have a bottle of Pepsi-Cola in his hand. I had originally made his acquaintance while riding the bus back and forth to school. My initial motiva-

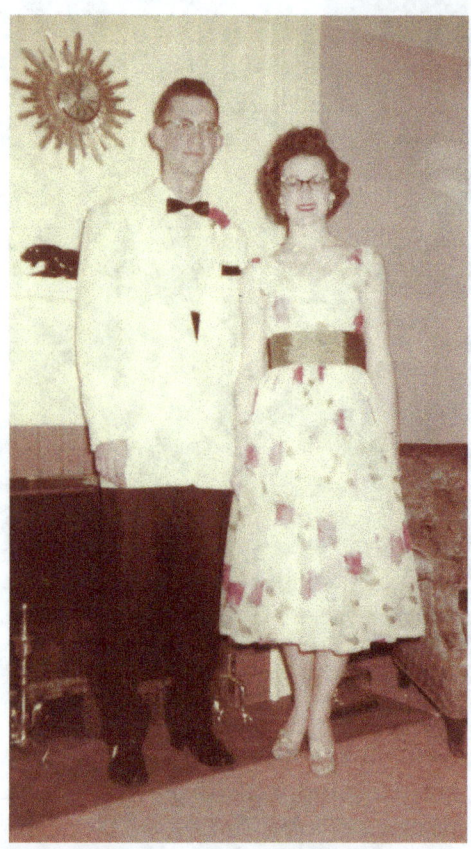

With Harriette, my Junior/Senior Prom date. I cringe when I realize how much she was like my mother.

tion for befriending him had been to be a good Christian and help him see the evil, particularly of his smoking, and perhaps convert him. But I was too self-conscious to be a very good witness and soon discovered that we had a lot in common. He was passionately interested in music, played the piano dramatically if not well, and composed music that I thought was amazingly good. We would listen endlessly to recordings and discuss the music for hours. In due course, I also discovered we shared a common sexuality.

David lived with his mother, a diminutive, scrawny woman approaching middle age, who was outspoken and forward to the point of being offensive. Her name was Corrine, and she would say whatever was on her mind. If you didn't like it, you could kiss her posterior; her words were more colorful and to the point. She had divorced David's alcoholic father years

before, and I gather, from the way she talked about him, that the split had not been amicable. She and I got along quite well, but my mother disliked her intensely. The fact that I spent most afternoons and evenings after school with David didn't help.

Corrine was of the opinion that except for herself, the whole world was crazy. Some years before, she had seen a psychiatrist who at some point had told her there was nothing further he could do for her. She took this as a validation of her own sanity, though I suspect the good doctor may have meant she was beyond his ability to help.

One weekend David's mother had gone to Canon City to visit her mother, and David invited me to sleep over. We listened to music and drank Pepsi late into the night. As we were getting ready to turn in, one thing led to another, and we found ourselves exploring each other's bodies. It was tentative, and we didn't know exactly what we were doing, but it felt good, more open and honest than the furtive experience I had had with Reverend Bill.

At one point in my involvement with the Presbyterian Church, I had briefly expressed an interest in becoming a minister but quickly became disenchanted with the idea. About that time I was working on the requirements necessary to receive the "God and Country Award," a prestigious honor given by the Boy Scouts. Part of the process was to do volunteer work at the church and to have someone there mentor a program of reading and study. A member of the church staff, a woman named June Pauline, assumed the duties. Though probably in her late 30s or early 40s, she was already an old maid. She had a saccharine phoniness about her that I found repugnant.

In addition to such menial tasks as folding the Sunday bulletins, I was given required reading. One of the books June Pauline assigned was a small cat-

echism of Presbyterian beliefs. In some small but significant way, this little book changed my life. The first chapter was about God, and in it was the statement that God was "omniscient, omnipotent, and omnipresent." All well and good! Several chapters later came the topic of Hell that was defined as "eternal separation from God." This created a logical impossibility, for if God were truly omnipresent, one could never be separated from him, and if one could, God would not be God. Perhaps this experience marked the beginning of what would become a life-long spiritual quest.

For a period of several months during high school, I worked for a family-owned boys' clothing business. The Lees, who owned the shop, were members of the church. I soon learned that the sweetness that they so generously slathered upon people on Sunday was just an act. In business, they were anything but kind and treated me with haughty disdain. The middle-aged mother was the worst. No effort on my part could please her or was ever good enough. In due course I was fired.

This marked another small turning point in my life. For years, I had suppressed so much of myself. I had tried desperately to be a good Christian and control my sexual drive. I never cursed and had, with limited success, suppressed the urge even to do so mentally. I tried to be kind and to love my fellow man, to emulate Jesus and turn the other cheek. In an instant it suddenly didn't matter any more. If I were damned to hell, then so be it. I didn't care.

Something inside me snapped. I left the store seething with anger and a smoldering hatred for a lifetime lived under the crushing rule of an implacable god overseen by his groveling minions, my parents included. It all came to focus on old lady Lee. As I stood on the street in the gathering darkness waiting for the bus, I could no longer hold back all the rage and the rising torrent of feelings. A swell of obscenities began pouring out of my mouth. "You fucking bitch!" I raged, and every other vile word I could think of soon followed. I half expected some divine retribution, but none came. As the anger subsided, the realization gradually dawned that the deity I had feared for most of my life was impotent. Soon after I stopped going to church with my parents.

For a brief period of time, I gave serious thought to becoming an atheist—some of the other kids in school thought it was cool—but I lacked the conviction necessary to pursue such a radical change of direction. As my high school years drew to a close, I became increasingly hostile to the religion of my family. David was an Episcopalian. I began going to church with him and, to the consternation of my parents, eventually converted. I loved the ritual, the music, the incense, and most of all, the refreshing lack of emphasis on sin, damnation, and hell. The happily married parish priest never condemned me for my sexuality when it was brought up in confession.

The Episcopal Church was in a little tourist town called Manitou Springs. Across the street from it was a very nice little gift shop that didn't sell the usual tacky souvenirs. Instead, it sold beautiful local crafts plus fine china, glassware, and the like. John, the owner, was quick to spot a young gay man, and discovering my lack of experience, set about introducing me into the local gay community, such as it was in 1959. I worked for John that summer and was taken under the wing of a kindly older gentleman named Frank, who introduced me to the various expressions of gay sex, at least the non-kinky variety. I was beginning to blossom.

It is rather amazing to me that by this time I was already beginning to acknowledge and accept my sexual orientation. I certainly had not chosen to be this way. If God had, in fact, made me, then presumably he knew what he was doing.

One night, I returned home late from spending the evening with Frank. The house was dark, and I made my way downstairs to the basement where I slept. As I was starting to undress, I heard mother's footsteps on the stairs. Clad in her nightgown, she came down and sat on the landing, a pained expression on her face. "Are you a homosexual?" she asked.

"Why do you ask?" I replied.

She then proceeded to explain that she had found and read my diary. Faced with the evidence, I made no effort to deny it. Assuming her very best Saint-Marjorie-the-Martyr tone of voice she then said, "You know we'll have to send you to a psychiatrist." Since I felt there was nothing wrong with being who and what I was, and that there was no point in discussing the matter with an unsympathetic outsider, I vehemently objected. These were the days when homosexuality was still considered a mental illness.

As the conversation came to a close, the strangest thing came out of my mother's mouth: "I wonder if you're the way you are because I enjoyed sex too much."[1] It took a great effort of will on my part to keep from laughing.

With graduation approaching, the subject of the draft raised its ugly head. To tell the truth, I was terrified at the thought of having to join the army. Being neither strong nor athletic, I envisioned the abuse I would have to endure especially if it were discovered that I was gay.

John and some of his friends had talked about gay men they knew who had "checked the box." There was a question on the form they received prior to being drafted asking if they were homosexual. By checking the box they had been declared 4-F, unsuitable for service.

When I subsequently received the form, I decided to come out, although that term would not be in common use for several decades. However, being excused from military service was not that simple. Selective Service required that I have an evaluation by a psychiatrist.

I was referred to a doctor in Denver and saw him several times. He gave me a number of common psychological tests, the Rorschach inkblot test and something called the Thematic Apperception Test. I was shown a number of pictures, and was supposed to make up a story about what they depicted.

Apparently nothing indicated mental illness or severe psychological problems, although the doctor felt I should still consider therapy for my homosexuality. This was hardly surprising considering the *Diagnostic and Statistical Manual of Mental Disorders* (*DSM*) would continue listing it as a disorder until 1973.

I thanked the doctor for his help and recommendation, told him I saw noth-

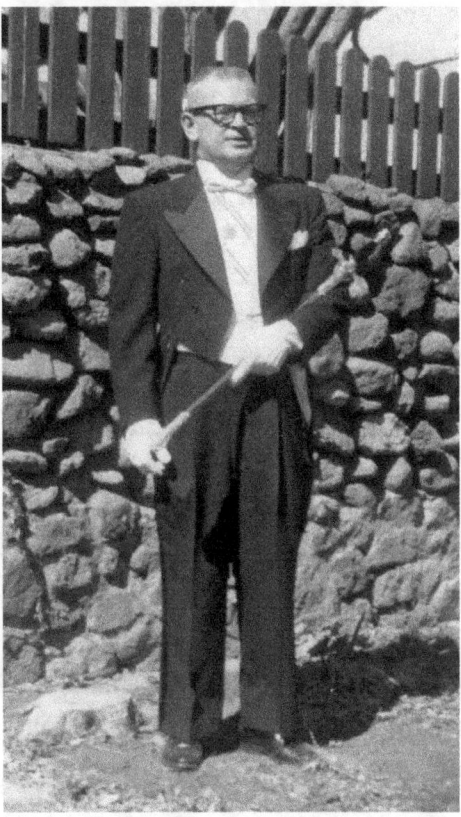

Frank, the gentleman who brought me out, in his Knights of Columbus regalia

ing wrong with being gay, and never saw him again. Soon after, I received my draft card in the mail and was relieved that I had been classified as 4-F.

Once I left the Presbyterian Church, I lost contact with Reverend Bill. His proclivities eventually got him into trouble. He ended up marrying a woman some said was old enough to be his mother—I don't know if he ever had a child—and moved to a church in the Seattle area. Some years later, I learned he had died of AIDS.

As high school drew to a close, I, like all my classmates, had begun giving serious consideration to a career. We had been given a battery of tests in an attempt to help us find our calling. One teacher, who I disliked intensely, decided that I should consider becoming an architect because of my interest in art and my decent though unremarkable math scores. At that time of my life, my passion was music. I dreamed of becoming a composer and making my fame and fortune as a musician. With encouragement from my violin teacher, I applied to the Eastman School of Music in Rochester, New York. I was accepted and even offered a $500 scholarship.

My parents weren't exactly supportive of my pursuit of a musical career. They invited one of the church deacons to come to the house and talk to me. Since I was no longer interested in joining the clergy, he encouraged me to consider becoming a minister of music and applying to Whitworth College, a Presbyterian school in Spokane, Washington, but there was no dissuading me from the path I had chosen. My parents finally relented.

I graduated from Colorado Springs High School, class of 1959. Historically speaking, it was not a particularly momentous year, the most notable events

including Alaska and Hawaii becoming states, Fidel Castro assuming power, the premiere of *The Sound of Music*, and the debut of Barbie. At the time, a postage stamp cost four cents.

My first year out of high school, I attended the Eastman School of Music, studying violin and composition. During that year I also took up the harp. Several run-ins with the homophobic dean made it clear that I would not be allowed to return even if I wanted to—I didn't. By this time, it was clear that I lacked sufficient talent and abil-

ity to ever be anything more than a mediocre musician. I applied to and was accepted at the New York School of Interior Design, and over the course of the next several years bounced back and forth between there and the University of Colorado at Boulder trying to find a vocation. Unfortunately, I was so emotionally fucked up I couldn't stick with anything. An art professor at the University once wrote in my sketchbook, "Just an inch more commitment." Those five words could easily serve as my epitaph.

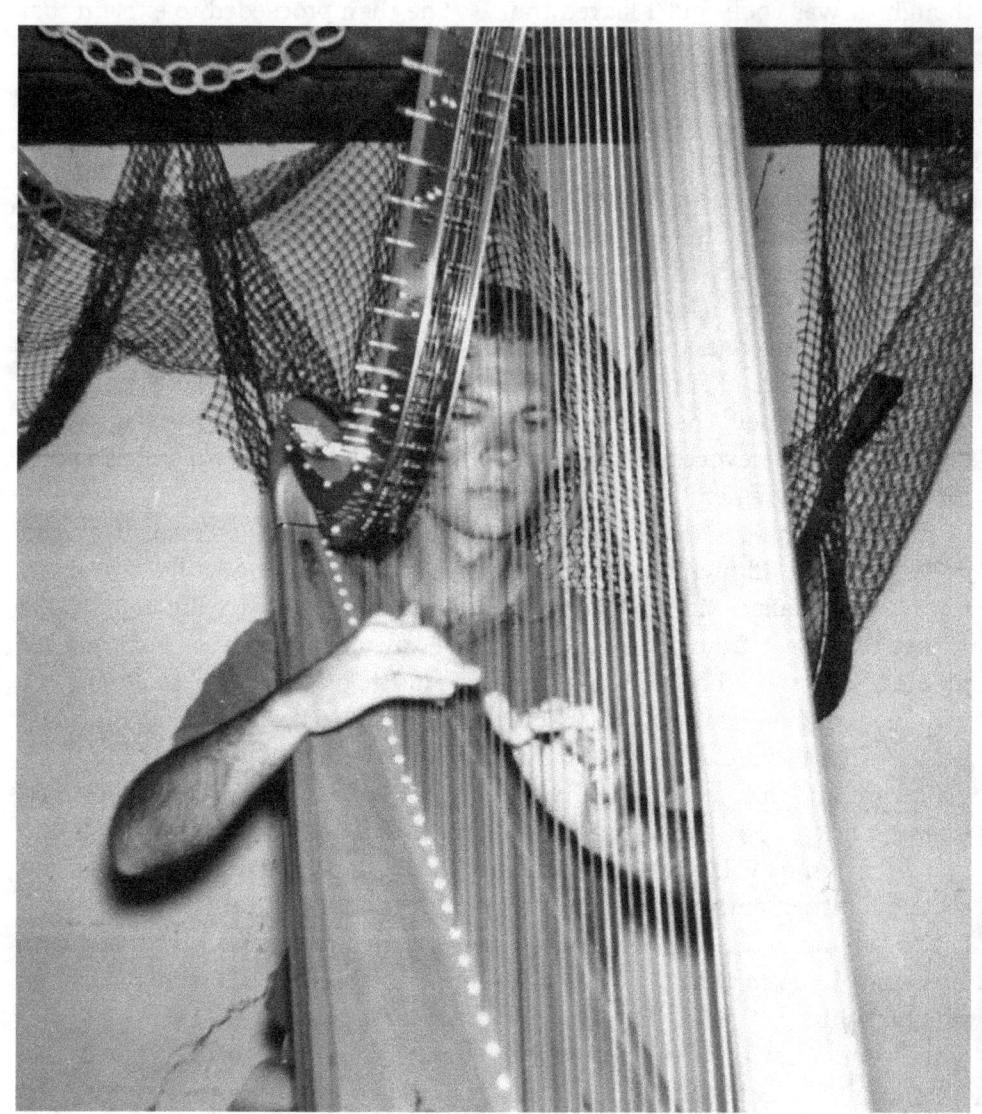

Practicing on a rental harp in the summer of 1960. I began studying the previous year at Eastman School of Music and developed a life-long love of the instrument.

---

[1] Modern research seems to suggest there may be something to this. Some scientists hypothesize a "man-loving gene" that passionate women might pass on to their sons.

Chapter 2

In the mid-1960s I moved to New York City to pursue a career in interior design. It soon became apparent that just being a good designer—and I was—wasn't enough. Far too many clients were rich, pampered neurotics. Those designers who excelled were consummate salespeople in the guise of best friend, confidant, psychotherapist, and father/mother confessor. The profession demands a certain level of ruthlessness, and at that point in my life I was too shy and self-conscious to succeed. My talents lay elsewhere.

But two things are noteworthy about this period, for they set me upon the path that led to my calling. First was training in jewelry making and manufacture. The second was discovering the demimonde of gay S/M and through it, body piercing.

My journey into those worlds began in 1967, when I was 26 and living in Brooklyn Heights in an ancient brownstone apartment building at the foot of Joralemon Street, known to the local gays as "Vaseline Flats" because of the sexual orientation of many residents. From my bathroom window, I could look down on the Brooklyn-Queens Expressway and the East River.

A few blocks away on Montague Street, there was a small bookstore owned by two gay guys named Steve and Marc. A friendship developed, and as we became better acquainted, they revealed that they were into leather and sadomasochism (S/M) and belonged to the New York Motorbike Club (NYMBC), an organization of like-minded men.

For years I had wrestled with my own S/M feelings, carefully keeping them concealed from others and acting them out only in private. My attraction to S/M was intense, but was restrained by fear: fear of losing control, fear of being harmed, fear of revealing who I really was behind the mask, and fear of

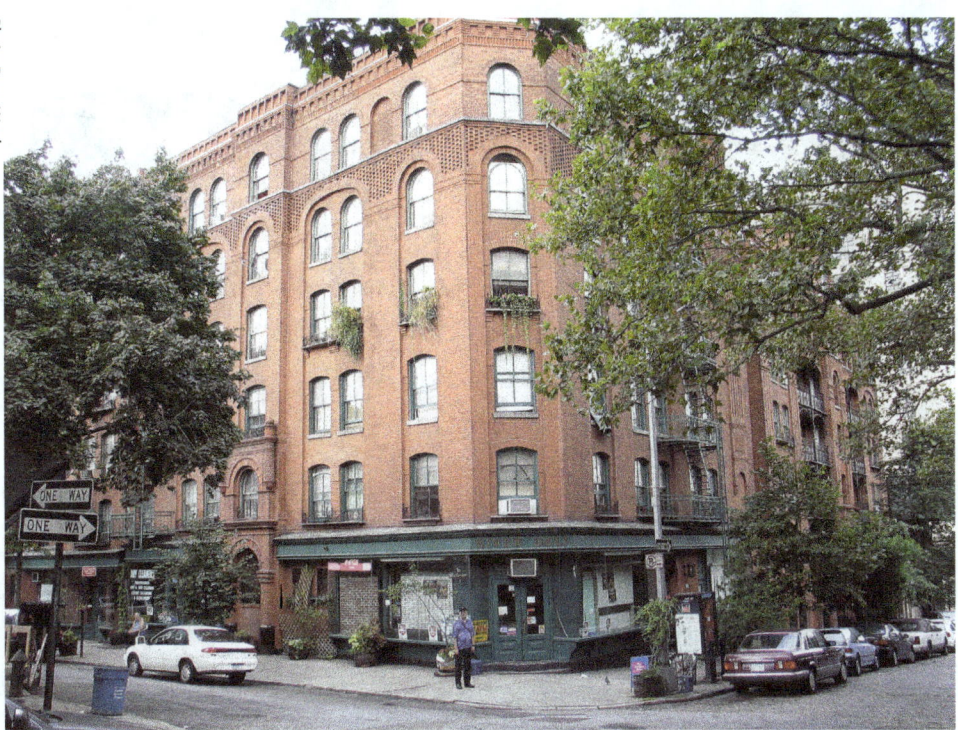

Photo: Drew Ward

"Vaseline Flats" in 2003. It's had a face-lift since I lived there in the late '60s. In those days, it was a grubby, rent-controlled building.

being rejected by friends and family.

Over two hundred years have passed since the Pilgrims set foot on Plymouth Rock, yet this country has made amazingly little progress in casting off the bonds of prudery that landed with them. The degree of intolerance still surrounding issues of sex is truly staggering. We see it daily in our government. The faithful will turn a blind eye to every form of political corruption, but let there be sex involved, and it can easily end a career.

Like so many aspects of sexuality that diverge from the mainstream, sadomasochism is particularly misunderstood. Unlike homosexuality, which has not only become much more visible in mainstream society, but also has gained far greater acceptance and understanding, S/M has not fared as well. Fueled in no small part by film and television, the preconception of S/M is of forced rape, violence, abuse, and even murder. Erotic S/M is none of these. Instead, it is a combination of psychodrama and intense physical stimulation and is always consensual. In a time before any-

one had heard of political correctness, I once described S/M as "cowboys and Indians for adults."

Pain and pleasure are frequently inseparable. Ask any of the countless people who consume a bowl of fiery chili or some other incendiary delight and relish every burning bite. S/M is to sex what hot sauce is to food. Both stimulate the body to produce pleasurable endorphins. And while both may be slightly addictive, there is nothing inherently dangerous or life-threatening about either.

As my friendship with Steve and Marc grew more comfortable, I was finally able to acknowledge my true S/M feelings. As a result, they introduced me into the local leather scene, keeping a careful eye to make sure I didn't go home with anyone who might be dangerous. The experience was liberating. I felt much like I did when I discovered I was gay and that I wasn't alone. Here were others who shared the same drives and longings.

At that time, the gay S/M scene was nothing like it is today. Things were far less codified, or perhaps codified in a different way. No one ever discussed "safe words." It wasn't even clear whether wearing one's keys on the left meant you were a top or a bottom. On the East Coast, it was said it meant you were a top, but if you were from the West Coast, it meant you were a bottom. The bandana color code to signal one's particular sexual proclivities—more on that in the next chapter—was still several years in the future.

Among some older S/M players, there were strict guidelines governing one's initiation into this subculture. But within the circle I found myself a part of, there was considerably less formality. It's even difficult for me to say just how much actual S/M was going on. In my own experience, what passed for S/M was often little more than rough sex with some role-playing and bondage thrown in on occasion.

Regardless, it was mandatory to adhere to a certain dress code. This usually included a black leather motorcycle jacket. The "leather boutique" where

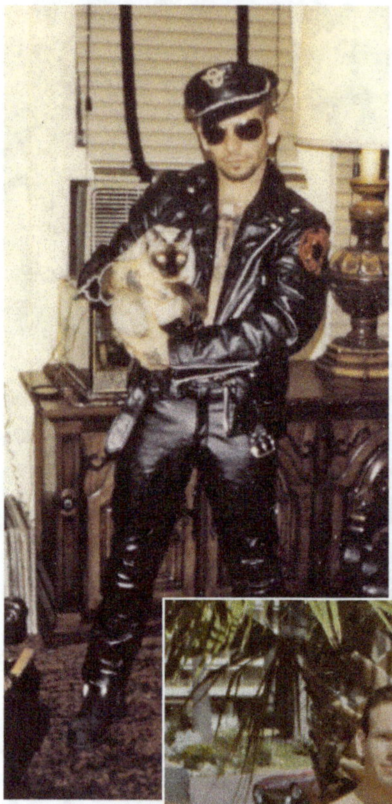

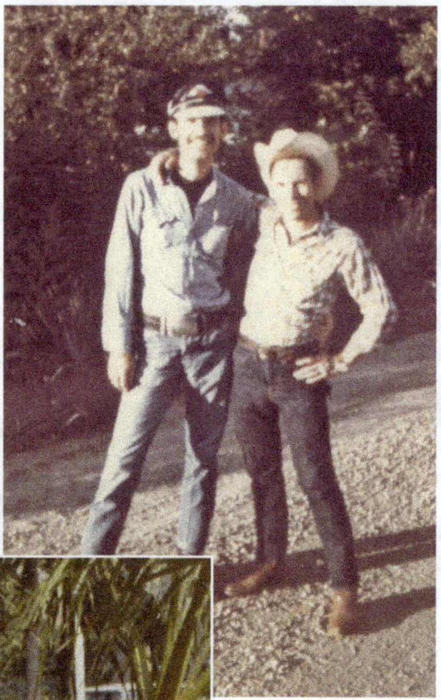

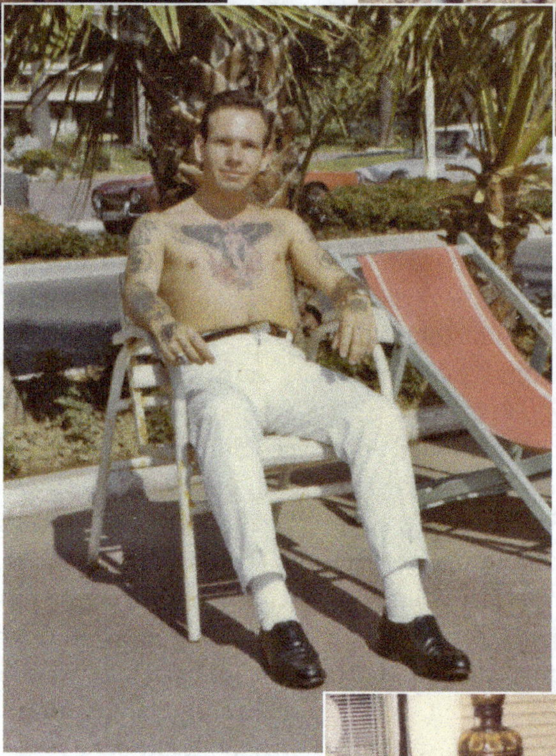

Ron, a pal and fellow NYMBC member. He pierced my ear.

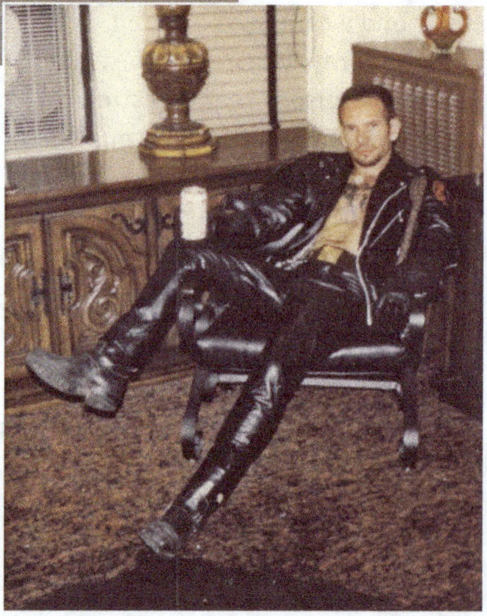

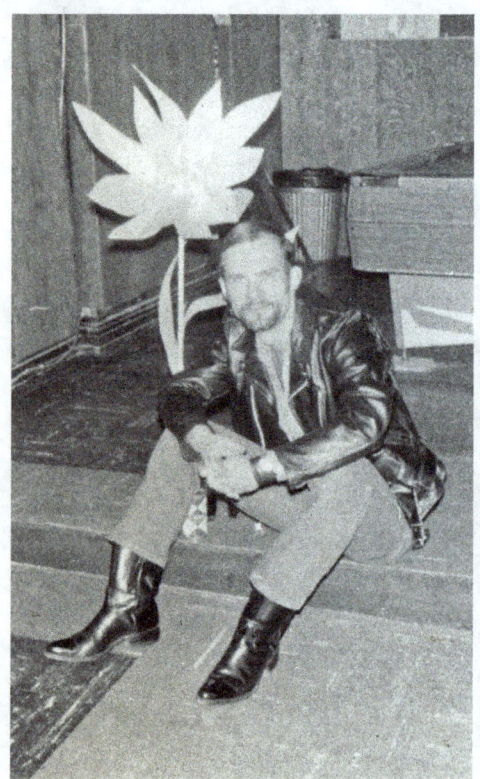

In my new finery at the New York Motorbike Club

14

you could outfit yourself and build your toy collection was hardly commonplace. The Leather Man on Christopher Street was one of the few, but catering as they did to a small, select clientele meant their prices were high. A fellow member of the motorbike club gave me the address of a shop on Delancey Street where I could pick up a motorcycle jacket at a reasonable price. The shopping experience was one I'll never forget. Delancey Street is one of New York's colorful ethnic neighborhoods, home to an orthodox Jewish community. It seemed an unlikely place to shop for fetish wear. The store itself was tiny, but there was, in fact, a rack of shiny motorcycle jackets of decent quality. A very orthodox-looking merchant waited on me and, unfazed, helped me find one that fit. If memory serves me correctly, the price was $35.

My next stop was a western wear store, where I purchased a pair of Levi's, a pair of Wellington boots, and a black cowboy hat. Having grown up in orthopedic shoes, I expected the boots to be uncomfortable, but to my amazement they weren't. With my purchases in hand, I could hardly wait to get back to my apartment. I immediately took off all my clothes, put on the boots and jacket, and jerked off in front of a mirror, the feel and smell of the leather fueling my lust. It felt like a rite of passage.

Unfortunately, there was some validity in my fear of losing friends, as I discovered all too soon. I had two acquaintances, Armand and Jerry, with whom I'd developed a close relationship. It never crossed my mind that they wouldn't embrace my new self-discovery with enthusiasm. Had the situation been reversed, I would have been thrilled to watch their own personal growth.

Dressed in my new finery, I went to visit them one evening. If the doorman was surprised at my appearance, he gave no indication and admitted me as he had on numerous other occasions.

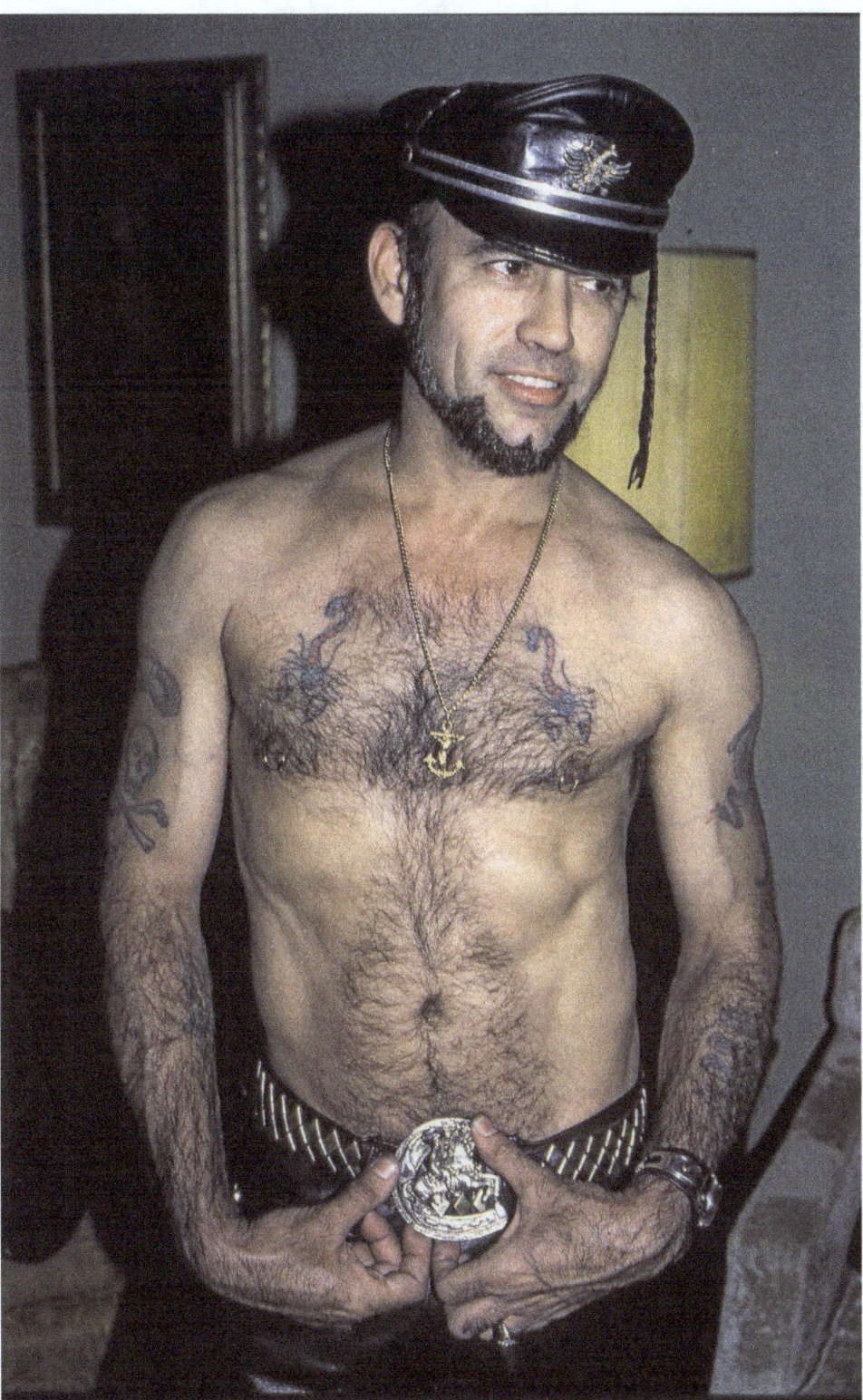

Fernando, the first person I ever saw with pierced nipples

I was not prepared for the reception I received when I knocked on Armand and Jerry's door. They were horrified, and there was no mistaking their displeasure. Armand made it very clear I was not welcome in their home until I came to my senses.

I was stunned. I had overlooked their own idiosyncrasies: their alcoholism and Armand's pretensions to being a bishop in some obscure offshoot of the Catholic Church, swishing around their apartment celebrating Mass in high ecclesiastical drag. Who were they to

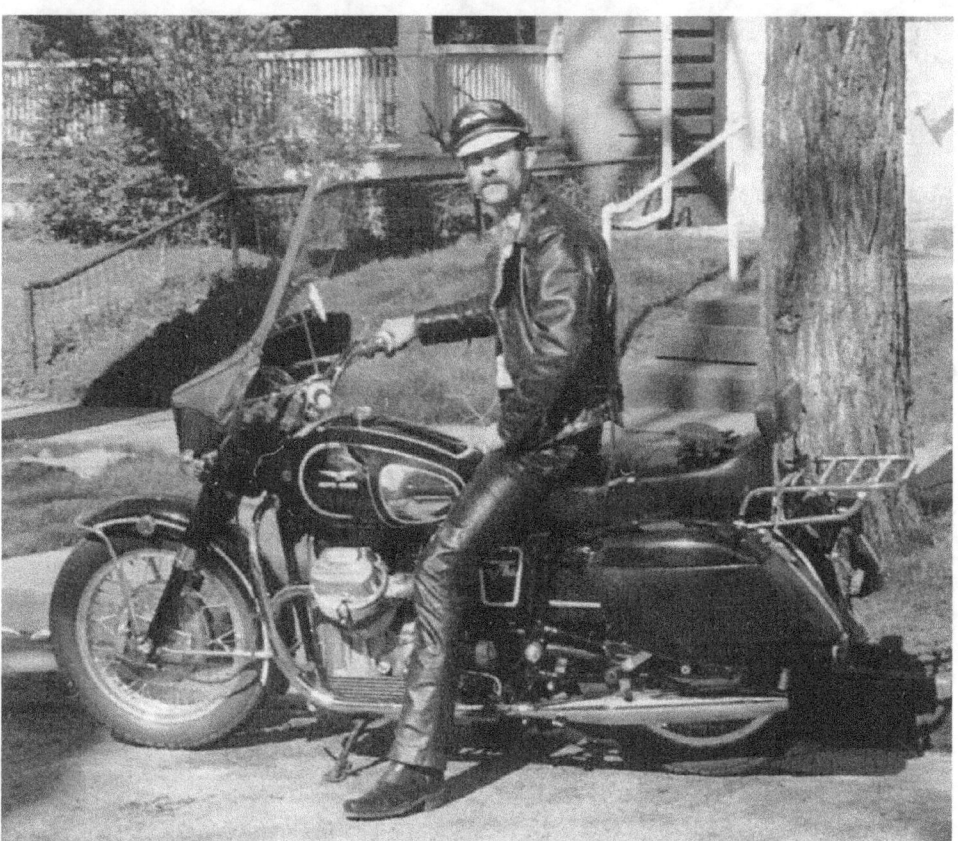

Road ready in my leathers astride my new Moto Guzzi

judge me? Without a word, I turned and left and never saw either one of them again. I went home and cried over the experience, not from shame, but that I had wasted several years of my life on two people who could pass judgment so quickly with no compassion or effort at understanding. I had been demonized based on some preconception, the same kind of prejudice gay people so often face from the society in which we live. It was a painful awakening, a reminder that gay people can be just as mean and petty as anyone else, and that being gay does not make someone my brother or sister—or friend.

About this time, I chanced upon an article in *Gentlemen's Quarterly* about a man who had made an extensive sea voyage. To mark the occasion, he had had his ear pierced.[1] Reading this article triggered something in my psyche. I felt compelled and had to have an ear pierced. It didn't matter that it was 1967, and openly wearing an earring

was the equivalent of saying, "I'm gay!" This was just something I had to do.

The New York Motorbike Clubhouse was located in a storefront near the foot of Christopher Street, a short distance from the docks and the leather bars. With Steve and Marc's sponsorship, I became a member and made friends with a number of the others. One of them was a man named Ron, an ex-merchant seaman with the tattoos in keeping with that profession. His earlobes were tattooed with stars, in the middle of which were piercings. The tattoos and pierced ears turned me on, and led us to share some sexual exploits. We ended up as good buddies. Once I made the decision to have an ear pierced, it seemed natural to ask Ron to do it. One weekend we got together, and Ron pierced my ear using a large sewing needle. With a bit of maneuvering, he was finally able to insert a small gold ear stud through the piercing. It was done.

At the time, I was working in a deco-

rator showroom that sold tacky pictures and statuary to interior designers. There was every likelihood that my pierced ear would not be acceptable to my employer. Still, it was necessary to leave something in the piercing for at least six weeks until it was sufficiently healed to be able to leave the stud out through the workday. Every morning before I left for work, I would carefully clean the piercing and put a Band-Aid over it. If anyone asked, I reasoned, I could always say I cut myself shaving. No one seemed to notice. At the end of six weeks, I was able to take the stud out before going to work and insert it again when I got home. The piercing healed and is with me today.

In my late teens, I had discovered the erotic pleasures of nipple play. Soon after getting my ear pierced, a fantasy began taking shape of piercing my nipples and wearing gold rings in them. It was a fantasy that never ceased to turn me on, even though it was as scary as it was erotic. I found myself unable to confide this secret desire to anyone, even Ron. But I could stave off the inevitable only so long. Finally, one Saturday afternoon I gathered the courage to attempt piercing my own nipples.

An ex-lover and neighbor of mine was a watchmaker. In his small toolbox filled with various materials that he used in his trade was a small roll of thin gold wire. I snipped a few inches of it and from them fashioned a couple of small gold rings about ⅜" in diameter. Although I filed the ends so there would be no burrs or rough edges, they still had no closure and were way too thin for the job, but at the time I had no way of knowing this was problematic.

That fateful Saturday afternoon I took the gold rings, a cork from a bottle of wine, and a pushpin, and soaked them in a small dish of alcohol. After cleaning my nipples with some of the alcohol, I pressed the cork against one side of my nipple, the point of the pushpin on the other. Taking a deep breath, I forced the pin through and into the cork. It hurt, but not that badly. By this time, I was sweating and feeling a bit light-headed. After lying down for a few minutes, I recovered sufficiently to proceed. Of course, it would be necessary to remove the pin to insert the ring. When I did, the wound began to bleed a little, but fortunately not enough to be a problem. The difficult part was trying to maneuver the round ring through the straight hole. This took several harrowing minutes, but I finally succeeded. All that remained was to do the other nipple. Somehow I managed. It was a testimony to my determination that I finished. But after the erotic rush had past, I freaked out a bit at what I had done and removed the rings. By the following morning, were it not for the pleasurable tenderness, I would not have known what had happened the previous day.

But the fantasy of pierced nipples would not go away. Finally, after a few weeks, I gathered up my determination and my trusty makeshift tools and repeated the ordeal. This time I

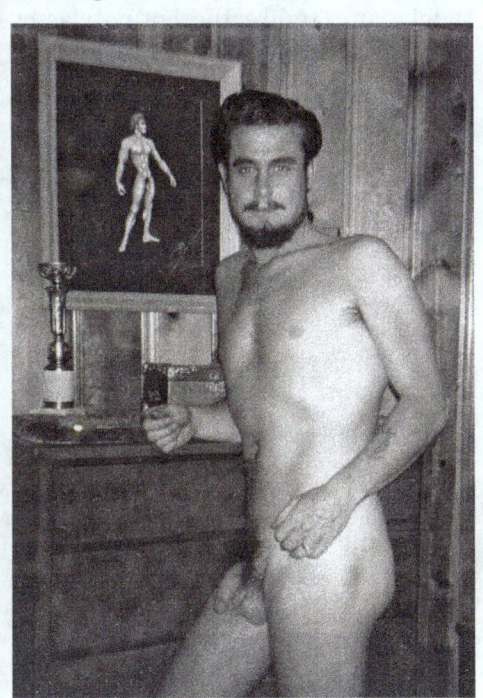

Bud, my Denver roommate and occasional fuck buddy

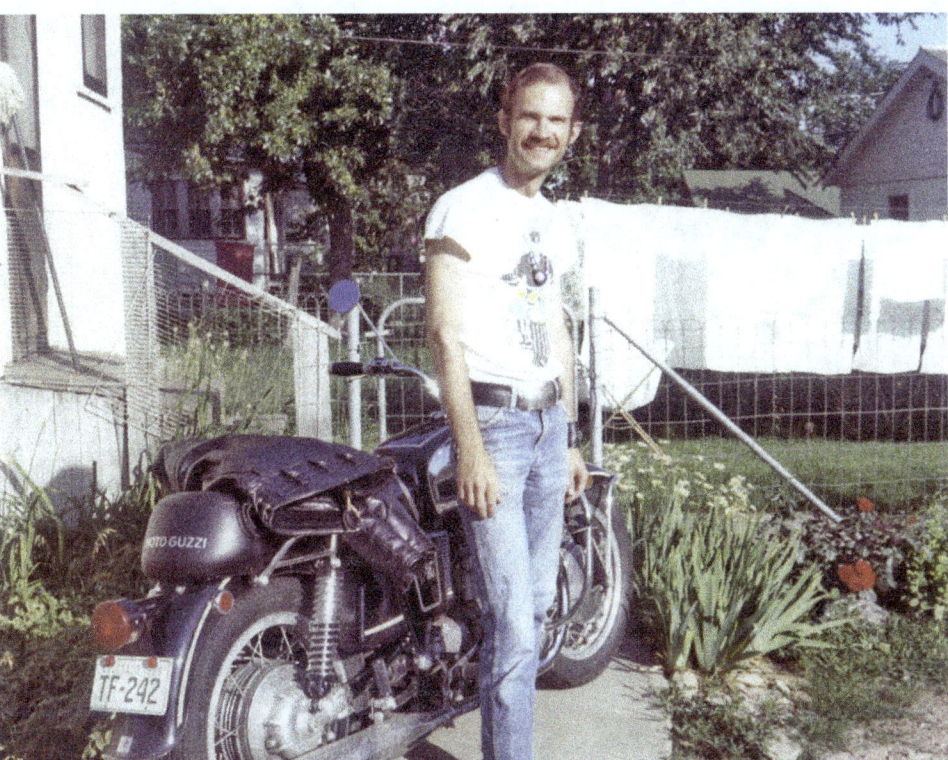

Behind the Denver house with my Moto Guzzi, summer of 1969

left the rings in place, though I was very closeted about having them and carefully removed them before going to bed with anyone. After sex I would get dressed, go to the bathroom, and secretly reinsert the rings.

At this point in my life, I had never seen or heard of anyone with pierced nipples even in the pages of *National Geographic*. That was soon to change. One weekend night I went to the Village to hang out at the NYMBC. It was a quiet night, and several of us decided to wander down to one of the leather bars on West Street. Standing shirtless by the bar was a hunk of a man. Even in the subdued light there was no missing the glint of gold on his muscular chest. His nipples were pierced. I learned that his name was Fernando and that he was something of a local legend. Though I was never fortunate enough to enjoy the intimate pleasure of his company, I was comforted to know that someone else shared my lust for this form of body adornment.

The year 1968 marked another turning point in my life. One weekend eve-

ning, I met up with my friends Steve and Marc to head into Manhattan to cruise the leather bars. Much to my surprise, Steve had a trick in tow, a man named Bud who I had had an affair with when I'd been a student at the University of Colorado at Boulder. The old passion between us was rekindled, and by the time Bud had to return to Denver, I had decided to pull up stakes and move back to Colorado to be with him. Thanks to major challenges—his long-term lover, primarily—the love affair was short-lived, though I stayed on sharing the house with him, said lover Tom, and Bud's aged mother Viola.

By this time, I had become much more comfortable about my nipple piercings, and made no effort to conceal them from my sexual partners and close friends. The lust for another piercing was beginning to take hold of my psyche. I visited a local jeweler and had him make a small abutted ring in white gold about 1/16" thick with an inside diameter of 3/8". The chosen location for the piercing was my frenum, that thin web of tissue that connects

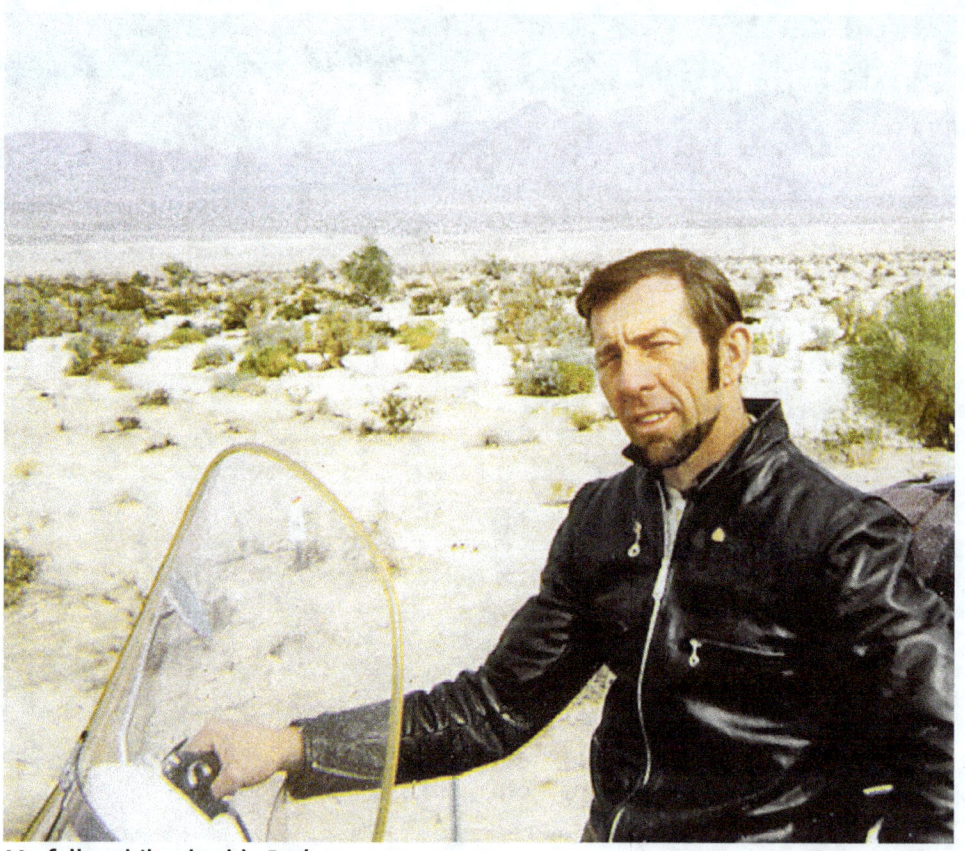

My fellow biker buddy Rod

the underside of the penis head with the shaft. Somehow I managed to accomplish the piercing and insert and close the ring. But, alas, the piercing was doomed. Unwise in the ways of the body in those days, I had no idea that the placement was wrong and that such delicate tissue would not accommodate a piercing. It healed quickly, but within a short period of time the hole began to enlarge until the thin tissue finally split, and the ring fell out.

By now Bud was bitten by the piercing bug. One weekend he decided to do a surface piercing on himself in the center of his chest at the base of his throat. Years later, a Gauntlet piercer would dub this the Madison after a local porn star. Bud's piercing actually healed, and he wore a ring in it for a couple of years until it inexplicably began to migrate to the surface and soon suffered the same fate as my frenum piercing.

Denver had a small but active leather community, and a number of its members got together and decided to start a

motorcycle club. It was called the Rocky Mountaineers, and is still in existence. I was one of the charter members, and eventually I purchased a Moto Guzzi motorcycle and learned to ride it.

During the years of my sojourn in Denver, the club organized a number of motorcycle runs and invited men from other clubs all over the country to participate. For one of these a couple of guys came from Omaha. I became intimate with one of them, and by the end of the weekend, he wanted me to pierce his nipples. This was the first time I ever pierced anyone else. We managed to find a pair of earrings that would work, but I had no idea of a better way to do the piercing than the way I had done my own. Although the outcome was ultimately successful, there was little doubt in my mind that there had to be a better technique.

The Sixties had spawned the Human Potential Movement, resulting in the widespread popularity of many kinds of psychotherapies. I was not immune

to the appeal, and joined a gay encounter group that met weekly at a local church. A chance remark by a fuck-buddy of mine named Victor, who was also a member of the encounter group, led to my saying goodbye to Colorado and moving to Los Angeles to pursue Primal Therapy.

Once I'd settled down and my therapy was well underway, the time came to do something about employment. A fellow patient named Diane came up with the idea that we should take up court reporting. After all, it was a well-paying profession with great job security. We enrolled in a Los Angeles court reporting school and started learning the fundamentals of stenotype.[2] It didn't take Diane long to lose interest and drop out. I stuck with it for almost a year before realizing just how deadly boring the life of a court reporter could be.

But my stint at court reporting school was not a total loss. In addition to developing typing skills, students were required to take and pass a comprehensive class in English grammar and punctuation. The class was well taught and, unlike the boring classes I'd suffered through in high school, held my attention and actually made sense. When I eventually started publishing a magazine about body piercing, the skills I learned came in very handy.

For my first year or so in California, most of the friends I made were people who were also in therapy. The main exception was my friend and fellow Rocky Mountaineer Rod from Denver. He had been married for some years and had several grown children. Approaching middle age, he was no longer willing to deny that sexually he preferred men. The year before I moved to L.A., he packed a few essentials, said goodbye to wife and family, climbed on his Harley, and headed for California, settling down in Los Angeles with a succession of male lovers. Soon after

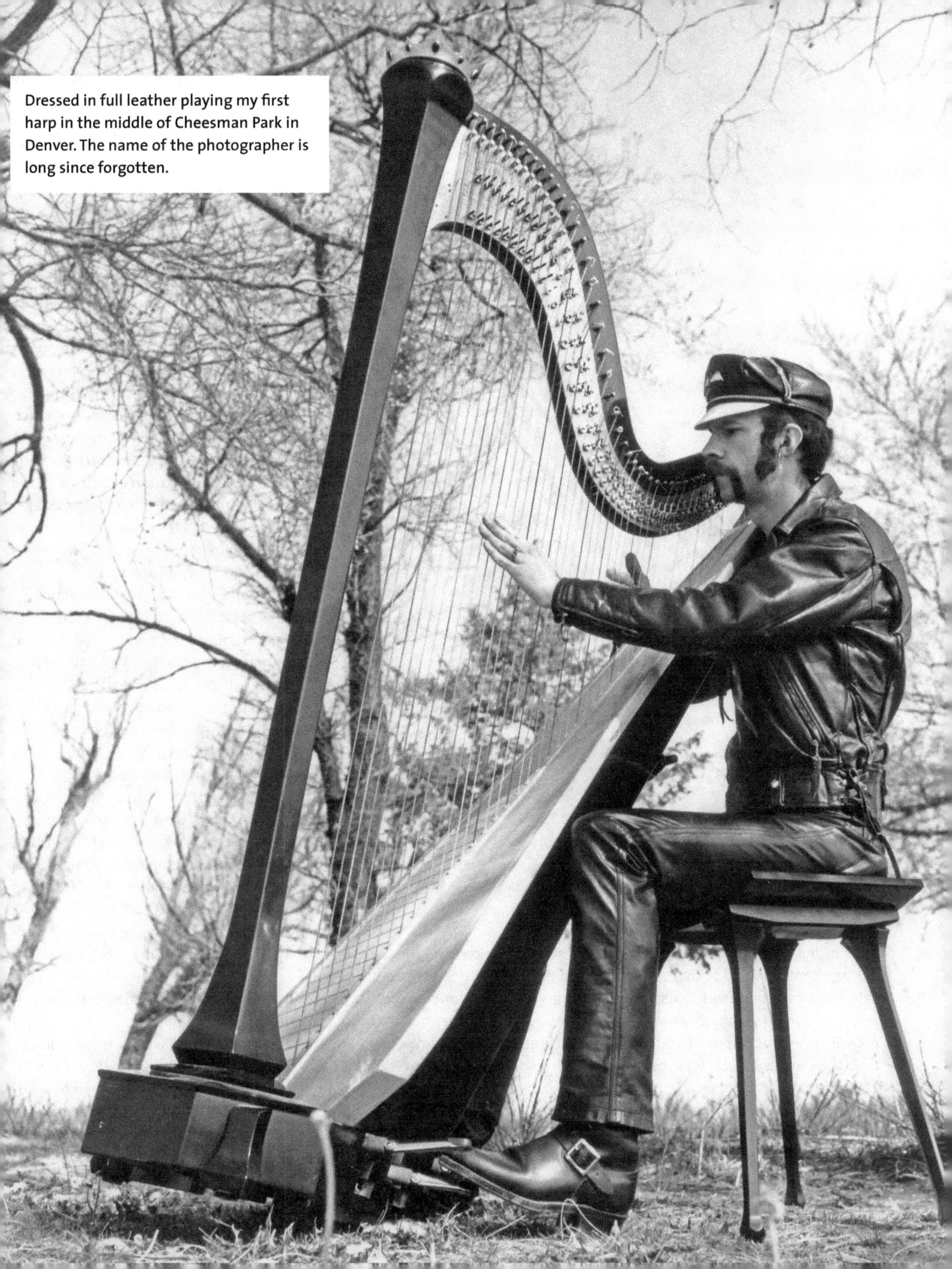

Dressed in full leather playing my first harp in the middle of Cheesman Park in Denver. The name of the photographer is long since forgotten.

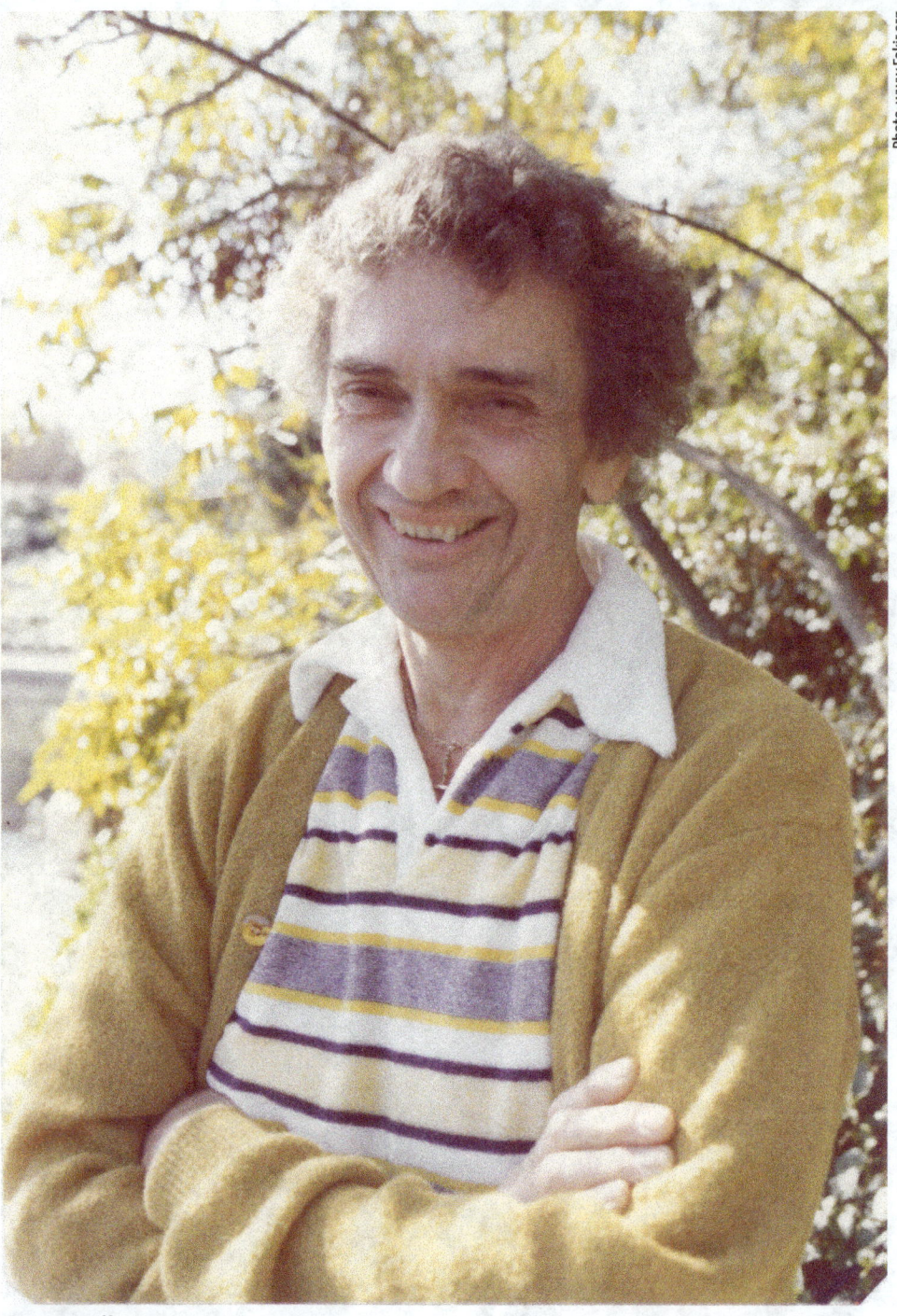

Doug Malloy

arriving, he took a job as a bus driver.

I've often marveled at that thing we call fate. Does such really exist, and if not, how do we explain those amazing coincidences that happen in our lives?

Rod's regular route was between Hollywood and downtown Los Angeles. One day among his passengers was an amiable longhaired gentleman who, taking a seat near the driver, struck up a conversation. The man's name was Tom, and he worked as a librarian at the downtown public library. Tom became a regular commuter, and one morning as they were chatting en route to downtown, a man with a pierced ear boarded the bus. The conversation turned to the subject of piercing, and Rod said, "I have a friend with pierced nipples," to which Tom replied, "I'd like to meet him."

I must confess that I secretly hoped that Tom would be a sexy hunk, but instead I met a rather plain, round-faced, slightly heavyset man in need of dental work. Whatever he lacked in looks was offset, to some extent, by a sunny disposition and a passion for piercing. He shared with me a collection of letters and photographs from a number of fellow enthusiasts who, at the time, were unknown to me. Among these was one Rolly Loomis, who would, in due course, make a reputation for himself as Fakir Musafar. The photographs of him that Tom showed me were truly awesome. I'd never seen anything like them. There were pictures of reenactments of the Native American Sun Dance and Hindu Kavadi ceremony as well as a profusion of images of the most unusual body piercings I had ever seen. They made me aware that there were many more piercing possibilities than I had ever dreamed of.

Another of Tom's correspondents was a man named Doug Malloy. He was supposedly some well-traveled expert on the subject of piercing. Since he lived locally, Tom arranged for us to get together one evening so I could meet him. We were to rendezvous at the public library where Tom worked and then go out for dinner.

Doug arrived with a guest, a man named Alan Oversby. Over dinner, I learned that Doug had recently written a short autobiographical account of his piercing exploits called *The Adventures of a Piercing Freak*[3] and had used the money from selling the book to a publisher to pay for Alan's plane ticket.

Alan, it turned out, was from England where he worked as a tattoo artist who also did body piercing. His professional name was "Mr. Sebastian," an homage to the Catholic saint who was martyred by being pierced with arrows. Doug had corresponded with him, and Alan had shown a great deal of interest in learning more about the art and technical aspects of piercing.

It was a pleasant evening. We parted company, and I heard nothing further from either Doug or Alan.

At this point, I had been a patient at the Primal Institute for a couple of years. A friend and fellow patient named Jim decided it was time to get on with his life and moved to San Francisco. Periodically, I would fly up to spend a weekend with him. He would show me the sights. Sometimes we'd smoke a little grass and hit the gay nightspots.

On one of these outings, a guy named Eric came on to me. We spent some time together. Though the chemistry wasn't perfect, he pursued me, and we started to see each other on a regular basis, sometimes in San Francisco, sometimes in L.A. We eventually became lovers.

Eric was very turned on by my nipple piercings and called me to see if I would pierce his nipples the next time he came to L.A. While I was certainly willing, I realized that my pushpin-and-wine-bottle-cork method left a lot of room for improvement. I also knew from my brief meeting with Doug that earrings were not the right jewelry for the job. With a knowledgeable source so close at hand, it made sense to see if I could get a little guidance.

I called Tom and, after explaining the situation, asked if he would give me Doug's phone number. This he did, and I gave Doug a call, asking if he would be willing to share some of his piercing techniques with me and tell me where I might be able to purchase appropriate jewelry. He was gracious and most accommodating. The techniques he'd developed over the years were at my disposal. All I needed to do was let him know when Eric would be in town and we'd make the necessary arrangements.

As for jewelry, there weren't many choices. Doug knew of a jeweler in San Diego who would make gold rings, but the guy was asking $200 apiece for them—that's $200 in 1975 currency!

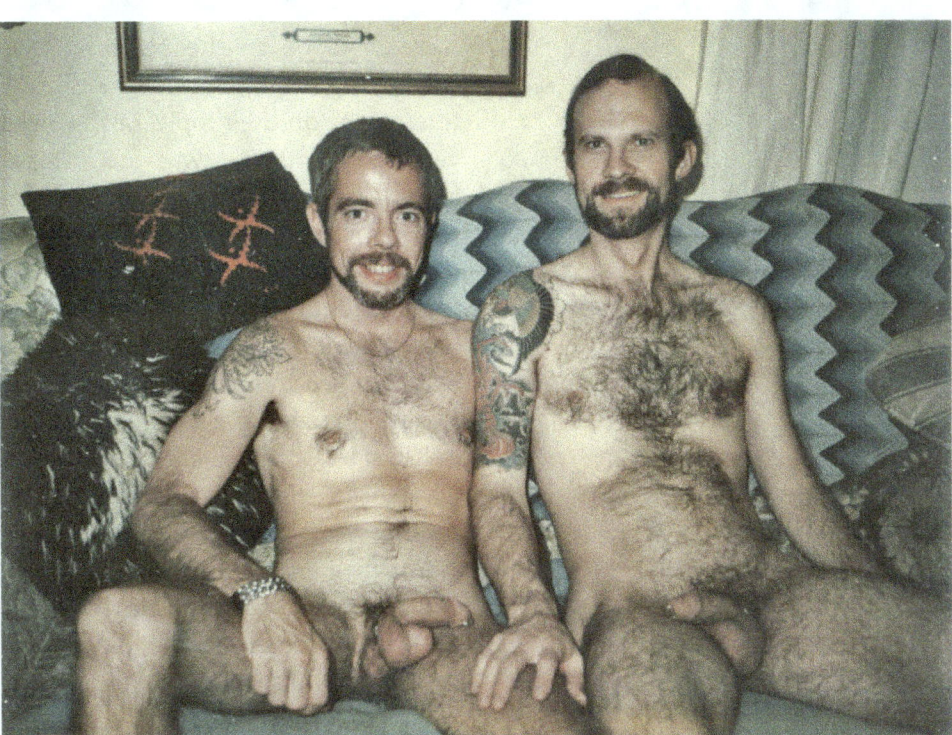

On the couch with my lover Eric

This was much more than I was willing to pay. Having taken several jewelry making classes in New York, including one for professionals, I had a pretty good idea what it would take to make a pair of nipple rings, and it wouldn't cost anywhere near $400. For a fraction of that amount, I could buy the raw materials and the necessary tools as well.

Doug and I had several discussions about the best kind of jewelry to use for new nipple piercings. There was some question whether they would heal better with a curved ring or something straight. In the end, we decided that the latter would be the better choice. With that in mind, I set out to create an appropriate design. Thus came into being my first pieces of body piercing jewelry. I called them "nipple retainers."

Consulting the Yellow Pages, I discovered a lapidary shop in nearby Hollywood where I was able to purchase enough 16-gauge gold wire for the project and the various tools I needed, all for under $50.

Once the jewelry was made, Eric arranged to come down to L.A. for the piercing. We set up a time for Doug to

come over and supervise. He brought his "kit" of implements. These included a pair of Pennington forceps. These are now an industry standard, but at that time were something pretty exotic. There was also an assortment of heavy gauge hypodermic needles, the kind used on livestock, and what in the 1950s had no doubt been a state-of-the-art ear-piercing gun. This latter contraption consisted of a plunger on the end of which was mounted a pointed piece of wire about ¾" long. Over this wire was fitted a metal sleeve called a cannula that was short enough to leave the point exposed. By pressing firmly on the plunger, this needle and sleeve were forced through the tissue and between a fork-like stop on the opposite side. Once the pressure was released, a spring would retract the plunger pulling back the needle and, hopefully, leaving the cannula in the tissue. The jewelry could then be inserted by butting it against the end of the cannula and following it through the piercing.

My mother worked 25 years for an eye doctor, so I understood the impor-

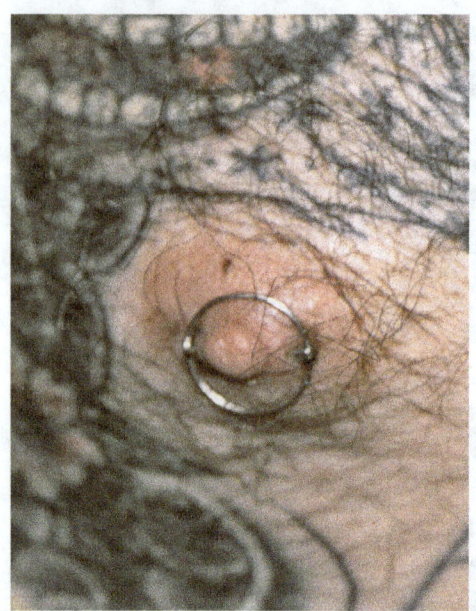

The Nipple Retainer, my very first jewelry design

tance of proper sterilization. Fortunately, I had a pressure cooker that I usually used for cooking, but it worked just fine as a stand-in for an autoclave. These were the days before AIDS, so we gave no thought to latex gloves. If, we reasoned, dentists and tattooists worked without them, why should we? Only doctors doing surgery wore them. We believed that a thorough hand washing would be sufficient.

Except for using the ear-piercing gun as part of the procedure, the piercing technique itself was much like it is today. The nipple was first cleaned. Since surgeons were using it in surgery, we had elected to use Betadine instead of alcohol. Next, using a fine-tipped marking pen, a small dot was made on either side of the nipple where we wanted the openings of the

piercing to be. In the beginning we tried just clamping a pair of Pennington forceps on the nipple, but realized very quickly that it was too painful, at least for most people. The problem was solved by wrapping a rubber band several times around the handle of the Pennington forceps and adjusting for the right grip. Next, the nipple was clamped into the forceps and the marks aligned in the same location on either side. Once the ear-piercing gun was placed in position, the needle and cannula were forced through the nipple. As the needle retracted, the cannula was left in place. After laying aside the gun, the forceps were removed and the jewelry inserted.

Though crude by today's standards, Doug's technique worked amazingly well, and the piercing went smoothly. Eric returned to San Francisco happy.

Not long afterward, Doug called me up and asked me to have lunch with him. He picked me up in his sports car, and we went to the Red Room, a little Swedish café in West Hollywood not far

from the picture frame shop where I was working. Over lunch the conversation naturally turned to our shared passion. To my surprise, Doug said he thought I should start a piercing business. After all, I already knew how to make the jewelry. The only thing that remained was for him to teach me what he knew about the various piercings and his techniques for doing them. I could start out working part-time from home, and he would share his private mailing list of enthusiasts from around the world as the basis for mail order. When I pointed out that I lacked the capital to launch such an endeavor, he told me he was prepared to lend me whatever it would take. He firmly believed that a need existed for such a business and told me that from the moment he first laid eyes on me at the library, he'd known that we were destined to do something together. This was it.

How could I pass up such a generous offer and the possibility of creating a career for myself doing something I loved? I said yes.

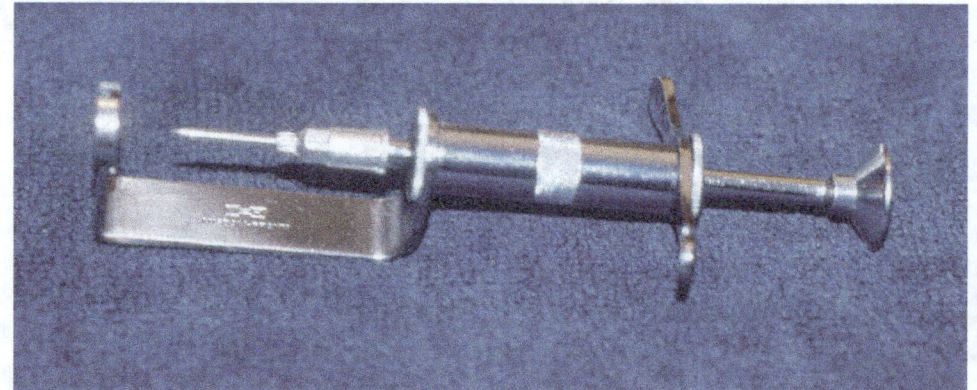

The original ear-piercing gun that we used to pierce nipples. It proved inadequate for the job, though we used it for years for other piercings.

---

[1] Though I wasn't aware of it at the time, there is an old Navy tradition of piercing a sailor's ear(s) upon crossing the Equator for the first time. An article about it appeared in *PFIQ* issue #21.

[2] This wacky system of machine shorthand is nearly a century old. Syllables, words, and phrases are transcribed onto a paper strip—nowadays onto computer—by pressing multiple keys simultaneously. The keyboard does not contain all the letters of the alphabet, and the missing equivalents are produced by combinations of existing characters.

People have tried for years to trick their state Department of Motor Vehicles into putting the "F word" on their vanity license plates. Someone actually succeeded by using stenotype. I laughed when I got behind a car the plate of which read TPUBGU. That spells FUCK YOU.

[3] The complete text appears in the Appendix.

CHAPTER 3

Starting any new business can be challenging, especially for someone who's never done it before. The challenge gets multiplied several times when one sets out into unknown territory: an industry that never existed before. To the best of my knowledge, no one before me had ever attempted to do body piercing exclusively as a profession. In the past, if anyone wanted an exotic piercing, they did it themselves, had a friend do it, or sought help from one of a small handful of tattooists who offered piercing services as a sideline.

I imagine the process of starting a new business is pretty much the same anywhere, but in California one has to file a fictitious name statement and run a notice in the newspaper to the effect that you're doing business under the chosen name. Next, one opens a business bank account and submits the necessary paperwork to the State Board of Equalization for the privilege of collecting sales tax. Plus there are lots of little odds and ends. It's not particularly difficult, but the task is time-consuming and fraught with aggravation. However, before any of these can be done, the business requires a name.

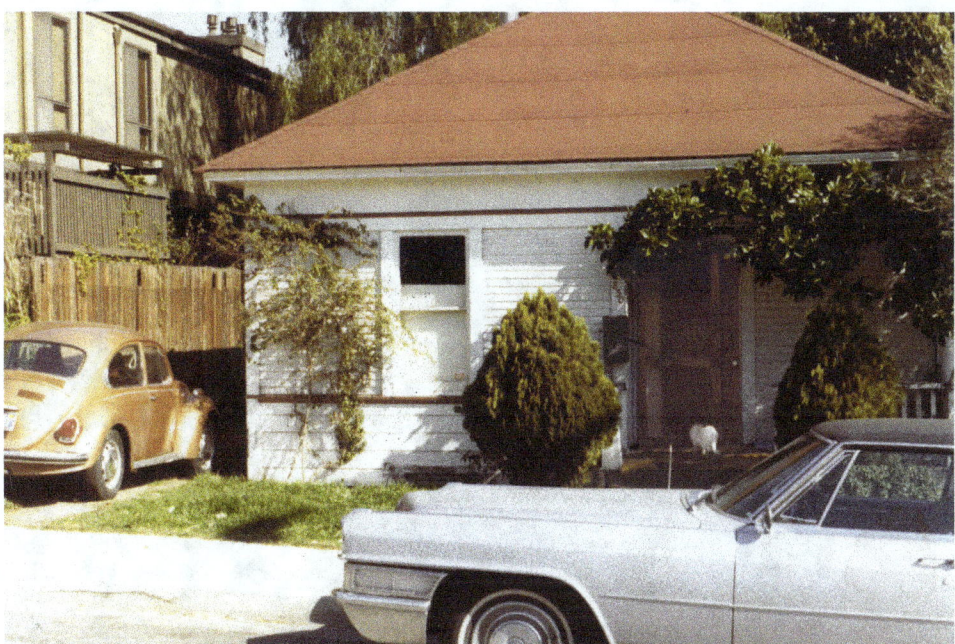

850 North San Vicente, Gauntlet's West Hollywood birthplace c. 1975

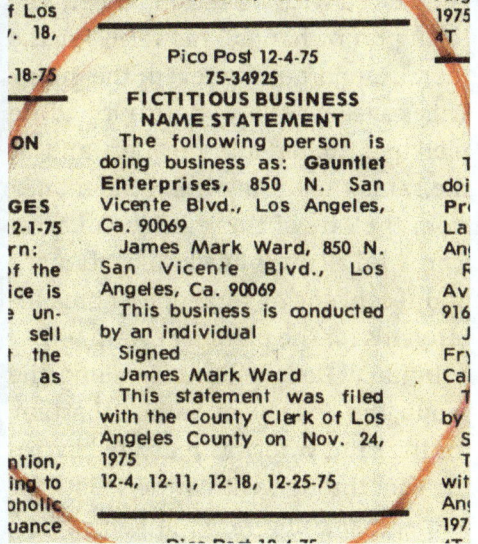

The newspaper notice that made Gauntlet official

Doug and I went back and forth trying to come up with something. He favored a mythological theme such as the name of a Greek god—Apollo comes to mind. I wanted something with a tough, masculine feel that would appeal particularly to the gay leathermen and S/M fetishists I perceived as my most likely customer base.

In the process of accessorizing my leather wardrobe, I had made a wide leather watchband edged with silver-colored, pyramid-shaped studs. While watching television one night, I removed my watch and set it on the end table. A short time later, I glanced over to see what time it was, and in a flash the name came to me. GAUNTLET! It was everything I wanted the name to be. In addition to being rugged and masculine, it also had metaphoric implications. In English, we have two sayings: "run the gauntlet," and "throw down the gauntlet," expressions for the ordeal and the challenge. Didn't that precisely describe this business venture? I did have momentary second thoughts about the name only because there was already a well-known leather bar in L.A. called The Gauntlet. But that didn't seem to

be a big problem since I'd be calling my business Gauntlet Enterprises and wouldn't be selling liquor.

Doug liked the name as soon as I told him about it. He was, however, of the opinion that I should incorporate. But since he didn't want to be a stockholder or to have any legal attachments to the business, I opted for a sole proprietorship.

It was November, astrologically the time of year Scorpio babies are born. Scorpios are supposed to be highly sexual, so I thought it would be an ideal time to give birth to my business. Since the sign ends around the 21st of the month, I needed to act soon. On November 17, 1975, I drove to the closest newspaper office, filled out the necessary forms, and filed the fictitious name statement, giving life to Gauntlet Enterprises.

There was now a flurry of activity. So many things needed to be seen to: the bank account, sales tax issues, setting up a place to make jewelry, developing jewelry designs, designing a logo... the list went on. Everything seemed to be happening at once.

My mental picture of the logo was of a stylized gauntlet forming the let-

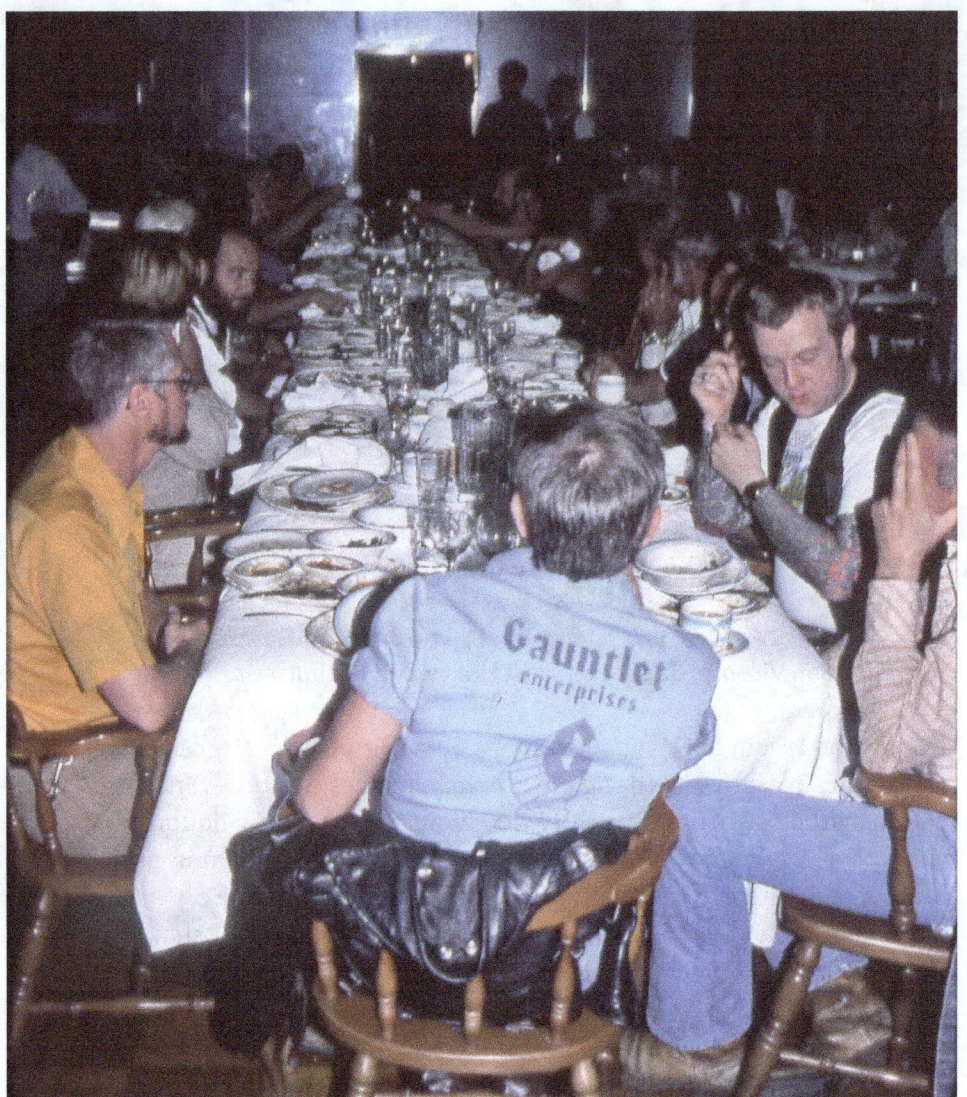

The T&P Group dining at a local restaurant. After the meal we would adjourn to someone's house where anyone who wished could get pierced.

ter "G." It could thus be used alone or combined with the remaining letters of the word. I found a rub-on capital "G" I liked in a font called "Hondo." Adding details with pen and ink and lots of patience, I finally produced a result that pleased me.

To be able to make jewelry, I needed a jeweler's workbench. Commercially made ones were very expensive, and I felt the money could be better spent. Using scrap lumber from construction sites and a piece of plywood from a packing crate, I made my own workbench. It might not have been much to look at, but it was functional and adequate for my needs. Amazingly, I still have it today.

Among some of today's young piercing enthusiasts, Gauntlet has a reputation for being "conservative," a dirty word usually used with a note of contempt. The same people who are quick to assume that I never took risks often fail to consider what things were like in 1975.

Because there was no precedent I was aware of, everything I did in those days was a risk. No one had ever attempted this type of business, especially on the scale I envisioned. There was no Internet providing vast informational resources at the tip of one's fingers. Every piercing technique, every jewelry design, and every material used for the jewelry or in the piercing

process had to be subjected to a trial and error process. That meant taking risks. Rather than calling me conservative, I prefer the word cautious. It was essential to me that every precaution be taken to assure the well-being of every person I pierced or who wore my jewelry. What would the fate of the entire piercing industry have been if I hadn't proceeded with care and someone had suffered serious harm? How quickly would everything I was building have collapsed in ruin?

Fortunately, starting out with such a small customer base I was able to personally keep tabs on my clients. If something went wrong, I had the opportunity to figure out why and immediately try an alternative. By proceeding with caution, I could progress slowly and minimize the risk of serious harm.

Primarily by placing classified ads in various gay and fetish publications, Doug had made contact with a couple of dozen gay men in the L.A. area who shared his fetish for piercing. As a means of helping get Gauntlet launched, Doug proposed that we start a social group for these men. We would get together once a month for a potluck supper. After eating and socializing, anyone who was interested could get pierced with what Doug called "the laying on of hands," his term for the moral support of the rest of the group. This gave me the opportunity to do piercings under his direction and at the same time bring in a little money from the sale of the jewelry. On occasion, we'd all meet at a local restaurant and reconvene at someone's home afterwards for the piercing event.

Initially, Doug proposed calling the group the Society of Saint Sebastian, for the saint who was martyred by being shot through with arrows. But that name, thankfully, never stuck. Instead, it ended up just being called the T&P Group, short for tattooing and piercing.

Back in my fine art days, I'd made some silkscreen prints. The skill came in handy for a bit of advertising and promotion. I silk-screened some T-shirts with the Gauntlet name and logo on the front. I also bought a button-making device and produced a series of buttons with drawings of various piercings, the Gauntlet logo, and the slogan, "We've got what it takes to fill your hole." We gave these out to the T&P Group and to clients who got pierced.

Of course, without Doug none of this would have happened. Over a period of years, he had managed to make contact with around a hundred fellow piercing enthusiasts. He provided a catalog of "traditional" piercings, along with their often-colorful histories, which lent them credibility and implied that they were all possible. However crude,

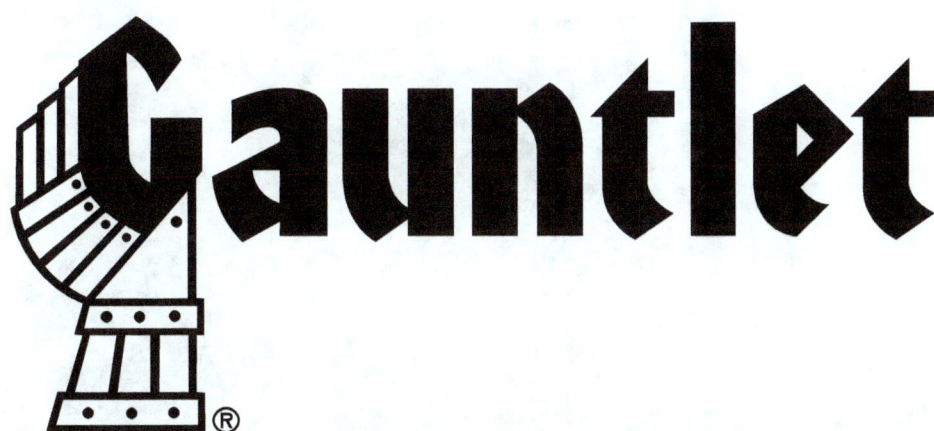

The Gauntlet logo could be used alone or in combination with the whole name.

he had assembled some rudimentary piercing techniques and equipment. These things, combined with my jewelry making ability, provided a foundation on which I could build my infant business, and, though I didn't realize it at the time, help set in motion the modern body piercing movement.

Doug's motives for setting me up in business were not entirely altruistic. He was married and had four adult children, but his heterosexual life provided no outlet for his piercing fetish or the expression of suppressed gay yearnings. By helping me start a piercing business, he was hoping to have the opportunity to fulfill both these needs. Many have assumed that we were lovers. Such was never the case. Early in our relationship, Doug had made advances that I declined. For my part there was no sexual attraction, and I didn't think it wise to mix business with sexual intimacy. Nor did I want to feel like a gigolo exchanging favors for money. Doug and I ended up in bed only once a couple of years later. It was a three-way Doug instigated with a friend of mine named Mike, who had a reputation for being a slut. I was pressured into participating and ended up playing with Doug's nipples while Mike gave him a blowjob.

"Doug Malloy" was what an acquaintance of mine once called the "nom de kinque" of a wealthy Hollywood businessman named Richard Simonton. I

was given to understand that Malloy was his mother's maiden name. Being an Irish name, I can't help thinking one of his forebears must have kissed the Blarney stone, for Doug had a remarkable flair for telling a story, and if it wasn't exactly true, it didn't particularly matter to him as long as the tale was a good one. He told wonderful stories, and the fact that many of them persist despite a lack of any supporting evidence says much for his ability to capture our imaginations.

I know little about his youth. From an early interview, it appears he was born in Chicago, and his family moved to the Seattle area when he was about three. By the time the Depression hit in 1929, he would have been in his early teens. I gathered the family wasn't exactly affluent. As a young man, he displayed an aptitude for music and audio engineering. Eventually, he ended up in Southern California and his fortune began to change. In the early 1940s, he struck a lucrative deal with Muzak, the ubiquitous background music company, which gave him control over the southwestern quarter of the country. It made him a very rich man.

Doug was quite interested in things metaphysical. He had been a personal friend of Ernest Holmes (1887–1960), author of *The Science of Mind* and the founder of the Religious Science movement. Thanks in no small part to Holmes's influence, he was very much a

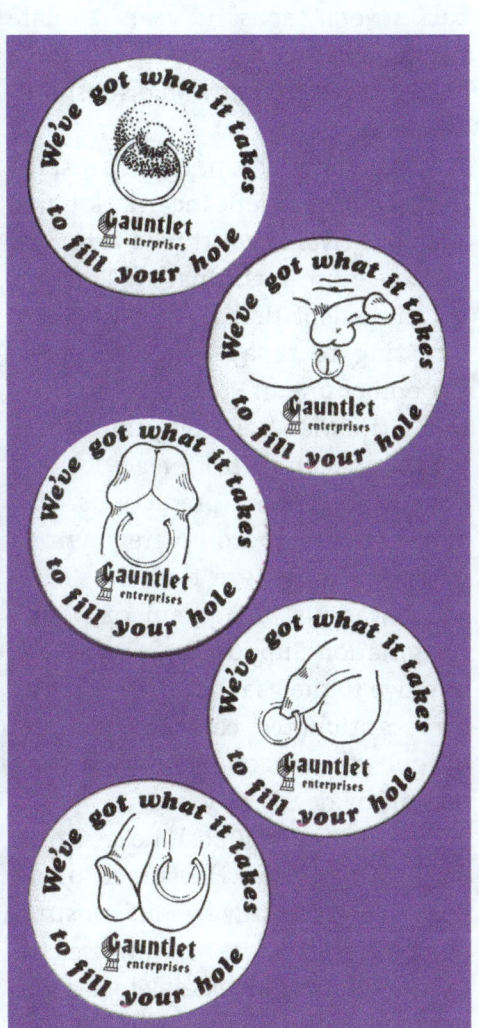

Advertising buttons.

25

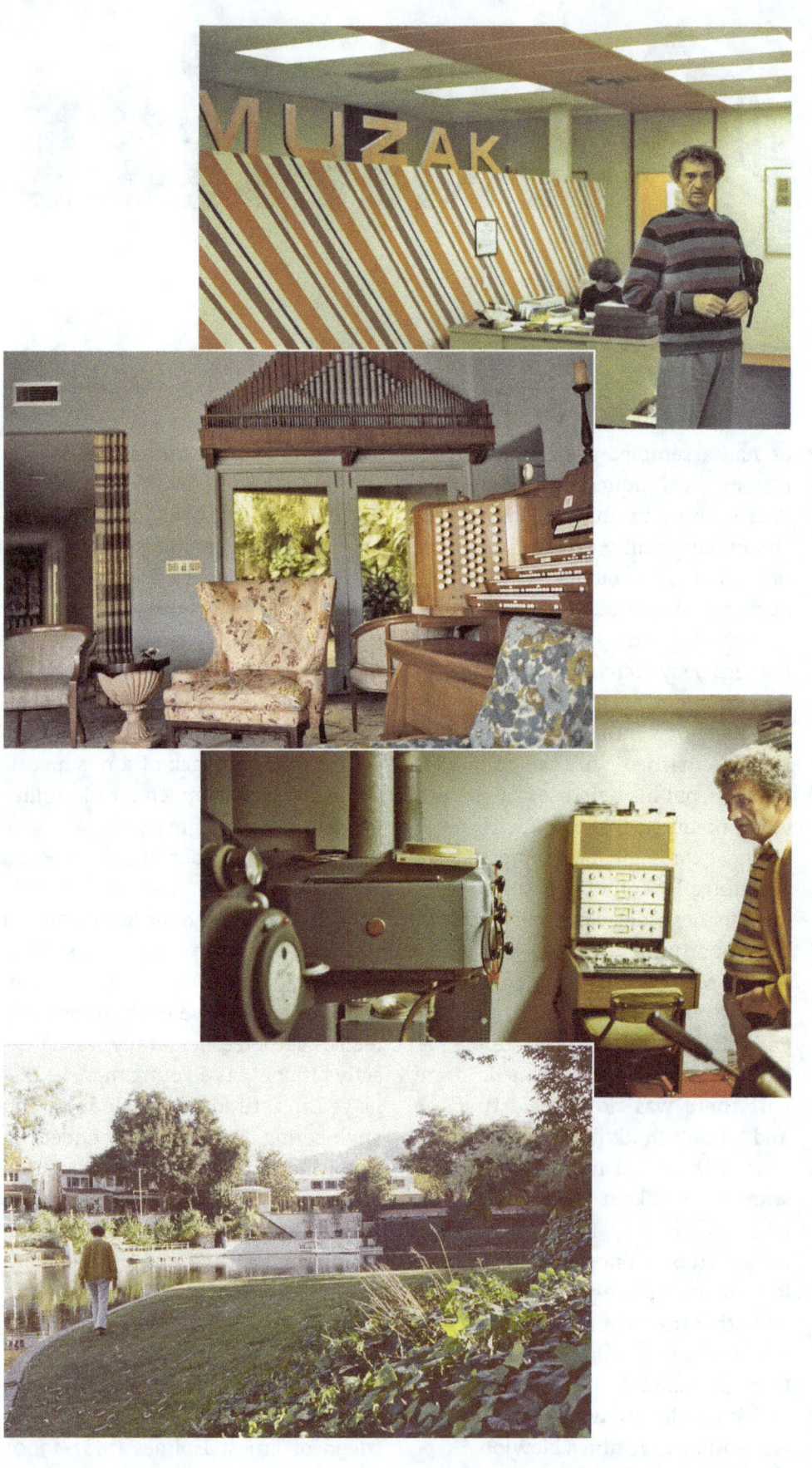

believer in what became known as the "power of positive thinking."

He also believed in reincarnation. According to Doug, it explained not only things like prodigies, but also why some people became passionate about things like body piercing. This, he claimed, was his own case. He remembered a past life during which he had been a highly-placed courtier in the entourage of Egyptian pharaoh Akhenaten.

According to Doug, navel piercing was common amongst the Egyptian aristocracy but forbidden to the lower classes. He claimed that the piercing could be seen in statuary, but try as I might I was unable to see it in the photos that he showed me. Within the last 50 years, archeologists have been able to construct an extremely clear and accurate picture of Egyptian life dating back several thousand years. To date I am unaware of any evidence having been discovered that would substantiate Doug's claim.

Meanwhile, back in Egypt's distant past, Doug's ancient incarnation had a jealous rival at court who arranged to have him assassinated. This left a karmic debt that the rival was attempting to repay in Doug's present embodiment. From time to time, the "Little Man," as Doug called him, would appear and offer advice and occasionally make predictions. One of these was so completely wrong it led me to believe that the "Little Man" was just a figment of Doug's imagination. Supposedly, he was told, he'd live to the year 2000. Perhaps by some antiquated calendar. At least by our modern one, the prediction was off by nearly 25 years.

Doug had a very posh home in the San Fernando Valley. He claimed to have been told psychically to start construction on it even before he'd amassed the fortune necessary to complete it. It was in an area called Toluca Lake, named after the small body of water on the edge

Top to bottom: Doug at the Muzak offices; the living room of Doug's Toluca Lake home; the projection booth in Doug's 99-seat theater; Doug walking the edge of the lake behind his property. All photos by Fakir Musafar (www.fakir.org) c. 1977.

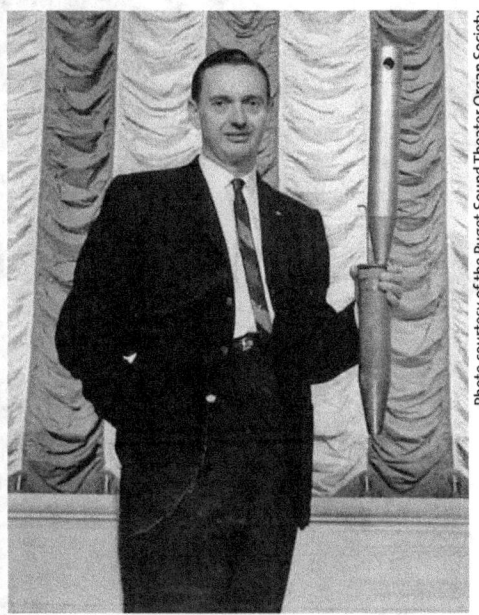

Doug holding a pipe for his Wurlitzer theater organ.

of which the house was being built. To the best of my knowledge, there is no public access to the lake itself because it is completely surrounded by expensive homes. Warner Bros. Studios are a short distance to the East. Doug's neighbors included Bob Hope and Olivia de Havilland, and Walt Disney's brother Roy lived next door.

From the street, the house itself was not particularly impressive. It appeared to be a modest, modern, one-level box. But inside, it was a marvel. There was an atrium with a roof that could be retracted. The house had not one but two pipe organs. One was a church-style organ in the living room. A narrow spiral staircase led downstairs to a small, 99-seat theater, in which there was a fully restored Wurlitzer theater organ dating from the 1920s. Wikipedia currently shows the number to be 63 seats, but Doug told me the number was 99 because any more would violate Actors' Equity regulations.

During the silent movie days, Doug's theater organ had graced a Paramount Pictures sound stage, though additional ranks of pipes were added over the years as old movie houses were demolished and their organs removed. Doug's interest in these musical marvels inspired him to help found the American Theater Organ Society (ATOS) in 1955. His theater also featured a rare Welte reproducing player piano that had been designed and built to reproduce the fine nuances of a live performance. The piano was wired into the organ from which it could be played.

The theater was equipped with state of the art projection and recording facilities. On several occasions, a few other Tattoo & Piercing Group members and I were invited to join Doug's family and some of his other friends for private showings.

Doug had been a very close friend of the comedy film star of silent movie fame, Harold Lloyd. When Harold died in 1971, Doug was the executor of his estate. This gave him access to all of Harold's old films.

Another close friend was an old theater organist named Gaylord Carter. Quite naturally, things came together for showings of several Harold Lloyd silent films accompanied live by Carter. These were truly once-in-a-lifetime experiences, and I'll never forget them.

Doug's interests were many and varied. In addition to organs, he had a passion for steamboats. In 1957 he and his family took a trip on the Mississippi riverboat the Delta Queen. On learning that the company was about to go under and this was to be its final season, Doug purchased controlling interest in the company in 1958. With his entrepreneurial skills, he quickly turned it into a highly profitable enterprise.

I was not fortunate enough to have met Doug at the height of his prowess. A few years previously, he had sustained brain damage from a near death experience. This had affected his ability to express himself. He confided to me that he had once been "an eloquent speaker," and was actually laying the groundwork to launch a political career when it all came to an abrupt end. The experience also forced him to take things easier and freed him to indulge his other great passion, body piercing.

During one of our many conversations, Doug confided in me that had he been of a later generation he might have been actively gay, but he was born at a time when such a lifestyle could easily make anyone an outcast. He had ambitions, and he also believed that he and the members of his family had been together in a past lifetime. He felt compelled to provide the means for all of them to incarnate together once again.

As mentioned previously, shortly before we met, Doug had written a short autobiography of his piercing exploits entitled *The Adventures of a Piercing Freak*.[1] He had subsequently sold the article to House of Milan, a publisher of bondage and fetish films and magazines. HOM issued it in softcover under the title *The Art of Pierced Penises and Decorative Tattoos*. Since body piercing was virtually unknown at the time, the publisher was hard-pressed to find suitable images to accompany the text. Consequently many of the photographs were male nudes that had little to do with the story. Here are some highlights:

• Doug's earliest fascination with piercing began as a small child, when he wondered how his mother's friends kept their earrings on their ears.

• In some ethnic communities, there was a belief that piercing the ears would improve eyesight. Hoping it might help, Doug's older cousin was taken to a neighbor lady to have his ears pierced. Doug witnessed the event with envy.

• Fresh from high school, the story continues, Doug went away to study marine biology. At the end of his freshman year, he got a job as a diver inspecting harbor pilings for marine worms. The gurgling of the

Body & Genital Piercing in Brief

written by DOUG MALLOY
illustrations by JIM WARD

Piercing of the body, for a variety of reasons, is an ancient, if not always venerable, art. For many years an underground phenomenon, it is at last emerging into the light.

Piercing of the nipples is not really new. The proud Roman centurions, Caesar's bodyguard, wore nipple rings as a sign of their virility and courage, and as a dress accessory for holding their short capes. The practice was also quite common among society girls of the Victorian era to enhance the size and shape of the nipples. Today the lure of piercing is primarily a sexual one. It provides a mechanical "tit"-ilation achieved by no other means. For many, especially the men and women into the bondage and discipline, and S & M scenes, there is a tremendous psychological turn-on. Where possible, piercing should be professionally done as placement determines the nipple's development, shape, and aesthetic effect. While difficult to obtain unless one knows a sympathetic doctor, anesthetics are available for the faint-of-heart. Healing normally takes 6 to 8 weeks and is quickest where a retainer with straight post is used.

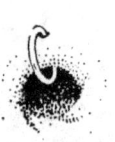
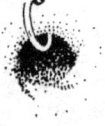

NIPPLE

Navel piercing, a sign of royalty to the ancient Egyptians, was something denied commoners. Hence, a deep navel was highly prized. But times change. Today this piercing is becoming increasingly popular especially with young swingers of the "In" set, male and female. Possible only to those with a well shaped navel, the piercing usually done through the little flap of skin above the opening and retained with a ring during healing, usually 4 to 6 weeks. Later the ring may be replaced by a decorative stud or bangle selected to suit the wearer's fancy. While not a sexually functional piercing, the visual effect is sensual and directs the viewers attention to the pelvic area.

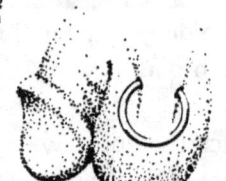

NAVEL

The Prince Albert, called a "dressing ring" by Victorian habardashers, was originally used to firmly secure the male genitals in either the left or right pant leg during that era's craze for extremely tight, crotch-binding trousers, thus minimizing a man's natural endowment. Legend has it that Prince Albert wore such a ring to retract his foreskin and thus keep his member sweet-smelling so as not to offend the Queen. Today its function is strictly erotic, providing the ultimate in sexual pleasure to men of both persuasions. Piercing is through the urethra at the base of the penis head. The procedure is quick; the pain, minimal; the healing, rapid, and the pleasure, lifelong.

PRINCE ALBERT

The use of dydoes seems to be of fairly recent origin. As they return much of the sensation lost with the foreskin, their emergence corresponds with the widespread practice of circumcision. Nor does the man alone benefit. During intercourse his dydoes provide delightful vaginal stimulation for his consort. The flagging sexual interest in many relationships has been revived with the use of these devices. Piercing is done through both sides of the upper edge of the glans. As proper placement is imperative, piercing should be done professionally. Small barbell studs, rings, "D" rings, or clamps may be inserted according to the wearers preference. While healing usually takes 4 to 6 weeks, continence during this period is not necessary.

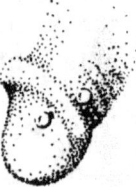

DYDOE

The ampallang, relatively unknown to the Western World but gaining foothold, is indigenous to the areas surrounding the Indian Ocean. Though sometimes done in childhood, the service piercing is usually done as part of a puberty rite, the service being performed by an old woman who places the ampallang horizontally through the center of the head of the penis above the urethra. A metal bar retained with metal discs may be used or studs of bone, ivory, or even gold, if the man is well-to-do. As this sexual device greatly enhances the sensual pleasure of both partners, many women may deny intercourse to a man not so pierced, or specify the size ampallang he should wear if he is.

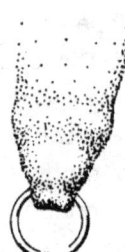

FORESKIN

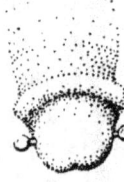

AMPALLANG

As described in the Kama Sutra, the ancient classic Hindu treatise on love and social conduct, the apadravya is any one of a number of devices (antique "French ticklers" and/or dildoes, if you will) used during intercourse to excite the woman. Among the Dravidian people of southern India, the word also refers to the device worn through the pierced male member. The piercing is generally vertical through the penis shaft behind the head, but sometimes in the head itself. It should be noted that this piercing is neither common or widespread

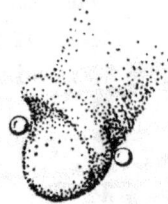

APADRAVYA

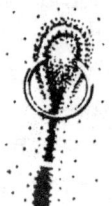
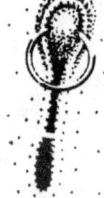

CLITORIS

...se piece of flesh beneath the ... having served, strange to ... and sexual stimulation. A ... event copulation. A special ... ge, secured at one end ... through a second piercing ... even masturbation. By ... the piercing and encircles ... bly in the groove around ... an be extremely erotic, ... cock ring. Many men ... the middle finger. Ring ... adily obtained using a ... quick and simple, and

... rab youth when he ... assage" is arranged ... f his gifts will be a ... remonial piercing ... e of the scrotum ... nis. Believed to ... roin from whence ... is called, gives ... forever a man ... with precious ... sian Gulf area) ... ionaires have ... l adornment, ... oth. Piercing ... the healing ... ost erotic of ... n stroked. ... common ... piercing is ... the ridge ... ld be the ... curately ... rimitive ... rice use ... ainers ... ks), a ... des a ... cings ... ure ... tle ... m. ... an ... e. ... as ... h

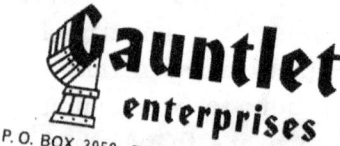

Gauntlet
enterprises

P.O. BOX 3950, BEVERLY HILLS, CA 90212
(850 N. San Vicente Blvd., Los Angeles, Calif. 90069)

water around the wet suit made him constantly need to urinate. This was a problem because he was only paid for the time he spent under water. Finally, one of the other divers shared a secret that would solve the problem. By having his penis pierced, Doug would be able to attach a tube running down the leg of his wet suit. This would allow him to urinate under water.

• In his junior year of college, his roommate introduced him to an organization called the Cyprian Society. It was made up primarily of Jewish men who rejected the practice of circumcision, and to compensate for the resulting loss of sensation, advocated piercing the glans of the penis and inserting small studs.

• The spring before Pearl Harbor, Doug graduated from college. For a graduation gift, he received a trip to Hawaii. While beach-bumming around, he saw his first navel piercing and had to have one for himself.

• After the war was over, Doug went back to school to study anthropology, specifically male initiation rites in Borneo. On a return trip from that country, he stopped in Tahiti where he met a gentleman who enlightened him on the native sexual lore. This included a male genital piercing called a "guiche," placed behind the scrotum about where the inseam of a pair of tight trousers would fall. Naturally, Doug chose to go native and returned to the States with an additional piercing.

Piercing Freak could hardly be described as great literature. It is told with masculine bravado and was clearly intended as "one-handed reading" for a primarily gay fetish market. Fantastic as parts of it are, Doug insisted the story was true. It's difficult to believe it was commonplace for divers to use Prince Albert rings to attach an external catheter, or that there was actually a college organization of Jewish men advocating dydoe piercings to restore sensation for circumcised males.

Doug authored, to some extent, promotional material for Gauntlet and articles for Gauntlet's magazine *Piercing Fans International Quarterly*. The truth is I was the ghostwriter for these, working from notes that he provided. One of the first promotional pieces we did was a flyer entitled "Body Piercing in Brief." It contained short histories and descriptions of a dozen piercings Doug considered "traditional." I drew two sets of illustrations to accompany them. The piercings included, in their original sequence, were:

• Nipple
• Navel
• Prince Albert
• Dydoe
• Ampallang
• Apadravya
• Frenum
• Hafada
• Guiche
• Foreskin
• Labia
• Clitoris

Of particular interest is the fact that, with the exception of the navel, all of these piercings have a largely sexual purpose. This reflected Doug's primary interest in body piercing as a means of enhancing erotic sensation.

The extent and significance of this document has previously gone unrecognized. Until recently, I failed to fully appreciate the influence the "Piercing Brief" has had and the enormous role it has played in the evolution of the modern body piercing movement. In my opinion, this brief document forms the "founding" or "charter" myths around which the entire movement was spawned and has grown.

According to Wikipedia, "A founding myth (Greek *'aition'*) is the etiological myth that explains the origins of a ritual or the founding of a city, the ethnogenesis of a group presented as a genealogy, and thus of a nation ("*natio*", "birth") and *the spiritual origins of a belief, philosophy, discipline, or idea.*" [Emphasis mine]. When Joseph Smith told the story of angels and golden tablets and lost tribes of Israel, he was creating the founding myths of the Mormon Church. Likewise, L. Ron Hubbard concocted the tale of Xenu and alien souls called thetans, and from it sprang Scientology. It doesn't really matter whether these stories or myths are true. What is important is their ability to captivate people's imaginations and appeal to an innate need they have to believe in something. With "Body & Genital Piercing in Brief," that is precisely what Doug accomplished. No one before him had ever presented such a specific palette of piercing possibilities complete with colorful history and lore. It didn't matter that he probably made up a lot of it, if not the piercings themselves. He'd at least done enough experimentation on himself to have some sense of their feasibility. This made it possible for him to speak with a confidence that lent credibility to what he said. It didn't hurt that it was a message a lot of people were ready to hear, whether they realized it or not.

The Wikipedia entry on Richard Simonton (Doug's real name) says, "Simonton's personal enthusiasm for body piercing as an erotic practice and his love of the fantastic came together in this document [the "Piercing Brief"], which contains some fictional and/or speculative information. Many of the theories regarding the practice and origins of various piercings historically have been distorted by the widespread circulation of this document or later documents which quote it."

There has never been any proof to substantiate, among other things, that:

• Roman Centurions wore nipple rings to which they attached short capes.

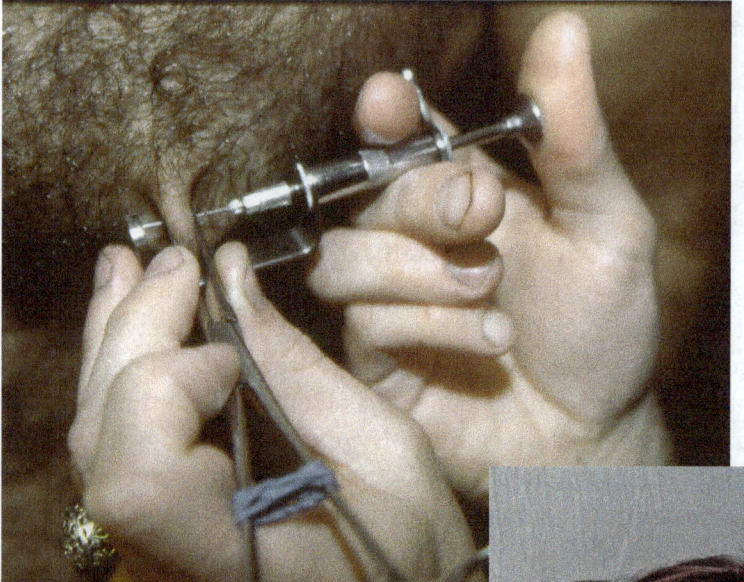

The vintage ear piercer proved incapable of handling tough nipples, but I continued to use it for many years for other piercings. Please note that what appears to be dirt under my fingernails was actually Betadine from cleaning the nipple.

Photo: Drew Ward

- Navel piercings were a sign of royalty in ancient Egypt.
- English dandy Beau Brummell and Queen Victoria's husband Prince Albert had their penises pierced.[2]
- Arab boys had the side of the scrotum pierced at puberty.
- Male South Pacific islanders did the guiche piercing as a rite of passage.

The evidence on which Doug based his Roman Centurions claim was a Baroque statue he'd seen in Versailles. He even showed me a snapshot he'd taken on a visit to that famous palace. I pointed out to him that Roman military men frequently wore breastplates sculpted to resemble a muscular male chest. The rings with cape attached were most likely in the breastplate, not the man. Doug paused for a moment to ponder my observation, then replied, "Well, it makes a good story anyway."

There are actually very few body piercings that have a well-documented history. The most extensively written about is the ampallang, which at one time was fairly common in and around Southeast Asia. There is one sole reference to the apadravya that I am aware of, and it is in the *Kama Sutra*. Doug maintained that the ampallang was horizontal through the head of the penis and the apadravya vertical. Gauntlet Master Piercer, researcher, and anthropology student Paul King, of Cold Steel in San Francisco, maintains that traditionally the

piercings are in fact one and the same and that either one could be oriented in either direction. Whatever the facts, most piercing enthusiasts have accepted Doug's designation, and the terminology helps make the orientation clearly understood.

Less extensively documented but much older are foreskin piercings dating as far back as the 12th century BCE. The practice, called infibulation, was introduced to the Romans by Arab traders. Usually the piercing was done to male slaves as a means of enforcing chastity. Women with pierced labia can also be infibulated, though the documentation of the procedure is scarce.

The second support on which the modern body piercing movement was able to build was, I believe, the combination of techniques and easily obtainable implements and equipment. Regardless of how primitive they might have been in the beginning, especially compared to those in use today, Doug had formulated a handful of piercing procedures that, with refinement, could be applied by anyone. The practice of using a clamp to hold and stabilize the tissue for piercing is ancient—Fakir even wrote an illustrated article about it in issue #3 of our magazine *Piercing Fans International Quarterly*. But by using modern implements, modifying and improving them as necessary, it was no longer necessary for would-be piercers to reinvent the tools of the trade. These also helped provide a basis for developing piercing techniques that were readily available and easy to duplicate.

Unfortunately, until I had sufficient experience to fully understand the limitations of Doug's basic techniques, they provided their own unique challenges. Thus far I'd followed Doug's lead, and aside from the occasional fumble, things were progressing fairly well.

For some time we continued to use

the ear-piercing gun to do nipples. This limited us to using only 16-gauge jewelry, pretty thin by today's standards, though certainly thicker than the earrings everyone was used to. On occasion, I encountered nipples that were on the tough side, but with a little extra muscle I always managed to get the piercing point to go through.

Then came the day that retired this technique. Doug called me up and told me that some guy in Hollywood who'd answered his classified ad wanted his nipples pierced. We arranged a day and time to go to the guy's apartment where I would do the piercings. Like many leathermen, myself included, he enjoyed heavy nipple play, something that, over time, had made them callused and tough. Everything went smoothly until the actual piercing. The point of the ear piercer scarcely penetrated the skin; it refused to go through. I could feel myself sweating partly from embarrassment, partly because I knew the guy was very uncomfortable. With every bit of strength I could muster, I made one final attempt. However, instead of going through, the needle bent. I then realized that the ear piercer was not a reliable tool for piercing nipples, since there was no way to tell how tough they were going to be.

By now I was soaking wet. Though uncomfortable, the client was bearing up incredibly well and was determined to persevere until he had the piercings. Doing my best to save face and keep the client calm, I quietly reassured him everything would be fine, set the ear piercer aside, and had Doug hand me a cork and one of the large hypodermic needles from the piercing kit. The nipple was still in the forceps. I placed the cork on one side and, placing the needle in position on the other, thrust it through the nipple into the cork. Though the going was still a bit rough, the nipple finally yielded.

I now encountered additional prob-

lems. The forceps couldn't be completely removed. I was able to open them and free them on the point end of the needle, but the syringe coupling was too large to pass through the remaining opening. I'd just have to work around them. It was also going to be tricky inserting the jewelry because the point of the needle was beveled, and I would have to insert the jewelry from left to right, a direction that was unnatural to me since I'm right-handed. Fortunately, we were inserting nipple retainers that had a straight post, so they managed to follow through with minimal difficulty.

At the time, I simply attributed all the fumbling and difficulties to my own lack of experience. This was partly true, but the tools themselves were actually a much more significant factor. This was about to be demonstrated most dramatically as I undertook my first Prince Albert piercing. Another one of Doug's contacts, a man named Jim A., was visiting from New York and had expressed a desire for this particular piercing. I remember well our visit to his hotel just off Hollywood Boulevard.

Doug's technique for doing the Prince

Albert was incredibly difficult. A small dab of topical anesthetic was placed on the end of a cotton swab (one with a wooden stick) and the swab inserted about an inch into the urethra. After waiting about ten minutes for the anesthetic to penetrate and do its work, it was time to do the piercing. The piercer would grip the cotton swab, position its tip just beneath the place where the piercing would go, and, with a hypodermic needle of suitable thickness, pierce into the tip of the swab. In order not to puncture more than one wall of the urethra, the needle and swab needed to be kept securely together until the needle was outside of it.

Any piercer who hasn't done this has no idea just how difficult it is. It's like trying to hit a moving target behind a curtain. Unless the piercer's grip is just right, the tissue can move around and the needle will miss its mark. Thankfully, I was able to master this technique in a fairly short period of time and a few years later figure out a better method.

Somehow I managed to actually do the piercing. It was now time to insert the jewelry, a 14-gauge bead ring, defi-

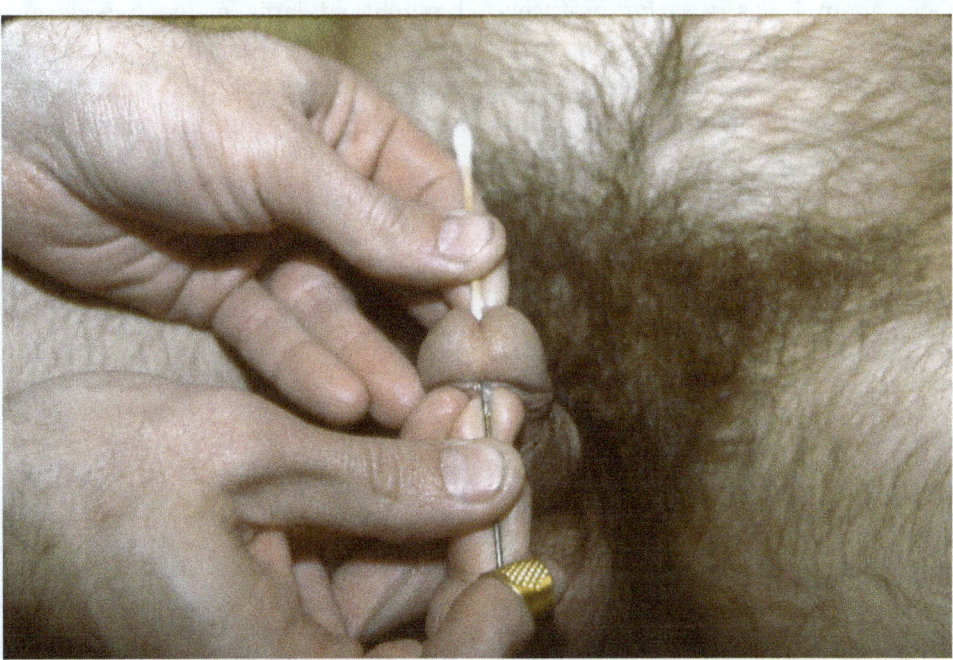

The original technique for Prince Alberts was very difficult and involved piercing into the tip of a cotton swab. Dull needles often required use of a thimble.

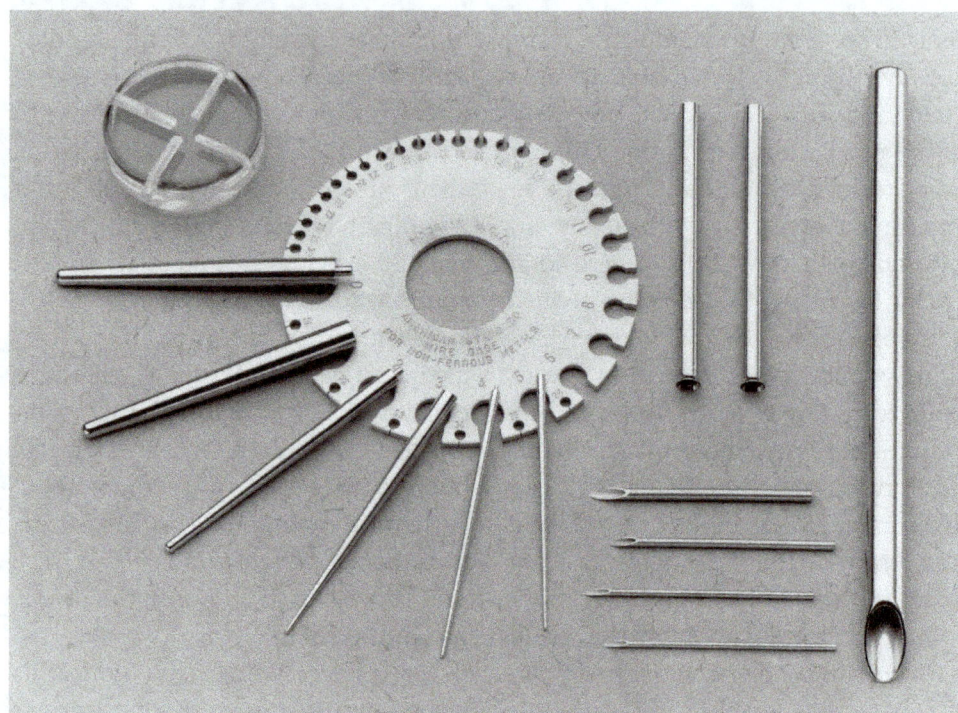

Piercing equipment. *clockwise from the upper left*: needle pusher, gauge wheel, needle receiving tubes, nostril tubes, piercing needles, and insertion tapers. Except for the gauge wheel, all of these were Gauntlet innovations. However, thanks to Gauntlet, the Brown & Sharpe system used for gold and silver has become widely used for jewelry of all metals, even those that traditionally use a different one. This eliminates the need for a whole additional range of piercing needle gauges.

nitely thin by today's standard. This necessitated getting a circular object to follow a straight one with a beveled point. Things weren't working well. Once again, I was sweating profusely and beginning to panic. Things were getting bloody. More by sheer force of will than anything else, I managed to get the ring in. Although the piercee was an incredibly good sport about it all, I felt terribly embarrassed. I knew that this method was too crude. Guys who had been around the S/M scene might take it in stride, but I couldn't expect that of others.

It was then that I had one of my "Eureka!" moments as the answer came to me in a flash. If I simply cut the syringe coupling off the needle, I would then be able to follow it through with the jewelry. In that instant, one of the most important revolutions in piercing technique took place. I had just invented the piercing needle. From then

on, at least one hurdle in the piercing process had been conquered.

The evolution of the piercing needle is an interesting one. For many years, I purchased large gauge hypodermic needles from a medical supply company in New York and then removed the syringe coupling. After filing away any

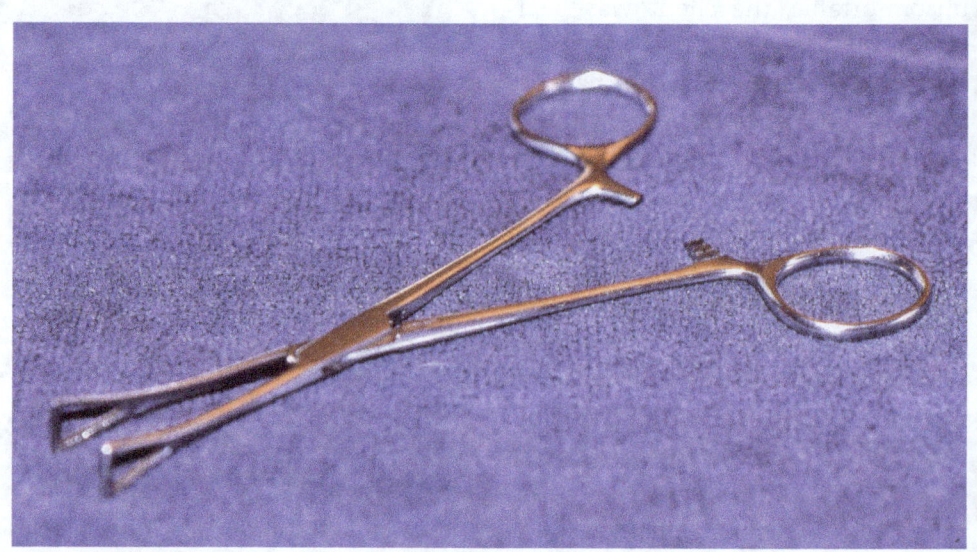

Pennington forceps

burrs, the needles were then placed in paper sterilization bags and processed, in the early days within a pressure cooker, after a couple of years, in a second-hand autoclave. The bags were printed with an indicator, and to the best of our knowledge at the time, if it changed color the contents were sterile.

For many years, we reused needles. Today's piercers may find this horrifying, but it's important to remember that at the time doctors also reused their needles. In fact my mother, who worked many years for an eye doctor, contracted hepatitis from a needlestick acquired while cleaning used needles. To avoid a similar incident, I sterilized needles twice. The first time was just to make them clean enough to handle. Then a wire would be run through each one to remove dried blood and any other gunk that might have accumulated inside. In fact, every box of hypodermics I purchased in those days came with half a dozen pieces of wire specifically for that purpose. With the debris removed, the needles were then re-bagged and sterilized a second time.

As role models for issues of sterility and hygiene, we turned primarily to some of the more responsible tattooists of the time, especially Cliff Raven, who had recently moved from Chicago and opened a shop in West Hollywood and who was a member of the T&P Group. Autoclaving instruments after each use was a given. But the use of latex gloves didn't occur until the AIDS epidemic hit nearly 10 years later.

Needless to say, every time a needle was used it became duller. Some of them weren't even that sharp to begin with. In cases where the tissue was particularly tough, this made it very difficult to get the needle through. I developed a thick callus on my piercing finger and sometimes even used a thimble. Some piercers wrapped their fingertips with a Band-Aid. In time, we designed and sold a needle pusher as a piercing aid. It never occurred to us that the difficulties we experienced might be because our needles were dull. We simply attributed the problems to tough tissue.

Even though I was always very conscientious about implement sterilization, once the AIDS epidemic began in earnest I felt compelled to find disposable piercing needles, partly to further reduce the risk of accidentally passing the virus to an employee via a needlestick, and partly as a reassurance to my customers, who were understandably nervous. With a great deal of effort and after many phone calls—these were the days before the Internet—I discovered I could buy hypodermic needles without the syringe coupling. The manufacturer called them "cannulas." At the time, they seemed like such an advance over what we'd been using in terms of sharpness, but even though these came from a major supplier of medical equipment, there remained room for improvement.

By the late 1990s, the piercing industry had grown to the point that it was profitable for companies to actually start manufacturing needles just for piercing. The basic design remained the same, but thanks to the ongoing quest to make them ever sharper, the toughest tissue now offers little resistance for the piercer. No more calluses;

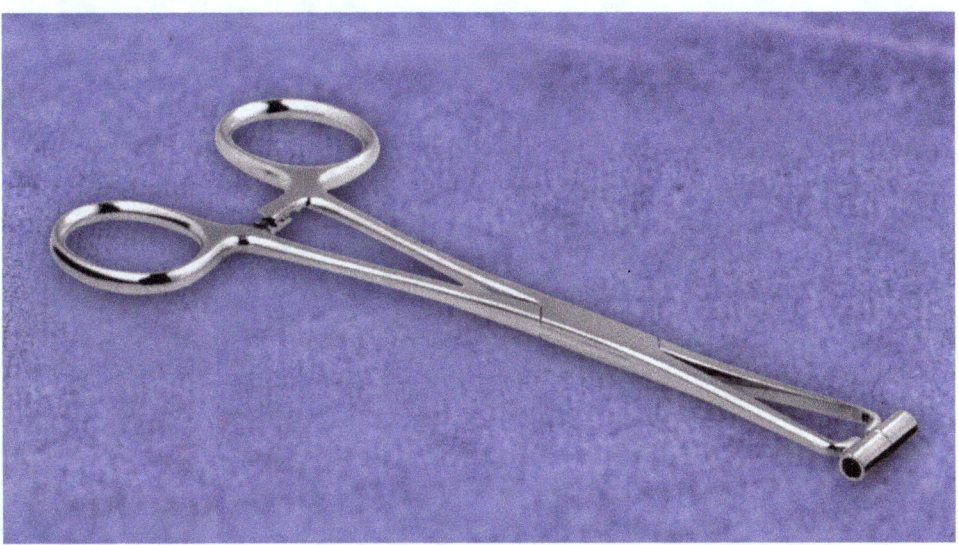

Septum piercings can be difficult to get straight, which inspired me to invent these special forceps. It came as a surprise to discover they're sufficiently popular for someone to actually manufacture a disposable plastic version.

no more thimble; no more Band-Aids; no more needle pushers.

The other piece of equipment that has become industry standard is the Pennington forceps. I've no idea what purpose this instrument was initially designed for. There was a pair in Doug's original tool kit, and I used them from the beginning. Gauntlet offered them for sale practically from its inception, but for years they were sometimes difficult to acquire, and the quality was uneven. Nowadays, they seem to be abundant and the quality has greatly improved.

Another Gauntlet innovation common in the piercing industry is the insertion taper. Its evolution began with the dull needles that are used for needlepoint. These were used when people removed their jewelry and needed to reopen the hole after it shrank. The metal corroded during autoclaving, and they were very thin, but they served as inspiration. The second generation utilized the points of knitting needles, but the taper was too abrupt. Next came pieces of aluminum knitting needles clamped in a drill press and tapered using a file and smoothed with a succession of fine abrasive paper. They didn't stand up well to steril-

ization either, were too rough, and way too time consuming to make. Eventually, as the industry and demand grew, they became just another manufactured stainless steel product.

There is one additional piece of equipment that I proudly consider my brainchild: the needle receiving tube. When the time came that I had to train additional piercers, teaching them how to do Prince Alberts using the cotton swab in the urethra method was a particularly difficult challenge, and the piercings these apprentices did were sometimes scary. A man who I attempted to groom as a manager for the L.A. store once I'd decided to move to San Francisco in 1988 did a job so bad, it's memorable. The entry was in the correct location, but somehow the needle never made it into the urethra, instead following between layers of tissue before emerging at the edge of the urethral opening. I had not been on hand to supervise the piercing and only saw it a day or two later when the client came back into the store complaining of discomfort and that the piercing wouldn't stop bleeding. At first glance, everything appeared normal, but upon closer examination I realized the problem and was able to correct it without much difficulty or further pain.

But this particular mishap bothered me. There had to be a better way. I had known for years that English piercer Mr. Sebastian did PAs from the inside out and had personally resisted this approach for several reasons. First was the matter of accuracy; second, I didn't like the idea of inserting a needle into the urethra. Mr. Sebastian used a short piece of tubing in the urethra as a guide and means of protection, but it still wasn't an approach I felt comfortable with.

One day while out driving, the answer came to me in a flash. I went back to our shop, had one of the jewelers cut me a 4" length of ³⁄₁₆" stainless steel tubing, smooth the ends, and polish it. After a thorough cleaning and autoclaving, it was ready. The first time I used it as a replacement for the cotton swab, I was thrilled at how easily the piercing went. The circular impression of the tube inside the urethra was clearly visible. The needle went through the tissue and into it so quickly and smoothly there was almost no pain. The new technique was so much easier for apprentices to master.

Another Gauntlet piercer modified the needle-receiving tube design, adding a flare to one end to make it useable for other applications such as septum piercings. Yet another piercer came up with a totally separate idea, a much thicker tube with a beveled end that proved useful for nostril piercings.

As time passed and more piercers became part of the Gauntlet team, I began to see slight variations in the techniques they used. My feeling was if it worked and posed no threat to the client or piercer, why not? With minor modification, I personally continued to utilize Doug's ear-piercing gun for some years to come for tragus piercings, though others pre-

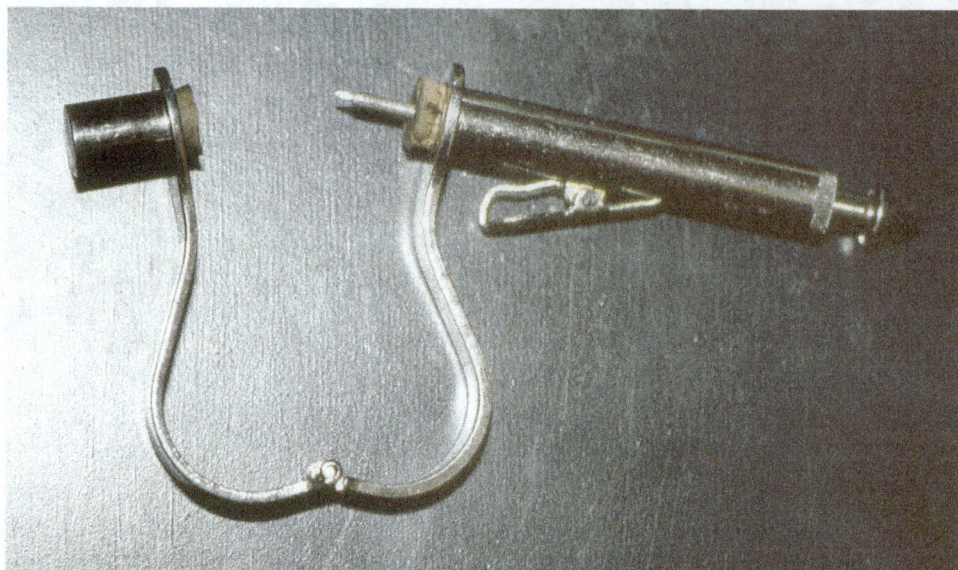

Two piercing tools devised by Tattoo Samy of Frankfurt. Above is a spring-loaded gun similar to the ear piercer on page 30. Below is a pair of pliers designed to pierce and insert a barbell stud. The piercing was accomplished by a small, triangular point that screwed into one end of the post. Once the stud was in place, it was extremely awkward to remove the point and the tool itself. Neither device proved worthwhile.

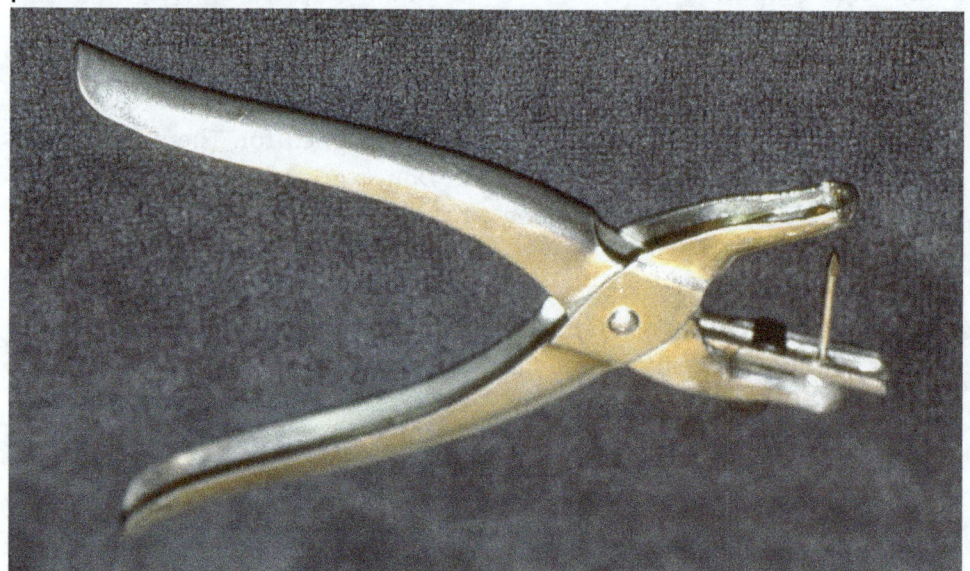

ferred their own methods.

Not every implement that came into my possession or that I imagined proved capable of standing the test of time. Some were quickly consigned to the scrap drawer. Doug had a friend, a tattooist and piercer from Frankfurt in Germany, who would show up from time to time with some new pierc-

ing instrument that he had designed. These were beautifully machined, but inevitably proved awkward to use and unsatisfactory.

We now come to the third leg supporting the foundation of the modern body piercing movement. In my opinion at least, that support is appropriate jewelry.

---

[1] The complete text appears in the Appendix.

[2] See "The Versatile & Sensual Prince Albert" in the Appendix.

CHAPTER 4

Today's well-stocked piercing establishment provides a feast for the eyes. The display cases brim with a dazzling array of jewelry to meet almost every need and whim, ranging from precision-machined items of stainless steel to rings and studs of colorful niobium or titanium to beautiful hand-crafted pieces of gold, many sparkling with gemstones both real and man-made. Most studios today carry a vast assortment of exotic creations, mostly for enlarged ear piercings, fashioned from semiprecious stone and a variety of organic materials including wood, bone, horn, and amber.

It would be easy to assume it's always been that way. What's difficult to conceive is that before Gauntlet, most piercing enthusiasts had no choice but to make do with earrings or some makeshift contrivance of twisted wire. There was virtually no way to easily provide a closure that would not snag on clothing, bedding, or on the edges of the piercing itself. Frequently the material was "mystery metal," perhaps silver- or gold-plated but hardly suitable for the purpose. I was personally responsible for introducing many of the jewelry designs and piercing innovations people often take for granted. When Janet Jackson flashed her breast at the 2004 Super Bowl, creating a firestorm of controversy, she was wearing a Gauntlet nipple shield. The sunburst design was one I created in the mid-70s.

Earrings were a common choice for early piercing enthusiasts, but they were universally too thin. Many people fail to realize the danger. Because of their thinness, if they catch on something, they can cut through the tissue like a knife or, more specifically, a cheese cutter. Heavy earrings with thin wires can also, over time, gradually slice through the earlobe.

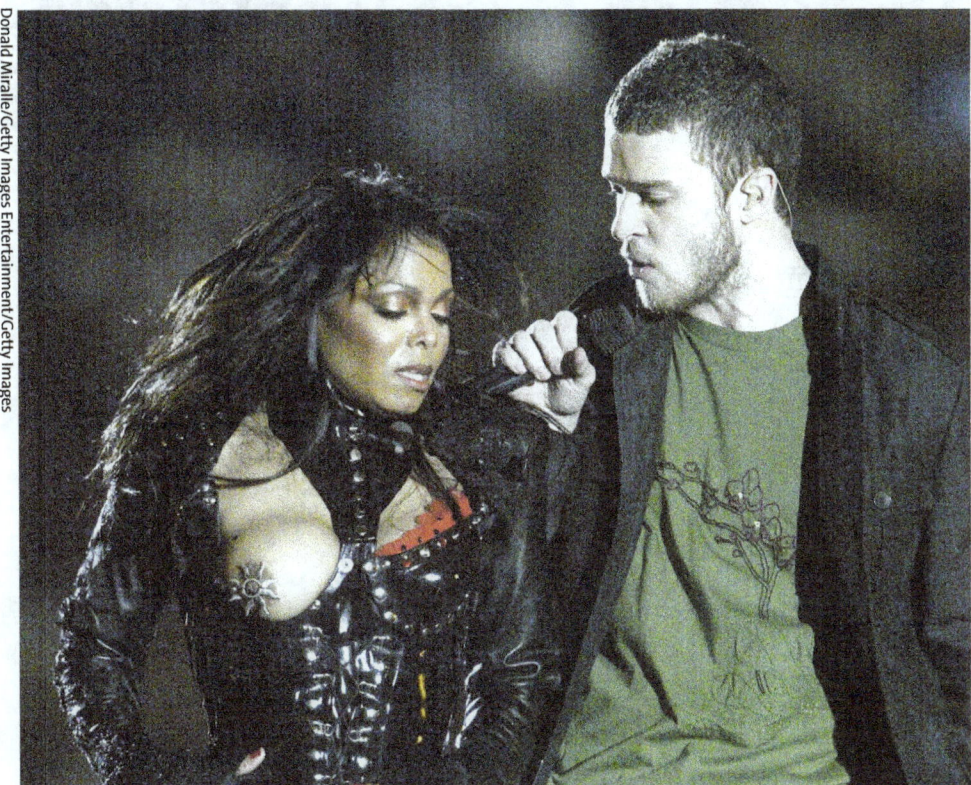

The nipple shield Janet Jackson was wearing when her wardrobe "malfunctioned" at the 2004 Super Bowl XXXVIII halftime show was one I designed around 1977.

In those early days, as now, there were some loop-style earrings consisting of a fairly thick tube with a thin wire that was intended to go through the piercing. Some hardy individuals managed to work the thicker loop through their piercings, a process that would have been uncomfortable to say the least. If the ring rotated, the sharp edges that remained could irritate and cut the tissue.

From the beginning, there was interest in stainless steel as a material for piercing jewelry, primarily because it was perceived as inexpensive and because many men preferred its silver color. Unfortunately, I had no knowledge or experience with the material; every piece of jewelry I'd ever made was of gold or silver. Consequently, the majority of my early jewelry was made from gold. I did design some pieces from silver, but while that metal may be tolerated in well-healed piercings, it is unsuitable for fresh ones. For these I offered gold.

Those who insisted on silver-colored metal had to settle for white gold.

Our knowledge of jewelry materials was quite limited. At that time it was legal to sell 13.5-karat gold as 14-karat, and many manufacturers did. In Great Britain, one could even find earrings of 9-karat. I had no idea just what effect the unknown components in various gold alloys had on people's bodies, and finding answers proved elusive. Today it's possible to get Material Certification Sheets (Mill Certs) from metal companies that provide a breakdown of a particular alloy. I'm not sure when these became commonly available. Even though I was using 14-karat gold, some people still had bad reactions to it. In those cases, our usual recourse was to insert monofilament nylon fishing line or weed-eater line. We had no idea that nickel was a common allergen in alloys and was frequently a component, especially in white gold. I'm not proud to admit it, but Gauntlet's first

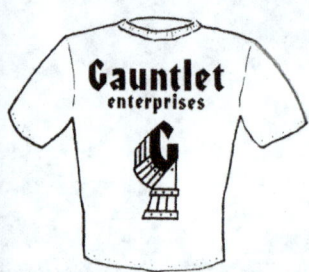

THE T-SHIRT

No. TS The GAUNTLET ENTERPRISES insignia silk-screened in black on white cotton. Available in sizes S, M, L, and XL.

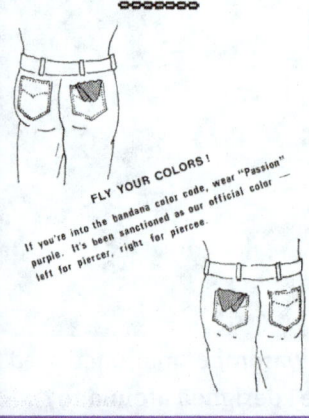

FLY YOUR COLORS!

If you're into the bandana color code, wear "Passion" purple. It's been sanctioned as our official color — left for piercer, right for piercee.

PER ITEM PRICE LIST

BEAD RINGS

	18 ga.	16 ga.	14 ga.	12 ga.
3/8	12.00	16.50	—	—
1/2	15.00	21.00	28.50	—
5/8	18.00	25.00	34.00	52.50
3/4	21.00	29.00	40.00	61.00
7/8	24.00	33.00	45.50	69.00
1"	27.00	37.00	51.00	77.50
1 1/8	—	—	57.00	85.50
1 1/4	—	—	62.50	94.00

"SEAMLESS" RINGS

	14 ga.	12 ga.
1/2	32.00	—
5/8	37.00	52.50
3/4	43.00	61.00
7/8	49.00	69.00
1"	55.00	77.50
1 1/8	61.00	85.50
1 1/4	67.00	94.00

insertion needles

.25	.30

TRIANGLE BEAD RINGS

gold	16 ga.	14 ga.	12 ga.
1/2	21.00	28.50	—
5/8	25.00	34.00	—
3/4	29.00	40.00	—
7/8	33.00	45.50	69.00
1"	37.00	51.00	77.50
1" gold - plated nickel silver		15.50	

LOCKS – either style

broken shackle	solid shackle 14 ga.	12 ga.
75.00	75.00	80.00

KEYS	NECK CHAINS
7.50	6.50

NIPPLE RETAINERS

1/2"	21.00
5/8"	25.00
3/4"	29.00

NIPPLE SHIELDS

all styles
37.50

"D"-RINGS

1/2"	30.50
9/16"	34.00
5/8"	37.00
3/4"	43.00
7/8"	49.00
1"	53.00

GUICHE WEIGHTS

GW-1	10.00
GW-2	3.50

BARBELLS / HORSESHOES

	BARBELLS	HORSESHOES gold	silver
1/4"	28.00	—	—
3/8"	29.00	—	—
1/2"	30.00	28.50	14.25
5/8"	32.00	34.00	17.00
3/4"	34.00	40.00	20.00
7/8"	36.00	45.50	22.75
1"	38.00	51.00	25.50
1 1/8"	40.00	57.00	28.50

T-SHIRTS

3.50

15 August, 1976

OFFER TO SELL GOLD & SILVER JEWELRY
TERMS, CONDITIONS, & GENERAL INFORMATION

1. Items are offered as jewelry, that is for use as articles of personal adornment. Items are not offered as an investment.
2. Gold is guaranteed to meet U.S. legal requirements for solid 14K gold. Silver is guaranteed to meet requirements for sterling. Many items will not be stamped with a "Quality Mark" as there is no suitable place to stamp it.
3. Gold and silver prices fluctuate daily, consequently, our jewelry prices are subject to change without notice.
4. All items are made to order. Allow four to six weeks for delivery.
5. Add $1.50 to your order to cover handling, postage, and insurance.
6. California residents must add 6% sales tax. Bay area residents must add 6½% sales tax.
7. Enclose check or money order in payment with your order. COD's cannot be accepted. Do not send cash.
8. Articles are not returnable.
9. Customer must assume all responsibility for use of our merchandise.
10. Inquiries regarding custom work are welcome. Send specifications for price quotation.
11. The item size you need is determined simply by measuring the distance between openings of an existing piercing or dots used to mark an intended one. New piercings may swell slightly, and an allowance of up to 1/8" should be made.
12. As a general rule new piercings heal better around a straight rather than curved wire. We suggest keeping this in mind.

WIRE GAUGES

6 8 10 12 14 16 18 20

WATCH FOR FORTHCOMING DESIGNS ESPECIALLY FOR THOSE INTO STRETCHED PIERCINGS.

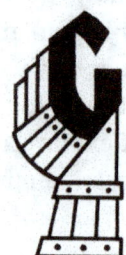
Gauntlet's first jewelry promotional brochure dated August 15, 1976.
The terms, conditions and prices are especially interesting.

THE BEAD RING

No. BR Our most versatile and comfortable ring. Since the bead closure cannot enter the piercing, irritation and discomfort are minimized. For a new *Prince Albert* this ring is ideal, however, it is handsome and serviceable wherever it is worn.

Hand-crafted of 14K white gold in a variety of gauges and diameters, yellow gold available on special order. Specify inside diameter desired.

THE NIPPLE RETAINER

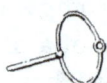

No. NR To facilitate speedy healing of newly pierced nipples, this retainer is difficult to rival. The 16 ga. center post and 20 ga. outer ring is hand-crafted of 14K white gold. Yellow gold available on special order. Specify inside diameter desired.

THE "D"- RING

No. DR This bold half circle of 14 ga. sterling silver with 14K white-gold post is built for action and looks. Works well in many piercings, new or old. Order by post length.

THE BARBELL & HORSESHOE

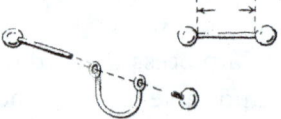

No. BB The ever-popular standby of the piercing *aficionado*, the GAUNTLET ENTERPRISES Barbell is precision constructed of two threaded balls and an internally threaded post, both of 14K white gold. Internal threading eliminates the irritating, abrasive factor common to so many barbells, past and present.

With its companion horseshoe (**No. HS**), the barbell is unmatched for ruggedness and durability in heavy action.

The barbell post is a sturdy one-sixteenth inch, and the horseshoe is 14 ga. (sterling silver or 14K white gold). Order by barbell post length. Add one-eighth inch if barbell is being used with horseshoe.

THE TRIANGLE BEAD RING

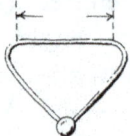

No. TBR This variation on our popular bead ring was initially created solely to provide maximum comfort during the wearisome healing process of a new *guiche* piercing. As the piercing heals, the fit of the ring gradually loosens, and when healing is complete, should be replaced. As it is intended for temporary use, it is crafted in gold-plated 12 ga. nickel silver, however, for those who want to go first class all the way, 14K gold, white or yellow, is available on special order. The one inch size fits all.

A scaled down versions of this ring in 14 or 16 ga., 14K white gold (yellow available on special order) has been added to our line for use in other piercings. It is both serviceable and handsome. Sized by length of long side.

THE "SEAMLESS" RING

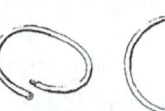

No. SR This ring, primarily intended for use in the well-healed piercing, is hand-crafted of a heavy 12 ga. and a lighter weight 14 ga. 14K white gold (yellow available on special order) in a wide range of diameters. The closure is precision constructed to be as close to seamless as possible. A special needle is available to facilitate smooth insertion. Specify inside diameter desired.

NIPPLE SHIELDS

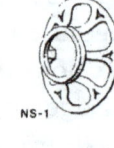 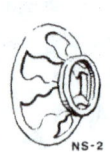

NS-1 NS-2

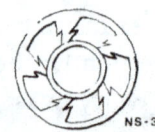

NS-3

No. NS These hand-crafted, sterling silver shields provide a striking focal point for any chest or breast. They are easily held in place with a ring, retainer, barbell, or lock. Three styles are available, outside diameter: 1¼", inside diameter: ½". Depth varies—style NS-1 is 3/8" deep, styles NS-2 and NS-3 are ½" deep.

LOCKS

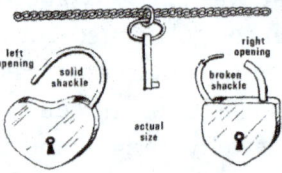

left opening / solid shackle / actual size / right opening / broken shackle

HEART shape   **SHIELD shape**

No. WL Completely hand-crafted of sterling silver and 14K white gold, the uses for these working locks are as limitless as your imagination. Currently crafted in two shapes with two shackle styles available. The broken shackle is made exclusively for use in the ear; the solid shackle (of 12 or 14 ga. white gold) is intended for body use. Locks open right or left. Specify choice as well as shape, shackle style and gauge.

Sterling silver keys (**No. LK**) and 18" neckchains (**No. NC**) to wear them on are sold separately.

GUICHE WEIGHTS

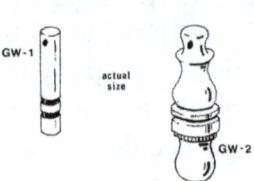

GW-1 / actual size / GW-2

No. GW After installing a permanent *guiche* ring, a small weight is usually added to provide further sensual stimulation. Two styles are currently available, and more designs will be forthcoming. Style GW-1 is a cylindrical weight of sterling silver with two black racing stripes. Style GW-2 is of turned and polished brass.

jewelry brochure actually included a piece of gold-plated, nickel silver jewelry. It didn't take long to recognize its incompatibility and discontinue it immediately.

Although Gauntlet officially became a business in November of 1975, it took nearly nine months before things began to come together for me to issue Gauntlet's first jewelry "folio." To call it a catalog would be stretching things. It was simply a legal-sized piece of heavy paper printed on both sides and folded into quarters. But to the best of my knowledge, it was the first time any collection of body jewelry designs had ever been offered for sale to the public.

Despite Doug's financial help, my budget was still very lean. I had little knowledge of photography, especially taking pictures of jewelry, which is an art unto itself. Since I couldn't afford to hire a professional photographer, and printing photographs would have been more costly, I chose to illustrate the first brochure myself with line drawings. In these days of desktop publishing, younger people have no concept of what was involved to produce printed materials before the advent of the home computer. Let's just say it took a whole lot of old-fashioned art supplies, time, and perseverance.

I was still groping my way. It took a while to design and "test drive" the nearly dozen items that appeared in the first brochure. As mentioned earlier, my first design was the nipple retainer. The bead ring, a scaled-up version of a fairly common earring design, followed this.

In the months and years to come, jewelry designs were always being developed and refined. Some became classics that are still being reproduced today; some were consigned almost immediately to history. Others lasted for a while, eventually fading into obscurity for lack of interest by customers. Still others ended up on the scrap heap because experience proved a particular design was not appropriate. Regardless of their longevity, many of them have an interesting story.

The one piece of jewelry that became Gauntlet's "bread and butter" was what I called the Bead Ring. It has become known in the industry as a Fixed Bead Ring since the bead that acts as a closure is soldered to one side of the ring's opening. In more recent years, the Captive Bead Ring, in which the bead simply snaps into the gap in the ring, has supplanted the design in terms of popularity. The CBR is easier and cheaper to manufacture and allows the wearer to choose a variety of bead materials, shapes, and designs. But since my primary focus was always on piercing as a means of sexual enhancement, I felt the fixed style was a safer choice. One never had to worry about losing the bead inside a body cavity or in the carpet or bedding if the activity got a little rough.

I can't claim that the Fixed Bead Ring design was my own. Back when I first pierced my nipples, I had found a pair of earrings of that design in a department store. What made them a unique Gauntlet design was the fact that they were scaled in a variety of larger diameters and thicknesses suitable for body wear. We were even sufficiently foolhardy to offer these in thick gauges and small diameters that required pliers for opening and closing.

The first barbell jewelry I recall seeing came from a tattooist and piercer from Frankfurt, Germany, one of Doug's contacts known as Tattoo Samy. Over the years, Samy came to the States a number of times and frequently showed up in L.A. to visit Doug and to stop by Gauntlet to buy jewelry. The easier way to make barbells is to thread the post externally, but this can make insertion difficult and even painful. Whenever I had to insert one, I would dip the threads in

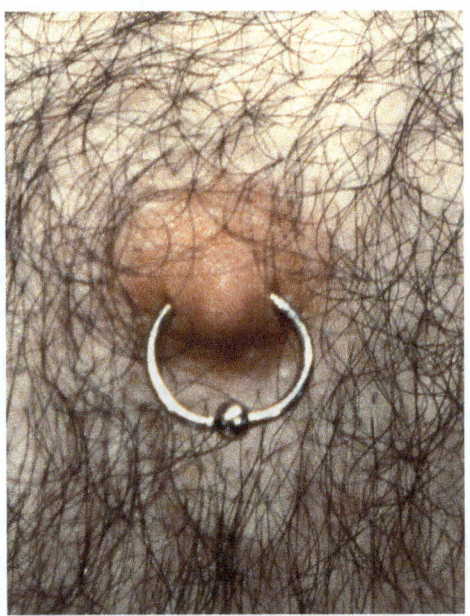

The Fixed Bead Ring, Gauntlet's bread-and-butter for the better part of two decades.

melted wax. This made for smoother insertion, and the wax flaked off when the ball was screwed on.

On one of his first visits, Samy showed us the barbell studs that he liked to use. They were internally threaded, a feature that made so much sense that I immediately set out to recreate them for my own customers.

This was a particularly difficult challenge. With no money for expensive equipment, the biggest problem was how to do the threading. One of my gold suppliers offered 1/16" gold tubing, the equivalent of 14-gauge. This worked great as the post, but how could I tap it? One of the jewelry equipment vendors solved the problem by providing me with the appropriate size taps and dies. They had to be used by hand, and unfortunately the taps were brittle and broke easily. Making the male-threaded pin that attached to the ball posed its own challenges. There was no standard wire of the necessary thickness, so I had to draw my own; it wasn't easy. The die that cut the threading had to be adjusted precisely or the pins would either be too thin or too thick to fit properly. It took

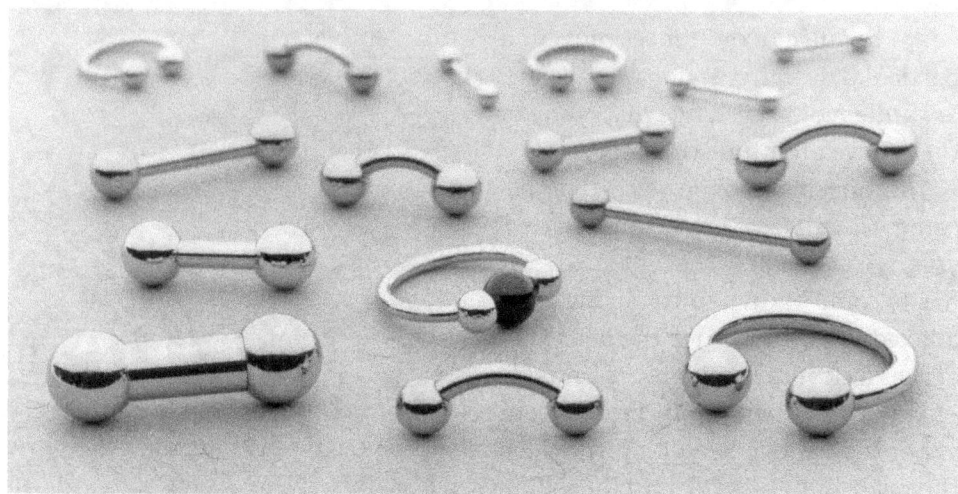

A selection of Gauntlet barbells. Over the years we pioneered a number of variations including the L-bar (center bottom) and circular barbell (right).

a fair amount of trial and error to get everything to mate just right.

Next, I had to find suitable balls for the ends. Initially I used those ear studs that are just a gold ball attached to a post. I cut off the ear post and soldered the ball to the barbell post or threaded pin. This proved completely unsatisfactory. First, there was an unsightly flange where the post was attached to the ball. Second, the ball had a tendency to explode when it was heated with a torch. That wasn't much fun. Lastly, the material was so thin that after it was heated it became so soft it could easily be dented with a thumbnail. This wasn't something I could sell. What to do?

Fortunately, fate intervened. On the elevator at the jewelry mart one day, I was discussing the problem with a friend. There was another man next to us who overheard the conversation and gave me the name of a findings company where I'd be able to purchase "no-hole" balls that would meet my needs. The lead proved invaluable, and for many years Gauntlet purchased balls from the company for a number of our jewelry designs.

Once I'd overcome the manufacturing problems, it seemed natural to design some decorative variations. The first was what I called the Arrow of Eros. To maximize comfort I didn't

want the head to be sharp, so I modified the shape to something like a Native American arrowhead. The two ends were forged out of metal. These were then taken to an engraver, who cut the details. Rubber molds were made so that the pieces could be cast. Though never a best-selling design, it nonetheless remained in the Gauntlet line for over 20 years.

Other barbell variations followed. The second brochure includes what I called Jeweled Studs. These had semi-precious stone beads set in pronged pearl settings. They were never very popular and eventually disappeared from the line. Over the years, many other variations were introduced. None of them were ever as popular as the initial one with the round balls that made it much more versatile.

The standard bead ring with the attached ball may have been our bread and butter, but some members of the T&P Group and others wanted a design that appeared to be continuous. Had it been practical, they would have been quite happy to have the rings permanently soldered shut.

One of Gauntlet's early competitors was a short-lived business called Whatever Rings. It was run by a couple of gay guys who were heavy S/M players. They operated out of their West

Hollywood apartment and solicited business through ads in the local gay press. The business was primarily a thinly-veiled enticement to lure men into an S/M scene.

The "jewelry" sold by Whatever Rings consisted of gold wire formed into simple rings. There was no closure. While they looked nice, I personally considered them impractical if not dangerous. I knew from experience it was difficult to get the ends to line up perfectly, particularly after the ring had been inserted into a piercing. This could mean discomfort, and that gap, no matter how small, would also trap debris and quickly become a breeding ground for bacteria that could lead to infection, especially in a fresh piercing.

Still, some people liked the look and insisted they wanted it. So I tried to make something at least a little more practical. I called it a "Seamless" Ring. It still had the small gap, but I perfected a way of crafting a pin coupling which, if nothing else, would keep the ends in alignment. To minimize the risk of in-

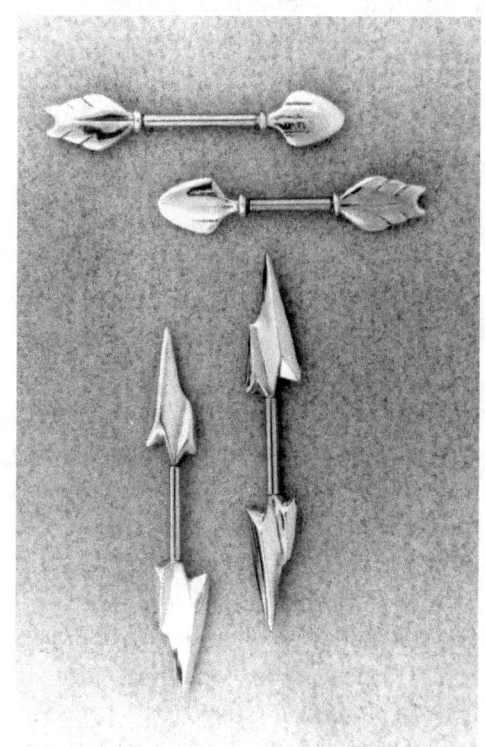

Two of my original designs: the Arrow of Eros and the Thunderbolt.

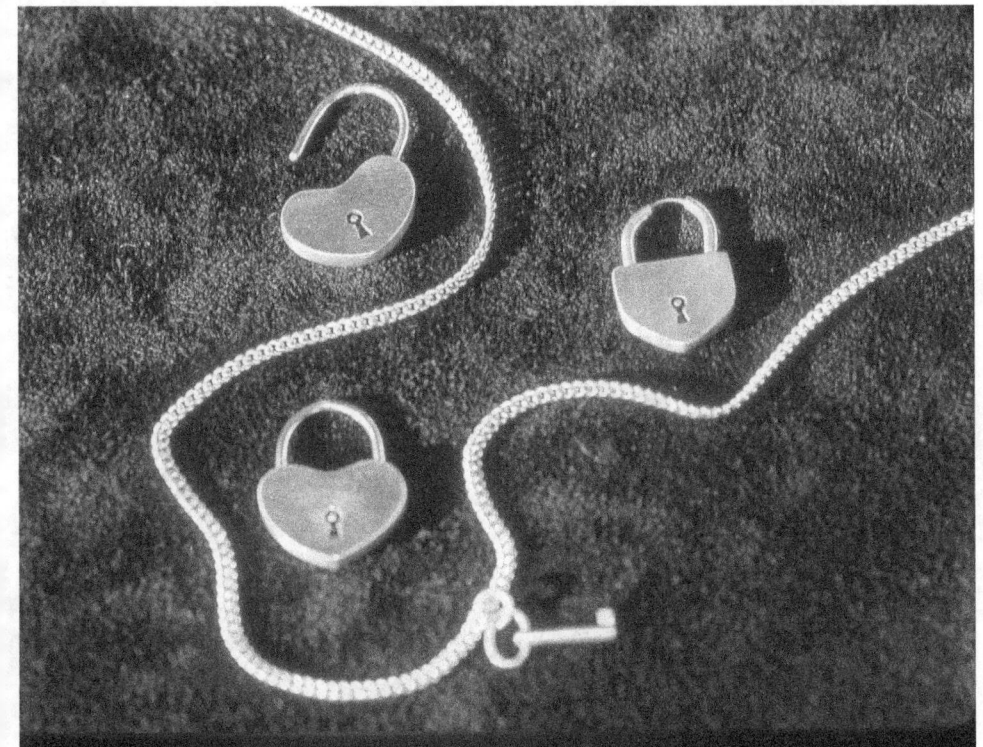

They looked great and were a psychological turn-on for some, but these hand-crafted locks were never practical and were quickly discontinued. The shield-shaped one was intended to be worn in an unstretched ear piercing.

fection, I insisted that customers wait until their piercings had healed before wearing this type of jewelry.

Unfortunately, one of my customers discovered the shortcomings of the design not long after I'd inserted them into his nipple piercings. His name was Alden, and he was a member of the T&P Group. He also enjoyed rough sex play. Early one Monday morning, he showed up on my doorstep looking haggard and distressed. It was obvious something was wrong. Apparently he'd gotten into some pretty heavy action on Saturday night. Someone he was playing with got too rough with his nipple rings and one of them had sprung open inside the piercing. He couldn't rotate the ring or remove it and was in great discomfort. I had to open the ring out with a pair of ring expanding pliers in order to free it. After that, he understood the benefits of wearing a ring with a closure, especially if he was planning on an intense play session.

As many of my early clients came from the local BDSM community, a common request was for a piece of jewelry that could be permanently installed and that would act as a chastity device. For most people this was nothing more than a fantasy. They still wanted something that could be removed whenever they wished it. So I set out to see what I could do with locks.

Before actually attempting to make a lock I searched in vain for something commercially available, ideally made of stainless steel. Almost everything was made of brass with a chrome-plated shackle. Even if I had found something that wouldn't corrode, the mechanism wasn't waterproof and there was no way to prevent a disgusting accumulation of bodily fluids and secretions. Unable to find a commercially satisfactory solution, I turned a blind eye to the obvious problems and set out to produce something by hand.

Back when I'd lived in Denver, I'd wanted to put a lock in my ear piercing. In the early 70s, it was uncommon for a man to have an ear piercing at all, and stretched piercings were something you saw only in *National Geographic*. There was no way to realistically get the thick hasp of a regular lock through my ear.

I had an assortment of basic jewelry making tools and was able to get some silver sheet and wire. Using these, I constructed a crude working lock. This design had what I called a broken shackle and gave the illusion of being much thicker than it actually was. Somehow it and another lock with a solid shackle made their way

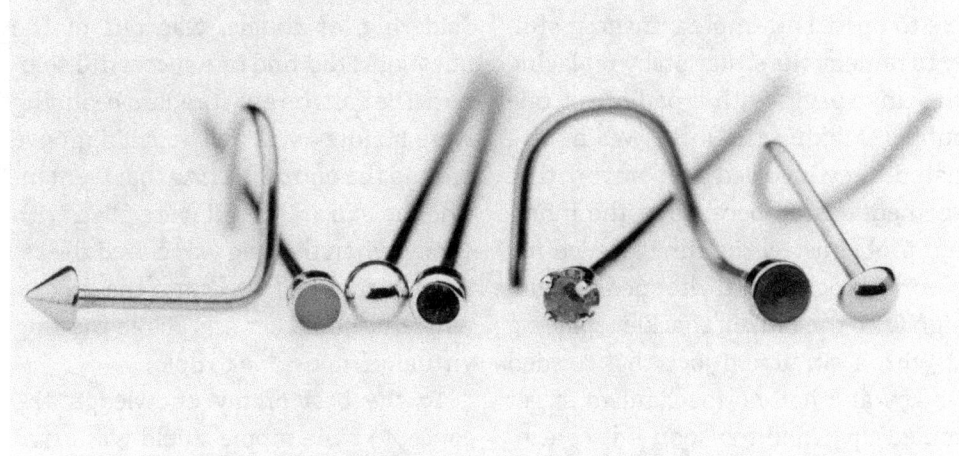

The nostril screw, a Gauntlet reinterpretation that I based on the verbal description of an East Indian design. All piercers must master the technique of custom shaping these to fit the individual nose.

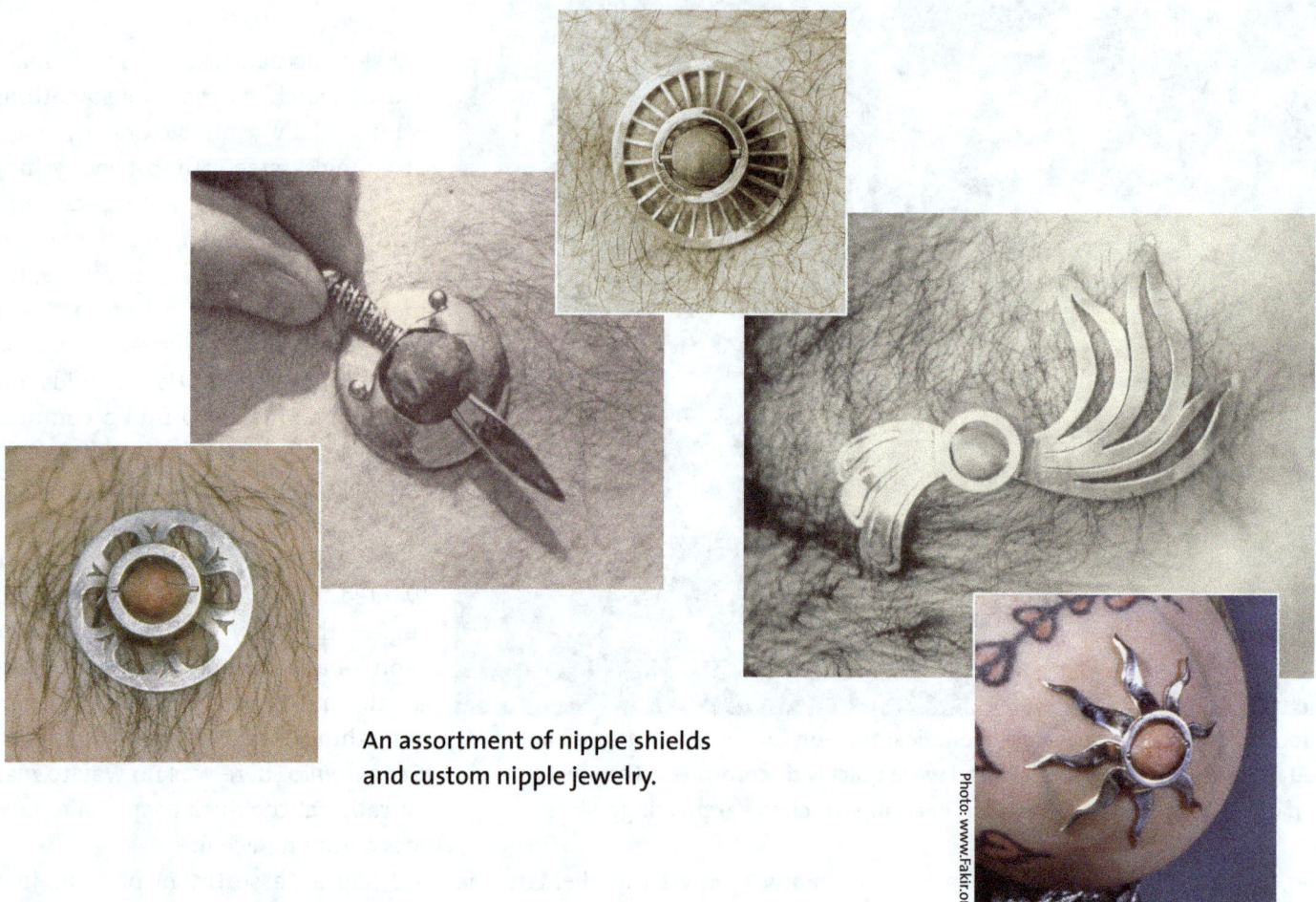

An assortment of nipple shields and custom nipple jewelry.

into my first jewelry brochure.

Unfortunately, these handcrafted locks weren't practical and should never have been included. If worn on any semipermanent basis, they would soon become bound up with disgusting gunk and rendered nearly impossible to open. I attempted unsuccessfully to remedy the situation by replacing the tiny spring with a pad of silicone rubber. Making the locks was a job I hated. They involved a lot of work that seemed wasted because of the inherent problems. By the time I issued my second brochure, I'd dropped the design with the broken shackle replacing it with a simulated lock that needed no key and had no mechanism to get fouled up. None too soon I discontinued locks altogether.

Other attempts at permanently installable jewelry were made. One was a triangular ring, a point of which had two eyes, one threaded, that could be secured with a small lock. Even commercially manufactured locks weren't practical for long-term wear since they weren't waterproof.

There were a few hardcore souls who still insisted on something permanent. Soldering, of course, was out of the question. I did find one successful solution. The balls on our standard bead ring were hollow. I was able to cut a groove around the end of the ring that went inside the ball. If the ball were filled with epoxy, when the ring was closed the cement would be forced into the groove, where it would set and make the ring virtually impossible to open.

To the best of my knowledge, the concept of the nipple shield was original to Gauntlet. The idea was to offer something more decorative that would appeal especially, though not exclusively, to women. As a gay man, I still had a lot to learn about female anatomy because at the time many of the first designs had an inside diameter that was too small for most female nipples.

For a while I tried using stainless steel, spring-loaded watchband pins to hold the shields on, but these proved cumbersome and unnecessary. The tension of the stretched nipple proved to be sufficient to hold the shield in place in most cases.

S/M also influenced one design in particular. Even in the early days, there were people into play piercing, inserting needles through the skin temporarily just for the sensation. For them, I came up with something like a spoked wheel that had a bit of depth. This drew the nipple out so that hypodermic needles could be inserted through the spokes.

One customer wanted a custom nipple shield. He told me he had a thing for feathers and wanted this reflected in the design. It was something of a challenge. Not wanting it to be big or heavy, the feathers had large cutouts and were counterbalanced by complementary shapes that were weighted with extra metal. He seemed pleased.

In the early years, when I made almost all the jewelry myself, I had a number of clients who asked me to create something custom just for them. One of the first was Jim A. He wanted a simple gold nipple shield that would be held in place by a gold sword. I made the blade from quarter-inch gold tubing that was pounded flat on one end, soldered shut, and shaped. A brass plug was soldered into the other end. This was drilled and tapped. The handle was wrapped with wire and a bit of flattened chain and ornamented with gold balls. Jim stretched his piercings up to quarter-inch just so he could wear his new jewelry.

Multiple ear piercings weren't exactly common in the early Gauntlet days. One customer with two ear piercings came to me and wanted an arrow made that would go through both of them. The post was not straight but shaped to accommodate the piercings. The arrowhead was drilled and tapped to screw onto the post. It was so tiny that the only way I was able to screw it on was to use a pencil eraser with a slit cut in it to hold onto the arrowhead.

One of my more colorful clients was a Hungarian doctor who showed up on

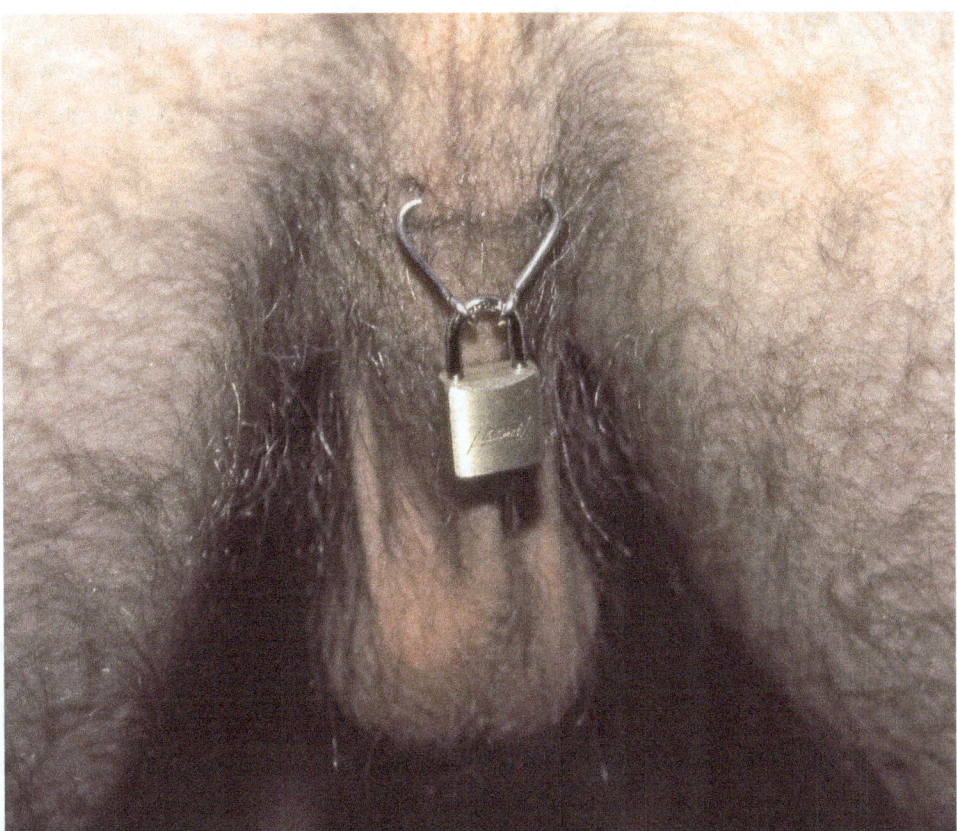

Another design for my BDSM customers. It proved impractical.

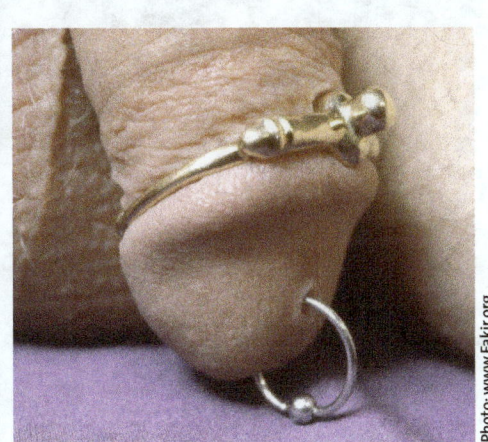

Dr. C's custom frenum ring

my doorstep one day. I was still working out of the house at the time. He'd been referred to me by the Pleasure Chest, a sex shop that had recently opened in West Hollywood.

Dr. C. was impeccably dressed in a suit and tie and had the bearing of a European gentleman. He explained that he wanted a frenum piercing. This was accomplished without a great deal of fuss.

I must confess I was a bit more nervous than usual. Although clean, the house and furniture were shabby. He was, after all, a doctor, and I was concerned that he would be uncomfortable being pierced in such an environment. Still, I brought out a clean bath towel and spread it on the couch for him to lie on. I laid out the bagged and sterilized equipment on a stainless tray. When I was finished, he complemented me on my technique as well as the cleanliness that I observed. It was a particular validation coming from him.

With casual European sophisti-

cation, the good doctor told me that he and his wife were no longer sexually active. He had a young girlfriend who he particularly wanted to keep satisfied. To that end, he commissioned me to make a cast gold frenum ring that would incorporate two penises and a ball on top that would stimulate her G-Spot during intercourse. He quipped that he wanted to pleasure her with three penises.

Dr. C. was quite happy with the finished piece of jewelry. Unfortunately he didn't feel comfortable wearing it all the time, especially at the health club. Consequently, he took it on and off frequently.

Eventually, the post would break off, and he would bring it to me for repair. The last time this happened, he gave me the pieces and chatted amiably about what a wonderful device it was. I told him how long it would take to re-solder, and everything seemed satisfactory. I never saw him again, and never found out what happened to him. After hold-

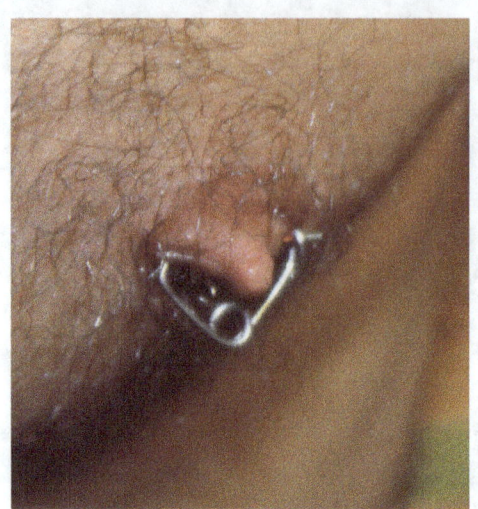

The triangular safety pin, my first effort at making stainless steel jewelry. It proved unsatisfactory, easily snagging on clothing and bedding.

ing onto the piece of jewelry for several years, I eventually sold it.

Although many clients wanted stainless steel, I lacked both the necessary skills and equipment to make it. Early on, I attempted a design I called a triangular safety pin made out of stainless steel wire. It was abandoned fairly quickly because the hook closure tended to snag on clothes and bedding.

Gauntlet's transition to stainless production was not an easy one. I resisted as long as possible and finally gave in only because circa 1979 the price of gold began to rise alarmingly. The situation was so bad with the gold prices fluctuating wildly from one day to the next that it made pricing the jewelry very difficult. At one point I created a price list with a complicated formula for calculating the price of a piece of jewelry on any given day. It was too complex for most people, and as the price of gold began to stabilize, I was able to make a list where the prices remained in effect as long as gold remained within a certain price range.

By the time Gauntlet began making stainless jewelry in the early 80s, there was already a company that had been in production for several years. It was called Spain's Custom, run by a man in

Lawton, Oklahoma, of all places, who used the alias Ray Spain for doing business. I probably could have made my life a lot easier had I worked out a deal with Ray to simply sell his jewelry. For one, I was just too independent and for another, I really didn't care for his quality. He offered primarily captive bead rings and barbell studs. I didn't like the captive bead ring design, and because the metal was extremely stiff, the rings couldn't be bent easily, which made trying to insert them into a wide or fresh piercing difficult. The barbells had externally threaded posts, a feature that I considered unsatisfactory. Thus, I set out to introduce Gauntlet's own line of stainless steel.

Ray Spain remained in business for some years to come, but severe back problems finally forced him to retire. A colorful character named Sailor Sid Diller (see chapter 7) purchased the materials and equipment and began duplicating the designs and offering them under the Silver Anchor brand name.

The challenges of manufacturing stainless steel jewelry were many. First and foremost, it was necessary to determine which of the hundreds of stainless steel alloys were appropriate for wear in the body. These were the days long before the Internet, so research was much more challenging. The best information I was able to gather was that the material needed to be low-carbon and nickel-free, qualities that matched the material being used at that time for some surgical implants. As a selling point, we called this material surgical stainless steel. Depending on availability, we made jewelry of 304 and/or 316 stainless. The industry standard today is ASTM F-138. That's always subject to change, as the industry is constantly evolving.

Then there was the matter of gauge. The standard gauge system used for steel wire is different from the Brown & Sharpe gauge system used for gold

and silver. For the sake of consistency and to eliminate the necessity for more sizes of piercing needles, I felt it was necessary to have all the stainless steel wire custom produced to corresponding thicknesses.

Purchasing stainless steel wire, especially of a custom size, requires a significant minimum quantity. The huge coils of wire arrived from the mill, and I quickly discovered that it was much too stiff to be easily shaped, necessitating a process called annealing. With gold and silver, heating them red-hot and quenching them immediately in cold water easily accomplish this. The same process will temper steel making it tougher and stiffer. To soften steel requires it be heated in a vacuum to a specific temperature and then cooled slowly at a precise rate. This is beyond the capabilities of any jewelry craftsperson, as is the ability to apply gold fabrication techniques to stainless steel, something I would soon learn.

Peter, my head jeweler, was one of the sweetest, kindest men I've ever known and an extraordinary craftsman of gold and silver. To him fell the

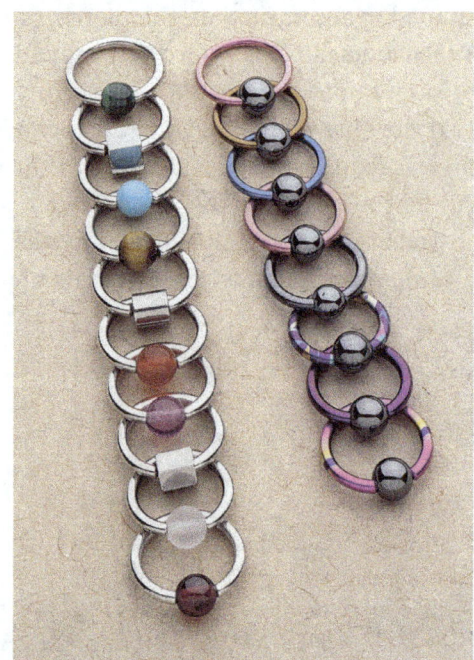

Once we began making niobium jewelry, I finally embraced the captive bead ring in a big way.

unfortunate task of making our first stainless pieces: bead rings. He spent a futile afternoon attempting to fulfill the job he'd been assigned. After several frustrating hours, he stormed up to my desk, threw a handful of ugly black rings on it, and quit. After a year or so—including a stint as a porn performer, being involved in a disastrous love affair, and fighting a battle with cocaine addiction—he asked for his job back, but only on condition that he would never have to make a piece of stainless jewelry again. Since he was such a delight to work with and had managed to kick his drug habit, I couldn't say no.

It was obvious that unless I was willing to spend vast amounts of money on equipment just for fabricating stainless, our product would have to be manufactured for us. There simply wasn't sufficient demand in those days to warrant such an investment. Eventually, I found a company that was able to silver solder drilled stainless steel balls onto rings of the same material and then electropolish them. For some reason the quality of the electropolishing was never consistent. Sometimes the surface was dull and on occasion the process removed too much metal, leaving the rings measurably thinner than they should have been. Had I not been convinced that the captive bead ring design was unsatisfactory, I could have avoided these problems.

Stainless steel barbells presented their own difficulties. Again, the limited demand was a major drawback. So I went looking for a machinist to produce the jewelry in quantities that we could afford. To minimize cost, I made the decision to have them produced in only one thickness: 14-gauge. A significant challenge was how to locate the right person for the job. I eventually tracked someone down, but was less than happy with him. He managed to persuade me to ac-

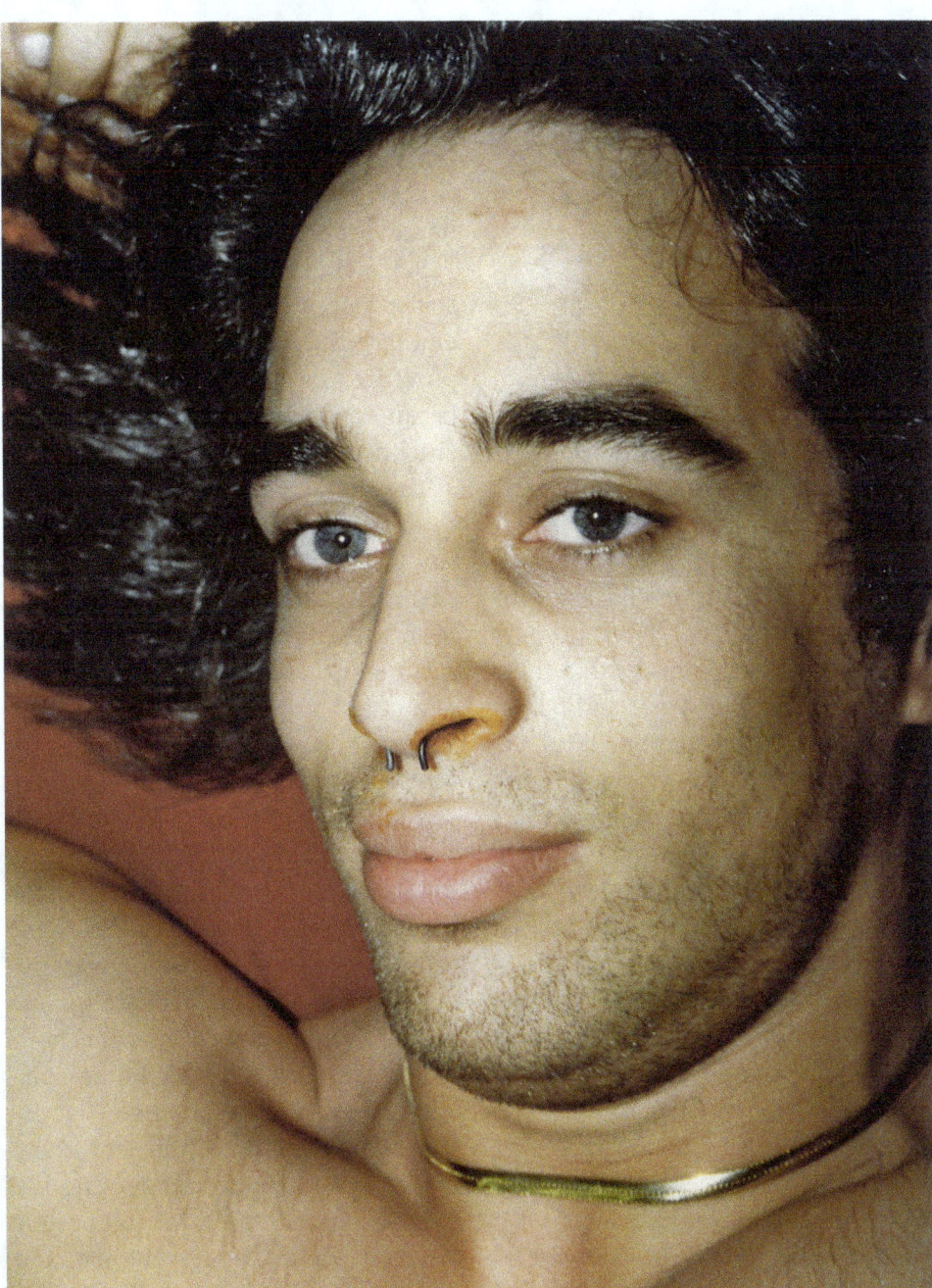

Photo: Drew Ward

The septum retainer, another Gauntlet innovation.

cept what I did not want: studs with externally threaded posts and internally tapped balls. The first order of barbells should never have seen the light of day, much less been offered for sale. In order to insert them without causing discomfort or damage to the tissue, the threads first had to be dipped in melted wax. It was a compromise I hated, and I vowed I would never offer this design again.

Even before the stock began running low, I started looking for another

machinist. This one had the same problems as the first, but managed to come up with something more practical. The internally threaded barbell posts posed no difficulty. The balls were drilled half way through and the holes tapped. Into these were inserted short, externally threaded pins that had to be screwed in and secured. We tried various kinds of cement without success and ended up having to silver solder them. It was a solution that worked, but was less than satisfying.

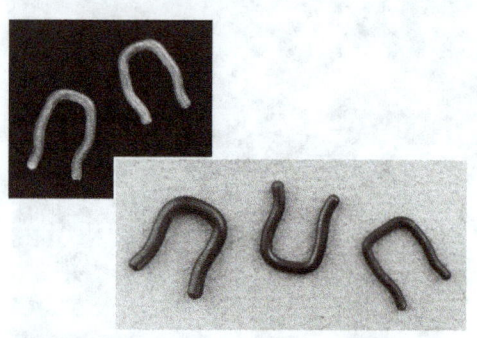

Septum retainers. The originals were made of blackened copper wire covered with Teflon tubing (top). They were superceded by ones made of anodized niobium (bottom).

On occasion, clients would ask why Gauntlet's stainless steel jewelry was so expensive. I always told them that they could buy a nut and bolt at the hardware store for pennies because they were manufactured in the millions. At that time, there simply weren't enough people who needed or wanted stainless steel body jewelry to mass-produce it like hardware. All that has certainly changed!

Niobium body jewelry, another Gauntlet innovation, has been wildly popular for many years and widely available. The first pieces I ever saw were at a craft fair in the early 80s, when craftspeople began making regular jewelry from anodized niobium. It was incredibly beautiful, and when I learned just how inert the metal was, I realized its great potential. The material was fairly inexpensive and could be anodized in an array of bright colors, though it took some effort to perfect the technique.

The anodizing process requires that the metal piece be attached to an electrode and submerged in a solution mostly of water. The more oxygen the solution could make available to the process, the better the results. Different craftspeople had their own secret formulas. I heard of someone who used Coca-Cola. After extended experimentation, I discovered what worked best for me was a solution containing non-chlorine bleach. Altering the voltage used in the process created the various colors. A rich, dark charcoal gray can be produced by carefully heating the metal.

Since there is no practical way to solder niobium, I finally was forced to embrace the captive bead ring. These proved to be extremely popular and became a stock item in Gauntlet's jewelry line and widely copied ever since.

The characteristics of niobium lead to experimentation with titanium, a similar metal. Though Gauntlet never developed it into a product line, a number of manufacturers offer it today and many shops carry it.

While it might not exactly qualify as jewelry, another early Gauntlet innovation was the septum retainer. You might be able to go to work with a septum piercing today, but in the 1970s it would have been unthinkable. It's hard to believe that not so many years ago the business world was universally hostile to facial piercings and people could lose their job over them. Still, there were people who passionately wanted the piercing. That inspired the creation of the septum retainer. It was shaped something like a thick, narrow staple, the flat bottom of which went through the piercing, and the two ends flipped up inside the nostrils. The first septum retainers were made of oxidized copper wire covered with Teflon tubing. They were virtually invisible. Eventually, these where replaced by an anodized niobium version that continues to be offered by a number of manufacturers today, though the shape is less elegant, at least in my opinion.

Over 30 years have passed since the inception of Gauntlet, but the ideas and innovations that it pioneered and the jewelry designs it introduced are very much with us today. Were I receiving royalties, I'd be a very rich man.

Early personal computers were pretty primitive machines with very limited memory and minimal data storage. Anyone remember floppy disks? I was impressed when they were able to hold one megabyte of data. These limitations required that the early applications be pretty stripped down as well.

One of my first exposures to the shortcomings of that early software came when Gauntlet acquired its first mail order computer program. I needed to come up with item codes for all the different styles and sizes of jewelry that Gauntlet offered. That particular field in the program could contain letters or numbers but not more than six characters. I could have made up random codes, but it would have made remembering them very difficult if not impossible. It seemed to me that the most desirable codes should incorporate all the information about the item: the jewelry type, the gauge, the length or diameter, and the material; but how to compress all that into only six characters?

I pondered the problem for some time before inspiration finally struck. The first two characters of the code would designate the design: BR for Bead Ring, BB for Barbell Stud, etc. Somehow the gauges had to be reduced to a single digit. The heavier gauges 0, 2, 4, 6, and 8 were no problem, but what about those with two digits? In what seemed like a stroke of genius at the time, I realized that I could add the two together. 14-gauge became 5, 12 became 3, etc. The fourth and fifth characters of the code number designated the size of the jewelry in sixteenths of an inch, and the final character represented the material, for example Y for yellow gold, S for stainless steel, etc.

Thankfully, by the time we started producing jewelry thicker than 0-gauge, at which point numbers would begin to repeat, software programs were capable of handling longer part codes.

CHAPTER 5

While working from home may have been convenient in the beginning, it also had its drawbacks. In essence, one never leaves work, so it's hardly surprising when drunks show up on the doorstep at 3:00 in the morning wanting to get pierced. It also doesn't help one's credibility. For some time I realized that if piercing was ever going to be taken seriously, I'd have to move the business to a storefront.

By the middle of 1978, I was able to generate enough cash flow to be able to seriously consider looking for a suitable location. Several factors were essential. Of course the rent had to be reasonable. For location West Hollywood seemed like an excellent choice. Since the majority of my clients at the time were gay men, it was logical to be in the heart of the "gay ghetto."

I briefly considered the Silver Lake area because a lot of leathermen lived in that neighborhood. There were also a number of leather bars. Unfortunately, it lay within the jurisdiction of the rabidly homophobic Rampart Division of the LAPD under an equally homophobic police chief, Ed Davis. Notorious for his raids on the area's gay bars, Davis made headlines and enemies on the city council when he squandered a sizable chunk of the police budget marshalling a large force, including helicopters, to raid one of the

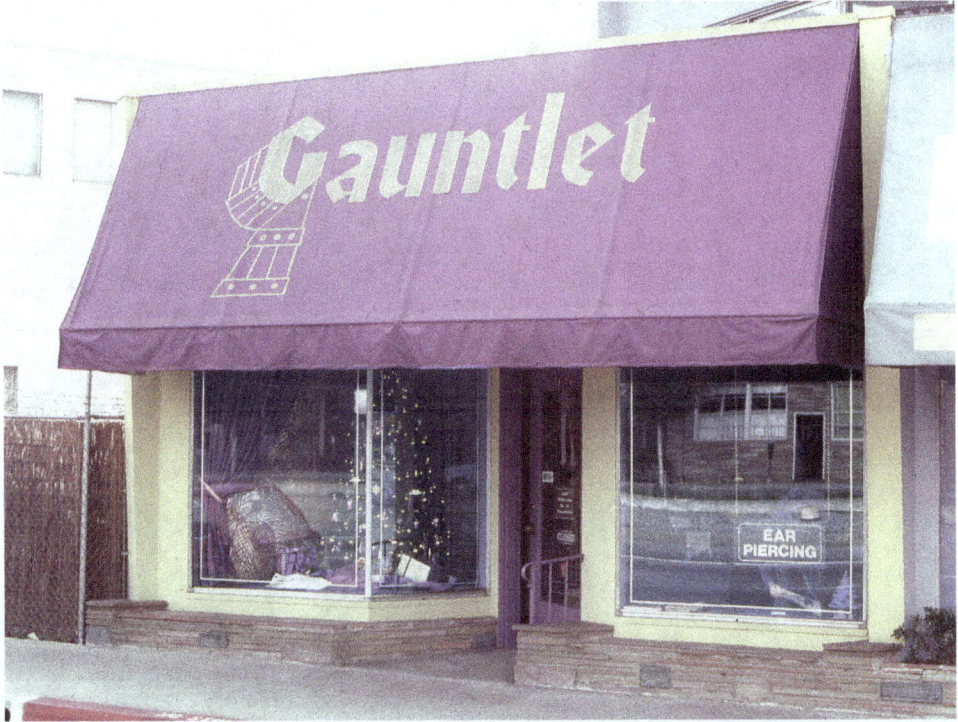

The world's first body piercing studio, 8720 Santa Monica Boulevard at Huntley Drive in West Hollywood

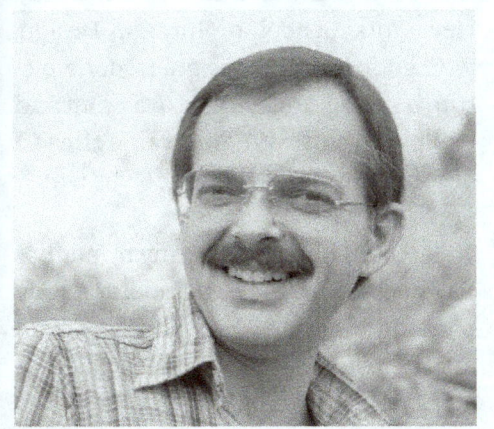

My friend Phil

leather bars that was having a "slave auction" to raise money for charity. He reasoned they were breaking the law because slavery, even if voluntary and temporary, is illegal. Were I to locate in Silver Lake, how long, I wondered, might it take for my fledgling business to fall victim to some cop with an agenda? At least West Hollywood had a sheriff's department that was pretty mellow and seemed to get along well with the area's residents and business owners. Because I hated driving in L.A., I was perfectly happy to find a location within walking distance of home.

In 1971 a New Yorker named Duane Colglazier opened The Pleasure Chest, a waterbed store that quickly became one of the first adult boutiques in the U.S. Forget the sleazy, dirty bookstore of yesteryear and the plain-brown-wrapper mail order business advertised in the back of a shady men's magazine. Here was a clean, well-lighted place where anyone with a modicum of sexual liberation, male or female, could feel comfortable exploring and expanding their erotic universe.

I was still looking for a shop location in 1975 when a large Pleasure Chest branch store opened just a block down Santa Monica Boulevard where the L.A. Gauntlet would soon take up residence. It was a beautifully decorated, erotic department store managed by a buxom redhead, open and friendly and with an easy sense of humor. I had introduced myself to her, given her business cards, and told her if anyone ever inquired about body piercing, to please send them my way.

That's how I met Phil. He showed up on my doorstep one hot summer afternoon intent on having his nipples pierced. I was in the process of making body jewelry and was dressed only in a pair of grubby, cut-off coveralls, my pierced nipples very much in evidence.

A good-looking man with a fair, round face, Phil could easily have passed for some kind of business professional, neatly dressed, short-cropped dark hair, wire-rimmed glasses, and cleanly shaven except for

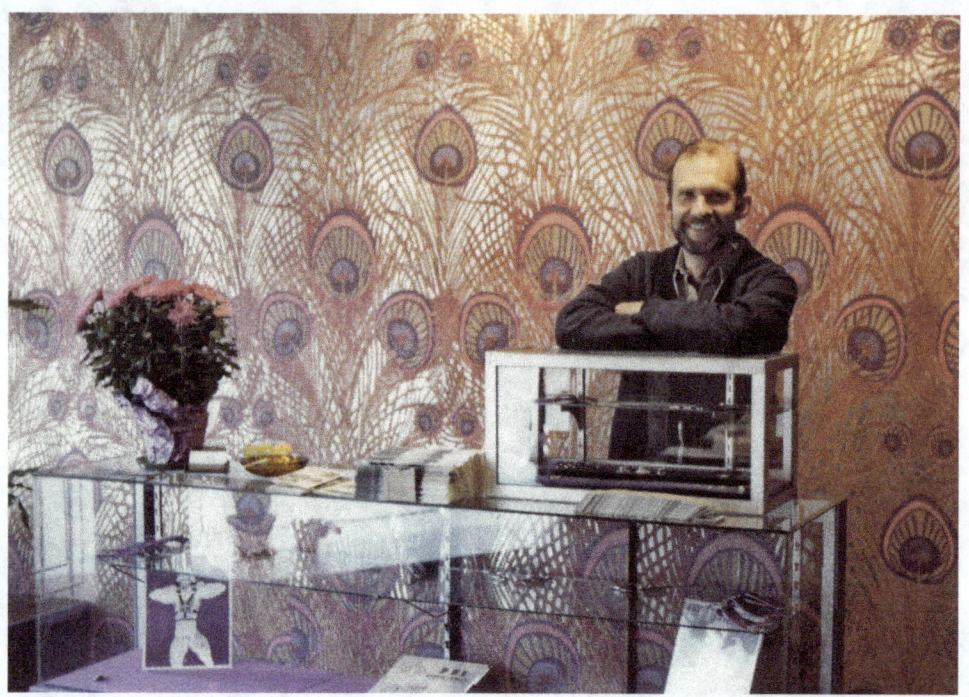

At the front counter of the new shop. The wallpaper was certainly dramatic.

a carefully trimmed moustache. He was a recent transplant from Phoenix looking for love—and lust—in Southern California. Phil got his nipple piercings, but he made it quite clear that there was more on his mind. It wasn't long before we'd shared a joint and were romping in bed.

We had a brief affair, but between both of us being bottoms and my being a bit kinkier than he, it didn't last. However, a close friendship developed, and despite having a spat and falling out for a few years, we reconciled and are still in cordial communication.

Doug had several automobiles. His everyday car was a blue Datsun 280Z, but for very special occasions he drove a black and burgundy vintage Rolls Royce. It was an elegant vehicle worthy of a film star. The upholstery was dark blue plush, and many of the fittings were of highly polished wood: burl or birdseye maple. The backs of the front seats were wooden panels that could be tilted down into tray tables similar to the ones in airplane seats.

I don't know who first proposed it, but Phil wanted a Prince Albert pierc-

ing, and someone came up with the idea of doing it in the back seat of Doug's Rolls Royce. Doug jumped at the opportunity. So, one warm summer afternoon the three of us went looking for a spot where we could park and be undisturbed long enough for me to do the piercing and for Doug to take some pictures.

We drove around for a while before finally deciding on the deserted parking lot of the John Anson Ford Theater in Hollywood, overlooking the Hollywood Freeway. It might not have been the most glamorous or romantic of settings, but it gave us the advantage of privacy, and we could easily see if anyone showed up unannounced.

Just in case there might be some bleeding, we spread a blanket on the back seat. I set up my equipment in elegant glass dishes on one of the tray tables while Phil nervously lowered his jeans. With Doug documenting everything, I proceeded, and in a matter of minutes a delighted Phil had his new piercing.

West Hollywood, in those days before it became an anti-business,

incorporated city, was a genial community on the Eastern edge of Beverly Hills. Then, as now, the area was liberally dotted with showrooms catering to the interior design trade.

As fall approached, fortune smiled on me. On a corner of the main thoroughfare (Santa Monica Boulevard at Huntley Drive), about three and a half blocks from home, I saw a "For Lease" sign. The space was only about eight hundred square feet, but the rent was within my budget and it provided everything I needed at the time.

The building owner was a crotchety, middle-aged lush named Sid. At one time he'd had a design-related business on the premises, but had reached retirement age and wanted to let his property be his source of income. At the time, there were three other businesses in the building: a gay-owned vintage clothing store on the corner, a dominatrix for hire on the second floor, and briefly, a gay sex club run by the landlord in the basement. It was certainly a colorful location for my business.

I signed the lease in September and began the process of decorating and furnishing. Although he was frequently difficult, Sid and I got along well through the years, and Gauntlet had a presence in his building until its demise in 1998. Sid died a year or so before Gauntlet did.

My years of interior design training and experience were about to come into play. I'd studied three years at the New York School of Interior Design, worked for several designers, done picture framing, and worked in a paint and wallpaper store. When it came time to decorate my own business, I was ready.

By 1978 I had made up my mind that purple was to be the color for body piercing. This had sprung directly from another of those products of gay creativity, the bandana or hanky code.

Evidently, the hanky code dates back

46

to Gold Rush days, when dancers in all-male mining town saloons would divvy up into "fellers" and "gals," those taking the women's parts wearing identifying kerchiefs tied around their arms. But in the hands of a few resourceful gay men, it manifested into a unique cultural phenomenon that is still with us today.

According to the Chicago Leather Club, "The hanky color code originated in the early 1970s primarily to distinguish specific sexual interests when the original S/M (or at least D/S)-orientated leather scene was enlarging—and clothing alone didn't reveal esoteric sexual interests. The first published hanky code was done by Ron Ernst who drew one up in collaboration with Alan Selby (the original Mr. S) for their San Francisco store Leather N Things; this code was published in the *Bay Area Reporter* in 1972."

The color of the bandana and the pocket in which it was worn signaled one's particular sexual interest. Worn in the left back pocket, it meant you were a top or active participant; on the right, a bottom or passive partner. Over the years the list of color codes became

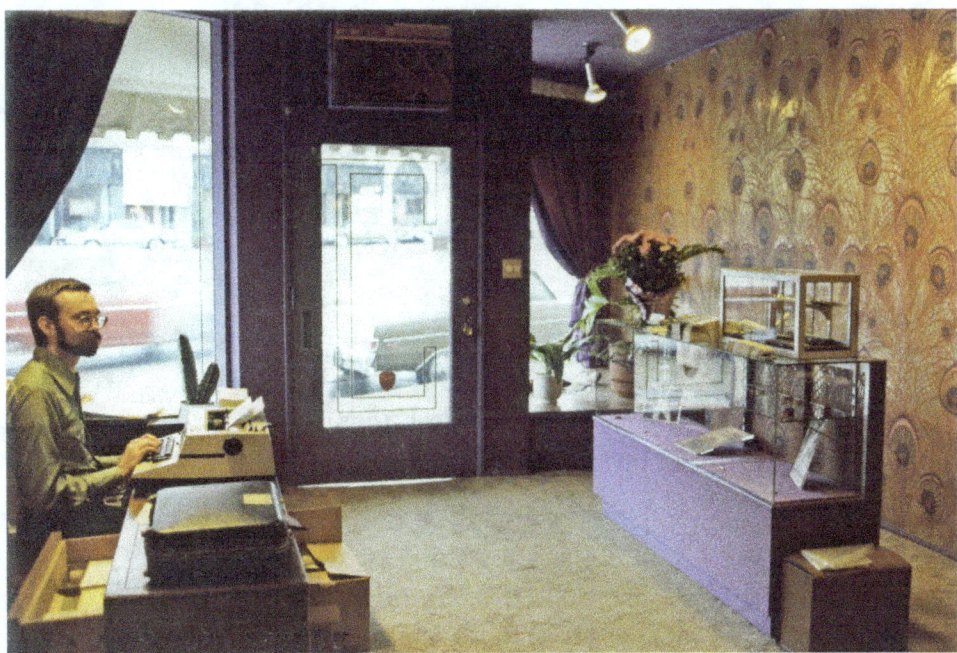
My secretary Gordon Finch at his desk in the new store

quite long. Some have quipped that a color chart is needed to decode all the subtle differences of hue and shade. In the early days, the list was fairly short. Dark blue indicated an interest in fucking, light blue a taste for cock-sucking. Red meant you were into fist-fucking, a sport that had begun gaining popularity in the mid 70s. Black meant S/M; gray, bondage. Yellow and brown need no explanation.

Drummer, a magazine for gay men into S/M that had begun about the same time as Gauntlet, had published an article listing the common hanky code colors. I reasoned that piercing fans ought to have a color of their own. But what color? I didn't have to look too far for inspiration—purple, the color associated with Jupiter, the planet associated in astrology with prosperity and good fortune; purple, the color draping Catholic and Anglican churches during Holy Week when they commemorate the day their deity got pierced. It seemed ideal to me, and so I fired off a letter to the editor of *Drummer* decreeing purple as the official color for people into piercing. My letter was published, and in time, by continually reinforcing the message, it stuck.

Quite naturally, purple had to be a significant element in my color scheme. While widespread today in fashion and design, in 1978 it was neither popular nor common. This presented me with a number of challenges from the start.

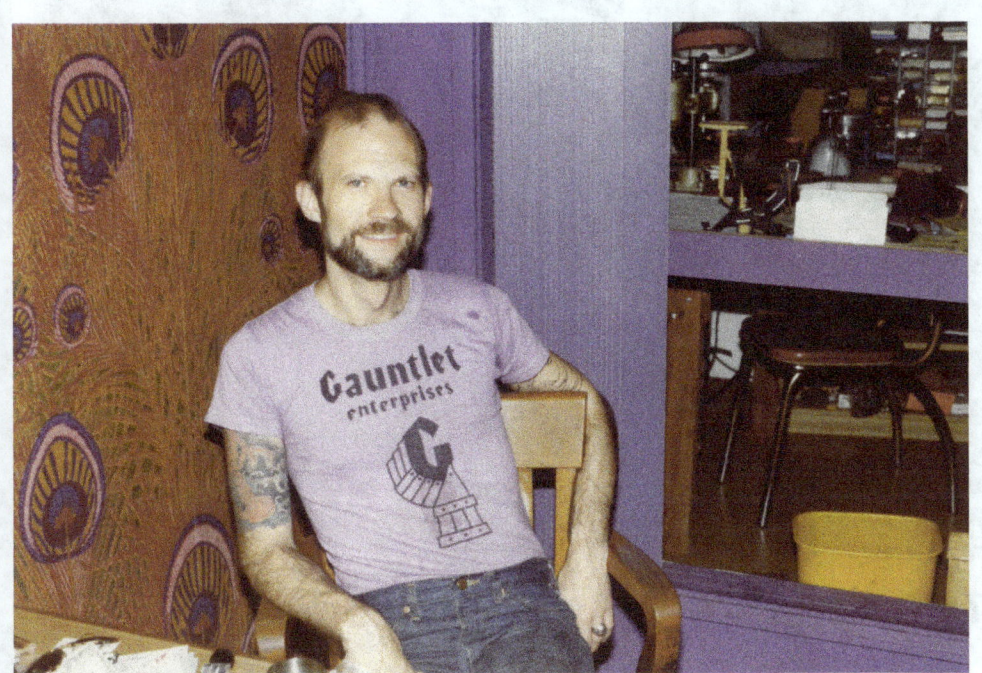
At my desk in the showroom area of the store. I silk screened the design on a hand-dyed purple shirt that unfortunately faded in the wash.

The business owner who'd previously occupied the store had put up a canvas awning. My original in-

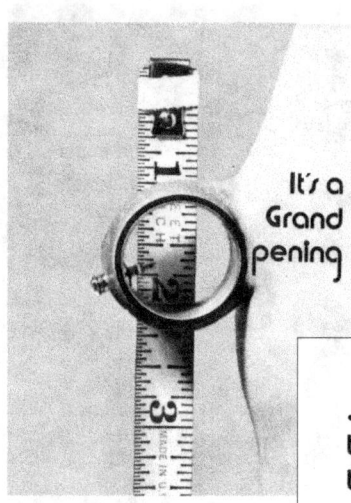

It's a
Grand
opening

... and you're invited
to the celebration at
the new shop of
**GAUNTLET
ENTERPRISES**
on its third birthday.
Friday, November 17,
8 to 11 p.m.

*8720 Santa Monica Boulevard
Los Angeles, California 90069
(213) 652-2385*

Top left to bottom, The original 1978 grand opening invitation featured a photo of Fakir Musafar's enlarged nipple piercing; I enjoy a photo op with Mistress Antoinette, owner of Versatile Fashions; in a similar opportunity Doug was caught at an awkward moment. The nipple photo is by Fakir Musafar and the others by Charlie Airwaves.

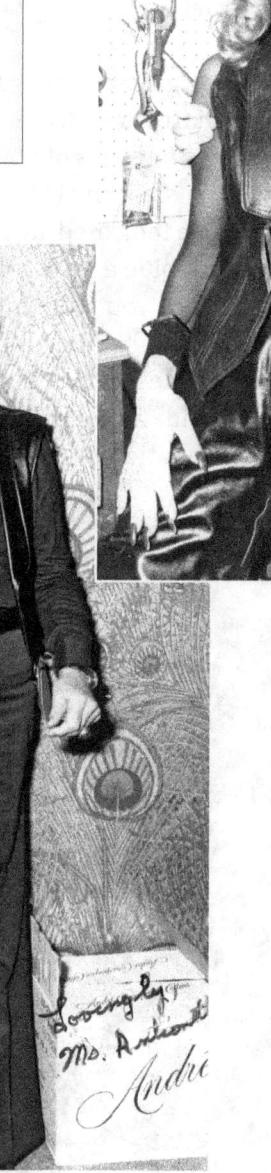

tent was to have a new awning made from purple canvas to fit the existing frame. On this would be painted the business name in gold. Unfortunately there was no purple canvas to be had. Rather than go with another color, I finally decided to have the existing awning painted and lettered instead.

As for decorating the interior, some friends and T&P Group members thought the motif should be "early dungeon"—dark with lots of black leather and chains. While certainly sexy for some, others would find it too intimidating. It might also create an impression of sleaze and a possibly unsanitary environment. For most people getting pierced is scary enough, and less edgy surroundings can help put them at ease. I envisioned a day when piercing would become popular with more than just gay S/M enthusiasts. I wanted a look that would be inviting to anyone who walked into the store.

A stylish wallpaper, something with purple as a major element, would certainly be a good starting place. From working in a paint and wallpaper store I was familiar with many of the designers and what they had to offer. So I got dressed up and, with business card in hand, headed for the newly opened Design Center in West Hollywood to play interior designer.

Finding what I wanted proved to be a bigger challenge than I had anticipated. Purple wasn't exactly a popular color in those days, and I found very little in which it was a significant keynote. While some companies will custom color a run of paper for a design job, it's expensive and reasonable only for a large installation. I needed only enough wallpaper to cover two walls.

What I finally settled on was beautiful, if a little over-the-top. It was a foil paper with an art nouveau motif of giant peacock feathers in shades of gold, orange, rose, and russet red with purple accents. The effect was rich and

quite dramatic. Some friends said it looked like a bordello. Others thought it was a little "too gay." But once applied to the walls, with the trim painted a complementary purple and the ceiling a shade of pumpkin, everyone had to admit the place looked elegant.

I really wanted purple carpet, but that was not to happen for several years. Until then, we made do with the sandy beige carpet that covered the floor when I took occupancy. At one point, a carpet dyeing service was called in to attempt to dye the carpet purple, but after they did a small, inconspicuous test area, the idea was scrapped. The best they were able to achieve was a sickly lavender that was not acceptable.

The back half of the store needed to serve double duty. There was to be an area for making jewelry and another screened off area for doing piercing. Fortunately, the existing floor was vinyl tile making it easy to clean and disinfect. I covered the back wall with a mottled silver and white wallpaper. The remaining walls were painted white. Good lighting and the white gave the area a clean, reassuring feel. Nowadays regulations probably wouldn't allow for jewelry manufacturing and piercing to be done in such close proximity, but in those days we simply didn't know any different.

As the decorating proceeded, plans for the grand opening were taking shape simultaneously. I designed invitations and had them printed. Fakir Musafar graciously provided a photo of his enlarged nipple piercing, which appeared on the front. Well over a hundred invitations were sent out to enthusiasts all over the world.

The grand opening was scheduled for Friday, November 17, 1978, Gauntlet's third anniversary. There was a whirlwind of activity in preparation. Refreshments had to be purchased, champagne iced, everything put in

order. Eric, my lover at the time and a gifted floral designer, produced lavish floral arrangements. A local photographer named Charlie Airwaves was hired to take photographs. It was one of the biggest days of my life.

Guests began arriving around eight o'clock. Doug and Eric were on hand to help me welcome them. Doug was in his element. For him, this was the manifestation of a long-held dream.

Throughout the evening, over a hundred people attended the festivities. It was a historical event. I doubt that many piercing enthusiasts had ever congregated in one location at the same time before. Among the many guests were my pal Rod and Tom the librarian, who had been so fatefully instrumental in bringing it all into being.

Members of the T&P Group were out in force. Mistress Antoinette, a pioneer in fetish fashion from Orange County, showed up and was photographed with both Doug and me.

One by one, the guests began to depart, and the opening night of Gauntlet, the first store in the world devoted exclusively to body piercing, came to an end. It was an event I will never forget. Who would have dreamed that in less than three decades there would be thousands of piercing establishments around the world following in its footsteps?

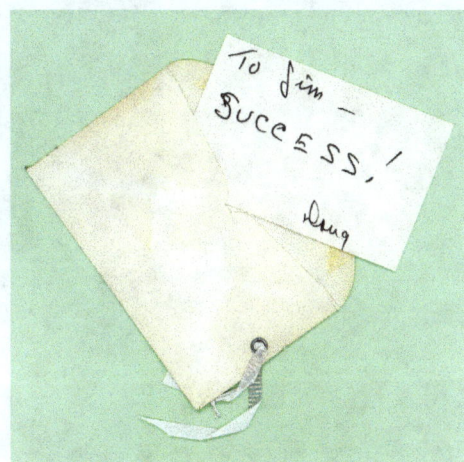

Doug sent flowers for the grand opening and enclosed this card.

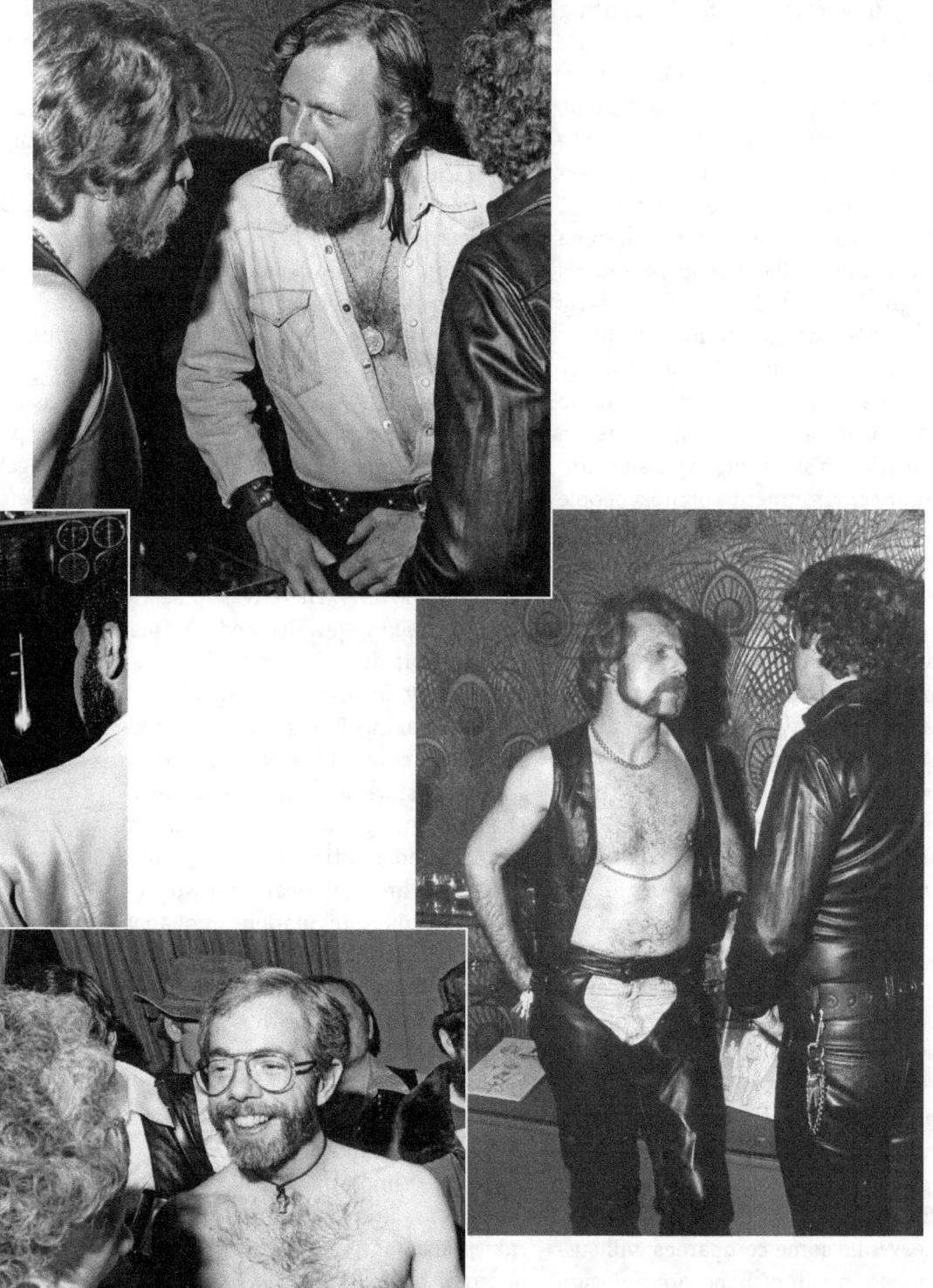

The grand opening celebration. *Clockwise from the top*, Viking Navaro, suitably dressed for the occasion, chats with David Z. who, in the next photo, converses with Dr. John; My lover Eric with Gauntlet's bookkeeper Alayne; Tom the librarian in conversation. Photos by Charlie Airwaves.

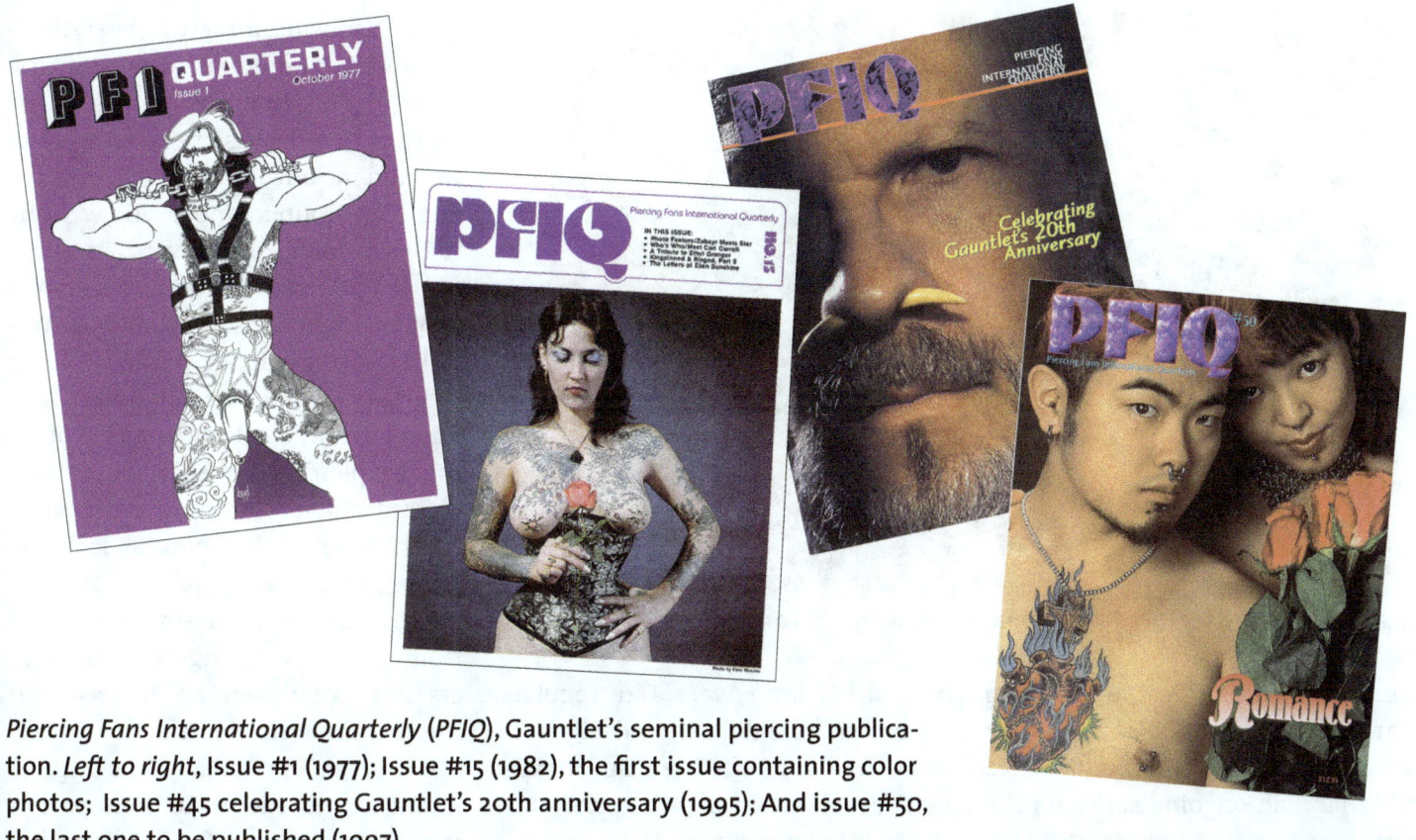

Piercing Fans International Quarterly (*PFIQ*), Gauntlet's seminal piercing publication. *Left to right*, Issue #1 (1977); Issue #15 (1982), the first issue containing color photos; Issue #45 celebrating Gauntlet's 20th anniversary (1995); And issue #50, the last one to be published (1997).

CHAPTER 6

When I first started Gauntlet, publishing a piercing magazine couldn't have been further from my mind. But it quickly presented itself as a very natural outgrowth of the work I was doing. Not least of its virtues was that it has preserved the stories of many early piercing fans.

As piercing enthusiasts began hearing about Gauntlet, a typical type of correspondence started to arrive in the mail on a regular basis. Up to that time, people who were into piercing were pretty much on their own. If they wanted a piercing they had to figure out how to do it themselves or get a sympathetic friend to assist them. There was no readily available resource for information on piercing technique or for the tools and materials to do it. In general, the results were less than satisfactory. Piercing enthusiasts were also widely scattered all over the globe and, for the most part, very closeted.

Consequently, many of the letters I received contained the same two questions: 1. How do I pierce my or my girl/boyfriend's [insert name of body part here]? 2. How do I go about meeting other people into the scene? This was in the day of the typewriter, so needless to say answering these questions repeatedly made it quickly apparent that there had to be an easier, more professional way to meet the demand. The solution that seemed best was to publish a magazine. Since there was clearly a growing interest in piercing, why not? I could also envision it as a powerful promotional tool. By seeing what other fans were doing, readers might be inspired to acquire new piercings and jewelry.

My background in the arts aside, when it came to publishing, I had no knowledge or experience. Perhaps if I had, I might have thought twice about pursuing the matter, but naïvely I be-

gan making plans and gathering the information and resources I thought I would be needing.

Early in the days of the T&P Group, someone had suggested we call ourselves "Piercing Fans International." The name never stuck, in no small part because the members were pretty much people who lived in the Los Angeles area. However, when I was trying to think of a name for the magazine I remembered the suggestion. Finding enough material to put out a monthly would have been a major challenge, but a quarterly seemed within the realm of possibility. So the magazine became *Piercing Fans International Quarterly* (*PFIQ* for short). It was a seminal publication, the first of its kind. From a historical viewpoint it is an invaluable resource. Every issue featured an interview with someone who was a trendsetter. They appeared in its pages, and some quietly slipped into obscurity. The contents also typically included

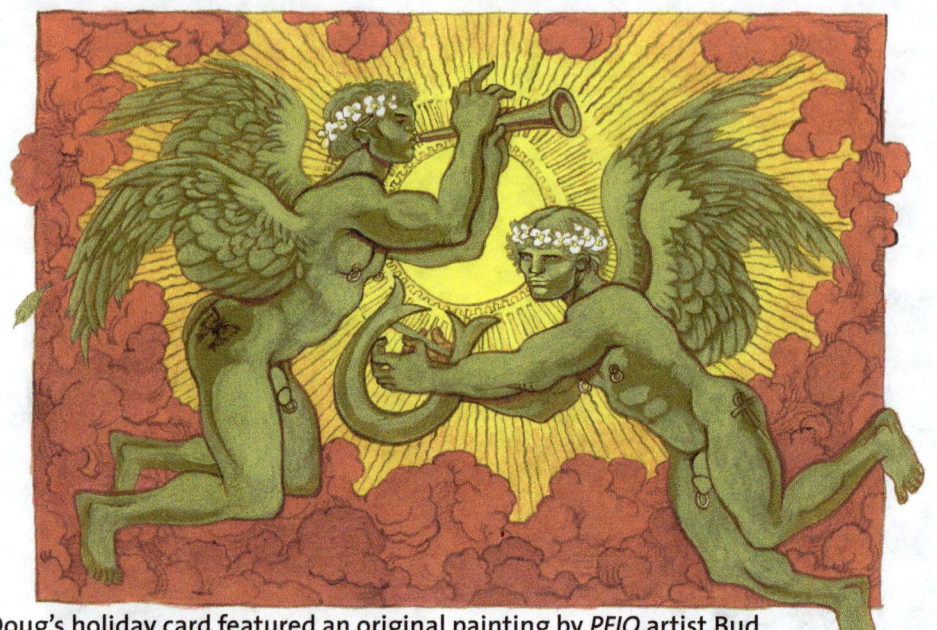

Doug's holiday card featured an original painting by *PFIQ* artist Bud

letters to the editor (great for knowing what readers were up to), a feature by Fakir on some rite or ritual, and "Pierce with a Pro," an ongoing series on the techniques Gauntlet piercers used for various piercings.

Doug Malloy was an avid photographer, especially where piercing was concerned. Although he had a fine camera and some basic skill in using it, his philosophy was that if you took enough photos, some of them were bound to turn out. Consequently, he spared no opportunity to take lots of pictures of piercings and pierced people whenever he had a chance. I had free access to these photos and figured that they would provide an ongoing source of material for the magazine.

Under Doug's influence I also went out and bought a good camera and spent some time learning how to use it. After all, Doug wasn't always around when a photo opportunity presented itself.

A regular contributor to the magazine was a local gay artist who went by the name of Bud. His work occupied 13 of the first 14 covers and, after we went to color, appeared regularly inside. I had seen his work in the gay S/M magazine *Drummer*. Though not pierced,

he and his lover were T&P regulars. On occasion he did tattoo designs for some clients of Cliff Raven. Bud's imaginative pen and ink drawings show the strong influence of comics, the graphic novel, and early fantasy and sci-fi art.

Doug was very taken with Bud's work and even commissioned him to do a watercolor Christmas card design to send out to his piercing enthusiast friends. It shows a pair of pierced cherubs playing musical instruments.

One of the primary contributors to and influences on *PFIQ* was Fakir Musafar. Without his input, the magazine would have been considerably less interesting, informative, and colorful. He has personally known many of the pioneers active before and after Gauntlet came into being. Photos and interviews with these people were regular features, as were articles on various tribal rites and rituals, many of which he emulated and documented. His contributions appeared in every issue from #2 through #36.

By September of 1977 I had managed to assemble what I thought would be enough material for the inaugural issue. It seemed only natural that this issue should contain an interview with Doug. He was, in my eyes at least, the

man responsible for setting everything in motion. There was also an article about male infibulation entitled "The Story of Nils." It was one of Doug's stories and included photos he had taken of a T&P Group member who went by the name of Viking Navaro. To round out the primary content, there were about a dozen photographs by an Australian photographer named Johnny Lee. Just how Doug had obtained them I don't know, but they were all of attractive pierced women, a couple with pierced nipples, but most with ear or nostril jewelry. They had the look and feel of photos dating from the Fifties.

With all the requests I'd received from people wanting to meet others into body piercing, it was clear the magazine needed classified ads. I called these "Pin Pal" ads. The original intent was just to make them part of the content, but on further consideration I realized it would be better to print them separately and mail them with the magazine, not as part of it. There were several reasons. Initially, we allowed people to include addresses and phone numbers in their ads. But since privacy was an issue, it would have meant not being able to sell the magazine on newsstands. The other reason was one of cost. It would have been a lot more expensive to put them in the magazine and much cheaper to just print them inexpensively at a local copy shop.

Not wanting to give any would-be competitor such easy access to my clientele, I soon stopped accepting personal contact information in ads altogether. From then on, we offered a mail forwarding service so subscribers could confidentially contact one another.

The next challenge was to get the material assembled into a magazine and printed. Through a T&P connection, I was introduced to a man in San Francisco named Lee, who owned a small print shop. He was known in fist-

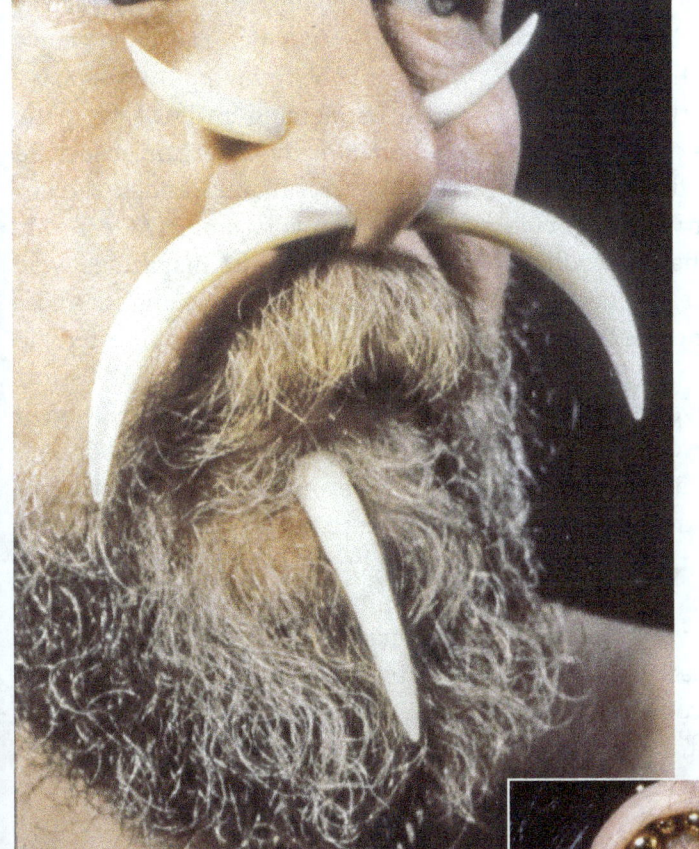

Photos: www.Fakir.org

Bud, a.k.a. A. Viking Navaro, was a member of the T&P Group. He was featured prominently in issue #13, though a photo of his pierced foreskin was used to illustrate a story about infibulation titled "The Story of Nils" in issue #1. His unusual multiple and enlarged piercings can be glimpsed in other issues, and he authored and appeared in the feature "Hans of Denmark" in issue #19.

If memory serves me correctly, by day he had a suit-and-tie job at one of the local universities. But few knew what lurked underneath the clothing. In private he was a self-described atavist, modern primitive, exhibitionist, and sensualist.

fucking circles as the publisher of the T.A.I.L. (Total Ass Involvement League) newsletter. At the time, he agreed to print the first issue of *PFIQ*, his shop was proudly printing a four-color image—four runs through a one-color press—of a muscular arm inserted into a tattooed male posterior. It came as no surprise that he wasn't squeamish about body piercing. In addition, Lee knew and introduced me to a graphic artist who was able and willing to assemble my collection of material into magazine layouts.

Materials in hand, I boarded an airplane for San Francisco. I'd made an appointment to spend a day with the layout artist, watching, overseeing the project, and proofreading the copy while he was typing it into his professional IBM Selectric. In that one day, I learned enough that when I returned home I was able to do the layout of almost every issue of the magazine that followed. The artist charged me a little under $200. It was without question one of the best deals of my life.

With the layouts complete, I returned to the printer. His shop foreman took the material and the photographs into the darkroom and produced the printing plates. From there, it was onto the press.

The premiere issue (October 1977) had 16 pages. Its original print run was 500 copies of the magazine and "Pin Pal" ad sheets. The cost of the printing was just shy of $500. The subscription rate, including postage, was $12.00 per year domestic, $14.00 overseas. The issue was soon being put into envelopes and mailed. There were copies left over. These eventually sold out over the counter and as back issues to new subscribers. In time, I had the issue reprinted.

The premiere issue featured an interview with Doug. While the magazine was in production and being printed, he was out of the country. I knew that he was very closeted about his piercing activities, but as a tribute to him I still wanted to use a photo with the article. There was no way to get ahold of him for his approval. I thought I could resolve the problem by having the printer "solarize" the image. That's a process of making it so high contrast that it's reduced to only a few tones, and I thought it would provide sufficient disguise so that he wouldn't be quite so recognizable. Nowadays, solarization can be done easily with a good computer program. Unfortunately, at the time I didn't even know there was a word for what I wanted, much less how to describe it. The printer tried to follow my instructions as he understood them, but the result was less than satisfactory.

Doug returned as I was preparing the first issues to be mailed. I proudly presented him with a copy of this history-making document, but my pride and enthusiasm were short lived. He was very displeased that I had included a recognizable picture of him. Caught between hurt and anger at myself, on the verge of tears, and knowing that it was too late and too expensive to have the magazine reprinted, I went to the hardware store after Doug left and bought a can of matte black spray paint. Returning home, flushed with upset and humiliation, I took a piece of thin cardboard and cut a rectangular hole in it the same size as the photo and started obliterating the evidence of my poor judgment by placing the stencil over the images one by one and spraying a swath of black paint across Doug's face. As soon as the paint dried, the magazines were hurriedly stuffed back into their envelopes. I couldn't wait to be rid of them as quickly as possible and immediately took the first batch to the post office just down the street. It's possible some of these copies still exist in someone's collection. If so, they now know why Doug's face is obliterated.

Several hours later, before I could deface any more photos, Doug called me. He apologized for overreacting and said that since the only people who would be receiving the magazine would be piercing enthusiasts, many of whom already knew him, it seemed silly to worry about. Besides, the circulation was very small. As a result, the remainder of the magazines were mailed out with his face unobscured.

Collectors may be interested to know that there is a subtle but distinct difference between the first edition of issue #1 and the reissue. The former uses purple and brown inks on some of the inside pages. To save money on the latter, only the cover has purple ink.

Issue #2 of the magazine came out in January of 1978. It featured both an interview with Fakir and an article by him. This issue also featured an article on nipple piercing, the first in a long-running series of articles on the basic techniques used for various body piercings. The series was initially called "Pierce Like a Pro," but was subsequently changed to "Pierce with a Pro." It's important to realize that the business was still in its infancy. As you learned in an earlier chapter, everything was new and without precedent. Maybe I was a bit paranoid, but I had no idea if "big brother" was watching, just looking for an excuse to intervene. As a result, I may have had a tendency to overthink things. After much consideration and consultation with Doug, we concluded that the word "like" might imply we were encouraging people to do piercing on their own, and the consequences of that were unknown. "With" put the reader in the neutral position of an observer, and that seemed a safer choice of wording. In the coming years Gauntlet made three videos based on the "Pierce with a Pro" series and used that name for them.

Rounding out issue #2 were several more photos by Johnny Lee, including

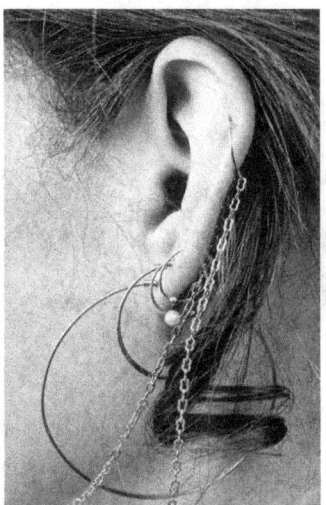

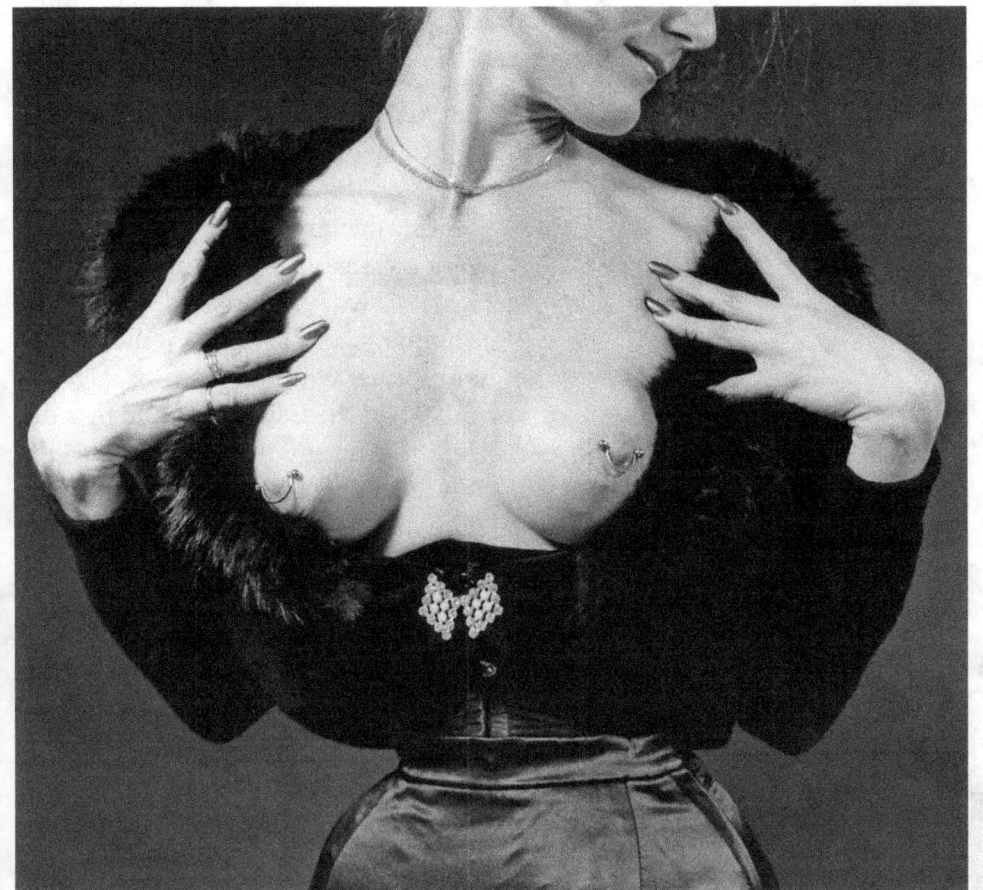

Issue #3: The 20-page issue featured an interview with Mike and Connie, an Orange County couple who went by Nick and Jennie Valentine in the article. They were an interesting male dominant/female submissive couple. At her husband's behest, the wife Jennie wore tight-laced corsets, extreme high heels, and nipple and labia piercings. Nick made a very good income selling chicken manure.

In 1978 when Gauntlet was in its infancy, I had my portrait painted by a wonderful friend and gifted artist named Sylvia Shap. The Valentines saw it, and Nick wanted to commission Sylvia to do a portrait of Jennie. They met with her, but the meeting didn't go well. Nick had an attitude that all women should be subservient to him. Sylvia told me later he was so rude and cheap, badgering her to lower her price, that she wanted nothing to do with him. Thenceforth, Sylvia always referred to him as "the chicken shit farmer."

Sylvia did paint one of the members of the T&P Group, a doctor named John who had his back, arms, and legs tattooed with a giant squid done by Ed Hardy. His portrait, called "A Doctor of Internal Medicine," as well as my own, can be seen on Sylvia's web site (SylviaShap.com).

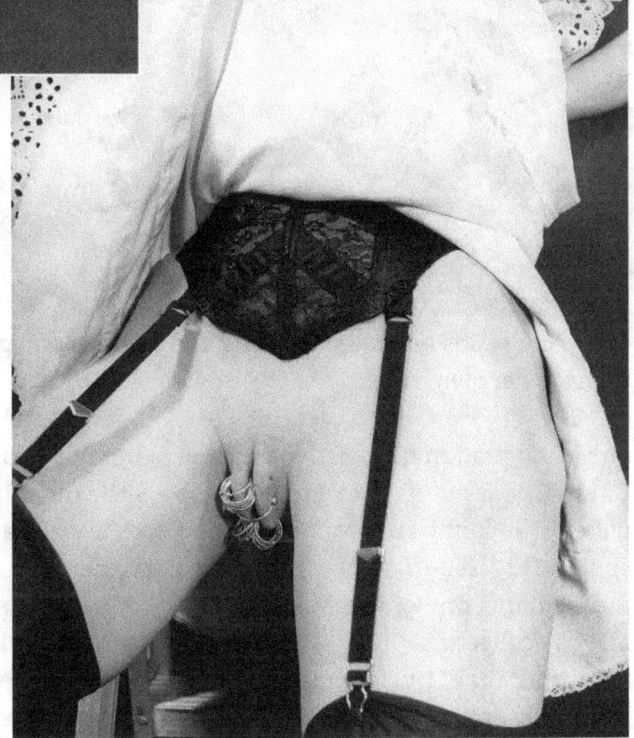

Photos: www.Fakir.org.

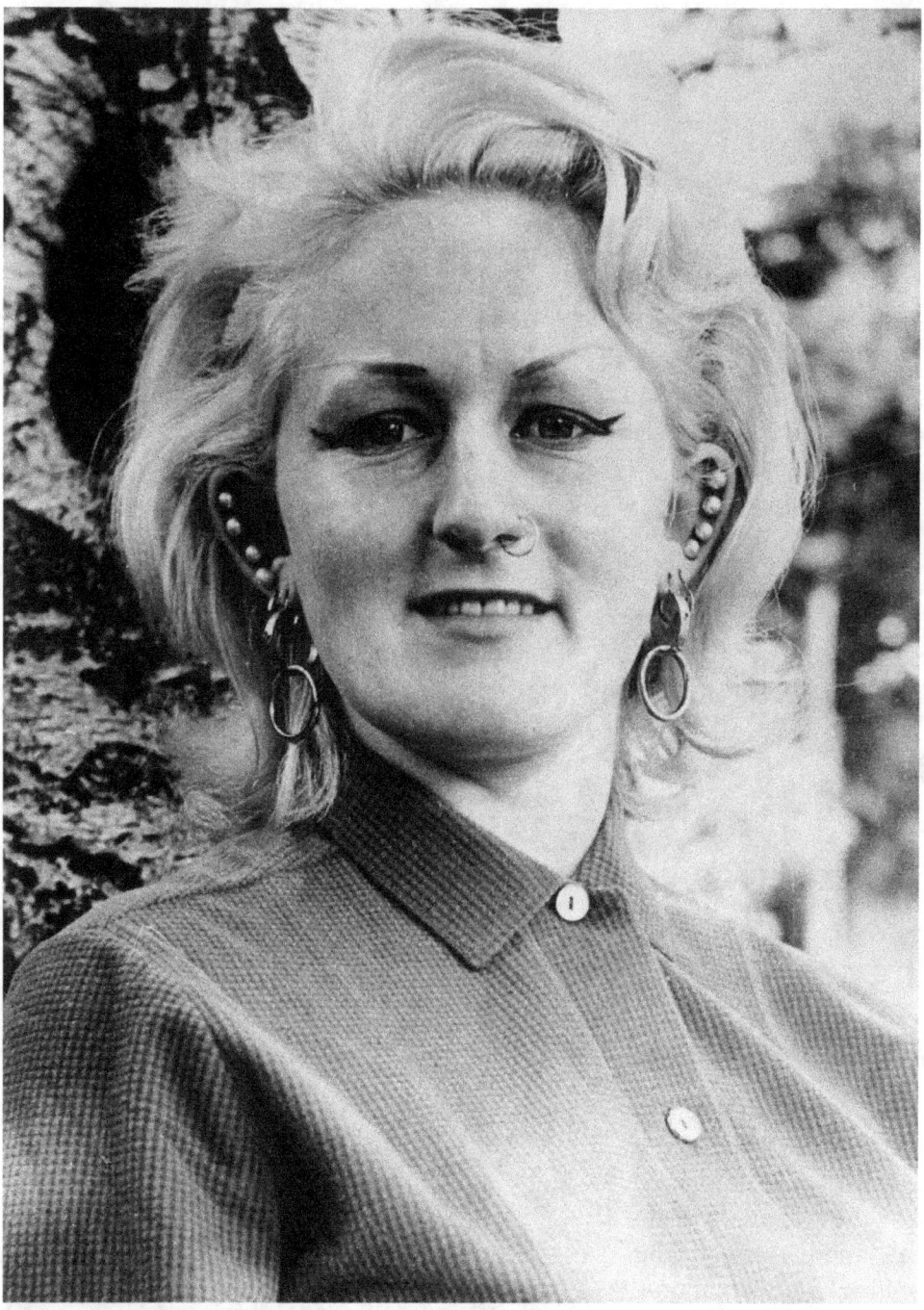

Cindy Ray, 1960s Australian piercing and tattoo pinup girl. She later became a tattooist in her own right.

point of view of my comparative lack of layout experience, the results were clearly sloppy and amateurish.

People who know me well are aware that I find it very difficult, if not impossible, to face confrontation, though I've gotten better with age and experience. My tendency is to distance myself from the offender. Had I been willing to confront Lee, I would have returned the magazines and insisted upon their being redone. Instead, although I let him know I was dissatisfied, I kept the shipment and sent the issues out to subscribers. When the supply ran out, I had the issue reprinted by a different printer with new layouts I did myself. Collectors take note: there are two distinct editions of issue #3. The revised edition is labeled as such on the front cover.

Issue #3 included another article by Fakir, and the second "Pierce with a Pro" feature on the Prince Albert, showing in graphic detail the extremely awkward and difficult technique in use at the time.

One of the major piercing pioneers, Alan Oversby from the U.K., better known in the piercing world as Mr. Sebastian, was the interview subject in issue #4. (He features prominently in chapter eight of this book.) By issue #5 I got around to interviewing myself.

In 1979 readers of issue #6 were introduced to a German couple named Bernd and Elke Schöbler. Doug and I had met them on a recent European tour. These were people who shared a common passion for piercing as a means of erotic enhancement that dated back to the late Sixties and early Seventies.

By the time issue #6 rolled off the press, it had become impossible to keep the magazine on schedule. From this point on they carried only the number. One T&P member even quipped that we should change the name to *PFIW*—

one of Australian tattooist and piercer Cindy Ray. Issue #2 had grown to 20 pages. The print run was only 1000 copies. This issue was never reprinted and remains one of the most sought-after by collectors.

By this time, I was already having trouble keeping the publication on a regular schedule. Not only was acquiring material a challenge, but there were all the other responsibilities of

the business as well. To give myself a little more latitude, issue #3 is the first to use a seasonal designation (Spring) rather than a specific month. When my printer Lee practically begged me to let him do the layout, I agreed.

I remember going to the Greyhound bus station in Hollywood to pick up the shipment of magazines from San Francisco. Upon seeing what Lee had done, my heart sank. Even from the

STAR THE ENCHANTRESS

Photos: www.Fakir.org.

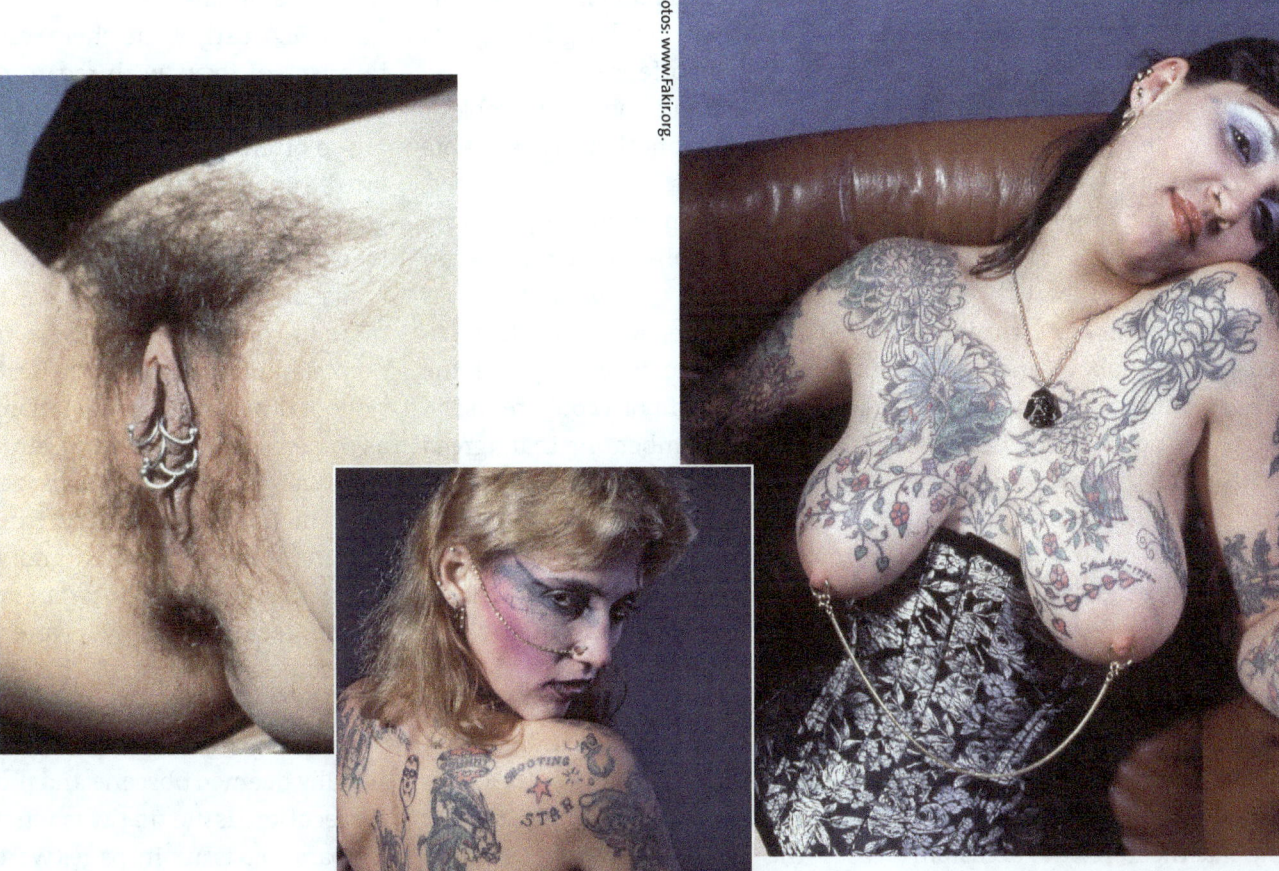

Below, Star with Zubayr.

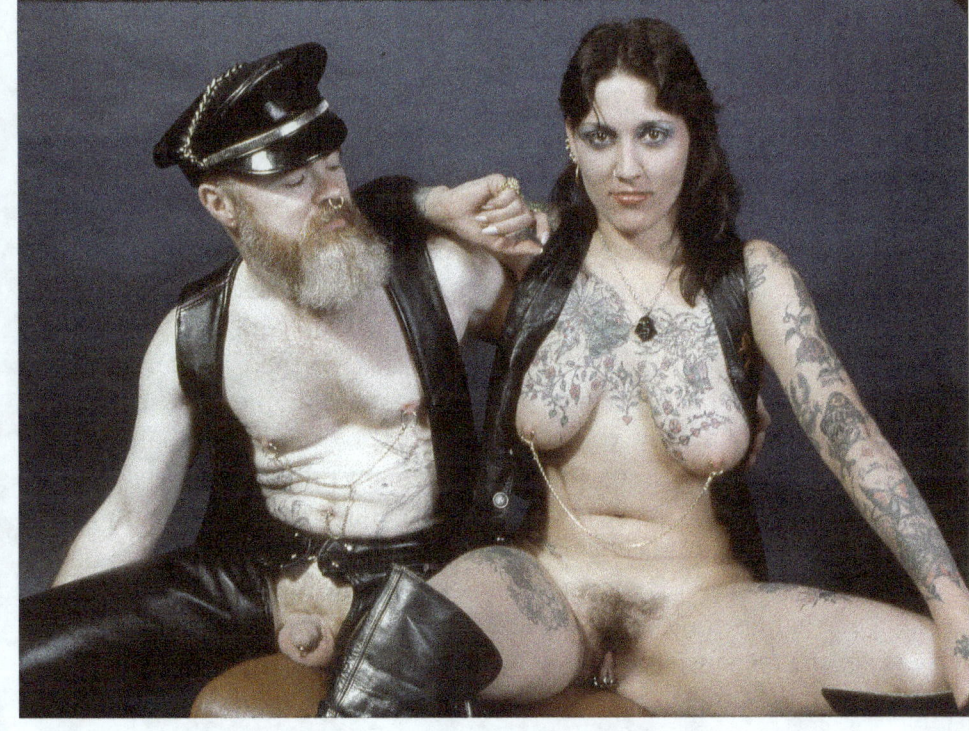

Issue #5 introduced Star, a.k.a. Star the Enchantress, who may have appeared more often in *PFIQ* than anyone other than Fakir. Her face or some other body part showed up with regularity for years. That may have been because she was one of Fakir's regular models. She was a tough-as-nails biker chic with a masochistic streak who'd gotten her first tattoo at age 13. More tattoos followed and eventually she started collecting piercings as well. She was the model for the cover of *PFIQ*'s first color issue, #14, and appeared in the centerfold with a friend of mine who appeared under the pseudonym Zubayr.

In time, Star drifted off the radar. According to Fakir, she moved to Florida and became a tattooist. He heard later that she had been murdered by a biker gang. I have no way of verifying this since I don't even remember her last name.

Piercing Fans International Whenever.

Fakir contributed an article to issue #8 entitled "Piercing: Modern Primitives." Historically, this is significant because it was the first time that the term, coined by him, had appeared in print. The article was about Ethel Granger, the woman who at the time held the record for the world's smallest waist: 13". She and her husband Will were pioneers from a bygone generation. Ethel got the spotlight with her tight-laced corset and piercings above and below the neck. Her biography was written by Will, who makes no secret that he did several penis piercings on himself.

The first 14 issues were essentially all black and white with an occasional second color on the cover. By 1982 Gauntlet had finally prospered to the point that it was financially possible to add full color to the covers and the center spread of the magazine. Even though it was only four pages of color, it was a big step forward. Fakir redesigned the masthead for the occasion. We were now getting enough content to be able to publish a 32-page issue, but it was still virtually impossible to meet any kind of schedule. We started listing subscription rates for four issues rather than a year.

As the business and magazine in particular grew, there were always new challenges. One was in finding printers willing to handle the material. Because of the unique content and the nudity, many printers wanted nothing to do with us. The first couple of printers were gay men who had no issues with the material, but their shops were only capable of handling one- or two-color jobs. Four-color printing requires larger, more expensive equipment, so I had to look for a new printer.

Unfortunately, in those days the only places willing to handle the magazine were printers of porn. The first one we used was a sleazy man who owned a print shop in Van Nuys, an L.A. suburb in the San Fernando Valley. He had a gimpy leg and walked with a cane, and I had visions of some mob henchman breaking his leg for some unknown offense.

Printers weren't the only problem. Binderies were another. These were the businesses that collated, folded, and stapled the printed sheets into a finished periodical. In some cases printers operated their own binderies. I was never able to understand how the bindery personnel who dealt daily with the raunchiest kind of porn could refuse to bind *PFIQ*. I remember one that agreed to do the job but only at night after their female staff had gone home.

Looking back through the years of the magazine, there's no questioning the invaluable contributions that we received from readers, most commonly letters and photos. It added a great deal seeing and reading about what people in other parts of the country and the world were doing. In most cases the piercings were the more common ones, but not infrequently the modifications some readers were doing to their bodies were so extreme they left us incredulous. It's difficult to forget Angel (issue #22), the man with an enlarged piercing behind his Achilles tendon that allowed him to be suspended from his foot. Or Til (issue #12), an Englishman whose split penis could be turned inside out and fastened into various configurations with a multitude of piercings. Or Mistress Noni (issue #20), whose stretched and pierced inner labia could be tied into knots.

Thumbing through 50 back issues and viewing some of these photos, it still amazes me that anyone could accuse Gauntlet of being conservative. In retrospect, perhaps it was my unconscious and somewhat schizophrenic attitude toward these extreme practices. On one hand, I continually urged readers to act responsibly and with caution and at the same time provided images of the most risky, freaky, and bizarre modifications imaginable for them to emulate.

In *PFIQ*'s early years, there was a certain lack of focus with regard to content. Since people into body piercing are so often into other similar and related things, we regularly received requests and material submissions that weren't exactly consistent with the magazine's theme. Tattoos were common, to some extent so were temporary/play piercing and S/M and a variety of other body modifications such as corseting, penis splitting, etc.

I must confess that there were periods in Gauntlet's history when the content made me a bit paranoid, fearful that some authoritarian agency might decide what we were doing was somehow criminal. This was not without justification. Even today the publication of piercing photos is occasionally deemed obscene and provokes prosecution. Issue #24 was what I call my paranoid issue. Its pages were filled almost entirely with articles about and images of pierced ears.

During the mid-Eighties, the government had started cracking down on S/M publications. I took a long hard look at the material I was publishing, asking myself if there was anything in *PFIQ* that might come under attack. After some consideration, I realized that by and large permanent body piercing could be defended as a form of body decoration not unlike ear piercing or even tattooing. Play piercing, however, was not. At this point I made the decision no longer to include play-piercing material in *PFIQ*. I also decided not to include images of any other form of body modification unless they were accompanied by a permanent piercing. Because of Fakir's influence, we continued the features on the various tribal rituals that included piercing, but my feeling was that they were not unlike some-

JIM A.

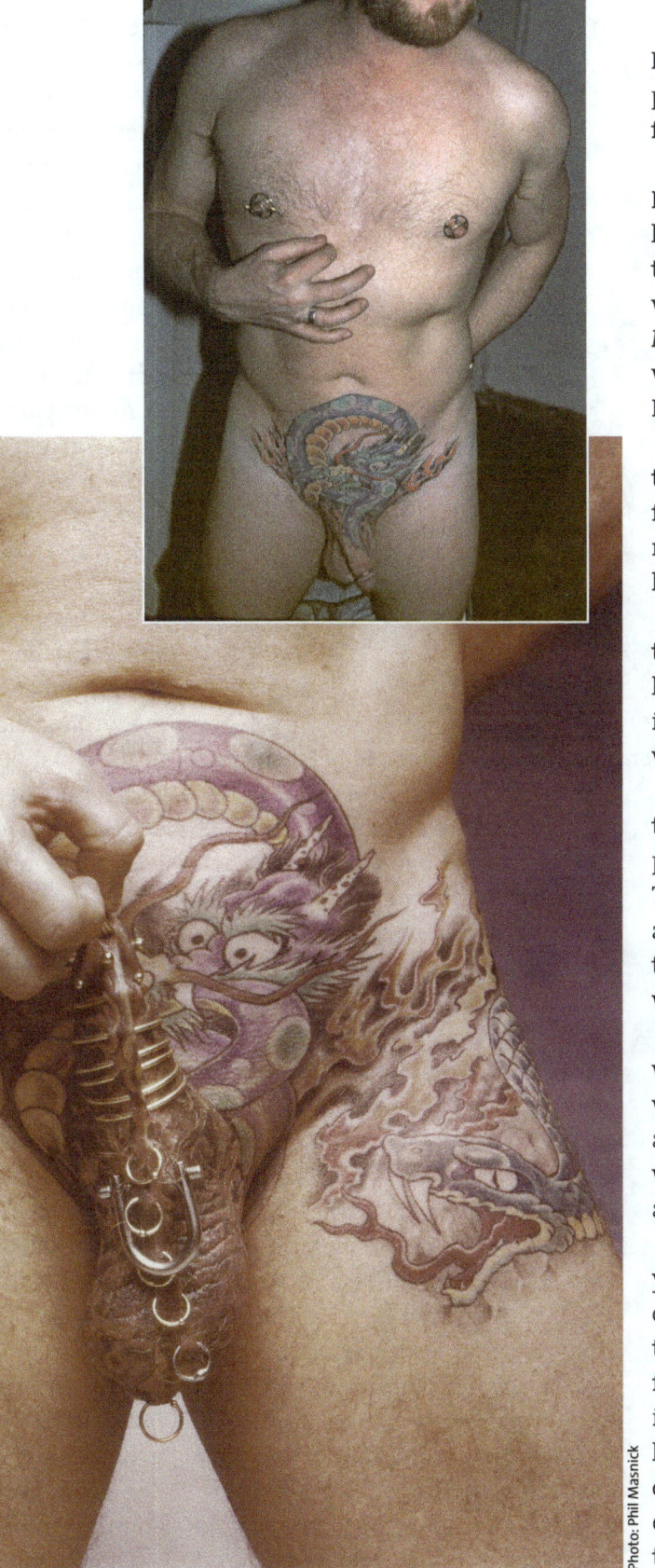

In issue #41 of the magazine (1993), I wrote the following tribute after the passing, much too soon, of my close friend Jim A.

"Gauntlet was still an infant when I first met Jim A. He was visiting Hollywood getting tattooed and wanted to get pierced as well. Arrangements were made, and one evening Doug Malloy and I went to his hotel room where I performed one of my first Prince Albert piercings.

"Jim became an avid piercing and tattooing enthusiast and a wonderful friend as well. We visited each other regularly, and with nearly every visit he acquired more piercings.

"In 1981 he was prominently featured in *PFIQ* issue #11 showing his collection of piercings. As was typical his interview sparkled with characteristic wit and humor.

"Jim was also a great crossword enthusiast. He was one of those bright people who could work the New York Times Sunday crossword puzzle in a couple of hours or less in ink. The themes for several of the *PFIQ* crosswords were devised by Jim.

"At the end of his interview Jim was asked, 'Did all that hurt?' to which he replied, 'Only when you ask that question.' I'd have to reply, 'It was nothing compared to the loss of a dear friend.'"

A crossword fan myself for many years, I thought it would be fun to include puzzles on piercing themes in the magazine. With a great deal of effort, I created a total of seven that ran in issues #36 through #42. With absolutely no feedback, good or bad, it became clear that readers weren't interested in stimulating their minds, and the feature was dropped.

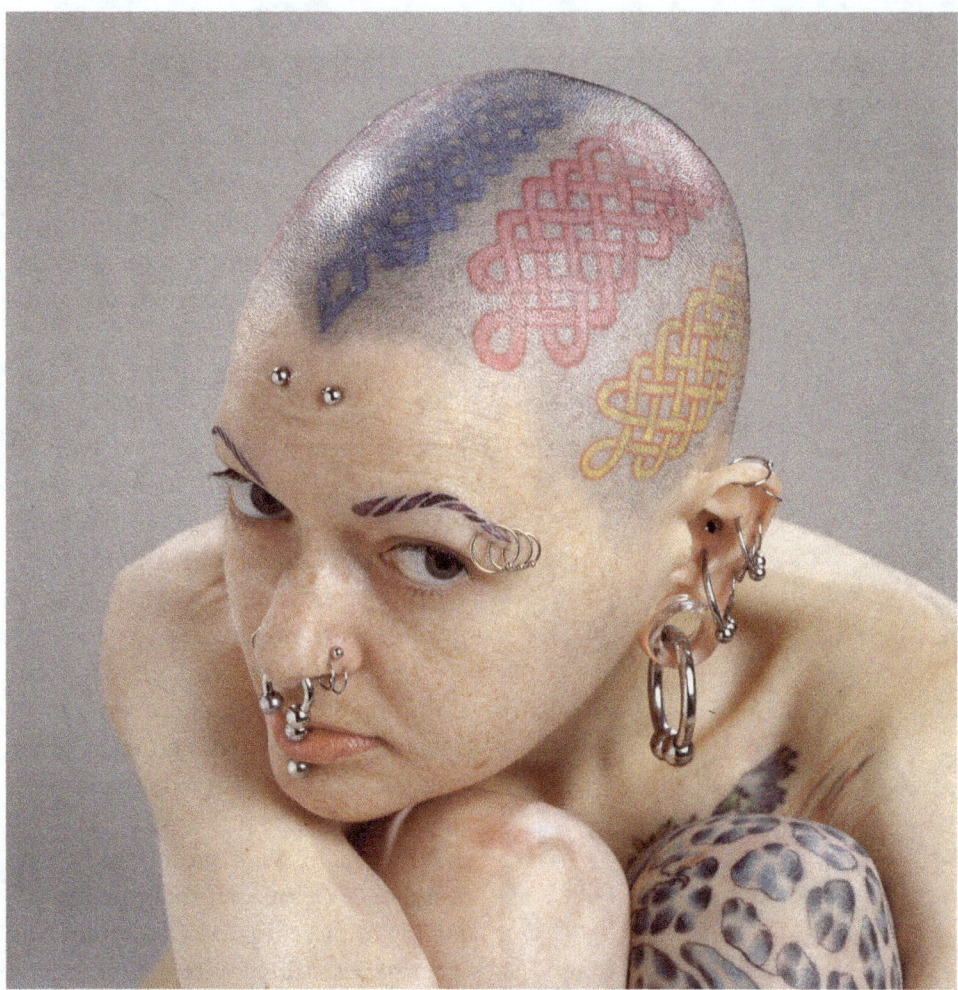

Jen (issue #39) worked in the L.A. store for several years. Photo by Todd Friedman

thing that might appear in *National Geographic*, thus defensible.

Nonetheless, through the years *PFIQ* did experience censorship, not in the U.S., but most notably in Japan, Great Britain, Australia, and New Zealand where customs agents regularly seized the magazine. In 1984 New Zealand's Indecent Publications Tribunal, not unsurprisingly, called it "indecent." The seizure problem was sufficiently bad that we had to advise overseas subscribers we could not accept responsibility for failed delivery.

One of my avid *PFIQ* collectors kept pestering me to get binders made in which to preserve the magazines. In 1983 I finally took him seriously and found a company that would make them to my specifications. The final product was very handsome, with cov-

ers of royal purple velour stamped in shiny gold with the magazine masthead on the front and spine. Unfortunately, many readers of the publication were less enthusiastic, and the binders sold poorly. I gave the last of them to a friend in 2004.

This wasn't the only time I discovered that my personal taste for purple and shiny wasn't something that appealed to all my customers. There were the T-shirts. When I first started Gauntlet I'd hand silk-screened some basic black on white ones. These sold out.

One of the members of the T&P Group became manager of the Pleasure Chest adult emporium in West Hollywood. He had a sideline business selling custom T-shirts. I had him make up some in royal purple with the logo in a glitter-impregnated gold heat transfer. They sold poorly and

took years to liquidate.

Also collecting dust was a burgeoning inventory of back issues. Printers required certain minimum quantities, especially to get a reasonable price break. There were always many more than needed to fill subscriptions. So, the back issues piled up. For a while they lined metal shelves in the manufacturing and mail order department that had been set up in a rented garage behind the store. Employees arrived one morning to find that the shelves had collapsed under the weight, leaving piles of magazines in the middle of the floor.

At one point, I rented a storage container in which to keep them. Some months went by before I returned to discover that termites had invaded the container and eaten the corrugated boxes. Because the magazines themselves were printed on coated paper, they were untouched. A couple of bug bombs put an end to the problem, but everything had to be re-boxed. Eventually we just built wooden shelves and had no further problem though some of the magazines continued to carry a lingering whiff of insecticide.

In addition to Fakir, *PFIQ* had a long history with a number of other gifted photographers. Todd Friedman, a member of the Southern California S/M community, began contributing photos in issue #32 (1989) and has told me he attributes much of his success as a photographer to appearing in the magazine.

Well-known porn star and performance artist Annie Sprinkle not only appeared in the pages of *PFIQ*, but was also a regular contributor. Piercing photos can tend to be on the dark side. Not Annie's. She had a lighter touch, and her images often brimmed with sunny humor. I am still in touch with Annie, and this book owes much to her constant encouragement and gentle prodding.

Photographer Michael Rosen has

In the world of modern politics, I've found no one more repugnant than Karl Rove, the man responsible for putting the evil Bush/Cheney regime in power. He succeeded in no small part by demonizing gay people. Until August of 2007, I never realized he was the adopted son of a close gay friend and avid piercing enthusiast.

Except for the most hardcore fetishists, the vast majority of my early clients were people who quietly went about their lives with their piercings discreetly hidden. If you met one on the street, you'd never know what secrets lurked beneath their clothing.

Louis Rove could easily have passed for anyone's grandfather. His gray hair was close-cropped in a buzz cut. He was clean-shaven and wore glasses. After many years as a geologist for Getty Mining, he had finally retired and was making the most of it by taking up a new passion: body piercing. He was featured in *PFIQ* issue #17 (1983) under the name "Indy." At the time, he had 37 piercings, mostly in his penis.

He was a member of the T&P Group and frequently hosted meetings at his lovely home in the Wilshire district of L.A., near the Los Angeles County Museum of Art.

Not long after I moved to San Francisco Louis sold his house in L.A. and relocated to Palm Springs. In the following years we talked a few times on the telephone. Years of smoking caught up with him, and the last time we spoke he told me that he had emphysema and was on oxygen. With his passing, the world lost an extraordinary individual.

I knew that Louis had been married and had several adult children, but had not realized that Karl was one of them. When the connection surfaced, Louis became the subject of several interviews I subsequently did for *Rolling Stone*, the *Advocate*, BoingBoing.net, and Rachel Maddow's show on the Air America radio network.

Louis was a warm, generous, caring man who just happened to march to the beat of a different drummer. Before his own health began to fail, he regularly visited and gave comfort to AIDS patients. I rarely heard him speak ill of anyone. The world would be a better place without his son, but we could use a lot more like Louis.

Photo: www.Fakir.org

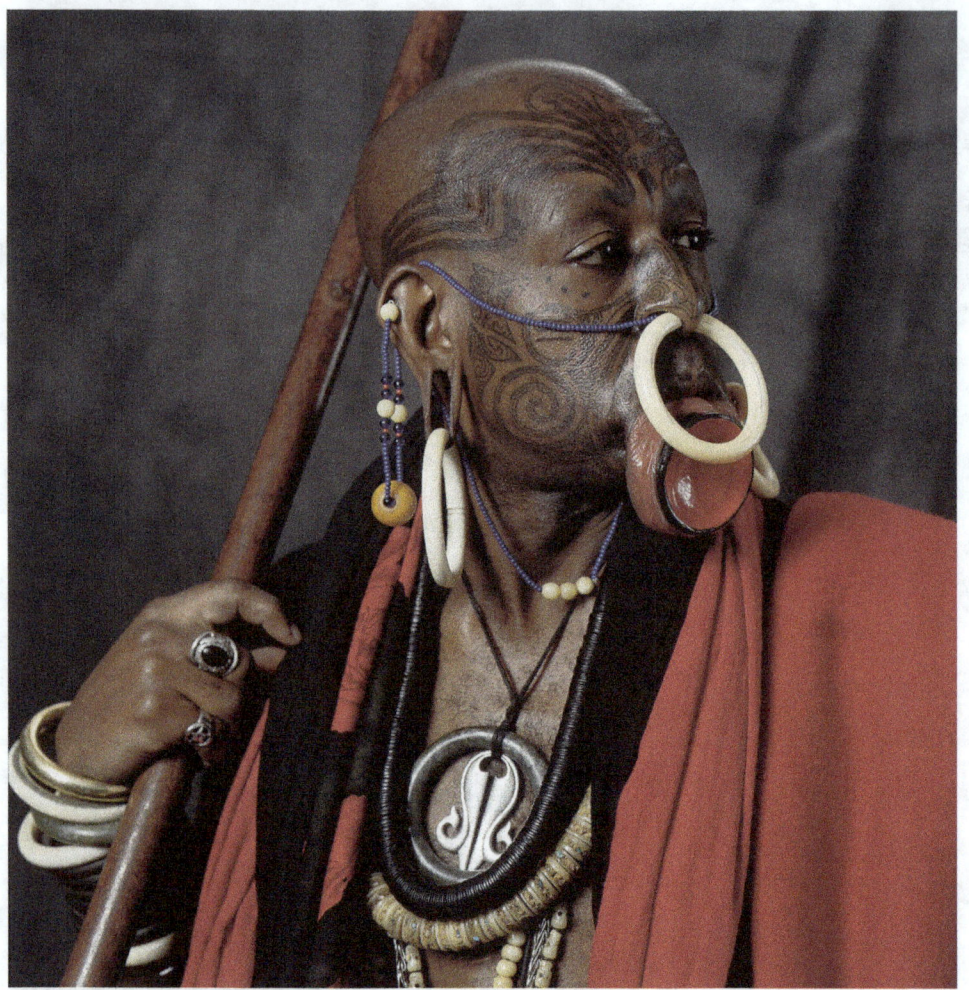

Baaba (from the cover of issue #47) by Todd Friedman

been doing sexual photography in San Francisco since 1977. His photos, some of which appeared in *PFIQ*, have, according to his web site, "encompassed a wide range of styles: stark and grainy nude landscapes; impressionistic, gritty, cinema verité images of S/M sex scenes; sharply focused, elegantly composed, studio sexual portraits involving S/M, erotic piercings, gender play and what he calls non-standard penetration. The latest work comprises soft and romantic images of explicit sex that challenge the concept of pornography."

Occasionally *PFIQ* featured photos by Sheree Rose. A significant portion of her work focused on her slave and lover of 16 years, Bob Flanagan, a writer, poet, comic, musician, and performance artist. They heard about Gauntlet through one of the S/M publications, and eventually Sheree brought Bob in for pierc-

ings, some of which she documented. He was also my willing victim for some demonstrations I did for the Society of Janus. Many of his performances included some kind of piercing, most notably nailing his penis or scrotum to a piece of wood or sewing up various parts of his body. He was a long-term survivor of cystic fibrosis, finally succumbing to the disease at age 44 in 1996. Bob claimed he was able to endure more than forty years of physical pain through masturbation, sexual experimentation, and sadomasochism. Sheree and Bob collaborated or appeared together in many different art forms. Most notable is perhaps *Bob Flanagan, Super-Masochist* (1993), the book of interviews the two of them did for Re/Search Publications; the performance art "Visiting Hours" (in 1993, 1994, and 1995); and the documentary film *Sick: The Life and Death of*

Bob Flanagan, Supermasochist (directed by Kirby Dick, 1997). Bob worked briefly at Gauntlet as his health permitted and was learning to do piercing. He was a kind and gentle soul, candid and frank, and imbued with a sly sense of humor.

There were a number of other photographers who submitted images over the years. Skip Williams from the Portland area created a yearly calendar he called "Angels of Steel," photos from which would appear annually in the magazine. Another regular contributor was Efrain Gonzalez, who has been photographing the New York kinky scene for decades. I also remember Jerry Rosen, whose lens was often focused on the pierced folk of Southern California.

There were two San Francisco photographers we called on regularly when we needed something special for *PFIQ*, a catalog, or an ad: Billy Douglas and Michael Adrianne. Both appeared in the later issues of the magazine. Billy did much of the photography for Gauntlet's last catalog.

Gauntlet published a total of 50 issues of *PFIQ*. As Gauntlet lay on its metaphoric deathbed, issue #51 was almost ready to go to press and the material for another had been assembled. Neither ever saw the light of day.

In Gauntlet's final days, all the inventory of back issues was sold for $5,000 to Last Gasp, self-described as one of the "largest and oldest publishers and purveyors of underground comic books in the world."

The story of Gauntlet's first "Pierce with a Pro" video series made in 1988 closely entwines with that of a gay porn film made the previous year, in which I had a cameo. One of my clients was a local businessman and occasional T&P member named Loren. He was what some gay men call a "bear," meaning beefy and hairy, and in addition, one of the rare men I knew who was uncircumcised. Loren had a taste for black men, and in due course became enamored of a fellow named James, a.k.a. Thor Johnson, who made porn films. James' company, Altomar Productions, specialized in videos featuring masculine, mature men—many of color—who were hairy, bearded, uncut, tattooed and/or pierced.

James had come up with the concept for a new video entitled *Cult of Manhood*. In the *PFIQ* review (issue #31), I wrote, "The plot of the video, such as it is, concerns Chad James's quest for the legendary tribe of lusty warriors, the Chumek. Piercing is an important part of Chumek initiation. During the course of the video, three initiates acquire new piercings. Unfortunately, the actual piercing procedure is not shown. Through the miracle of editing, the piercings appear magically. Because of concerns about the possibility of prosecution for obscenity, the piercing process was not shown.

"Although he does not partake in the sexual goings on, *PFIQ* editor and publisher Jim Ward makes a cameo appearance as the Elder. One sees the fruit of his handiwork if not the actual installation."

Like so many erotic movies, the plot was downright silly, the acting laughable. I never exposed myself, but I did get to participate in a group grope, and baptize the cast members by pouring water on them out of a geode.

If James could make a porn flick involving piercing, surely he could handle a piercing how-to. At the time, he was the only person I knew with the equipment and sufficient skill to create a video, and he was only too happy to oblige. I recruited the necessary volunteers who were willing to be pierced before the camera. Filming proceeded over a day or two; editing took a bit longer. Except for some pretty poor narration, I was quite pleased with the final product. Viewing it again recently, I was pleased to see just how well

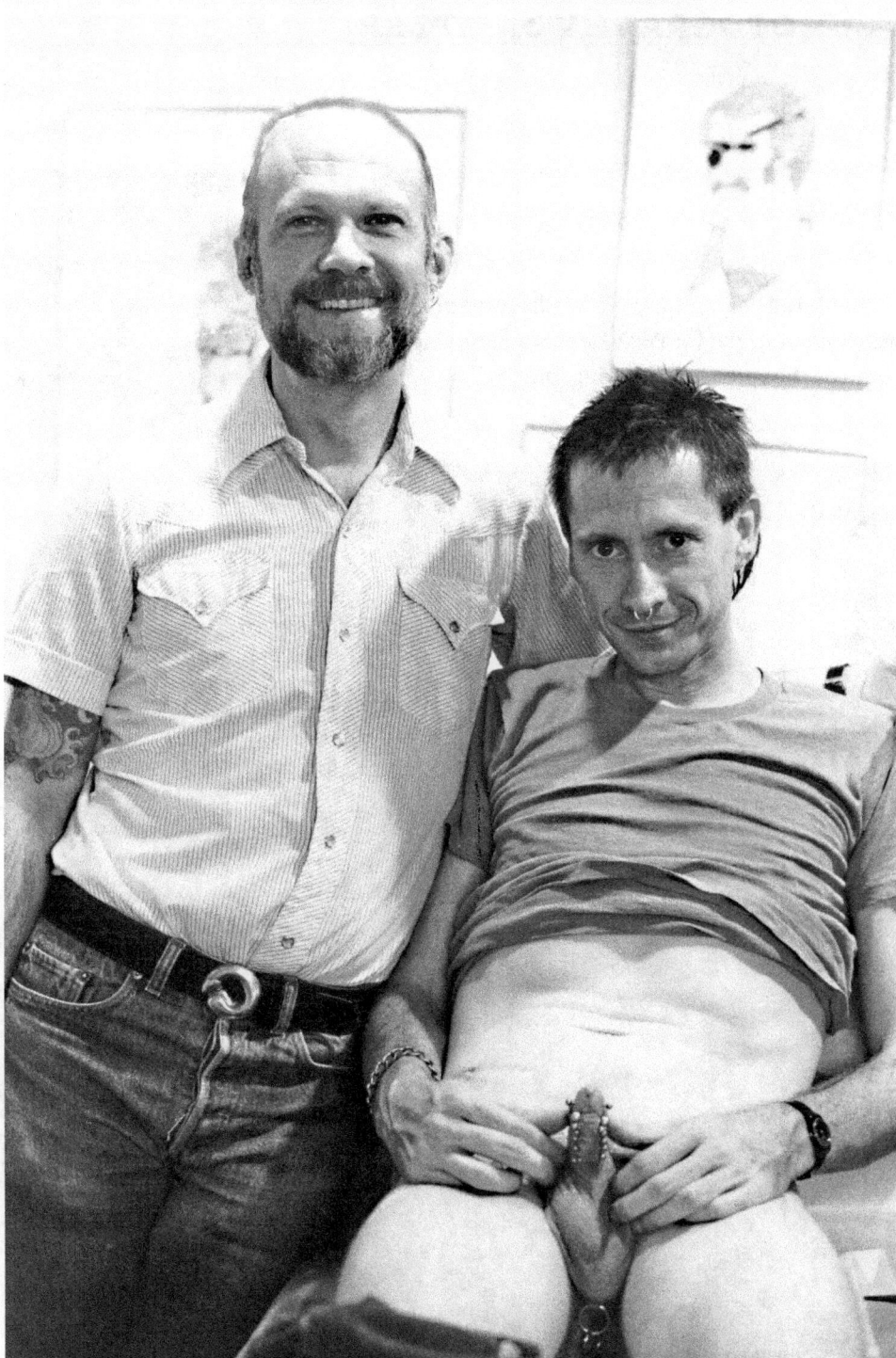

With poet and performance artist Bob Flanagan. Photo by Sheree Rose.

it has held up. Aside from the old cotton-swab method of doing the Prince Albert, the techniques remain solid. I did cringe watching how long it took the relatively dull needles of the day to go through some of the tougher tissue. The most significant improvements that have been made since then are sharper needles, newer and better skin

preparation and piercing aftercare, and the wearing of latex gloves for the entire procedure, including the cleaning and marking.

It's unfortunate that I didn't have a clearer grasp of who owned and controlled the film. While the copyright itself was and still is held by Gauntlet, Altomar produced all the copies that

A Photography Sampler

Through the years, many gifted photographers provided material for *PFIQ*. Here is a sampling from some of the more regular contributors.

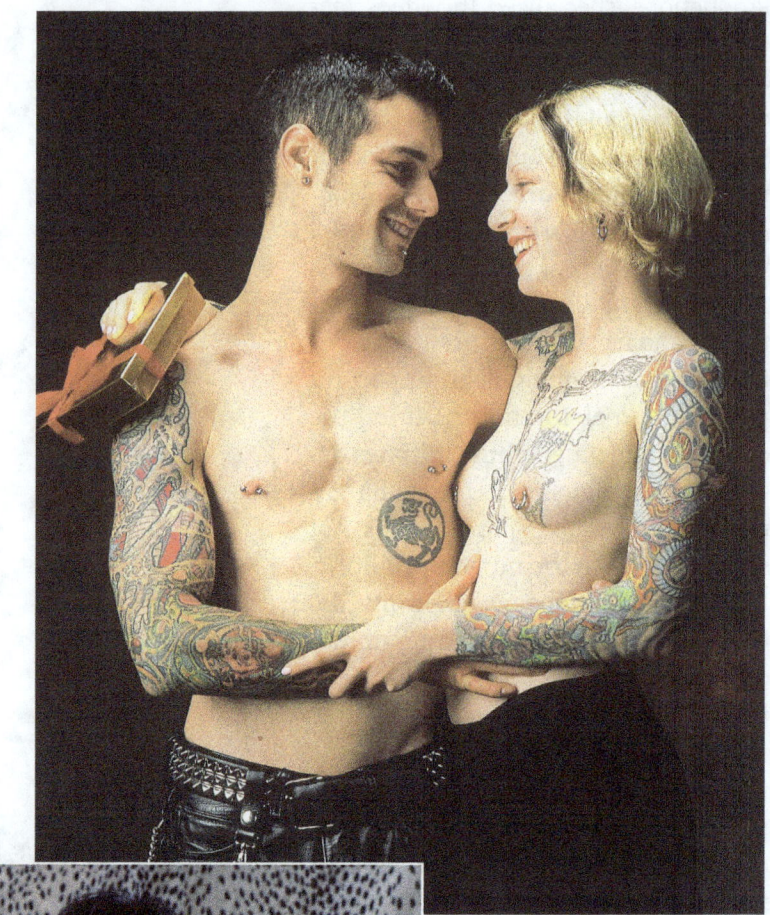

Hawk and Allison (issue #50) by Michael Adrianne

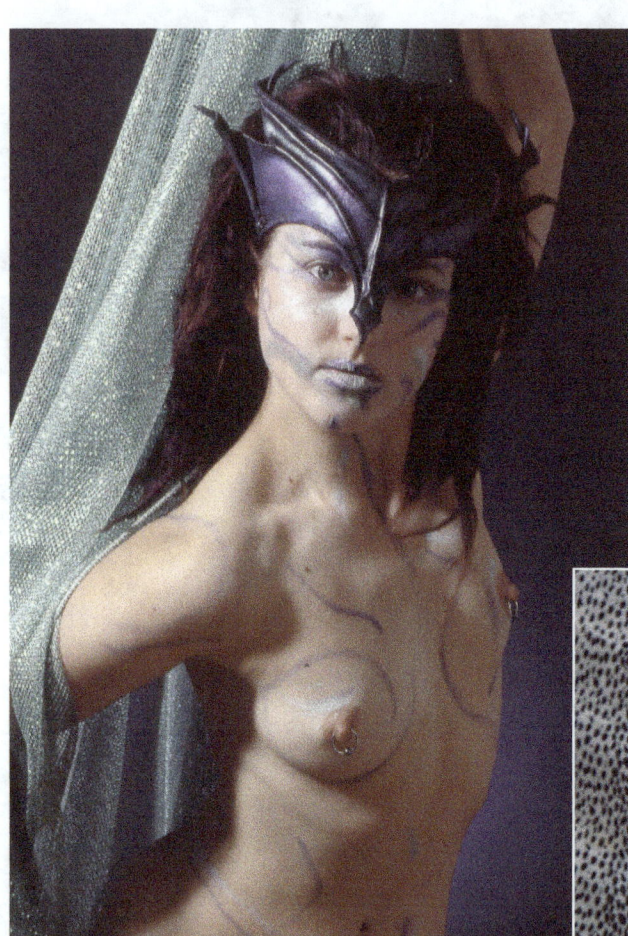

Kristi (issue #41) by Skip Williams

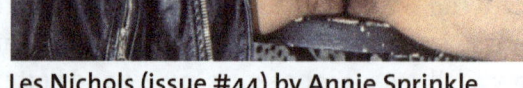

Les Nichols (issue #44) by Annie Sprinkle

Unknown model (issue #48) by Efrain Gonzalez

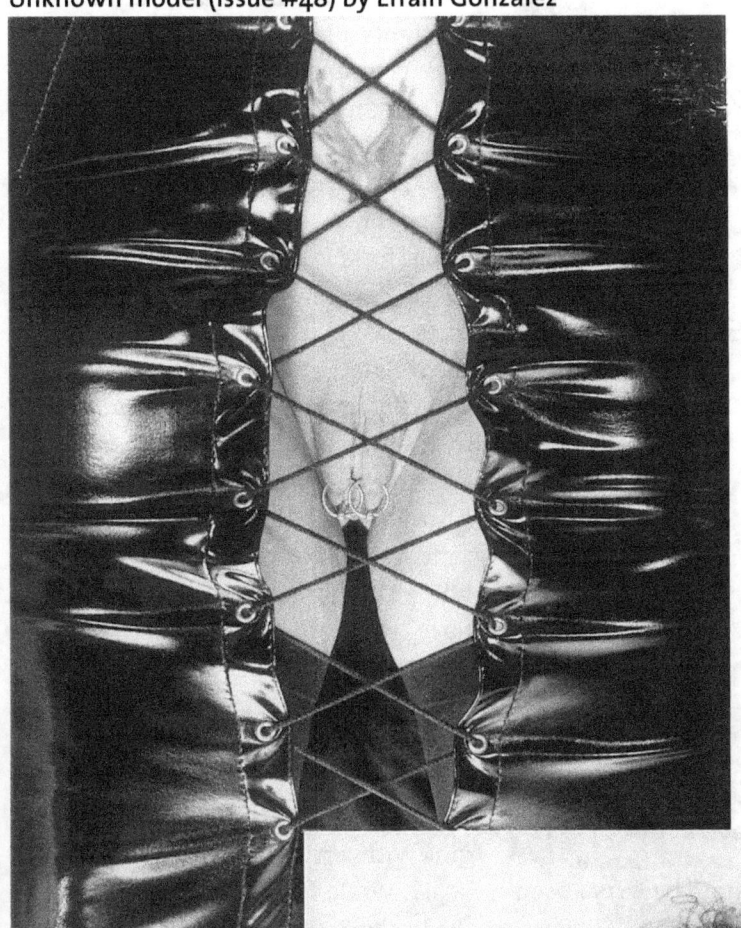

Meistro (issue #48) by Michael Rosen

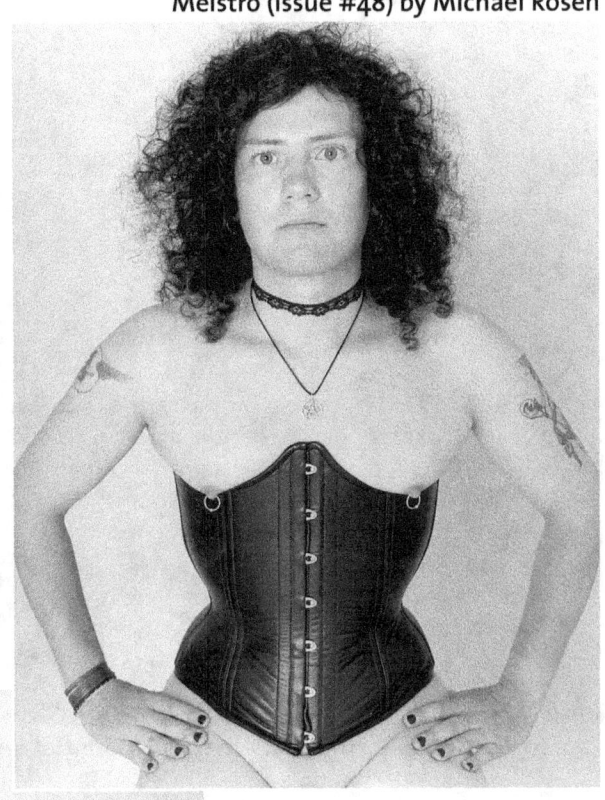

Cirus (issue #49) by Billy Douglas

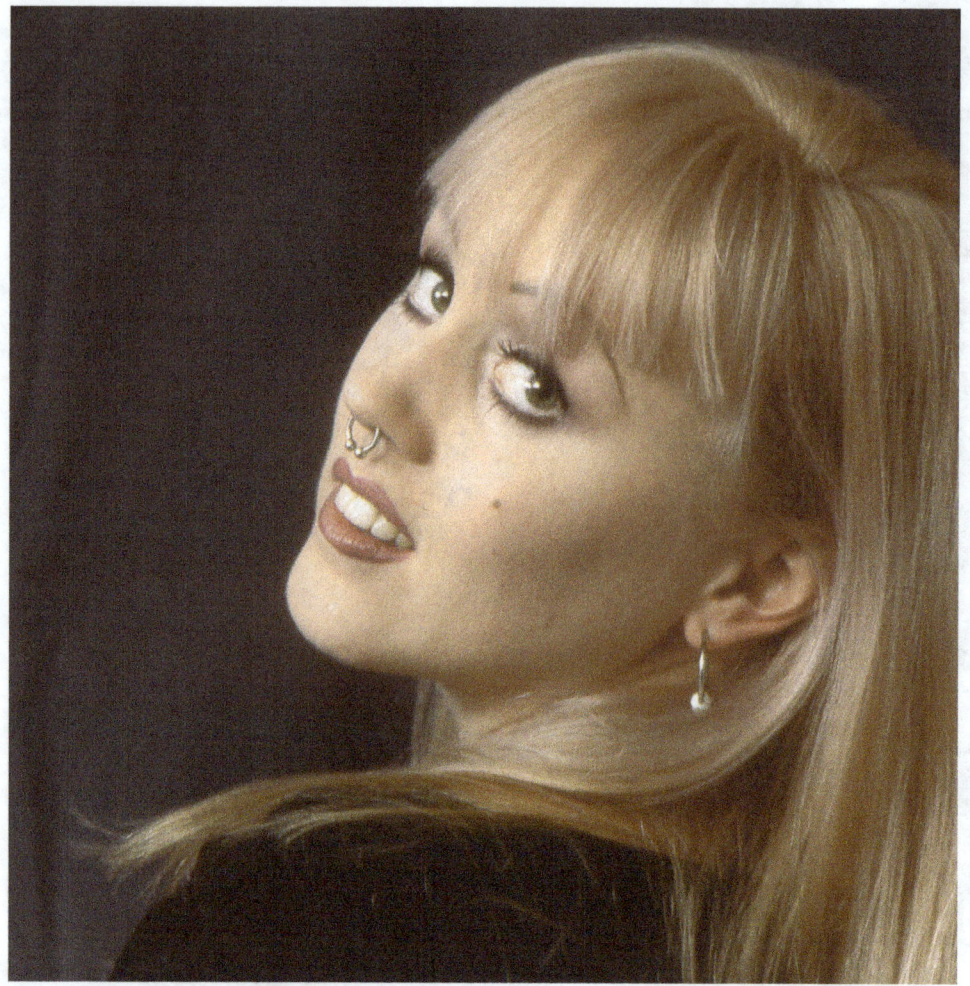

Lauren Pine (issue #41) was another L.A. Gauntlet employee. Photo by Jerry Rosen

were sold and never supplied me with a tape master. The company is no longer in business, and it's doubtful I'll ever obtain one.

My intent was eventually to produce a series of three videos, the second featuring female piercings and the third unisex. Six years later (1994), part two was released, though because there are fewer genital piercings for women it featured both female and unisex piercings. The last video (1996) was an updated remake of the male piercings video. Hrabba Gunnarsdóttir, a filmmaker from Iceland who was residing in the Bay Area at the time, filmed both. When George W. Bush came to office, she became disgusted with "the war machine" and returned to her native land, making occasional excursions to California for work.

James from Altomar was pissed off

to learn that I had hired someone else to make the sequels, but in turn I was unhappy that he kept control over the first video. Rather than fight with him over it, since it was out-of-date anyway, it was easier and more satisfactory to

simply remake. This time I knew how to avoid any conflict. Hrabba was paid for her work, and Gauntlet retained all rights. She was a joy to work with and a complete professional, devoting many hours to filming and editing the final tapes. Thanks to improvements in video technology in the intervening years, the actual high quality of these two efforts is visible.

It's a bit difficult re-watching these films today because the man who ruined Gauntlet did some of the narration and actually appeared briefly in the unisex aftercare section. Every time I see him or hear his voice again I cringe. Still, the basic information remains as relevant today as it was when the films were made. Yes, there have been many advances, but the core techniques are as viable as when they were first perfected. If I were to remake these films today, I would do something different with the opening sequences. The female/unisex begins with a trio of belly dancers on the beach while Idexa, a local tattooist in the background, peers resolutely out to sea. The last tape starts with a pierced guy in fetish gear swaggering down a dark alley. The voice over tells us he's looking for, "the Professional." It looks and sounds like the beginning of a porn movie or a TV commercial.

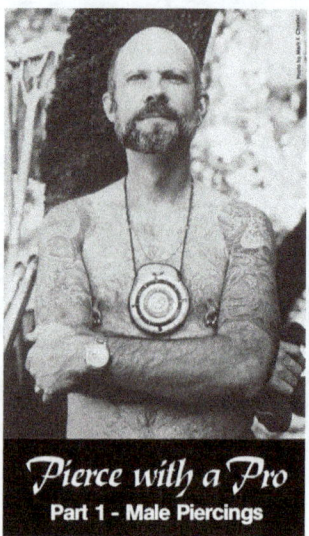
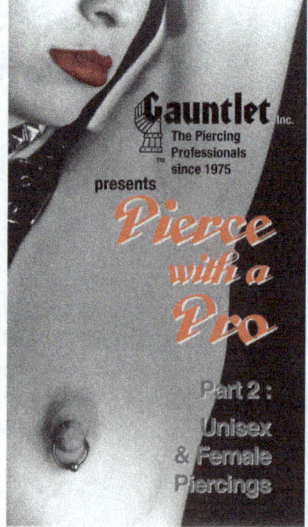

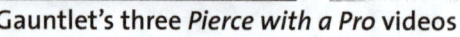
Gauntlet's three *Pierce with a Pro* videos

Chapter 7

A significant part of Gauntlet's success had much to do with the tireless effort I put into promoting not just the business but body piercing itself. Over the years, I traveled regularly, giving presentations for everything from S/M organizations to university human sexuality classes and art classes.

A lot of people take it for granted that they can go into almost any tattoo shop and get a body piercing. Hard as it may be to believe, that has not always been the case. To some of us, it seemed self-evident that tattooing and piercing go together like salt and pepper. But there was a time when many tattooists were outraged at such a suggestion. Having a personal interest in both and knowing many others who shared it, it seemed logical to me that the tattoo community was just waiting to embrace my efforts. It didn't take long for me to find out otherwise.

Early in 1977, the International Tat-

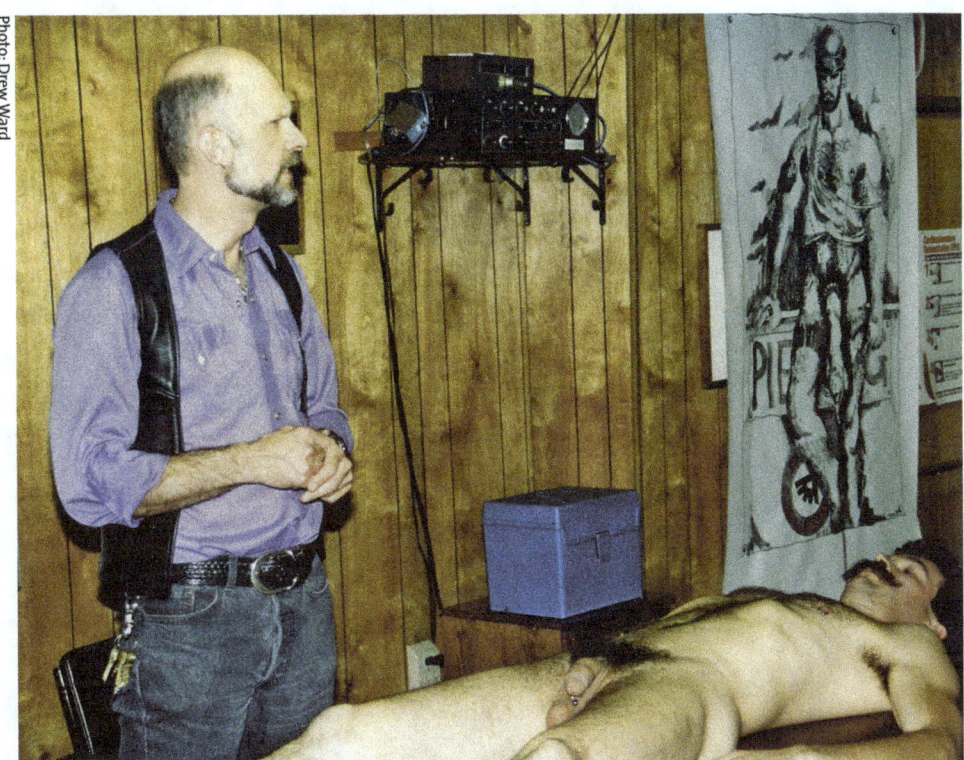

Doing a demonstration for a Southern California S/M club

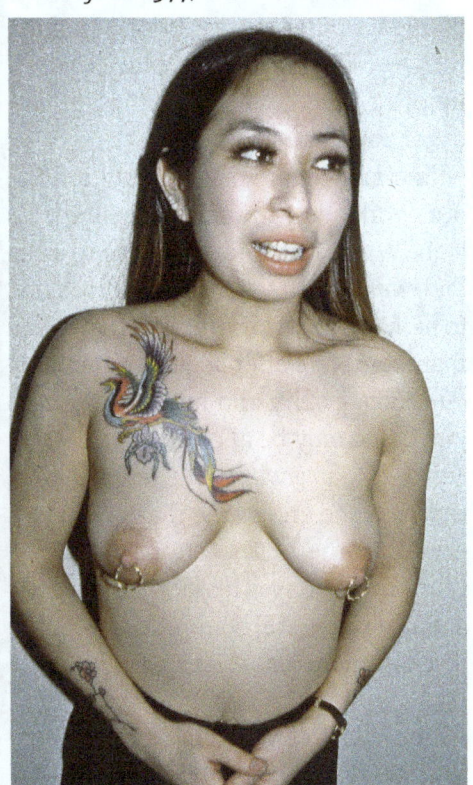

Karen Ryan, girlfriend of Chicago tattooist Dale Grande, got her nipples pierced at the 1977 ITAA convention.

too Artists Association (ITAA) held its first convention in Reno. In an effort to reach out and spread the word amongst the tattooed, Doug suggested that I get a vendor booth there. I submitted the necessary forms and was accepted. This would be one of our first public appearances.

I made up an assortment of jewelry and gathered a selection of piercing equipment and set off with Eric and Doug for Reno. We were greeted by a number of familiar faces. Cliff Raven and his lover were in attendance, as were old friends of Doug: Tattoo Samy from Frankfort and his wife Ella. We also met Ed Hardy, who was doing very extensive tattoo projects on a couple of members of the T&P Group. Fakir was present and had been asked to provide entertainment at the banquet.

Outwardly everyone was courteous and curious. During the course of the convention a number of people made arrangements to come to our room for private piercing appointments. Among them was the girlfriend of Dale Grande, who had done tattooing with Cliff Ra-

ven when he had his shop in Chicago. I was even asked to do a nipple piercing demonstration on the floor of the vendor area. A good-looking young tattooist named Steve Richards volunteered to be my subject.

The demonstration went well, and many people stopped by the Gauntlet table to ask questions and take literature. On the surface, it appeared we were well received. But unknown to us, there was trouble behind the scenes. A number of the big name tattooists, most notably Ed Hardy, were not pleased.

"Since Ed Hardy had brought the subject of piercings up at the ITAA. Reno Convention in 1977 (he felt, as did the overwhelming majority of Artists there, that piercing did not belong at a Tattoo convention and should not be linked to tattooing. ITAA Members voted there and then not to have piercing at future conventions) it was decided on (by the suggestion of Bob Shaw) not to allow facial tattoos or piercings at the National Tattoo Conventions. This was to be a Convention to promote Tattooing and only Tattooing."[1]

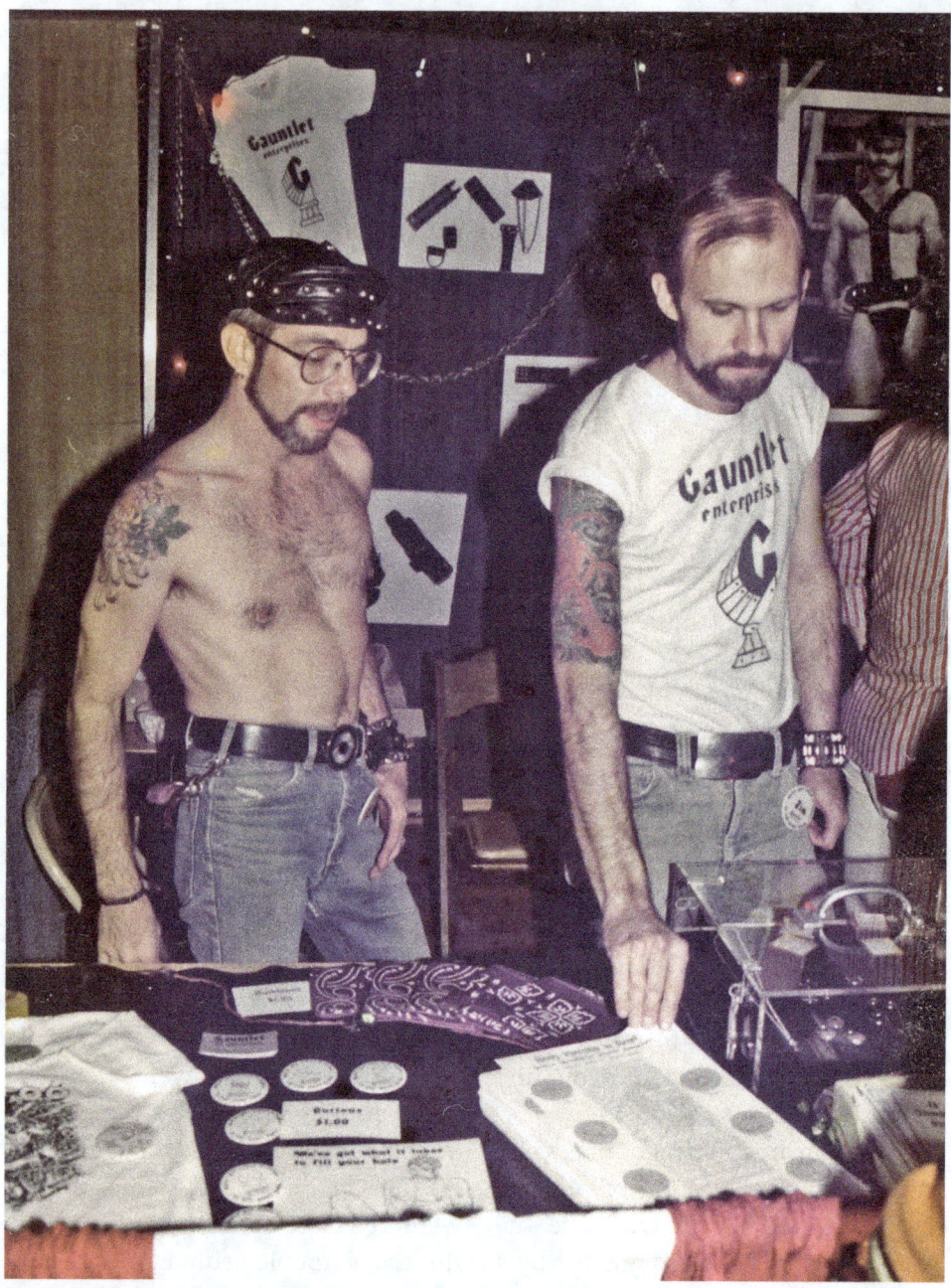

My lover Eric and I promoting piercing at a convention

Anyone with piercings has probably experienced discrimination in some form at one time or another. While it may be increasingly rare today, in Gauntlet's early years it was much more common, often cropping up when least expected.

In the early Seventies, a Florida company began to revolutionize fitness training with the introduction of a line of exercise machines. Their appeal was that they made it possible to get a good workout in a minimum amount of time. Within a few short years, health clubs featuring the Nautilus equipment were springing up around the country. Around 1977, one opened in West Hollywood. To draw business, the gym was offering one-month free trial memberships. My lover Eric and I decided to enroll and check it out.

The gym manager was a gay porn star named Paul Barresi, and given its location it was no surprise that the clientele was mostly gay men. The facility was clean and well-kept, open 24 hours—at least in the beginning—and it was a great place to tone up one's body while checking out the other patrons.

Eric and I were seeing results from our workouts and enjoyed using the club. When our free trial came to an end, we decided to join. Alas, it was not to be. Mr. Barresi informed us that other members were offended by the sight of our body jewelry and had complained. We would only be allowed to join if we removed our jewelry. We refused, and that was the end of the matter. Maybe it was for the best. Within a couple of years, the gym was history, replaced by another club—still going strong—just a block from the Gauntlet store.

The April following the Reno convention, another one was happening in Texas. Although vending was no longer an option, Doug convinced me we should go to hand out business cards,

Not all tattoo organizations were as hostile as ITAA and NTA (National Tattoo Association), but the Reno convention was the first and last tattoo event that I recall where Gauntlet vended. The whole attitude left a bad taste in my mouth. For years to come, the applications for at least some conventions carried a statement to the effect that, "we will not rent vendor space for piercing or anything else that might give tattooing a bad name." What I wanted to point out, but never did, was that bad tattooists and the behavior

of certain rowdy tattoo fans were far more likely than we were to give tattooing a bad name.

The hostility of some tattooists toward piercing persisted for a decade or longer until the late 1980s, when the popularity of body piercing exploded. Suddenly, some savvy tattoo artists realized there was money to be made doing piercing. Almost overnight, there was a huge shift in attitude, and tattooists around the world began setting up shop as piercers whether they were qualified or not.

meet people, and promote our favorite form of body adornment. I wasn't exactly excited about the prospect, but acquiesced knowing Doug was much more business-savvy than I.

Plans were progressing well until shortly before we were to leave for Texas. Doug approached me and said that after giving it some thought, he felt it wasn't worthwhile. Instead we should take a vacation to Key West and then go up to Fort Lauderdale and spend a few days with an outrageous piercing and tattooing enthusiast, Sailor Sid. I took him at his word and didn't think anything further about the change of plans. Later, it came out that the real reason for the diversion was that Doug had learned his youngest son Robert would be attending the Texas convention and that he wanted to avoid running into him. As far as his family was concerned, Doug was still very much in the closet, but before too many years passed it became apparent that he wasn't fooling as many people as he thought.

We flew into Miami, rented a car, and took to the road 160 miles south to Key West. Particularly memorable were the series of bridges that link the chain of small Gulf islands with the mainland. We passed through Key Lar-

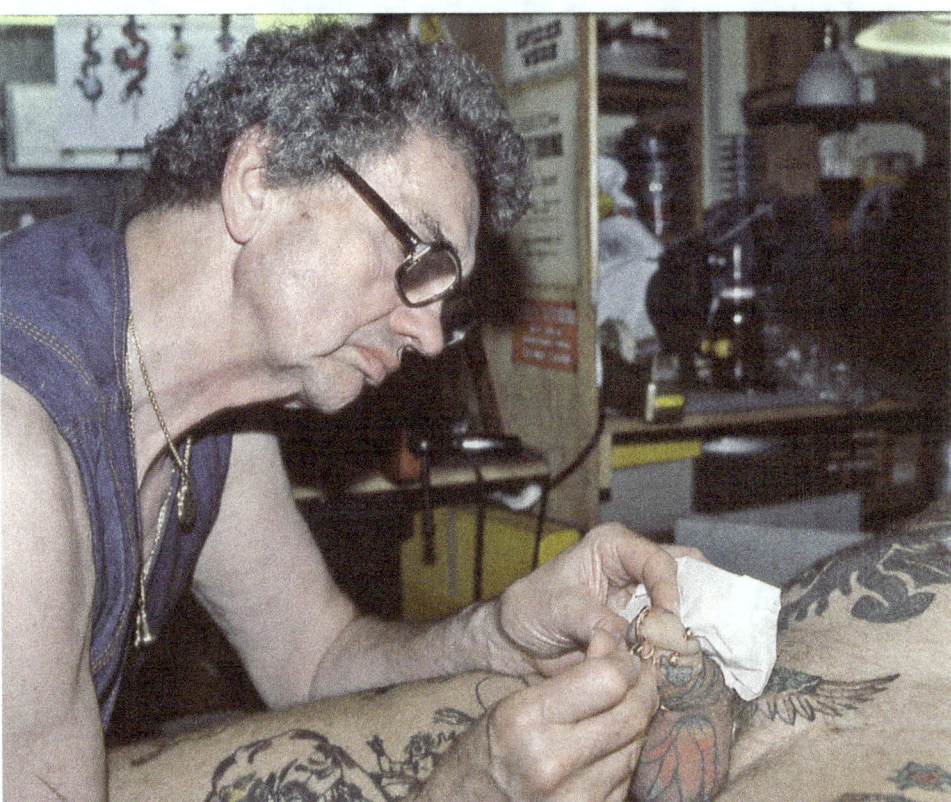
Doug piercing Sailor Sid.

go, an easily forgettable place whose name we'll always remember thanks to Bogart and Bacall.

It's funny how memory plays tricks on us. When I began this chapter, it seemed like Doug and I had made only one trip to Key West. But when I began looking through photos and examining the dates stamped on slide borders, I realized that we had actually made two trips to that sunny destination.

On our first trip, we were typical sightseers. We explored all the usual tourist traps on Main Street. I still have a handmade silver belt buckle of stylized male genitals that I bought on this trip. We visited the home of Ernest Hemingway and lunched at some roadside shack on the beach, where we ate stone crab—the first I'd ever tasted—simply prepared, fresh, and delicious. Doug also hired a boat for us to have an afternoon and sunset Gulf excursion.

Doug had a personal connection to this Southeastern tip of the United States. He told me that the island might well have belonged to Cuba, but in 1821

an ancestor of his had purchased it thus making it part of the U.S..

"In 1815, Spain deeded the island to a loyal subject and St. Augustine native, Juan Pablo Salas. In 1819, all of Florida was ceded to the United States. Salas had made no improvements to the island of Key West and sold it to John Simonton, an American businessman, for $2,000. Simonton understood the potential of Cayo Hueso's natural deep-water harbor and divided the island into four parts, selling three of them to fellow businessmen Whitehead, Fleming and Greene, and keeping one for himself. By this time, the island had been renamed Key West, probably as a result of an English language distortion of the original Spanish name."[2]

One of the sights we took in was an old fort that had been turned into a museum. In one of its many rooms we came across a portrait of Doug's ancestor, John W. Simonton.

After our Key West adventure came to an end, we loaded up the rental car and headed north to Fort Lauderdale

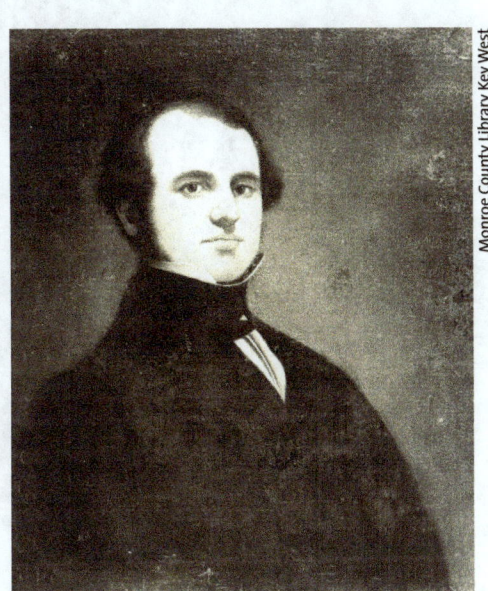

Doug's ancestor John W. Simonton

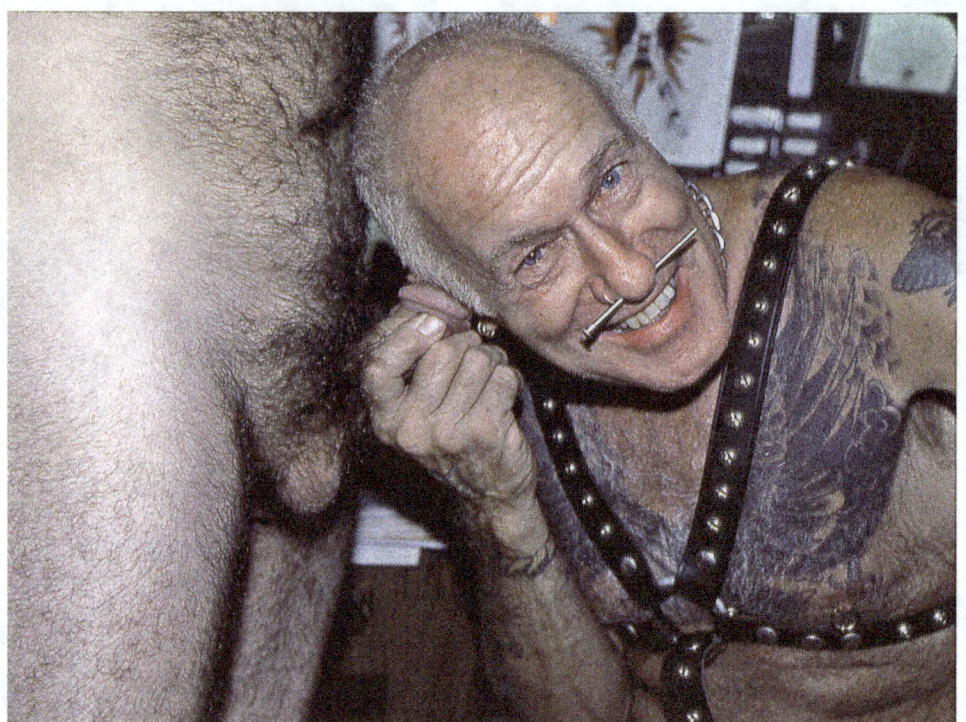

Sid clowning

to spend a few days with the self-proclaimed "freak nut" who went by the name Sailor Sid.

To say that Sid was a character is an understatement. Generally speaking, I think he was a kindly and good-hearted person. He could be a source of endless humor, although he had a tendency to repeat the same joke or bit of business, often to the point of painful irritation. Whenever we went out to dinner, he rarely passed up the opportunity to insert something—frequently the toothpick or swizzle stick from his cocktail—through his septum piercing and try to rattle the waiter or waitress.

I found him to be genial for the most part, but after spending some extended periods of time with him, discovered he could be quick-tempered, irritable, and occasionally petty, especially where money was concerned. From my perspective, he was a difficult man to get to know and warm up to. The freakish side of his persona was always on display. It was a façade that was firmly in place, and he rarely allowed anyone to see the real person behind the mask.

When I first met him, Sid was in his late sixties and had been fascinated with tattoos from the time he was pre-adolescent. During World War II, he had been a member of the Coast Guard that was a part of the Navy. It was in those war years, the early 1940s, that he got his first piercings—ear and frenum—and tattoos. He became an electrician after leaving the service and settled down in Ft. Lauderdale, Florida, where he eventually retired.

Sid's passions were tattooing, piercing, and very heavy S/M. He had managed to connect with a large number of other enthusiasts throughout the world and was a voracious correspondent, writing at length—on a typewriter, no less—about his experiences. Photos of his exploits and those of others were often enclosed. For their time, these included some of the most extreme S/M I had ever seen documented, including extensive play piercing scenes and some involving the opening of the scrotum and exposure of the testicles.

Doug's and my visit did not include any of these particular activities. Sid took us to a gay bar or two—pretty

tame ones by L.A. standards. He also arranged a big piercing party at his home for various gay friends and fellow motorcycle club members so they could drop in and get pierced.

Given the tendency of many gay men toward promiscuity, the reader may have assumed that "piercing party" is just a euphemism for "orgy," but such was not the case. These were primarily social events, and while men did meet and not infrequently hook up, actual sexual activity was rare. The atmosphere was too clinical and not appropriate, since new piercings are vulnerable to infection and must be kept clean. An orgy with the possible presence of bodily fluids is not a safe environment for a fresh piercing.

At this point in our history, the Jim Ward name had virtually no recognition. Sid didn't really know me, and his assumption seemed to be that Doug was the man in charge. Aside from acquiescing to Sid's desire for a piercing or two from the hands of the "Master," Doug very graciously sang my praises as his protégé and made it clear that I would be doing whatever piercing services were required.

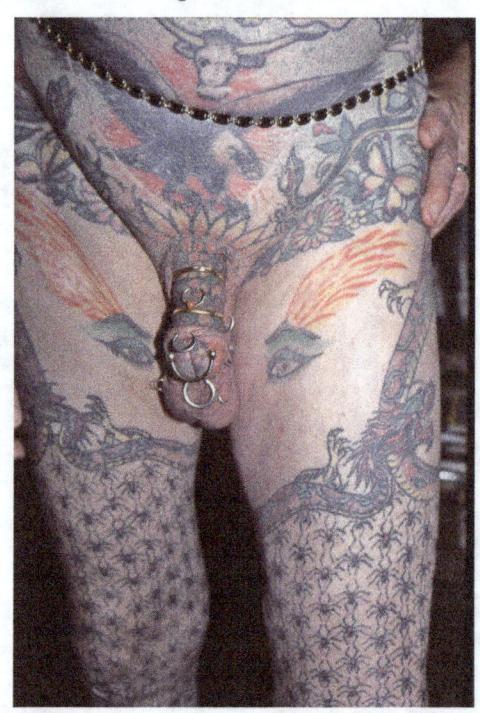

Sid's friend John K.

I pierced at least eight people that night, some having multiple piercings. Doug got into the spirit of the evening by letting me pierce his ear. Being as closeted as he was, it came as no surprise that he removed the jewelry by the time we returned to L.A. Sid got his wish when Doug added another piercing to his ear and gave him an apadravya. The atmosphere was congenial and supportive, and everyone seemed to leave on an endorphin high.

During our visit, Doug and I also met a kinky straight friend of Sid's named John. My impression was that John enjoyed cross-dressing, or at least expressing the feminine side of his nature. Both legs were tattooed with lace stockings made up of hundreds of tiny spiders. His toenails were painted. In many of his piercings he wore jewelry of a decidedly feminine character. John was probably the first man I ever encountered who had split the head of his penis. It wasn't difficult to understand why he and Sid were friends.

Our stay in Ft. Lauderdale was pleasant, and we returned to L.A. having made many new piercing friends.

Sid loved going through security at airports. Between the cock rings he frequently wore and his stainless steel body jewelry, he would invariably set off the metal detector. He would calmly pull up his shirt and display a nipple ring, then point to his crotch and say, "I've got a lot more down here. Would you like to see?" It wouldn't happen these days, but back then security personnel would invariably dismiss him and send him on his way.

I visited Sid again in 1980 to interview and photograph him for *PFIQ*. That interview appeared in issue #10. I've never considered my skills as a photographer to be particularly outstanding, but I have to say my pic-

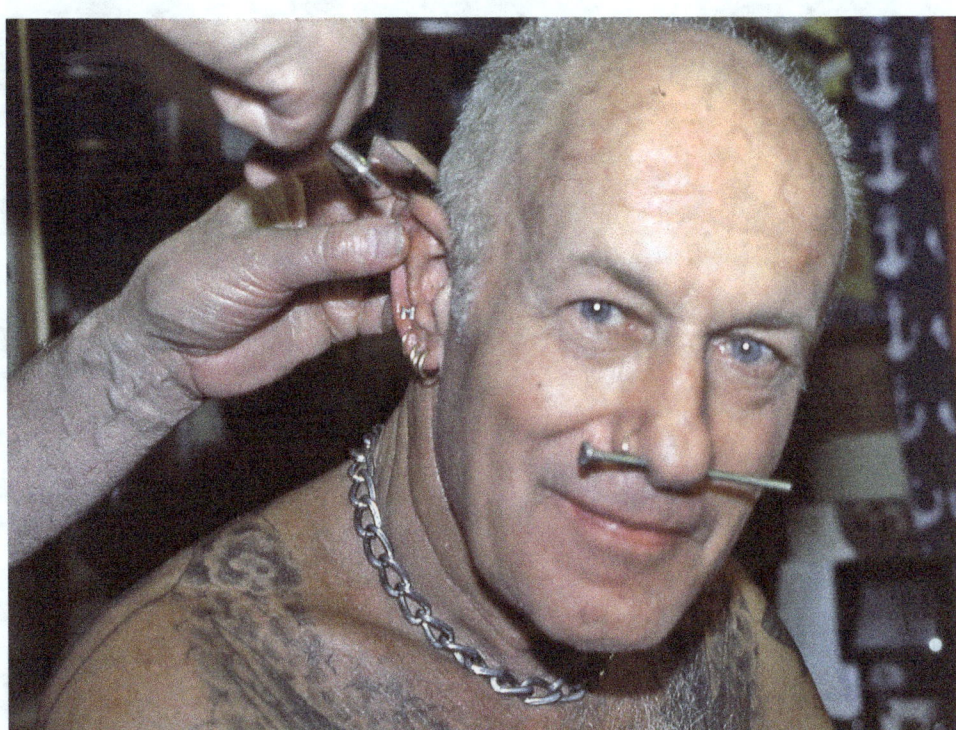
Sid gets another ear piercing

tures of Sid are among the best I've ever done. He was relaxed and open and never camera shy. The shots I took that day always remind me of one of the most unforgettable characters it's been my privilege to know.

Sid kept two collections of correspondence and photographs he'd accumulated over the years: one related to tattooing, the other to piercing. When he died on May 24, 1990—age 80 if my calculations are correct—he had already made provisions for his collections to go to people he trusted. The tattoo papers were left to his good friend Jack Yount. The piercing collection Sid left to me. A few months after his death a couple of large, heavy boxes arrived for me at Gauntlet's corporate office. In them were a number of three-ring binders filled with photos in plastic protectors, and a large stack of correspondence from his various and sundry friends. He'd also kept photocopies, on fading thermal paper, of his own letters.

For some time I pondered how best to preserve this unique collection and also make it accessible to interested individuals. I considered using some of the material in *PFIQ*, but since there were no photo releases, and I didn't know most of the individuals pictured or how to contact them, I abandoned that idea.

In the late 1990s, my health became somewhat uncertain, and my survival unsure. I was concerned about the future of the unique inheritance Sid had left in my care and felt the best thing I could do was to find a better home for it. Eventually, I made the decision to donate it to the Leather Archives and Museum in Chicago. It's clear from their web site that the collection is still there. I'm assuming anyone interested in exploring this resource can make arrangements to view and study it.

Sid was one-of-a-kind: a man who marched to a different drum and made no apologies for it. Despite any differences we might have had, I consider myself fortunate to have known him.

[1]Source: http://www.nationaltattooassociation.com/fullhistory.html
[2]Source: http://floridakeys.com/keywest/ key-west-history.htm

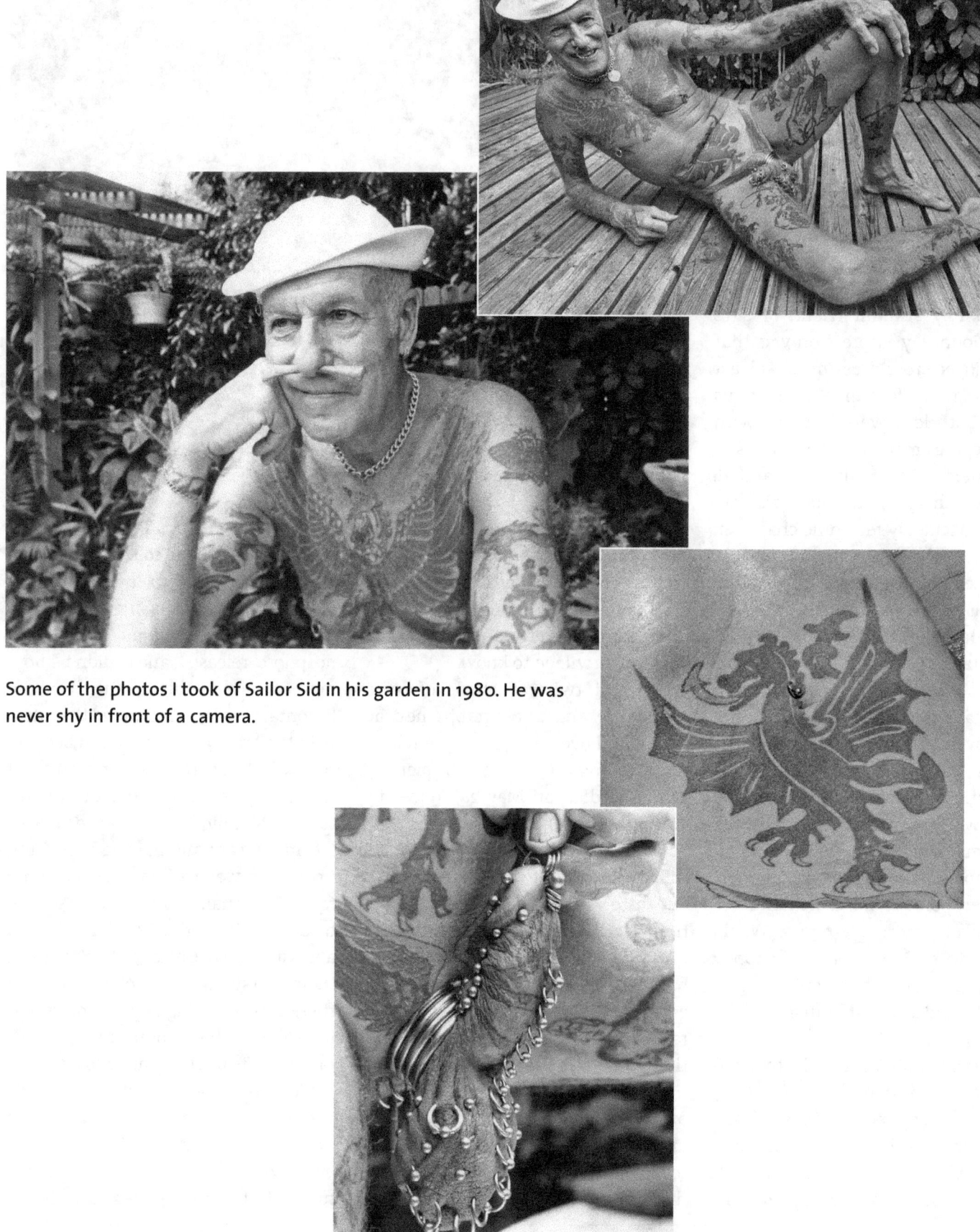

Some of the photos I took of Sailor Sid in his garden in 1980. He was never shy in front of a camera.

CHAPTER 8

In March of 1978, the ITAA put on another tattoo convention, this time in Amsterdam. Doug and I decided we would attend even though vending was not an option. It was, nonetheless, an opportunity to meet people and proselytize for our favorite form of body art. Somehow our plans evolved into a month-long vacation, with Sailor Sid and Elizabeth Weinzirl joining us through most of it.

My lover Eric wasn't included in the plans and sulked about it. The fact was I couldn't afford to take him along, and he had no source of income with which to pay his own way. By this time, our relationship was already on rocky ground.

Elizabeth Weinzirl had a reputation as the grandmother of the tattoo community. At the time of this trip, she was in her mid-seventies, though she could easily have passed for sixty. She was a widow, her husband having been dead for a number of years. She was a delightful, friendly woman, very comfortable in a wide variety of surroundings. Being around gay men didn't faze her. Truth be told, I think she was a bit of a fag hag. She seemed to blossom in their presence, and on this trip she had ample opportunity.

Elizabeth's husband had been a health inspector. She told the story of his going to inspect a Chinese restaurant. When he pointed out a mass of garbage that needed to be disposed of, the chef responded indignantly, "Not garbage. Soup stock."

When asked why she got tattooed, she replied that her husband wanted a tattooed wife. In this era of political correctness, some might find this offensive, but it was said tongue-in-cheek and with a twinkle in her eye. There was never any hint that she felt coerced, and my feeling was that she shared her husband's interest in and

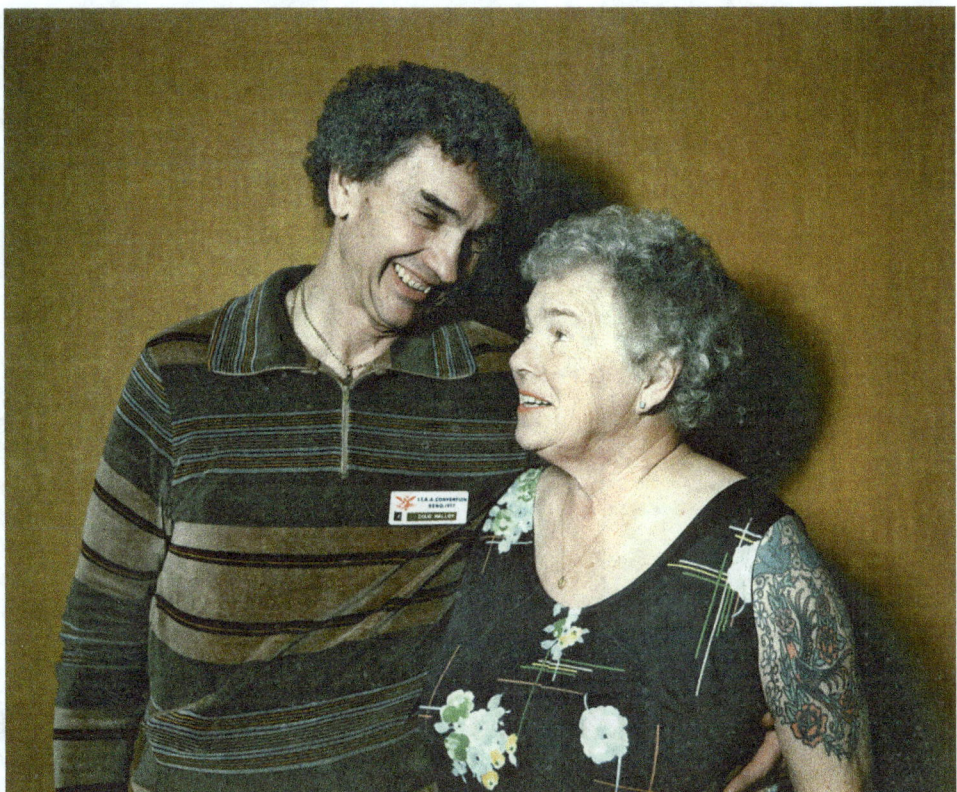

Doug with Elizabeth Weinzirl, the grandmother of the tattoo community

enthusiasm for body art. She even confessed that she had had her nipples pierced at one time, but for some reason had taken the jewelry out.

We arrived at Heathrow on Tuesday, March 7th for a week in London prior to moving on to the Continent. Our main reason for this lengthy stay was to spend some quality time with Alan Oversby, better known in piercing and tattoo circles as Mr. Sebastian. We also wanted to meet as many other British piercing enthusiasts as possible.

Accommodating the four of us wasn't possible in Alan's small apartment—or flat as he would have called it—so he had made arrangements for us to stay with different friends. Regardless of where we stayed, we were all treated as honored guests. Doug and I stayed with a delightful gay couple who lived in Clapham. Their names were Mike and Robin. I believe Sid stayed with Alan, and Elizabeth was housed with another friend, probably Rudy Inhelder, a client of Alan's.

Not surprisingly, Sid was his usual

boisterous self, never passing up an opportunity to joke around. While we were visiting with Alan, Sid happened to notice some folding chairs with clear plastic seats. It wasn't long before he had instigated a photo op: getting a picture of his guiche and tattooed ass through the seat of the chair. Pictures of the photo session remain, but unfortunately the snapshots of Sid's posterior are gone.

Sadly, also missing are most of the photos that were taken at a cocktail party that was given in our honor. A dozen or more of Alan's clients showed up. The men were anything but inhibited. They quickly got down to exhibiting their tattoos and piercings, chatting with each other about their work and who had done it. Elizabeth was the only woman present and was perfectly calm as the clothes came off and the cameras began clicking. She shed some of her own outer garments and posed along with everyone else. One of my favorite photos made the cover of *PFIQ*. It's a close-up of a man's pierced

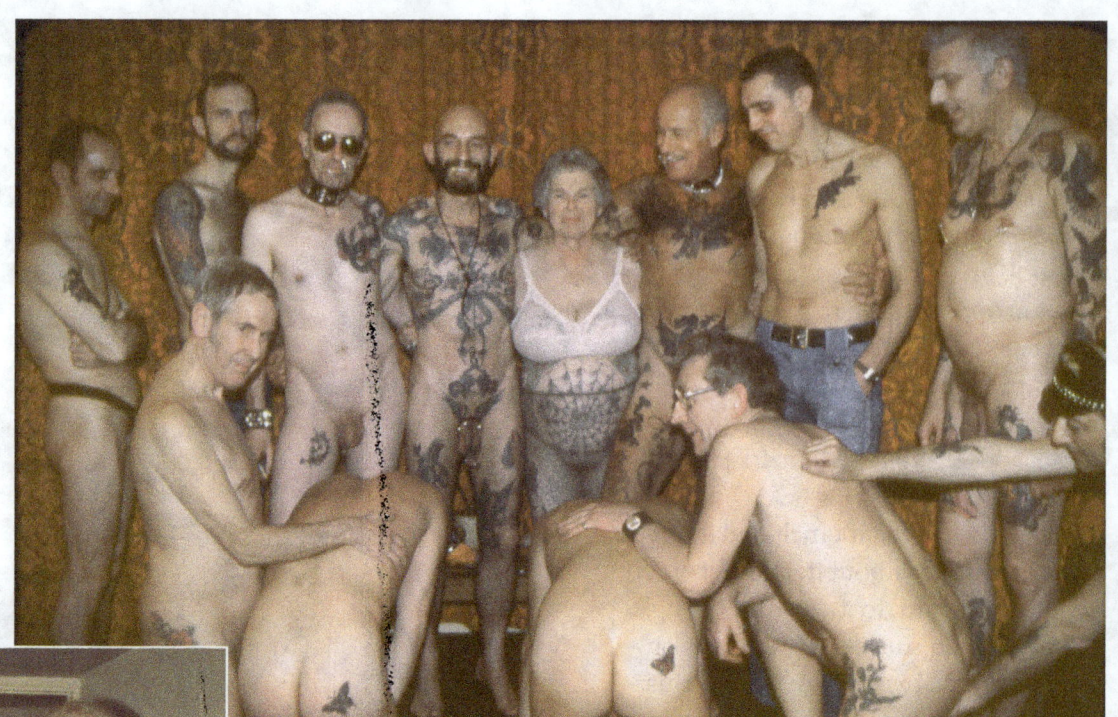

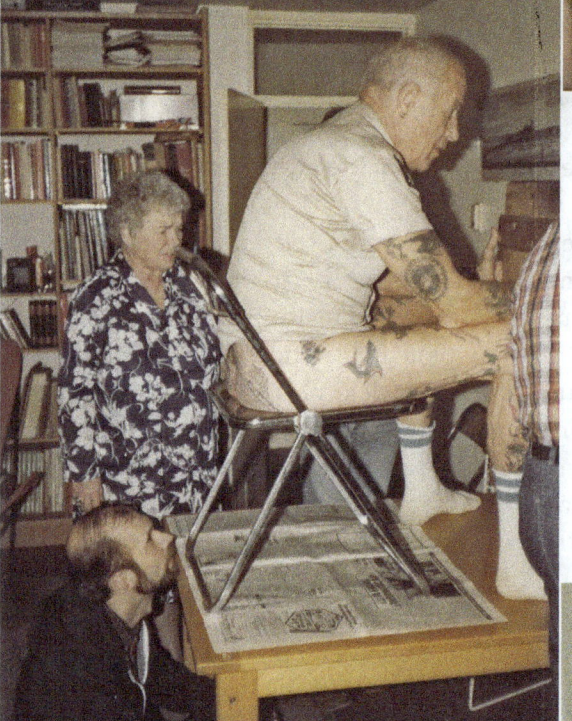

Top, Party of London and U.S. tattoo and piercing enthusiasts. Elizabeth Weinzirl is in the center. Alan Oversby (Mr. Sebastian) stands to her right with his slave boy Thing, Sailor Sid Diller is on her left. Standing to her far left is Rudy Inhelder, another client of Alan's who was active promoting tattooing and piercing in Europe. The two butts with the butterflies in the foreground belong to Mike and Robin, with whom Doug and I stayed. *Left*, Sailor Sid instigating a photo op. *Bottom, left to right*: Sailor Sid, Alan, Doug, Elizabeth, and me in Alan's London flat.

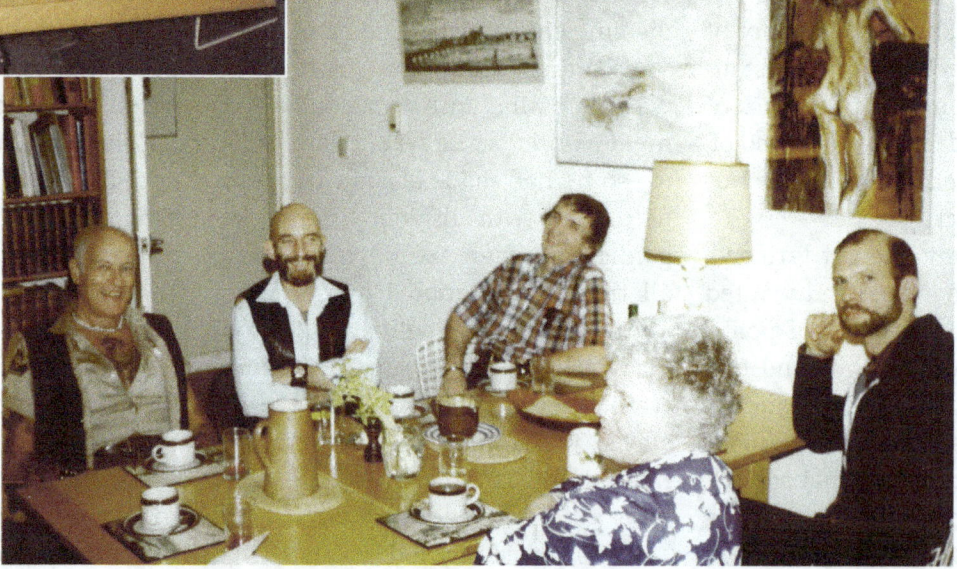

nipple tattooed with the head of a bull, the ring through its nose.

Alan was British to the core. My impression of him was of a rather private man who was a bit difficult to get to know. Not that he was particularly shy. He would casually disrobe and allow himself to be photographed, but there was always a reserved quality about his actions. He could converse with intelligence and ease, but to access the man behind the mask was a challenge.

During our stay in London, I took advantage of the opportunity to interview Alan for *PFIQ*. Prior to becoming a tattooist, he had worked as an art teacher. There's no doubt his background as an artist was of great benefit when he left teaching to pursue his passions for tattooing and piercing.

Aside from any living canvases who might still be alive, I don't know how much of his artwork survives. One of my little treasures is a ceramic egg that Alan made as a gift for Doug. It is sculpted with male pecs and prominent pierced nipples and finished with a shiny metallic glaze. Doug entrusted it to my care because he didn't want it around the house where a family member might find it.

In the mid-to-late 1950s, when Alan was in his twenties working on a sugar plantation in British Guiana, he observed a couple of field hands who were wearing little gold earrings in their nipples. This was the beginning of his fascination with body piercing. He returned to London with his own nipples pierced. Within a few years, he had acquired a number of tattoos and additional piercings as well. Over time, many of them were stretched to accommodate sizable jewelry.

On one of our days in London, Doug and I paid a visit to Alan's tattoo and piercing studio in Wandsworth. He shared space with a leather business called Leather Unlimited, owned by a man named Alan Selby, who was one

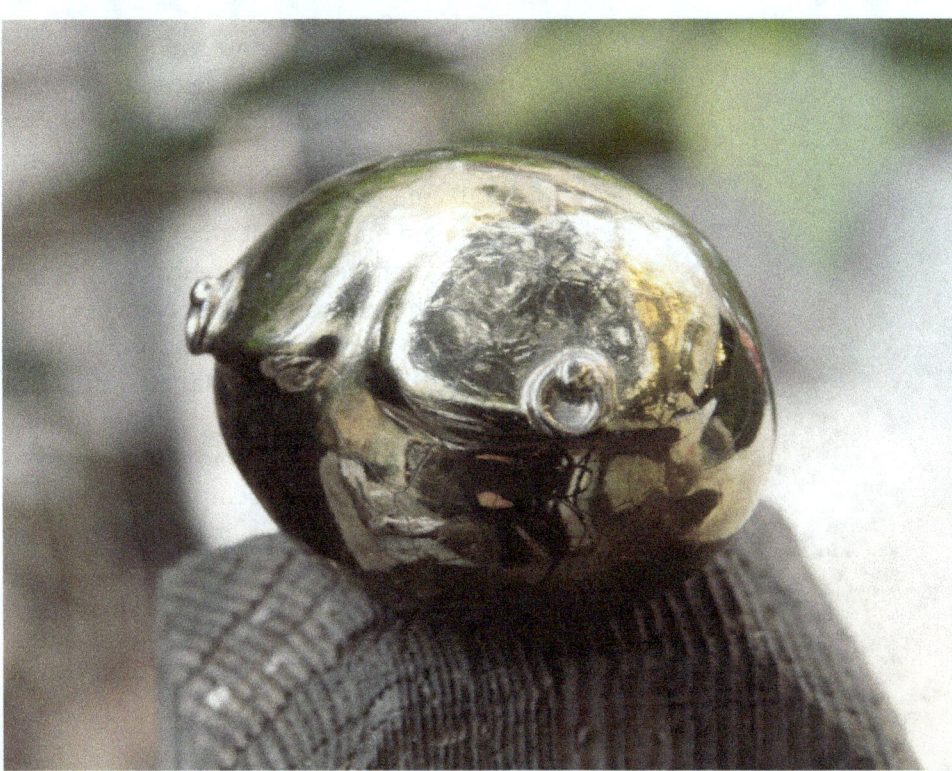

Ceramic egg with nipple rings that Alan made and gave to Doug

of the pioneers of fetish clothing for gay S/M enthusiasts. I recall that while I was living in Denver some years before, I had ordered a motorcycle cap from him. In 1979 he immigrated to the U.S. and set up shop in San Francisco as Mr. S Leather. His warmth and outgoing manner endeared him to the local leather community. He worked tirelessly raising money and awareness for AIDS charities up until his death in 2004.

Mr. Sebastian's space was meticulously clean and well-organized. I would have expected no less. While we differed in our viewpoints on a number of issues, he and I shared a commitment to cleanliness and proper hygiene.

Even as late as the 1990s, there was much debate on the subject of using anesthetics for tattoos and piercings. Especially in Gauntlet's early days there was nothing available without a prescription that was of much use. I had experimented with using topical anesthetics where a mucous membrane was involved, but found that they burned and irritated the delicate

tissue and were not very effective. From my perspective, they were hardly worth the effort.

I strongly rejected the use of injectable anesthetics, considering them too risky to be used by anyone who wasn't a physician or at least a nurse. They were dangerous for a couple of reasons. For one, they can pose a health risk to some people. That's bad enough, but a far more immediate concern was that in the U.S., their use is illegal in the hands of an unlicensed individual. Assuming I could even have obtained them, I would have been putting my fledgling business in jeopardy of being closed down and myself in danger of arrest for practicing medicine without a license. It just wasn't worth taking a chance. I also felt, and still do, that when piercings are done by a skilled professional, the pain is usually less than the anesthetic injection would be.

As the years went by and I observed other piercers at work, I came to the conclusion that oftentimes some used anesthetics to mask their incompetence. It became my firm belief that the

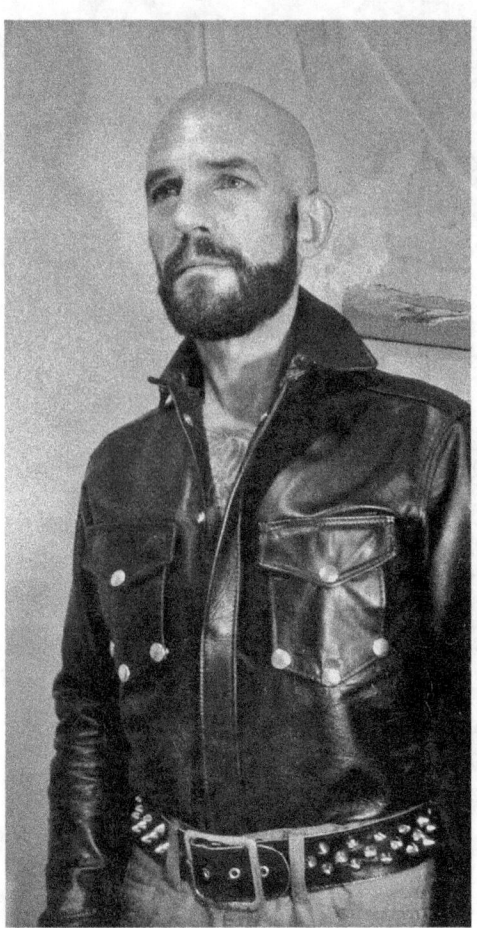

Young Alan

best thing a piercer could do to minimize pain is to master the necessary skills and be able to perform a piercing quickly and accurately. In my opinion, this eliminates the need for anesthetics of any kind.

Even though the legality of their use in Britain was not much different than in the U.S., Alan never seemed to be particularly concerned. He was able to obtain anesthetics through a physician friend and had no qualms about using them. Doing so became one of the charges against him when he was arrested in 1987.

I must be honest; I had very little opportunity to watch Alan at work. Some years later I saw a video in which he performed a Prince Albert piercing, and I was a bit appalled by his technique. The piercing was done within the context of an S/M scene, and perhaps the crudeness was for effect and to deliberately prolong the discomfort.

It took an inordinate amount of fumbling and time, and seemed to be more bloody than usual for this often bloody piercing. It left me wondering if Alan's technique could have used some refinement and if it might explain his regular use of anesthetics.

This may or may not have been the video that landed him in serious trouble, but in 1987, the Manchester police obtained what they thought was a "snuff" film, a video of what looked to them like people being tortured before being killed. In fact, it was of a group of heavy S/M enthusiasts at a play party. Alan was one of 16 men charged in what became known as the Spanner case, and even though everything that transpired had been consensual, the court ruled that a person doesn't have the legal right to consent to receiving what it considered to be bodily harm. Thus the convictions stood. Alan "received a sentence of 15 months, which was suspended for two years." Translated, that meant if he didn't re-offend in two years, he could avoid prison. However, if he were convicted of any wrongdoing inside that time, he would be incarcerated for 15 months.

The case was appealed to the European Court of Human Rights, but Alan didn't live long enough to hear the verdict. He died May 8, 1996. The final judgment in the Spanner case was handed down in February of 1997. In it, the ECHR found that the British government had not violated the right to privacy by prosecuting the men involved.

Mr. Sebastian is considered by many—and with good reason—as the father of the modern body piercing movement in Europe. Sad to say, living on opposite sides of the world wasn't conducive to our spending much time together. The Internet didn't become practical for public use until about the time of Alan's death, and with the pressures of our businesses and lives, we weren't very good correspondents, so

communication between us was minimal. Still, I am happy to have known him personally and to have shared the spotlight with him.

On March 14, 1978, our London excursion at an end, Doug, Sid, Elizabeth, and I caught a train for Harwick on the western coast of England, where we boarded a hovercraft that would take us to the Netherlands. Northern Europe in March is still in the grip of winter. The skies were overcast and gray. There was a cold, icy drizzle between rain and sleet, and the sea was rough and choppy.

Although born in a water sign, I much prefer the shore to the deck of a seagoing vessel. When it comes to seasickness a hovercraft may be some improvement over a ship, but I still felt a bit green for the duration of the crossing. I found a bench in a quiet corner, lay down, curled up, closed my eyes, and managed to reach the Continent without losing my lunch. After disembarking, a short train ride later found us in Amsterdam for the third "World" tattoo convention. The first had been in Houston, the second in Reno.

Although it certainly wasn't evident

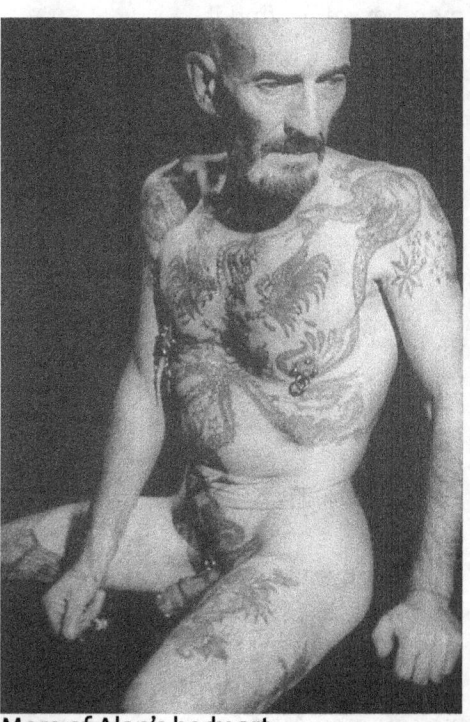

More of Alan's body art

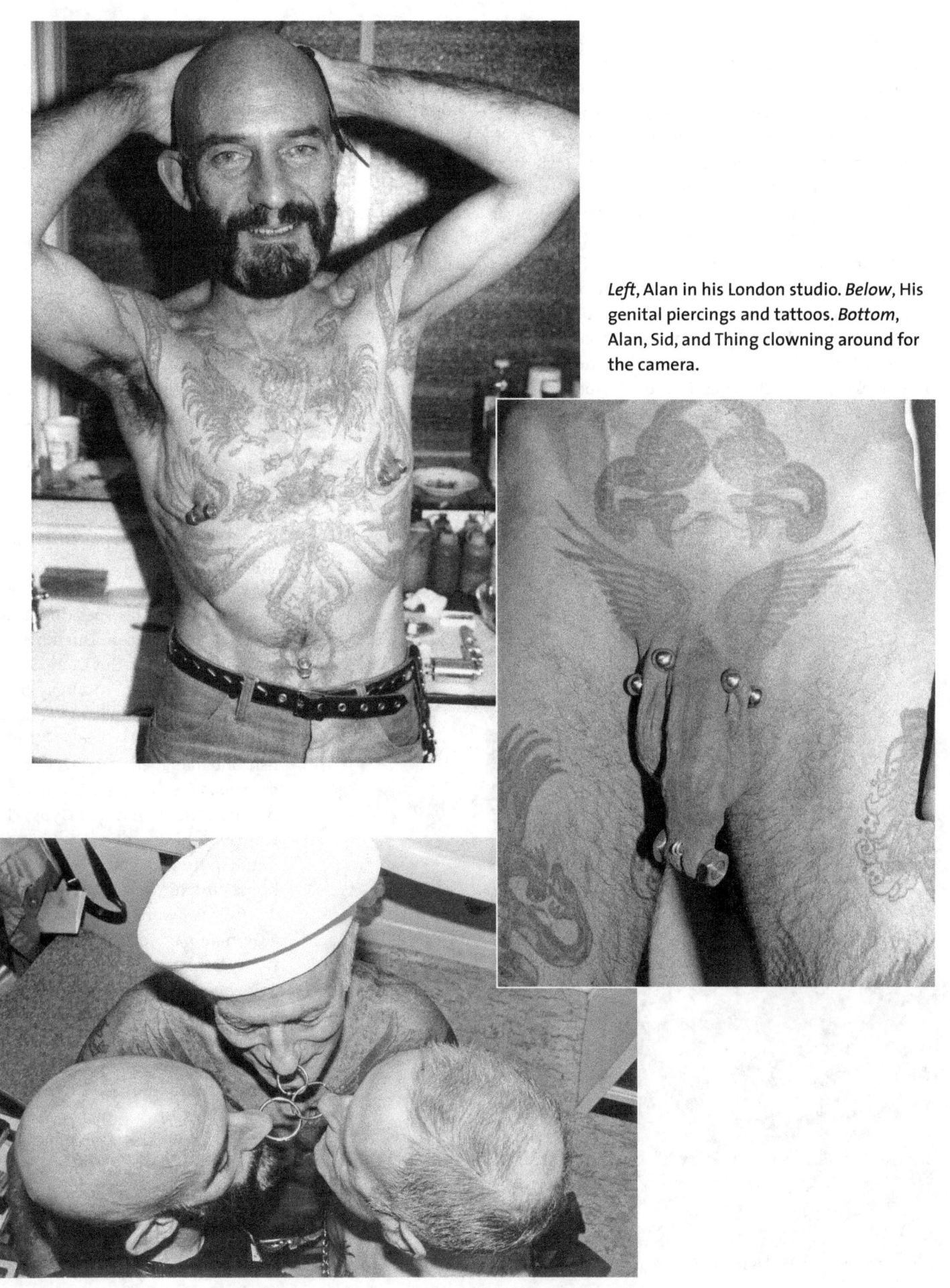

Left, Alan in his London studio. *Below*, His genital piercings and tattoos. *Bottom*, Alan, Sid, and Thing clowning around for the camera.

from the weather—both days and nights were often bitter cold, while snow still piled up along the streets and lay in random patches wherever there was open space—spring was beginning to stir. Already those hardy heralds of spring, crocuses and jonquils, were beginning to push their happy faces up through the snow.

The convention itself was disappointing, to say the least. On a postcard to my parents, I even described it as a poorly planned "disaster." The venue was Amsterdam's De Brakke Grond (The Brackish Ground)—what I'd call a

local cultural center. About 200 people showed up for the event. While the social and photo opportunities were virtually endless, from a business standpoint the returns seemed minimal. Still, I felt that every opportunity to expose people to piercing had the potential to result in clients and customers in the future, so I did my best.

During the course of our stay, I visited a local gay-owned leather and fetish shop called Rob of Amsterdam. I had seen ads for it in *Drummer* magazine and thought perhaps it would be a potential outlet for Gauntlet jewelry.

The shop's owner was, not surprisingly, named Rob. Alan (Mr. Sebastian) was a friend of his who made occasional visits to the city to do tattoos and piercings for Rob's clients. Rob purchased a few pieces of Gauntlet merchandise for his shop, but in retrospect I think for convenience if nothing else he preferred to have his few piercing needs met by his friend Alan, who sold stainless steel jewelry made by Ray Spain.

Rob was attractive, blond, and outgoing. Business issues aside, there was a mutual attraction, and I ended up spending a night with him. I also purchased a few items to bring home with me: a belt buckle that I have worn almost daily since I bought it, and two dildoes of unique design and shape that I wondered how I'd explain if some zealous customs official went through my luggage.

Nor was Rob my only conquest on this trip. Generally speaking, I didn't find the majority of Dutchmen particularly attractive. But Doug, Sid, Alan and I went out to a local gay bar one night where an unusually short man came on to me. He spoke little English but managed to convey that not only was he interested, but also he was half Dutch and half Gypsy. There was something exotic about him that I found quite sexy and I ended up going home with him.

While we were in London I had met a German named Rudiger, an architect from Hamburg and a friend of Alan's. Somehow we developed an odd, loose attachment that continued through much of our trip. He showed up in Amsterdam at the convention, and we spent an enjoyable time together there. Later on we met again in his hometown, where he generously acted as tour guide.

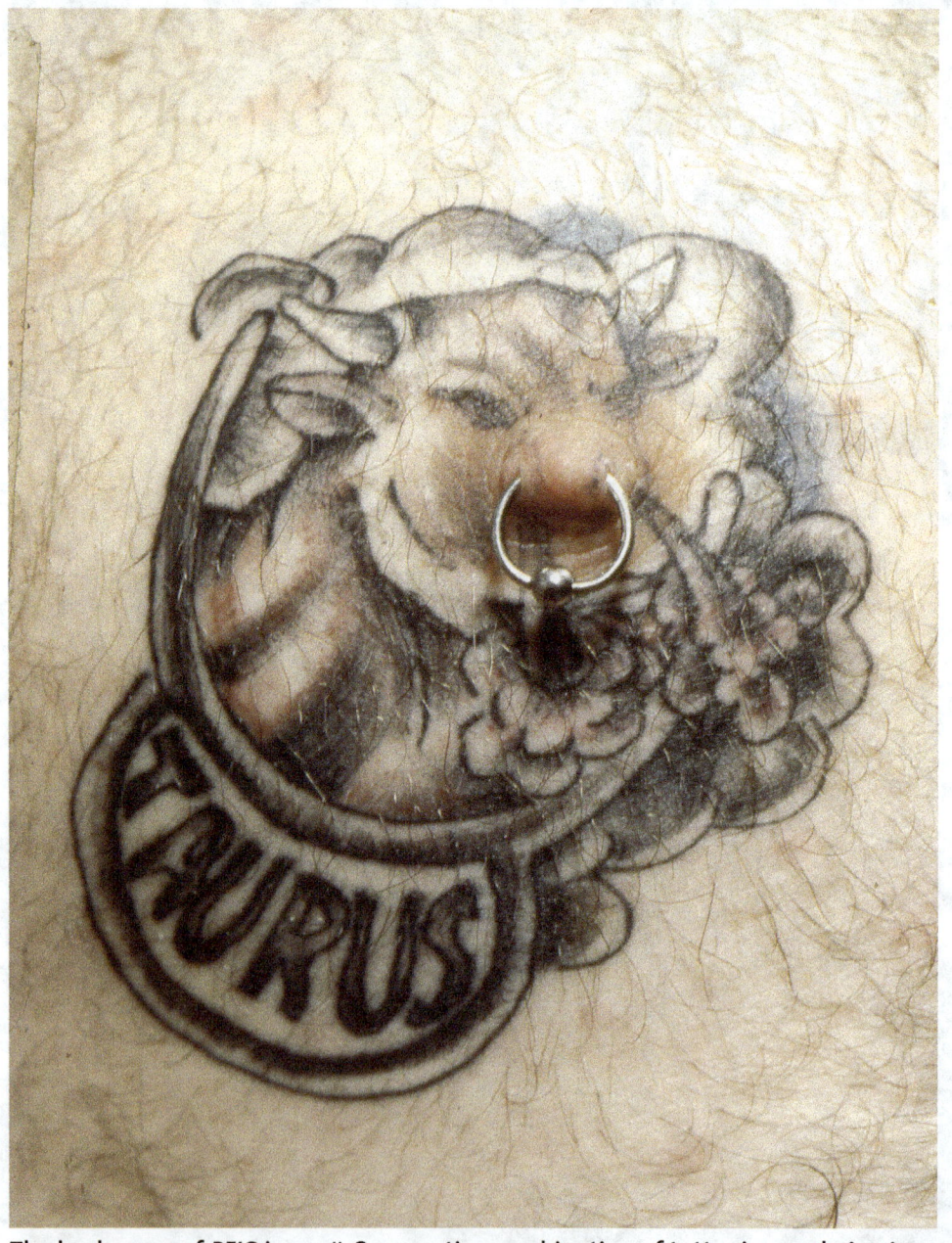

The back cover of *PFIQ* issue #18, a creative combination of tattooing and piercing

Some readers may think that I slept around a lot. By their standards, perhaps I did, and I make no apologies for it. Thanks in no small part to the Stonewall Riots and subsequent gay liberation, the unwritten credo of that time was that being gay and liberated meant that one could sleep with anybody, anywhere, anytime the opportunity presented itself. This freedom had a great deal to do with defining who we were as gay men, or at least how we saw ourselves. But when it came to "slutdom," I was no contender. Then, as now, I believed that there is much to be said for moderation. To most of my friends with whose voracious sexual appetites I could not compete, I must have appeared a bit reserved. It's my opinion that most men, straight or gay, are not inclined toward monogamy. And without the restraints of marriage or the nesting instincts of female companions to rein in their rampant desires, gay men tend to be more promiscuous than their heterosexual counterparts. This was especially true in the golden days before HIV/AIDS. We simply didn't think that we could catch anything life-threatening that a doctor's prescription wouldn't cure.

The freewheeling Sixties had also left a legacy of drug use that, in its own way, contributed to the promiscuity of the times. I remember well a friend named Michael with whom I occasionally played. He came to my house one night, and after we were finished, he shot up speed and went to the baths.

My own attitude towards drugs was pretty conservative as well. Like many others, I experimented, but always with caution. To this day I've never dropped a psychedelic. Having taken to heart the horror stories promulgated in the press, and being aware that too much or too strong marijuana makes me extremely paranoid, the risk simply seemed too great.

Back when I was living in Denver in the early 70s, I worked at a picture frame shop with a longhaired hippie named Craig, who was a pretty heavy

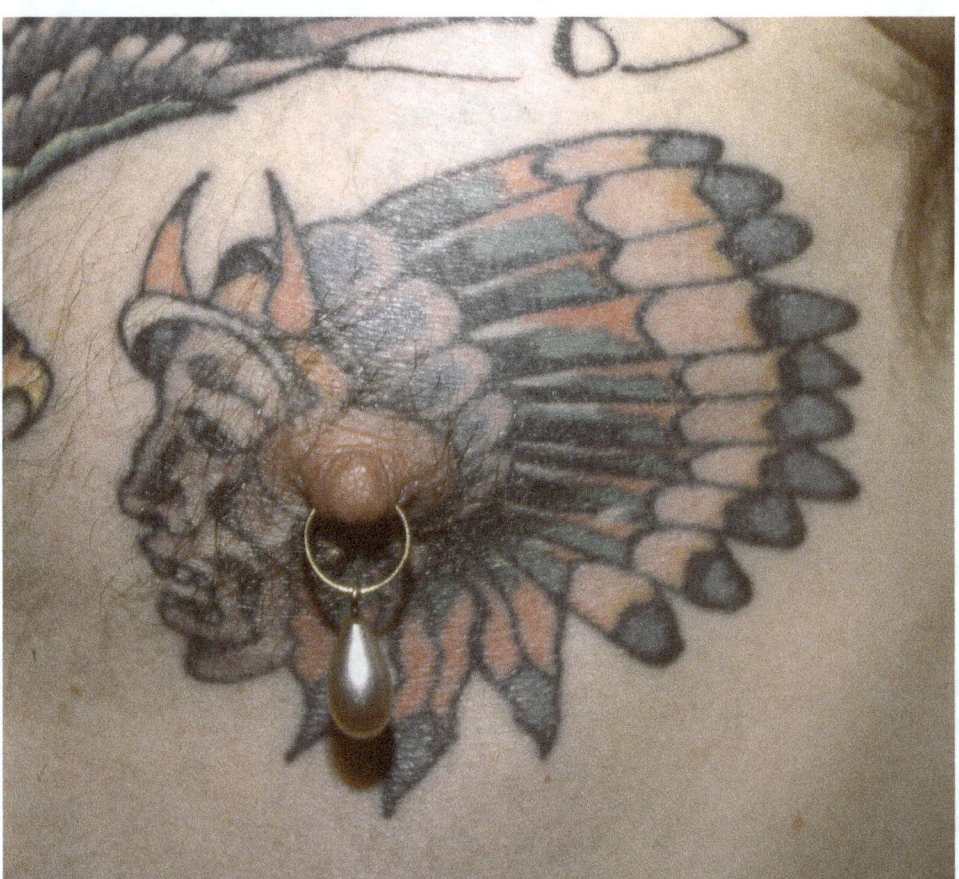

The cover of issue #23, another photo from our London adventure

drug user. One Friday night after work, we were hanging out, and he passed around a joint. The grass was particularly strong, and I got very stoned. At this point, someone realized that we needed to go to the bank and deposit our paychecks. We piled into the car and someone who was sufficiently functional drove us to the bank. Being Friday night, the place was busy. As I stood in line waiting my turn at the teller, I realized that I was having a difficult time staying focused. Paranoia began to take over, convincing me that everyone knew I was stoned. Somehow, I managed to make it to the head of the line and gave the teller my deposit. She noticed a mistake in my calculations, and asked me about it.

By this time, I was sweating and my brain was simply not functioning very well. The next thing I knew, I was lying on the floor with a number of friends and strangers standing around me. Craig was calmly explaining to people

that I was hypoglycemic, and since we hadn't eaten yet, I had passed out from a drop in my blood sugar. Apparently that was plausible enough to satisfy everyone. Concern on her face, the teller was kneeling beside me pressing some money and my deposit slip into my hand, carefully making sure I was aware what she was doing and at the same time offering me a piece of candy. The experience made my low tolerance to drugs quite clear.

In spite of what had happened, marijuana, at least in moderation, was still my drug of choice, and not infrequently I would have a few hits off my small water pipe in the evening when I got home from work or on those occasions when I had a hot date. I rarely smoked during the day and never partook of anything that would impair my judgment or abilities when I was piercing. To me that was unthinkable.

The other popular recreational drug at the time was amyl nitrite, better

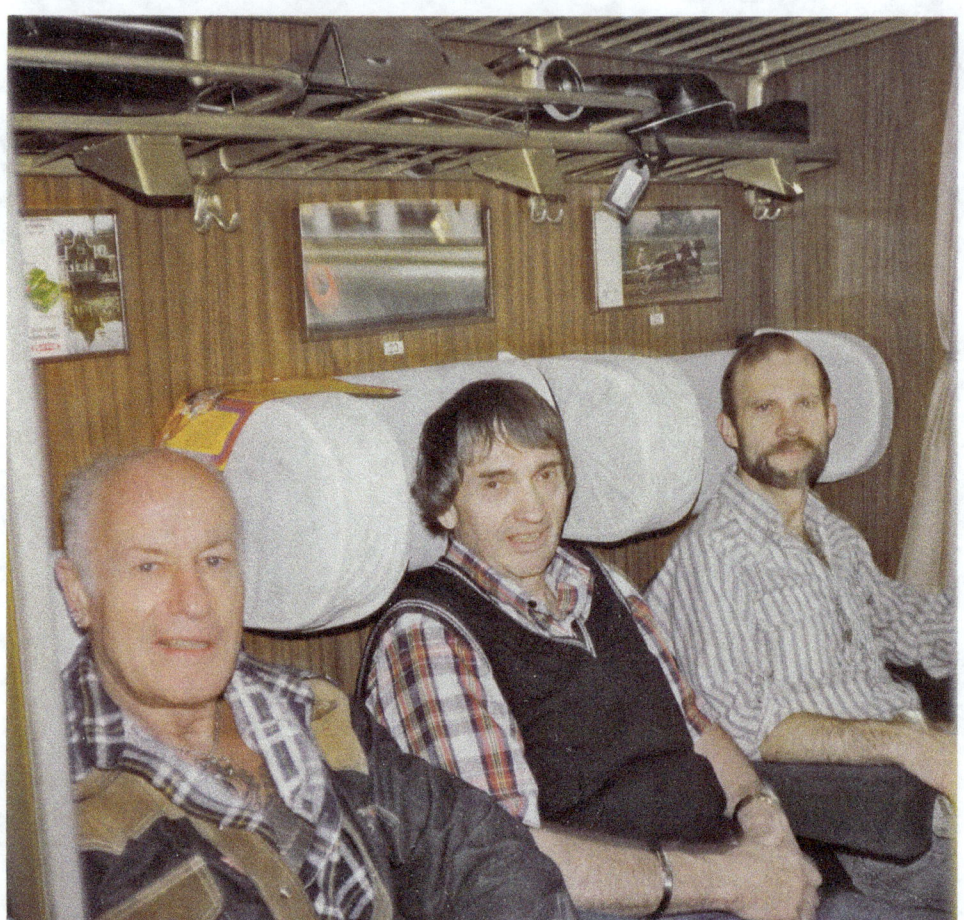

On the train somewhere between Amsterdam and Frankfurt

known as poppers. This inhalant, originally prescribed for angina patients, gained widespread popularity in the gay community, though its use diminished somewhat during the early years of the AIDS epidemic. Like many others, I indulged to enhance sex. Its telltale odor frequently wafted across the floor of a crowded disco as the dancers took hits to heighten their pleasure in the pulsating music and the sweaty, gyrating bodies. Many of the gay discos of the period had dimly lit back rooms where men would take a break between dances to indulge in a little anonymous sex.

Although I was certainly no puritan when it came to drugs, it didn't take very long for me to realize the wisdom of not piercing a client who was stoned or drunk. The rush of adrenaline and endorphins can be so intense that the likelihood of fainting, especially when the person is using poppers, is signifi-

cantly increased. Alcohol has a tendency to increase bleeding, and if one is doing a penis piercing and the man gets erect, the bleeding can be profuse. Doing piercings as part of a sex scene is generally not a very good idea either. Trying to maintain a reasonable degree of sterility is challenging, and attempting to keep things clean and orderly can quickly kill the spontaneity and put a damper on the mood.

One of Doug's many business ventures was a travel agency, and it was through this agency that we had booked our European trip. Part of the package was a Eurail pass. Our itinerary included taking the train from Amsterdam, first to Hamburg then down through Germany, with stops in Cologne, Frankfurt, Stuttgart, Munich, and finally, Vienna.

Rudiger met us in Hamburg and generously offered to show us the

sights. He also introduced us to a bit of local piercing-related history, the Hamburger carpenter. Hamburger is the German word for a person from Hamburg, Germany. This quote from an old issue of Time magazine provides the essential details: "When an honest young Hamburger seeks to enter the Hamburg Guild of Journeymen Carpenters, he faces harsh Medieval tribulations, searching tests. After suitable apprenticeship he must wander about Germany, carpentering, for three years. As a full-fledged member of the Journeymen's Guild, the proud young Hamburger wears a broad, black hat, extra wide black trousers, and heavy gold earrings." [1] This tradition actually dates back to the 13th century.

Earrings aside, I was particularly intrigued when Rudi showed up one day wearing a pair of Hamburger carpenter pants. These are heavy, bell-bottom trousers made from corduroy or canvas similar in design to those worn by U.S. Navy men. Their most notable feature is a front flap that closes with two metal zippers, whereas the Navy version is buttoned. Their uniqueness appealed to me, and I wanted to take a pair home with me. So on one of my free afternoons, Rudi took me away from the well-worn path of sightseeing into a blue-collar neighborhood to a shop that specialized in work clothing. I tried on several pair of the carpenter pants before purchasing some made of heavy, black canvas.

The trousers never wore out. I eventually had to give them away when HIV medications and middle age added several inches to my waistline.

Rudi also took me to one of the local sex shops and introduced me to the proprietor. It was an opportunity to show, and hopefully sell, some of my Gauntlet jewelry. I did sell a few pieces, but a big drawback to selling body piercing jewelry at that time was a general lack of piercers, experienced or otherwise.

Rudiger could not have been kinder or more helpful during our brief stay in Hamburg. Perhaps it was a matter of cultural differences, but despite the intimacy we shared, I was never able to really get to know the man. Some time later, I was saddened to learn from Alan that for some unknown reason he had killed himself.

From Hamburg we took the train to Cologne, where we stayed overnight, and then proceeded on to Frankfurt. Here we spent a couple of days visiting with Horst Streckenbach, better known as Tattoo Samy, and his wife Ella. In addition to tattooing, Samy also did a brisk piercing business. Although he had a local source for most of his jewelry, he turned out to be a very good Gauntlet customer. Traveling to the States at least once a year for a tattoo convention, he frequently made a detour through L.A., where he would stop by the shop and purchase a supply of jewelry to take home.

Samy was also something of an inventor. He produced a couple of piercing tools that I know of, and though I tried them out, I never found them to be very useful. While we were visiting him, Samy showed us a new tattoo machine that he had designed. It was built from the cylindrical body of a hypodermic syringe, and the needles were powered by the tiny motor from a handheld tape recorder.

Sid was particularly intrigued with this tattoo machine. He decided he wanted to return home with a souvenir, a small tattoo done by Samy with this device.

I'm no stranger to the tattoo experience myself, having had Cliff Raven apply fairly large ones to my shoulders and upper arms. Cliff was an academically trained artist. He was one of the first Americans to seek inspiration from the Japanese tattoo tradition. Before this influence had become so

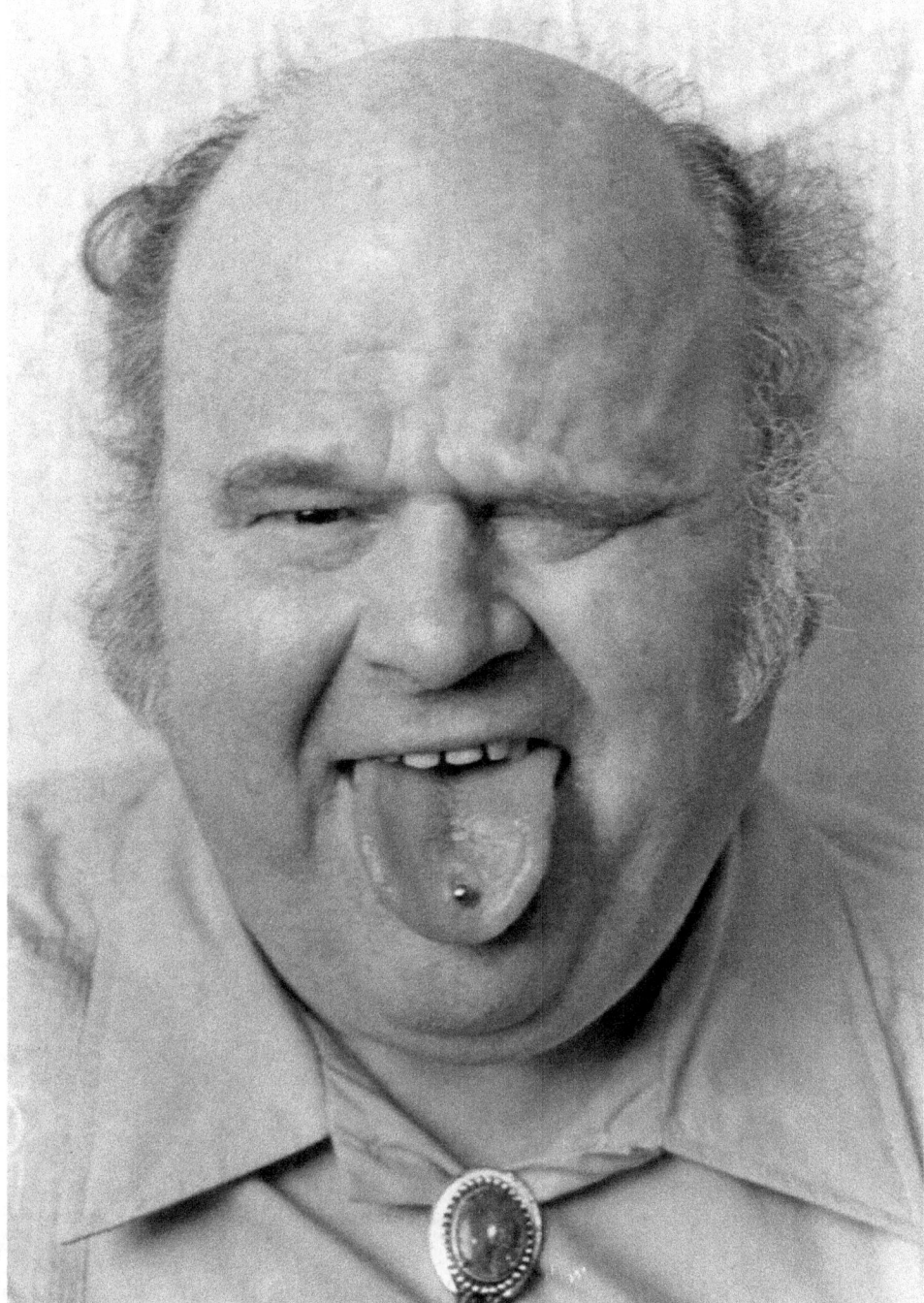

Tattoo Samy

widespread, tattoos tended to be rather coarse, with the applied appearance of a decal. Cliff's designs were carefully rendered works of art that fitted the contours of the body. He had a delicate touch, penetrating the skin no deeper than necessary, and although I didn't particularly enjoy getting tattooed, the discomfort was tolerable, and the tattoo healed quickly with minimal flaking and very little scabbing.

Sadly, such could not be said for

Samy. His designs were crude, but even worse was his technique. The inks were ground deeply into the skin, which caused significant bleeding. Sid was no lightweight when it came to tattoos and pain, but there was no mistaking from the grimace on his face that he was suffering. He later confided that it was the most painful tattoo he had ever gotten. Over the following days, it developed a thick, ugly scab.

Whatever he may have lacked as a

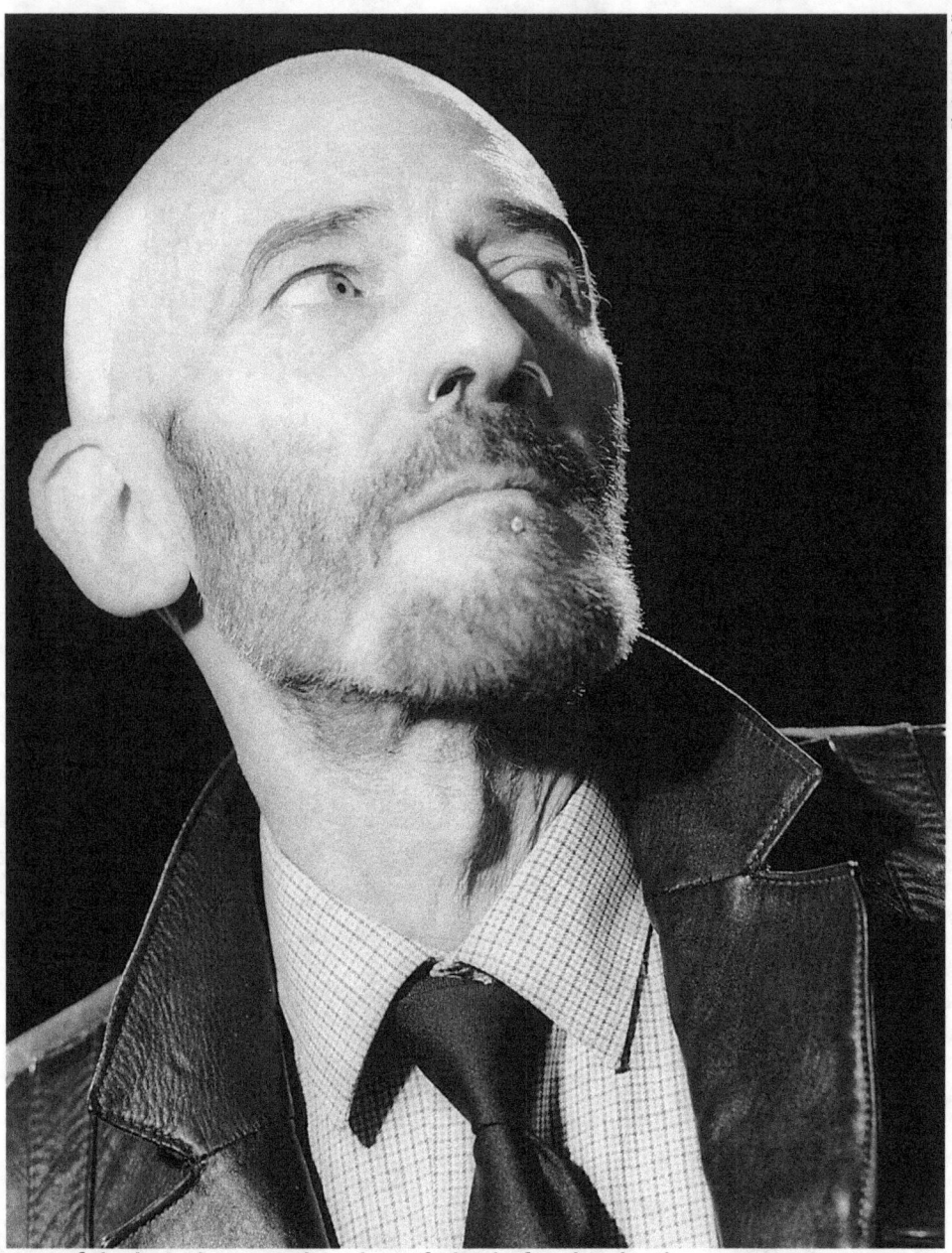

One of the last photographs taken of Alan before his death

tattooist, Samy was a gracious host. We were well treated and well fed, even though some of Ella's cooking, her pickled herring in particular, didn't exactly appeal to my palate.

The time came for us to depart Frankfurt. Elizabeth and Sid said their goodbyes and returned to the States; Doug and I were going on to Vienna. I was frankly relieved for Doug and me to be on our own. Traveling with more than two people is rarely easy. Trying to keep everyone together is frequent-ly frustrating. Elizabeth had been no problem, but Sid's presence had become wearisome. We could scarcely go anywhere without his attempting to shock the locals. When it came to matters of money, he could be incredibly cheap. After several weeks of this, I'd had enough and was happy to be out of his presence.

Doug and I boarded the train and set out for Vienna. We made a couple of brief stops on the way, but they are a blur. I have a cuckoo clock that I purchased in Munich. The trip itself, particularly through Salzburg and the Austrian Alps, presented us with some of the most breathtaking scenery we had encountered. Unfortunately, we only saw it from the train. I sometimes wish we had skipped one of the German cities and stopped in Salzburg for a few days.

All my adult life, there has been a special place in my heart for the lushly romantic music of Viennese operetta. One of my favorite arias is entitled "Vienna, City of My Dreams." Indeed, around that music I had formed an idealized fantasy of Vienna that, to my disappointment, fell apart in the face of reality.

By this time, Doug and I had been away from home for over three weeks. I was beginning to tire of the winter weather, feeling a little homesick, and at times crabby and difficult to please. This may have colored my experience of our stay in the Austrian capital.

I've no idea what Vienna is like when the weather is sunny and warm. When we arrived it was overcast, cold, and gray, and the sun never showed its face the entire time we were there. Most of the buildings appeared to have aged to a dull gray black making the city as monochromatic as the weather. Even the people seemed dour and inhospitable. We attended the opera, but the music was uninspired. We visited one of the local palaces only to find it faded and shabby. The dark, bitter Viennese coffee failed to warm me, and I found the famous local pastry, the Sachertorte, dense and excessively sweet. Fortunately, through it all Doug remained patient and took my ill temper in stride.

Finally our trip came to a welcome end, and we headed homeward to warm and sunny California. We had been away far too long. Thankfully, customs did not go through my suitcase.

---

[1]"Journeymen v. Crooks," *Time*, January 14, 1929. Source: http://www.time.com/time/magazine/article/0,9171,737207,00.html

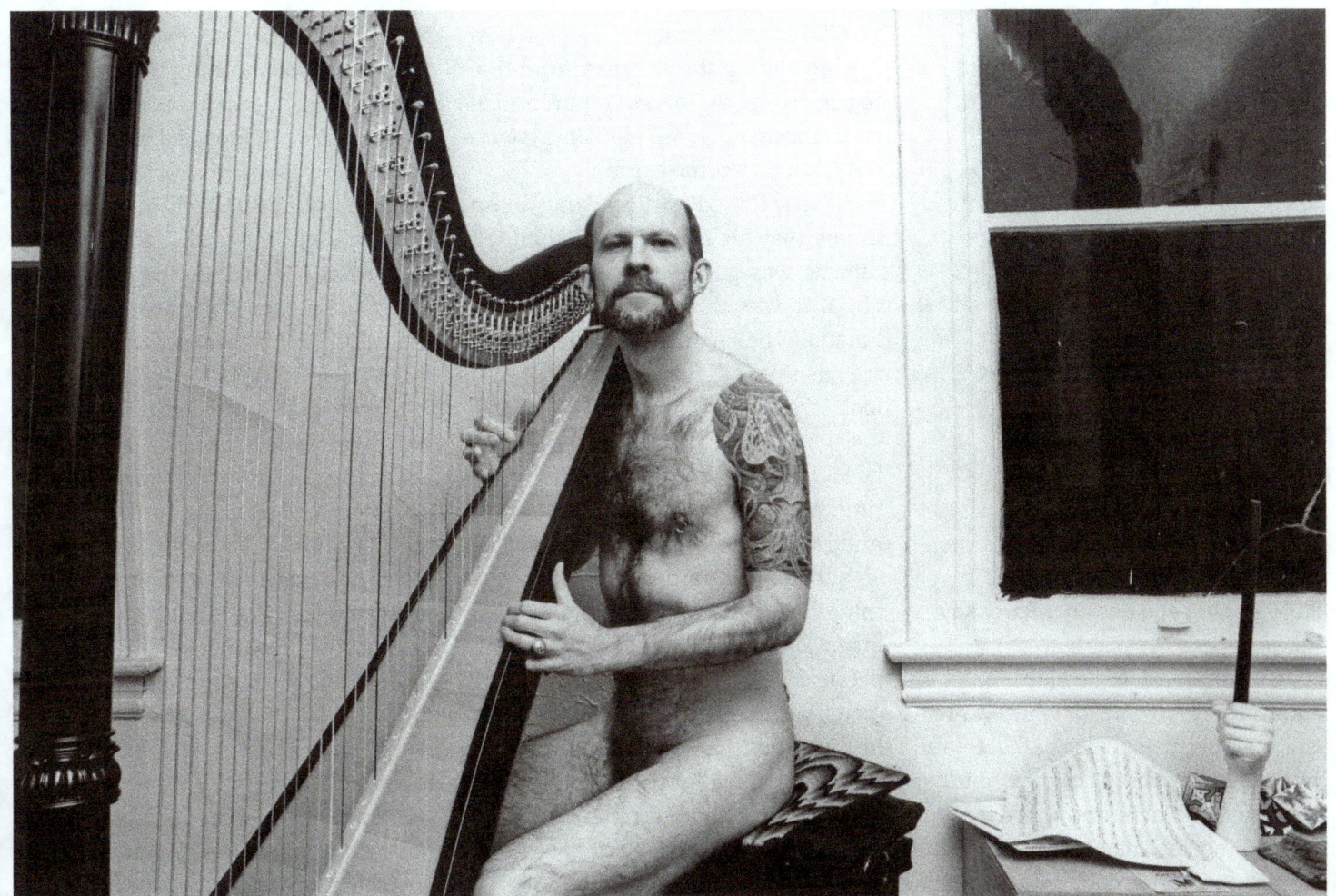

"Tattooed Male with Harp," portrait by Australian photographer Barry Kay (1979). Photo courtesy of the Barry Kay Archive, London

CHAPTER 9

Nothing had changed at home since my departure for Europe a month earlier. My lover Eric was still unemployed, and there was no evidence that he'd made any serious attempt to find work during my absence. Even before I had left, our relationship was deteriorating. As far as I was concerned, he was a pathetic, needy individual who desperately wanted to be taken care of. I had neither the means, patience, nor time to be a full-time babysitter for anyone. I tried without success to motivate him to find a job. All he wanted to do was to work for Gauntlet, but his clerical skills were abysmal, he had no facility with jewelry fabrication, and I didn't have the resources to cover what amounted to a full-time, unskilled employee.

A naturally gifted floral designer, Eric should have been able to find work with a florist. Unfortunately, when stressed and in unfamiliar or uncomfortable social surroundings, he was unable to appear relaxed and natural, and would assume a saccharine, prissy facade that put people off. Their immediate response was to distance themselves from him as quickly as possible.

One of the members of the T&P Group, a man named Jack, was an organist at a Hollywood church. He managed to channel some of the church's Easter floral design work Eric's way. For a while, it even looked as if he might actually develop a little business of his own. To that end, we started a short-lived division of the business called The Green Gauntlet. Sad to say, nothing ever came of it. On his own Eric simply didn't have the motivation or gift for

self-promotion necessary to make an enterprise succeed. The demands of building my own business made it increasingly difficult to deal with Eric's clingy neediness. I finally ran out of patience and called it quits.

When Doug talked about matters related to business, I listened. Body piercing was still an industry in its infancy, so there were no precedents for dealing with problems the business world at large had already figured out. One of these was the issue of liability. We were constantly evaluating everything we did, asking if it might perhaps put us at risk. In the beginning, I had included the cost of doing a piercing with the price of the jewelry, thinking that by not charging for the procedure, I could not be accused of practicing medicine without a license. But what if

83

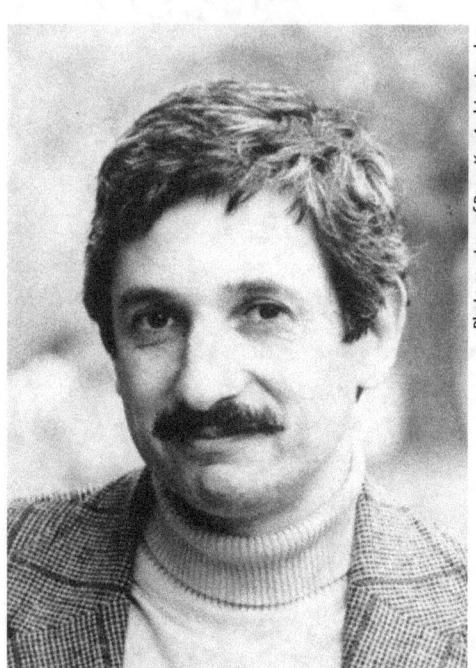

Photographer and designer Barry Kay

a client suffered some serious injury or simply decided to sue for whatever reason? I would personally be liable and could lose everything I owned, not that it was much. There are many reasons for loathing the manufacturers of the ear-piercing gun in common use today, but we do have them to thank for the idea of the release form. Fairly early on, in an effort to protect ourselves, we began having clients sign one. These have become standard for the industry.

Doug was very insistent that I should incorporate. The previous year he introduced me to his own attorney, a gay lawyer in Hollywood named Thomas Hunter Russell. Thomas was a member of the Log Cabin Club for gay Republicans and moved in exclusive circles. He was also one of the few people who knew about Doug's double life and his passion for piercing. He agreed to handle the incorporation. It had been agreed beforehand that I was to be the owner, and Doug was to be a shareholder. I wanted Doug to have a part of what he had helped create. Being a neophyte in terms of business, I had no idea how long the process should take, so when months passed without any movement on the matter, I didn't

think that much about it. I got on with my life, calling the attorney from time to time to get a progress report and always receiving some plausible excuse why it hadn't come through yet.

As mentioned earlier, Doug maintained that his psychic guide had told him he was going to live to the year 2000. It was now 1979. Gullible me, I actually believed we had 21 years of friendship and future adventures to look forward to.

One day Doug came into the store as he had done so many times before. This time he had something specific on his mind. Over the years, between our travels and the T&P parties and all the other things we had done together, Doug had taken a vast number of photographs. Because he was so closeted about his piercing interests, these had been left in my care. I had been through them countless times looking for photos to use in *PFIQ*, or slides for presentations I did for groups like the Society of Janus, a local S/M organization. Over time, everything had become pretty jumbled. Doug proposed that he take the collection back to his office and organize it. As fate would have it ,only some of the photos were at the store that day. Some of them were at my home. I gave him what I had on hand, scarcely noticing when the conversation briefly turned more serious.

In passing, Doug mentioned that he was going to the doctor for a checkup, making little of it before talking about other matters. Shortly thereafter he showed up at the store wearing a heart monitor. It wasn't anything to be concerned about he reassured me even though he had been stopped in the middle of a treadmill test when there was concern something was going on with his heart. It was probably just a glitch, but the doctor wanted to make sure everything was okay—absolutely nothing to worry about. Just routine.

Several days passed, and he phoned

to let me know that everything was fine. There was nothing to be alarmed about, or so he said. What actually passed between him and his doctor I'll never know. Perhaps the results really showed nothing. Doug's youngest son, with whom I've corresponded in recent years, has told me that to the best of his knowledge Doug never gave any indication to his family that his death might be imminent.

Not long after his heart issues had begun to fade from my awareness, Doug told me that he was going on a trip to New Zealand and would be gone for two or three weeks. It was a place he'd never seen before, and he was quite excited about going. New Zealand's indigenous people, the Maori, are renowned for their tattoo tradition, and Doug was thrilled that he would have a firsthand opportunity to learn more about it.

I'm sure Doug must have sent me a postcard or two while he was away, but given the distance, they probably arrived after he did. There was something different about the man who returned, and it was more than just a suntan. Doug was very relaxed, calm, and at peace. He glowed. There was a radiant, otherworldly quality about him that I simply attributed to a well-needed rest. The beauty of New Zealand had made a great impression on him, and he couldn't stop raving about it. It felt good to have him home.

During that summer, there was a man named Barry Kay visiting L.A. and taking photographs for a book he was working on titled *Changing Bodies*, which was to include images of people with tattoos and piercings and sundry other body modifications. I modeled for him myself, photographed naked in my living room playing my harp, my tattoos and nipple rings clearly visible. Barry, an Australian residing in London, had an extensive résumé as a set and costume designer for theater, ballet, and opera as well as other impressive credits,[1] though I wasn't aware of them at the time. Photography was just one of his many talents.

Barry was staying at the Cavalier Hotel on Wilshire Boulevard in West L.A., just southeast of UCLA. Doug and I had a friend, a fellow T&P enthusiast named Jack, who had been extensively tattooed by Ed Hardy. On August 22, 1979, a typical dry, hot summer day in Los Angeles, Jack was being photographed in Barry's hotel room, and Doug had gone to observe. In the early afternoon, Jack called me at the store from the hotel and told me that Doug had just died. I felt like I had just been kicked in the stomach.

Apparently they were talking and taking photos, and all of a sudden Doug "plopped down on the bed and keeled over." Jack told me, "At first I just thought he was being dramatic, but then I realized he was dead." He'd had a massive heart attack and was gone by the time paramedics arrived. Of course, I was devastated.

There was a young man named Gordon Finch who was my secretary at the time—I realize that job title is now considered politically incorrect. When I told him what had just happened he said, "Go home. I'll keep an eye on the store." Grief-stricken, I went home and mourned the loss of the man who had so dramatically changed my life. For the first time since he had come into it, I felt bereft and adrift. Doug had been my rock, not just in my business, but in so much else as well. Would I be able to make it on my own, or would the business fail without his guidance?

Issue #7 of *PFIQ* (September, 1979) was one of the most difficult I ever had to complete. In the midst of its production, I had received that phone call telling me of Doug's death.

It wasn't long after his passing that I realized part of our photo collection was still in his office. Although I had met his wife and other members of his

---

★ Los Angeles Times   Mon., Aug. 27, 1979

He Brought Muzak West, Saved Steamer for Carter

People either loved or hated Richard C. Simonton, a musically obsessed inventor and businessman who died in Los Angeles Wednesday of a heart attack at 64.

It was he who gave the West Coast Muzak, that omnipresent soft background music one encounters in stores, hotels, restaurants and offices.

Until 1941, Muzak was available only in New York City when Simonton founded Pacific Network, Inc., the franchise that brought the recorded music West.

Other Simonton interests included steamboats and pipe organs.

And if Simonton had not had that love for steamboats, President Carter probably would have not been able to take last week's cruise down the Mississippi on the Delta Queen.

Simonton and his family made a similar trip on the Delta Queen in 1957 and discovered they were among its few passengers. The family wanted to sail on the old steamer the following year but learned that the firm that owned her was about to go bankrupt.

So Simonton bought the controlling interest in the ship and started a publicity campaign which soon had her running at a profit. He sold his interest in 1969.

Simonton's interest in pipe organs went back to when he was a teenager living in Monrovia.

From 14 until he was 25 he worked in his backyard shop developing an electronic organ which could faithfully reproduce every harmonic and tonal quality of the pipe organ.

At Simonton's Toluca Lake home, he had two old pipe organs in a full-size theater. There he showed silent film classics and brought in such not-

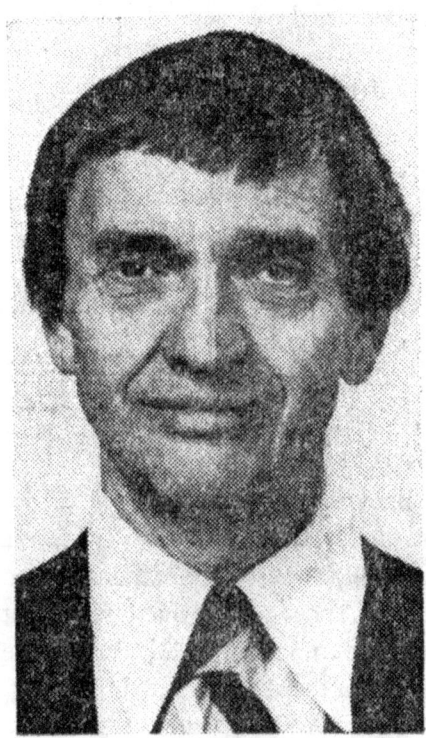

Richard C. Simonton

ed organists as Gaylord Carter, Jesse Crawford, Pierre Cochereau of Notre Dame Cathedral and Virgil Fox to accompany the films.

In 1955, he founded and became first president of the American Theater Organ Society, which now has 6,000 members throughout the world. The society restores and preserves old theater pipe organs.

Simonton leaves his wife, Helena; two sons, Richard Jr. and Robert; two daughters, Margaret and Mary, and one grandson.

Private family services were held Sunday.

—Dick West

Doug's obituary from the *Los Angeles Times*

---

family, I was certainly not in their inner circle of friends and acquaintances. As far as they were concerned, I was persona non grata. I wasn't invited to the funeral and didn't even know when or

where it was to take place.

In desperation, I called Doug's attorney Thomas Hunter Russell. He was very understanding and said that he'd approach the family about getting the pictures back. In retrospect, this was probably a conflict of interest on his part since he was representing not just me but the family as well. But thanks to Thomas's intervention I was put in contact with Doug's daughter Mary and spoke with her on the phone. She was sympathetic, acknowledged that several members of the family were aware of her father's interest in piercing, but said the fate of the photographs was not in her hands. She said she'd discuss it with her mother and some of her other siblings and get back to me. Not long afterwards, she called back and said, "There's nothing I can do. My mother put them in the fireplace and burned them." I was distraught, but there was nothing I could do. Under the circumstances her actions were understandable. It must have been difficult for her knowing that her husband was not only kinky, but cheating on her as well. Thankfully, at least some of the collection survived. Those photos that had been at my home on the fateful day Doug came looking for them were spared.

Losing someone dear is difficult in the best of situations. Not being able to attend the funeral, I was cut off and isolated in my grieving with no way to say goodbye or achieve any kind of closure. Over time, it resulted in some bitterness. The events of the previous year, like pieces of a jigsaw puzzle, began to create a picture unlike any I would have imagined. Though to the best of my knowledge he never confided the fact to anyone, it is my belief that Doug knew he was going to die.

In 2005 I was put in touch with an old, close friend of Doug's. I asked if Doug had ever indicated an awareness of his impending demise, he replied, "Dick [Doug's real nickname] was very tuned-in to the unseen side of life. He was very much both a spiritual and literal father

figure to me. We shared many thoughts and times together discussing and experiencing the Universe's realm of all that. As the years went by, I sensed a dissipation of his life force. It seemed he didn't have the same spark or interest in things, and I felt he was just going through the motions waiting for the final event."

He continued, "I do indeed feel that he knew it was time to go and something rather amazing (to me anyway) happened just a day or two before he left us. I was at the house and there was a big pile of clothes he had laid out. He looked at me with one of 'those looks' and said 'I won't be needing these any more, you can have them.' At the time, I thought nothing of it but thought it a little unusual in that the items were clothes he was currently using in his wardrobe and many of the items I could not wear, as they would not fit me. I think it might have been the very next day that he died! Of course, afterwards, I realized it was his way of saying goodbye to me! I believe this, as I knew him so well that way. I feel also that he went away from the house, like an elephant leaving the herd when they know it is time to go, so as not to cause undue stress for those around him."

I think it possible Doug wasn't even conscious of the inevitable. I also firmly believe he never intended for our photographs to be destroyed, and only wanted to sort through them and eliminate any images of himself to cover his tracks, but death claimed him before he was able to do so.

Within a matter of weeks after Doug's funeral, the papers for the incorporation unexpectedly came through. I think his paranoia had exerted itself making him change his mind about having his name associated with the corporation. In all likelihood, he told the attorney to stall

me. Perhaps on some level he was aware that his demise was not that far in the future. By the time the papers finally arrived, I felt that there was no longer a compelling reason to go through with the incorporation, so I didn't sign them. Gauntlet continued as a sole proprietorship for several years to come.

Sometimes I flash back to those times when Doug held the private screenings of old silent movies. Reflecting on the months following his death, I can't help feeling a bit like the tragic heroine caught in the clichéd love triangle in one of those silly old melodramas. In the end, of course, the philandering husband always returns to the bosom of his family leaving the "other woman"—man in this case—to go on and raise their "love child" alone.

Doug died believing that family and friends were unaware of his secret life and that he was protecting them, but in the end the joke was on him. Despite trying to isolate them from the truth, there was no way that it wouldn't eventually surface for the whole world to see. His attempt failed and could not erase whatever resentments his wife and family must have had knowing what they did. I felt abandoned and in some ways aggrieved that he had not left me so much as an envelope with a message that said how much our relationship had enriched his final years. After some time following Doug's death, I went to the Hall of Records and looked up his will. I never expected him to leave me anything. If he had, I would have long since received it. The will contained nothing out of the ordinary. I recognized the names of some of the people; some I had even met. In a small way, actually seeing this document gave me some sense of closure. It wasn't in the will, but I realized that he had left me an amazing legacy: Gauntlet.

[1]http://en.wikipedia.org/wiki/Barry_Kay and http://www.barry-kay-archive.org/BIOGRAPHY/BG_76_86.html#RS
Photo Barry Kay: Tattooed Male with Harp © Michael Werner 1985 by courtesy of Michael Werner Barry Kay Archive
www.barry-kay-archive.org

CHAPTER 10

The 1980s were turbulent years, both personally and in the evolution of the business, not to mention the world at large. By 1983 the AIDS epidemic was beginning in earnest. Over the next decade thousands of people died, most of them gay men. The plague cut a merciless swath not just through my friends and acquaintances but also too many of my clients. Though the emotional toll was significant, the impact on Gauntlet's business was actually pretty small. By this time my customer base had extended far beyond the gay leather scene. It hadn't taken long before the straight S/M fans became regulars. Then came the bikers, the punks, and the rockers. It was only a matter of time before we'd be discovered by the world at large.

As the '80s began, Gauntlet was prospering, and I was feeling less stressed financially. A realtor friend named Nick was determined to get me into a house of my own and found a small, two-bedroom house on Friar Street in Van Nuys, one of the San Fernando Valley communities. It was a flat, little box of a house with a vaguely Spanish Mission flavor, terra-cotta tiles ornamenting the roofline, and priced to sell. I took possession in April of 1982. With minor repairs and remodeling and a coat of paint inside and out, the place became a cozy haven to retreat to after a busy day at the store.

Once the fear and panic of the AIDS epidemic set in, I realized that I would be wise to become even less promiscuous and consider settling down with one person. Off and on for many years, I had occasional flings with an old fuck buddy from Denver named Victor. The sex was intense, and we were very compatible in many ways, among other things sharing similar tastes in music and the arts. At the time it seemed like an ideal match. I proposed, he ac-

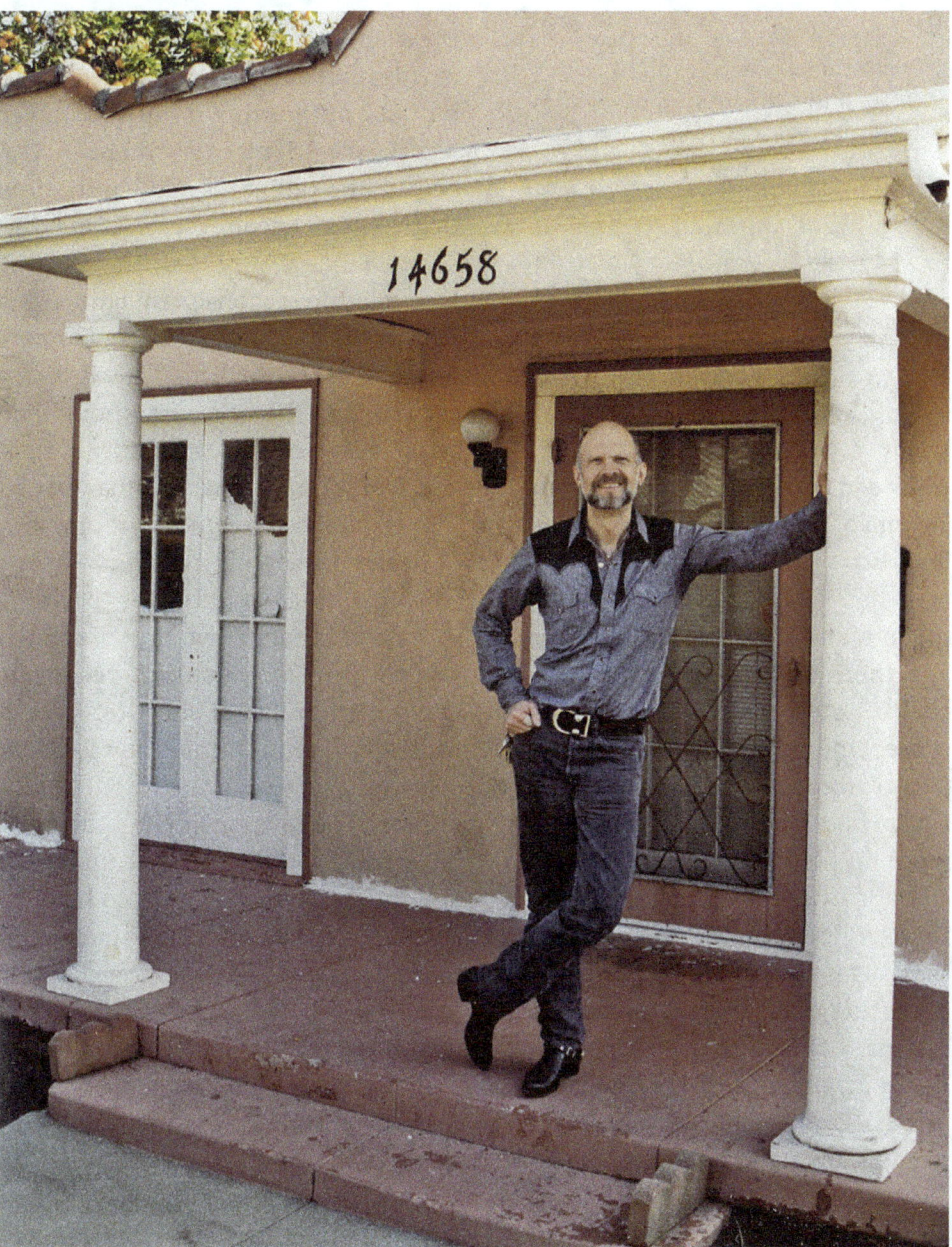

In front of my Van Nuys bungalow.

cepted and moved in with me.

By this time every gay person I knew was concerned about AIDS. People were beginning to die in earnest. Since I had never been as promiscuous as all the other guys I knew, I still thought it couldn't happen to me. When the HIV antibody test became available in 1985, Victor badgered me until I finally capitulated, and in January of 1986 agreed to take it. I was stunned when the results came back that he was negative, and I was positive. Even with the implication staring me in the face, I immediately went into denial, much

to Victor's chagrin. After all, my lab numbers were strong and my health was still good.

Though we were together for about five years, our relationship had been stormy from the start, and by 1988 the added stress of my HIV status had brought it to an end.

That same year, I met my current partner Drew, whose last name at the time was Nicholas. Drew pursued me. We laugh that if he'd done so any more fervently, he'd have qualified as a stalker. He came across a photo of

Drew and I made the leather gossip column of the *Bay Area Reporter*, San Francisco's gay newspaper.

me in an issue of *Drummer* magazine and there was an attraction that he couldn't put out of his mind. In order to meet me, he decided to have his nipples pierced, called the shop in West Hollywood, and made an appointment. In his enthusiasm, he failed to check if I would be working that day. He flew down to L.A. only to discover that, as fate would have it, I was doing a piercing clinic that weekend in San Francisco where he lived. Undeterred, he went ahead and had his nipples pierced. Over the next few months, he would show up at photographer Mark Chester's for piercing rituals or stop in at a piercing clinic, using it as an excuse to have me inspect his piercings to make sure they were healing properly, even though he knew they were.

In August we actually connected and had our first date. I was doing a clinic at Image Leather in the Castro area, San Francisco's gay ghetto. Drew hung around all day, catching me in between clients for a brief exchange of conversation. As my day came to an end, I asked if he would like to have dinner with me. Thrilled, he accepted and while I was finishing up, went back to his nearby apartment to dress.

A gay restaurant near the leather shop was giving a discount on dinner that night to guys wearing leather.

Drew showed up dressed in full "formal" leather but had managed to throw his back out putting on his boots. We went back to his apartment, and I helped him out of his boots into some that were more comfortable. Over dinner, he made it very clear that he was interested. In response, I told him I was HIV positive. His reply brought tears to my eyes. He told me that it didn't change how he felt, and though he wished it wasn't so, the reality wasn't a deal breaker. This began what turned into an intense slave/Master romance.

Over the following months, we spent as much time together as possible. Cards and letters went back and forth several times a week. We experimented with a number of short-term slave contracts, semi-formal agreements specifying how each of us would fulfill our role. The relationship rapidly escalated, and I decided to pull up stakes and move to San Francisco to be with Drew. I began making arrangements for the business, put the house up for sale, and scheduled the week following Christmas (1988) for my move.

As December approached, I wanted to do something that would symbolize a more solid commitment to Drew. As a sign of ownership, many slaves, both gay and straight, wear some kind of chain collar closed with a lock. Stainless steel chain may be impervious to water, but locks, I knew from experience, are vulnerable to rust and can clog up with crud. Drew and I liked the chain idea, but thought a heavy silver one that could be soldered closed would be more practical. Unfortunately, though I scoured the jewelry mart looking for it, I was unable to find anything ready-made that was as heavy as we wanted. The only option left was to make my own. Using thick sterling silver wire, I fashioned a chain long enough to be comfortable but too short to go over my head. I also made a silver "property tag" that I had engraved with a

glyph on the front that was meaningful to Drew. The back read, "Property of Master Drew Nicholas." Chuck Atmore, the husband of our jeweler Margie, soldered all the links save one and polished the chain. Arrangements were made for it to be soldered around my neck. Drew flew down, and one night the Atmores came to the house with the necessary equipment. The chain was secured around my neck and double-checked to make sure it wasn't twisted. After putting a cold, wet towel covered with aluminum foil between my neck and the chain, Chuck deftly and very carefully soldered the last link. All I felt was the towel and not so much as a hint of heat. Chuck polished the soldered joint, and it was done. The only way to remove the chain would be to cut it off. Thus was forged, quite literally, a special bond between my Master and myself.

Drew returned to L.A. to celebrate the holidays and help me finish packing everything. The plan was to rent a truck and load it. He would then drive the truck back to San Francisco, and I would follow in my station wagon.

Drew shared a three-bedroom apartment with a young gay man named Shawn. He was a genial fellow who made a comfortable living as a profes-

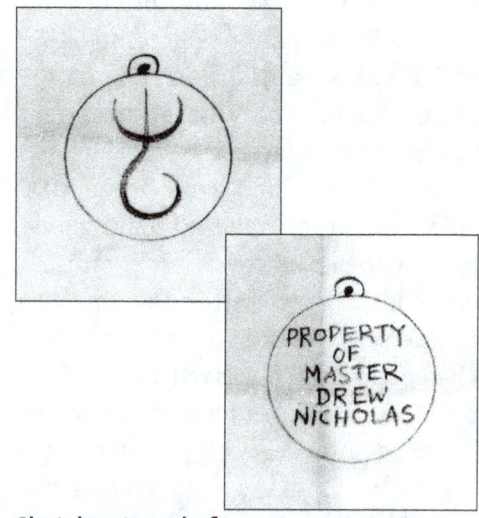

Sketches I made for my property tag. The glyph, Drew's personal symbol, represents a winged cobra.

sional "escort." He good-naturedly put up with boxes everywhere, even lining the halls, until I was finally able to make some order stacking most of my belongings in the third bedroom, recently vacated by a departing roommate.

Once things began to settle, Drew and I decided we wanted to have a bonding ritual not only to formalize our relationship, but also as a way for me to become more acquainted with the local Pagan and leather community. It evolved into an event on a sizable scale. For a venue, we rented a space on Shotwell Street where a number of the local S/M clubs held monthly play parties. We planned to have the ritual first, followed by cake and refreshments and a play party afterward. Those guests who weren't into S/M were anticipated to leave after the refreshments.

February first is a beautiful Pagan holiday called Imbolc or Brigid—spellings vary—in honor of the Celtic deity of that name. She is a goddess of healing, the hearth, and the forge. This seemed like a wonderful time for our celebration, but since the date fell in the middle of the week in 1989, we moved our rite to the following Saturday, February fourth.

As part of the ritual, we wanted to have a formal slave contract signing, and after consulting with several knowledgeable friends, were able to put together one with which Drew and I both felt comfortable. It wasn't too far removed from the "love, honor, and obey" that has often been a part of traditional weddings. The main difference is that it's in writing, and for Drew and me the oath is more "love, honor, and negotiate" with Drew getting the final word. Having our responsibilities to each other spelled out in this way is very liberating. It's a bit like ballroom dancing; one person may lead, but when both people know the steps, it's easier for them to move together gracefully and not step on each other's toes.

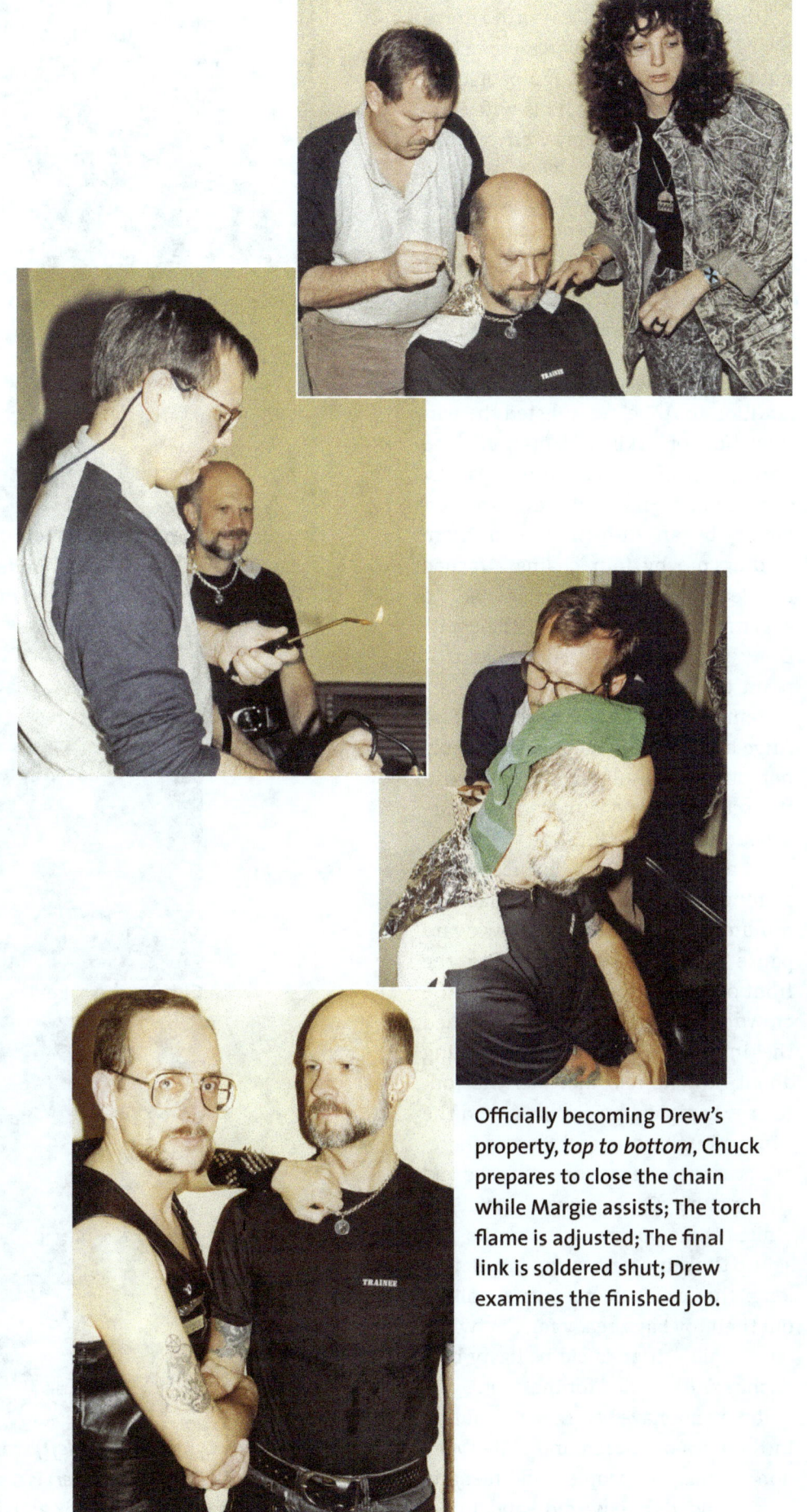

Officially becoming Drew's property, *top to bottom*, Chuck prepares to close the chain while Margie assists; The torch flame is adjusted; The final link is soldered shut; Drew examines the finished job.

I designed an invitation with a drawing of my property collar, and we sent out about 150 of them. 120 people, including my brother and his wife from Seattle, replied that they were coming.

For the ceremony itself, we still needed someone to officiate, and Drew called upon an old friend named Ange to act as High Priestess. An astrologer of Drew's acquaintance calculated an auspicious time—7:34 as it turned out—for the contract to be signed, and we planned the ritual accordingly. In addition to Ange, we enlisted the participation of Fakir and his girlfriend Carla (a.k.a. Cleo) and another Master/slave couple, Fred and Steve. The ceremony began with the four of them leading me by four chains attached to a leather collar around my neck to a platform in the front of the room. Drew and Ange awaited me. At that point, the ritual itself began.

Being the first sizable ceremony that Ange had led, she was understandably nervous. As a result, the stately pace of the script quickly launched into fast forward. Before we knew it, we had arrived at the point where the contract signing was supposed to take place... 15 minutes early. There was an awkward pause before Drew stepped to the front of the platform, explained to the crowd what had happened, and filled the intervening gap of time telling about how he had met me. The contract was signed on schedule, and the ritual brought to an end. Shortly thereafter came the reception with cake and champagne. Some guests socialized while others put away the chairs and set up the dungeon equipment. Before long, the kinky people were pulling out their toy bags, ready for play, while our "vanilla" friends bid us hasty best wishes and scurried for the door.

It may not have been a real wedding in the eyes of church and state, but I don't think two people could feel any more bonded than we did... and do.

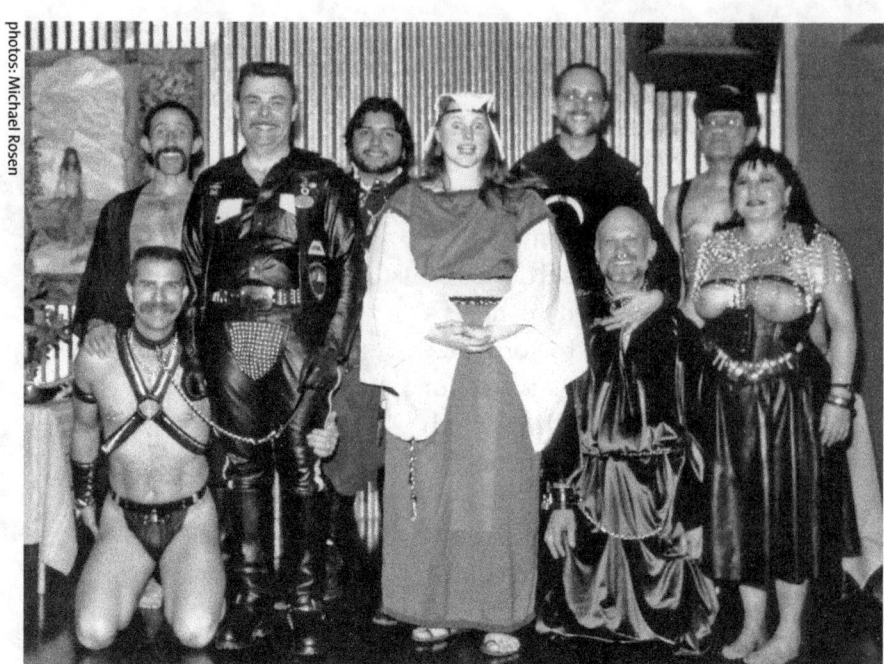

Bonding ritual participants, February 4, 1989. *Left to right, standing*: Gary a.k.a. "Ram" our High Priest, Fred, Tony, Ange the High Priestess, Drew, Fakir, Carla. *Kneeling*: Steve and myself.

Cutting the cake. The design is my property tag.

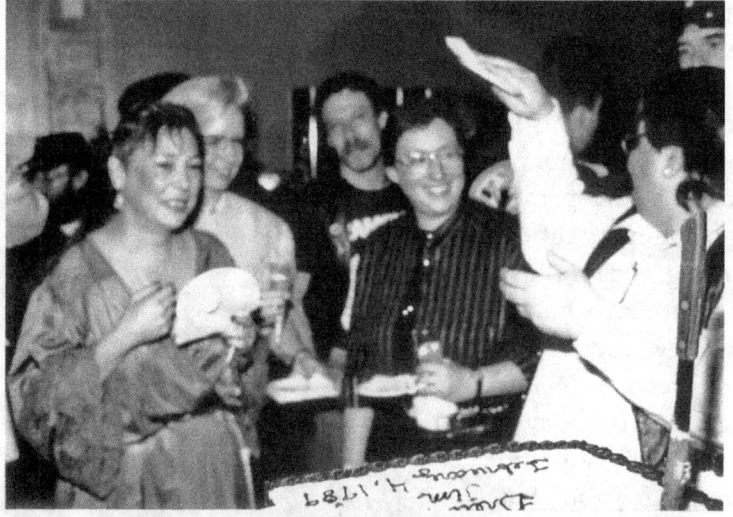

Guests socializing: Cynthia Slater (*left*) was co-founder of the Society of Janus. Gayle Rubin (*center*) is a social anthropologist, author, and prominent "pro-sex activist."

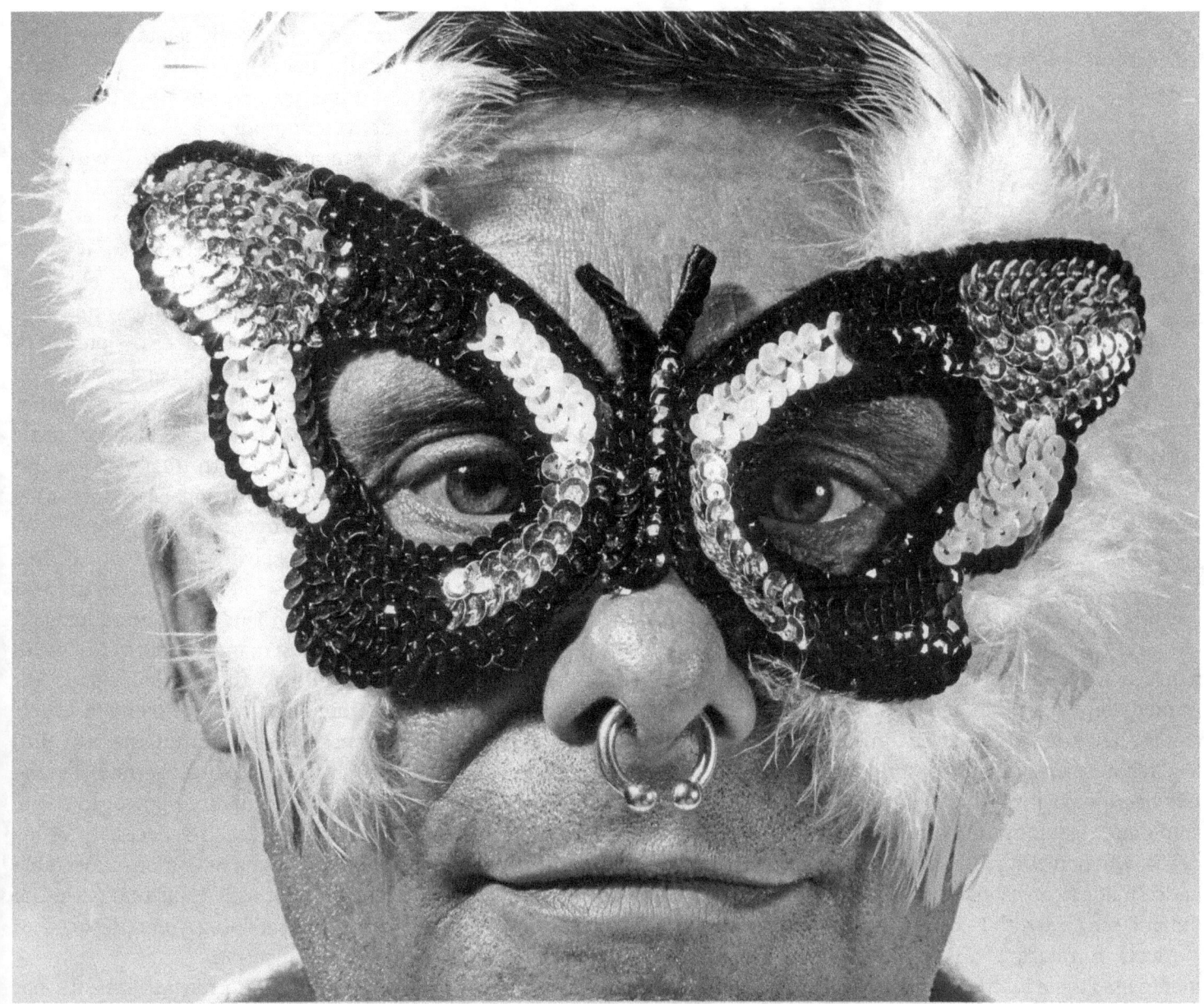

Cover photo of Fakir Musafar from his book *Body Play, the Self-Images of Roland Loomis, 1950-1980*

CHAPTER 11

Anyone who's gone through the acrimonious breakup of a marriage or long-term relationship knows how difficult it is to be objective when discussing his or her ex. Though we were never lovers, I find myself in a similar, awkward position regarding Fakir Musafar. We were very close for nearly 20 years when growing differences over core values and a mounting loss of mutual respect brought our friendship to a rather abrupt end. After little contact or communication for over 10 years, we recently reconnected through Facebook and have exchanged a few emails that have been cordial. We attended each other's presentations at the annual Association of Professional Piercers conference in 2010, where we each talked about our individual perspectives on the history of the modern body piercing movement.

Personal feelings aside, he has, in his own unique way, had a huge influence on many people, myself included. His guidance helped me find a direction and keep Gauntlet alive following Doug's untimely death.

Ours was, I think, a mutually beneficial friendship. He was a fount of information and experience and provided access to rare and unusual material to use in *PFIQ*, and in turn the magazine helped make him well known in body mod and kink circles and build a worldwide reputation. Gauntlet also provided him the opportunity to meet, interview, and photograph many of its more extraordinary pierced clients.

It was my friend Tom the librarian who first showed me pictures of and told me about the amazing Roland "Rolly" Loomis in the days before he, Roland, assumed the Fakir title. I met him early in my relationship with Doug, who invited him to come down

91

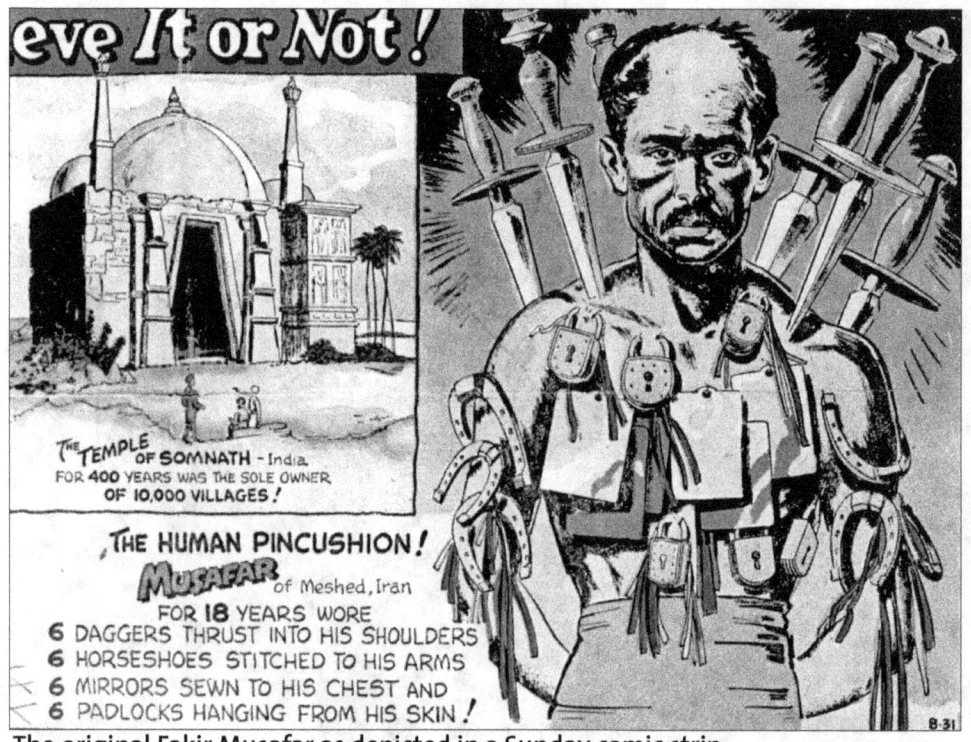

The original Fakir Musafar as depicted in a Sunday comic strip.

to L.A. so we could meet him. He didn't immediately warm to me and was distant and standoffish, later confessing his first impression of me had not been a positive one. Our friendship didn't blossom until after Doug's death, when, feeling lost and at loose ends, I made a conscious effort to reach out and connect with Fakir.

Much of Fakir's life is well documented,[1] so there is little point in reiterating it here. He was born Roland Loomis in Aberdeen, South Dakota on August 10, 1930. At an early age, he began doing extraordinary things with his body and has been doing them ever since.

"A fakir or faqir is a Sufi, especially one who performs feats of endurance...." That's one definition. The fakir is not unlike the East Indian sadhu. Both are ascetics who are known for their feats of extreme body mortification and modification. There are countless examples including hanging from flesh hooks, lying on a bed of nails, wearing weights of some sort sewn onto ones skin, and carrying a cage-like apparatus called a Kavandi or Kavadi through which spears pierce into

the flesh. Fakir has done all of these and more. He discovered his namesake in the "Ripley's Believe It or Not" strip in an old Sunday comics. According to it, the original Fakir Musafar was from Persia circa 1800 and for 18 years wore six daggers thrust into his shoulders, six horseshoes stitched to his arms, six mirrors sewn to his chest, and six padlocks hanging from his skin.

According to what I have read, the reason fakirs and sadhus perform all these rigorous rites and attempt to subjugate the body, especially the sexual desires, is to attain liberation from the necessity of reincarnating. I don't recall this ever being the goal of modern Fakir. Even his experiments in chastity seem to have been more about erotic bondage than stamping out sexual appetite.

As long as I have known him, Fakir's primary interest has been in promoting his own brand of shamanism, and his focus has been on body modification as rites of passage and a means of attaining altered states of consciousness. I have utmost respect for his approach, but since we parted ways my

own spiritual path has taken a different direction.

It has been known since the discovery of endorphins and similar neurochemicals in the 1970s that when the body is in pain—as happens with a body modification or when stressed as occurs in some extreme sports—the brain secretes natural drugs that can produce profound ecstatic states. This raises the question: does the pursuit of such pain or stress have any spiritual value, or is it just the quest for another drug high? Greater minds than mine have wrestled with this question and failed to reach a conclusion. I certainly don't have an answer.

Fakir has always had, to one degree or another, a following within the S/M community. This is easily understood considering many people in the scene comprehend the pleasure/pain dichotomy and the transcendence that intense physical stimulation can produce. As far as I'm concerned, if some get off on pain, more power to them. I just fail to see the necessity of attempting to make it more acceptable by turning it into a spiritual path. The same goes for doing a piercing or other body modification.

Here in California at least, it's not uncommon in Asian restaurants to see a small altar tucked away in some out-of-the-way corner. The proprietors make no issue of their spiritual or religious affiliations. From my perspective, that is as it should be, whether you're serving food or offering piercing services. During my Gauntlet years, I occasionally had clients who wanted to have their piercing done in some kind of ritual setting. I was always happy to oblige, but I required that they make an appointment for after hours.

The Fakir Musafar persona made his public debut in 1977 at the International Tattoo Artist's Association (ITAA) convention in Reno. Doug encouraged the then-named Roland Loomis to perform some of his feats as entertainment and suggested that he come up with a stage name. Roland took the name of his alter ego, and thus Fakir Musafar was born. His performance that evening included laying on a bed of nails and a rack of knives, various contortions, and all manner of carnival sideshow fodder. Earlier in the evening, there had been a performance by a heavily tattooed belly dancer. As a grand finale, Fakir pulled the dancer through the room on a hotel luggage cart attached to hooks in his chest piercings.

Over time, Roland Loomis seems to have been supplanted by the Fakir Musafar persona. By chance I stumbled upon something he wrote in *PFIQ* issue #8 (1980) that seems to explain what happened. "We, the 'Modern Primitives' find ourselves coping with dual and sometimes triple identities, living several lives at the same time, very seldom letting all the identities merge into one at the same time. We instinctively know the confusion that would cause—both to ourselves and to others. Sometimes, however, the 'primitive self' gets the upper hand and becomes so strong IT emerges as the primary self! Then the atavistic personality must either live in semi-seclusion (like Ethel Granger), or come out in defiance of prevailing customs (like Star in *PFIQ* issue #5 or Omi the Great, a carnival attraction of the 1950s in England)."

I learned a great deal from Fakir, especially about rites of passage and shamanism and their connection with body modification. Those rituals a society uses to mark the milestones in its members' lives have been common, especially in tribal groups, for millennia. Unfortunately, in American and Western European culture, such rites, at least the formal ones and especially those involving some form of body modification, are rapidly succumbing to the onslaught of modern "civiliza-

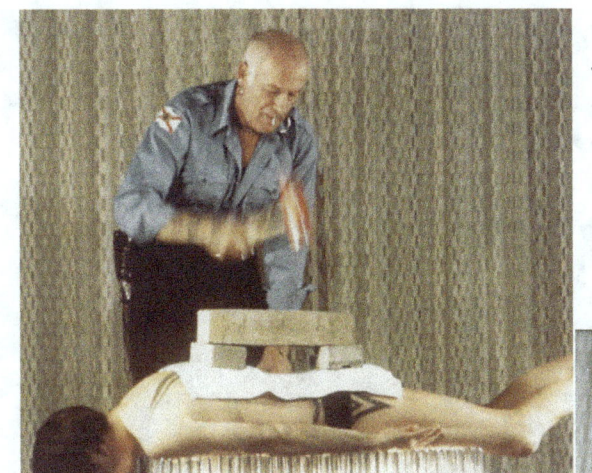

Photos taken by Doug Malloy of the entertainment at the Reno ITAA tattoo convention in 1977 where Fakir made his public debut. *Left*, Fakir lies on a bed of nails while Sailor Sid hammers a wooden block on his back.

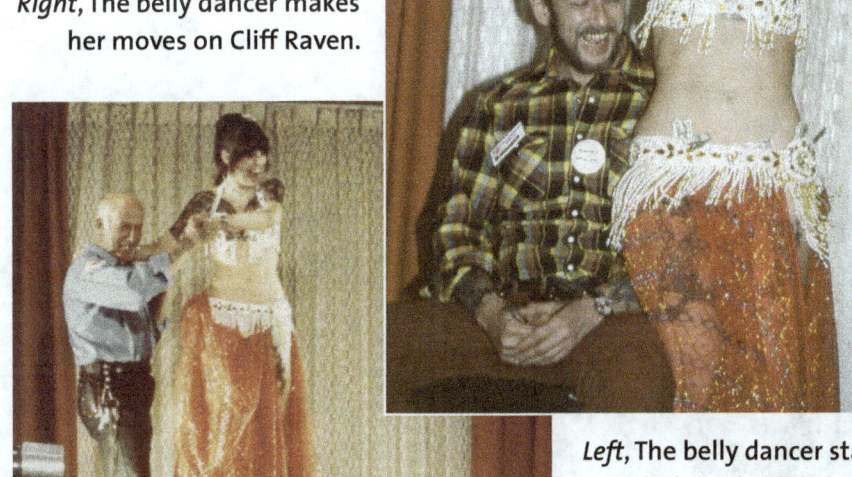

Right, The belly dancer makes her moves on Cliff Raven.

Left, The belly dancer stands on Fakir's back while he lies on swords.

Above, For the finale, Fakir tows the belly dancer from the room on a luggage cart attached to the deep piercings in his chest.

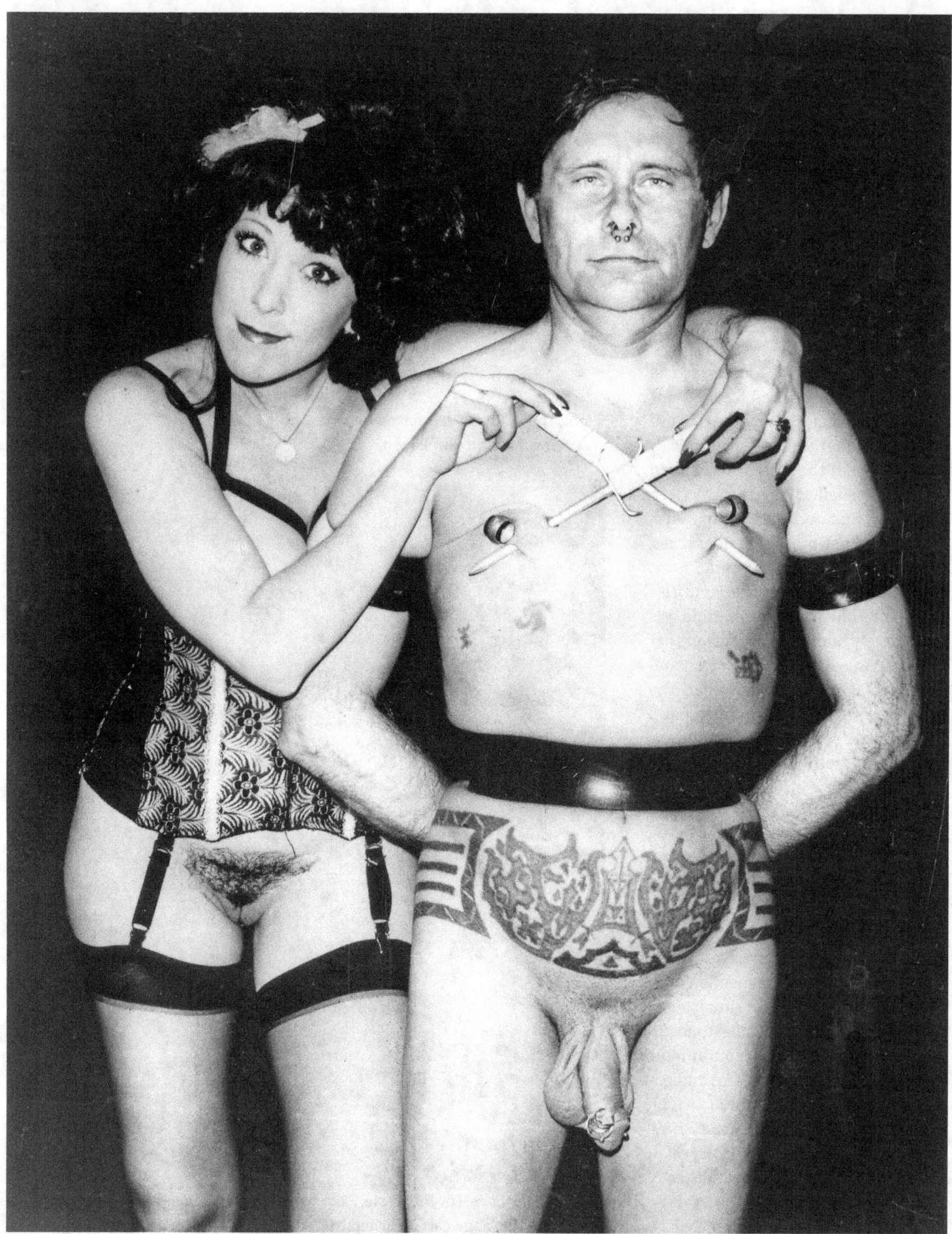

94

tion" and vanishing even in the tribal cultures, their last stronghold.

But rites of passage are an essential part of the human experience, and no matter how latent or unconscious, some part of our psyche craves them. All too often, if the society does not provide for them, the individual will find some way of fulfilling the urge, not always in a healthy or constructive way.

One of the most potent transitions in life is the one from child to adult. Where no rites to mark these transitions are provided, many people create or seek out their own, often unconsciously. How many young men of my generation joined the military, and/or got drunk with their buddies one night, and then on a dare decided to get a tattoo? Even if they awakened the next morning with a hangover and an ugly tattoo, there was no longer a question in their minds that they were now men.

When the impulse is thwarted, the scenario can be less benign. It frequently manifests in acts of vandalism and violence, the defacing or destroying of property or, even worse, attacking and beating up someone considered somehow inferior. Thankfully, the popularity and widespread acceptance of most body modifications over the last couple of decades have made it possible for both men and women, regardless of age, to mark the important transitions in their lives without resorting to violence.

But make no mistake, rites of passage that involve no pain tend to be less potent than those that do, and the indelible, visible alteration to the body becomes a badge of honor that unmistakably proclaims that the individual has passed a milestone in his or her life.

Another thing I learned from Fakir

Opposite, Annie Sprinkle with Fakir as photographed by Charles Gatewood for his book *Forbidden Photographs*

is that those who perform body modifications, whether they're aware of it or not, are functioning as shamans within society, overseeing important rites of passage for their clients. For the most part, I would agree. Even today whenever I perform a piercing, I still approach it with the same shamanic reverence and respect. But I always keep in mind that these experiences are not about me. They're about the other person, and it isn't up to me to determine what is right for them. My job is to follow their lead and never to intrude. The piercer is first, foremost, and always a professional in the eyes of the client. That doesn't mean that my place is to be at the mercy of their whims. Once I've determined that the person sincerely wants the piercing, it's my responsibility to usher them through the experience even if that means taking a firm hand.

Long before the endless deluge of email spam selling the impossible dream of greater endowment, Fakir experimented with elongating his own penis. He asserted that simply by stretching and by starting young, East Indian sadhu boys were able to achieve such length that their penises would no longer function sexually. Others have, in fact, corroborated his claim. Although Fakir spent a great deal of time with a weight hanging from his dick, I'm not aware of any significant increase in length. Maybe he just didn't start young enough.

His quest for the world's longest trouser snake had its interesting moments. At one point, he was in communication with a Dr. Brown, a Mexican doctor who claimed he could help. The suspensory ligament that holds the erect penis away from the body supposedly also keeps it from being stretchable. The doctor volunteered to surgically sever the ligament, and Fakir even considered it but ultimately (and wisely, in my opinion) decided against it..

Over the years that we were friends, I flew to the Bay Area on a regular basis to spend a few days training with Fakir, sometimes working on *PFIQ* or a new jewelry brochure, sometimes participating in what he called "body play" and simply being an apprentice shaman. Though we were never actually lovers—he indicated a preference for women at the time—our play sessions were very erotic with an unspoken sexual charge that smoldered just below the surface. I learned to lie on a bed of nails and in doing so drifted off into a kind of euphoria. To introduce me to sensory deprivation, Fakir strapped me blindfolded and with earplugs to a "witch's cradle," a kind of platform that could be rotated. At intervals he would rotate me to a different position. The disorientation, along with the restriction of movement, vision, and hearing is supposed to stimulate an out-of-body experience, though in my case it never succeeded.

Perhaps the most intimate thing Fakir and I ever did together was Sun Dancing in the summer of 1982. Dan and Mark Jury, two documentary filmmakers from the East Coast, initiated the project. Their original plan had been to make a film about anthropologist and gonzo photographer Charles Gatewood, well-known for his images of weird and unusual people in sometimes bizarre surroundings. During their research and preparation, they were introduced to Fakir who quickly stole the show. The Jurys wanted to shoot Fakir doing something impressive, and the plan quickly evolved for him to do two forms of the Sun Dance. I agreed to participate in one and assist in the other. The first, ripping flesh, would involve inserting a metal pin through a chest piercing, the pin then being tied securely to a rope attached to a cottonwood tree. After that, we would keep pulling back on the pierc-

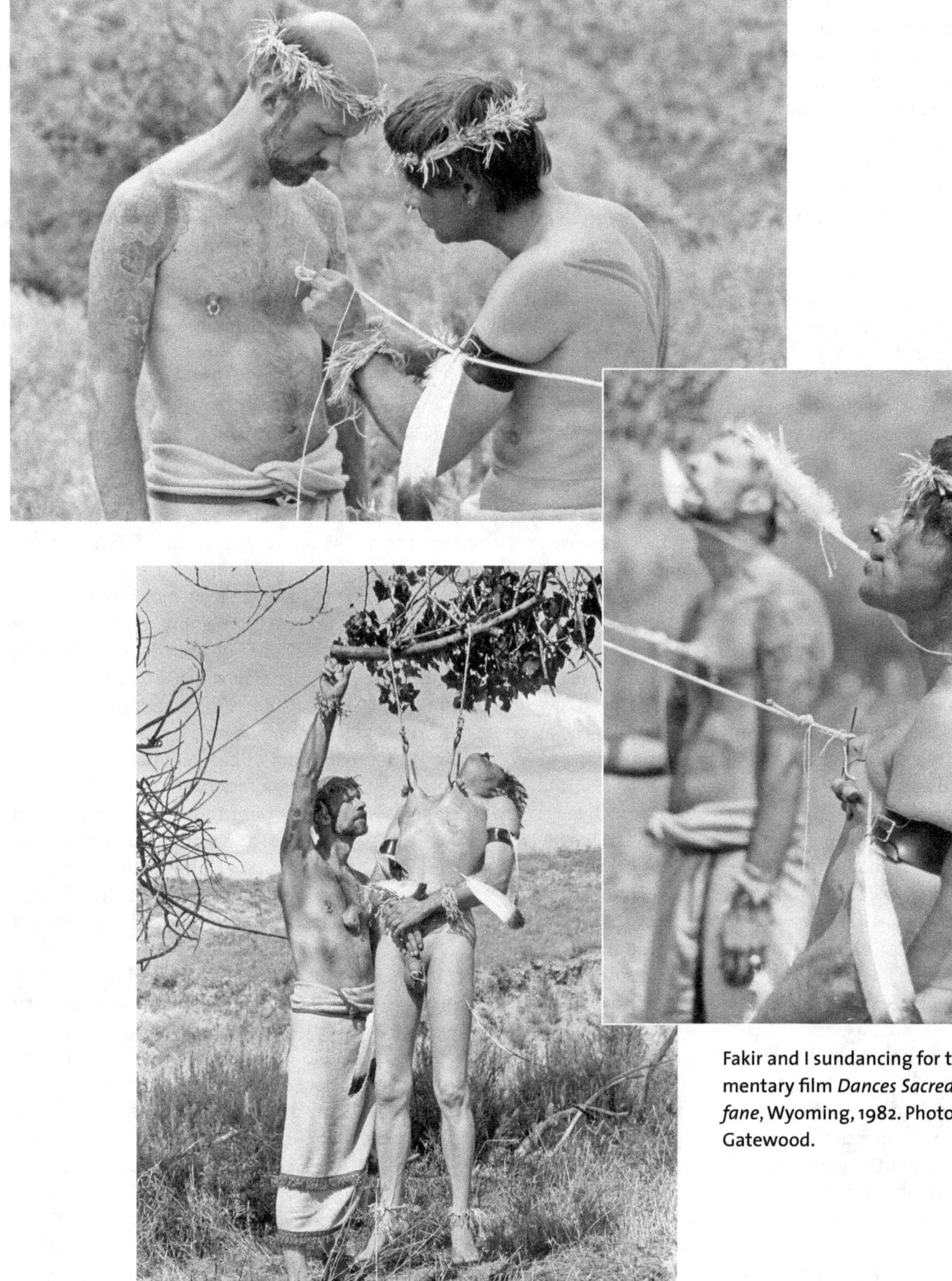

Fakir and I sundancing for the documentary film *Dances Sacred and Profane*, Wyoming, 1982. Photos by Charles Gatewood.

ing until the skin finally gave way and we broke free.

For the second Sun Dance, Fakir would hang from the tree by hooks through his deep chest piercings. I was to assist by gradually twisting an overhead rope until he was completely suspended above the ground. This form of Sun Dance had been seen in the 1970 film *A Man Called Horse* starring Richard Harris.

Fakir drove to Wyoming several days in advance to scout a location. This proved to be a challenge, for much of the state land had been leased to ranchers and was fenced off and private. Eventually he found what he thought would be a suitable spot.

The film crew, Charles Gatewood, and I arrived on July 5 at Rapid City airport. The following morning, we packed rented vehicles and headed for Devil's Tower to mentally and energetically prepare for the coming day. Afterward, we headed for the location Fakir had scouted out previously. Unfortunately, a ranch foreman with a yellow pickup truck, two dogs, and a shotgun ran us off before we could make camp. What to do?

The following morning, Mark started making frantic phone calls and eventually found a promising location in Little Thunder Basin National Grasslands near the Montana border. We packed up and set out hoping for the best. After too many false starts, heading down some dusty gravel road only to be confronted with yet more fences, we finally decided to leave the road and take our chances out in the barren terrain. Fortune smiled on us, and not too far away Fakir spotted the type of location he had envisioned, a deep gulch with a flat, dry riverbed surrounded by cottonwood trees and patches of sage. We pitched our tents and prepared for the following day.

Dawn came, cloudy and gray with the threat of rain. Although the situation appeared less than promising, Fakir and I began our preparations

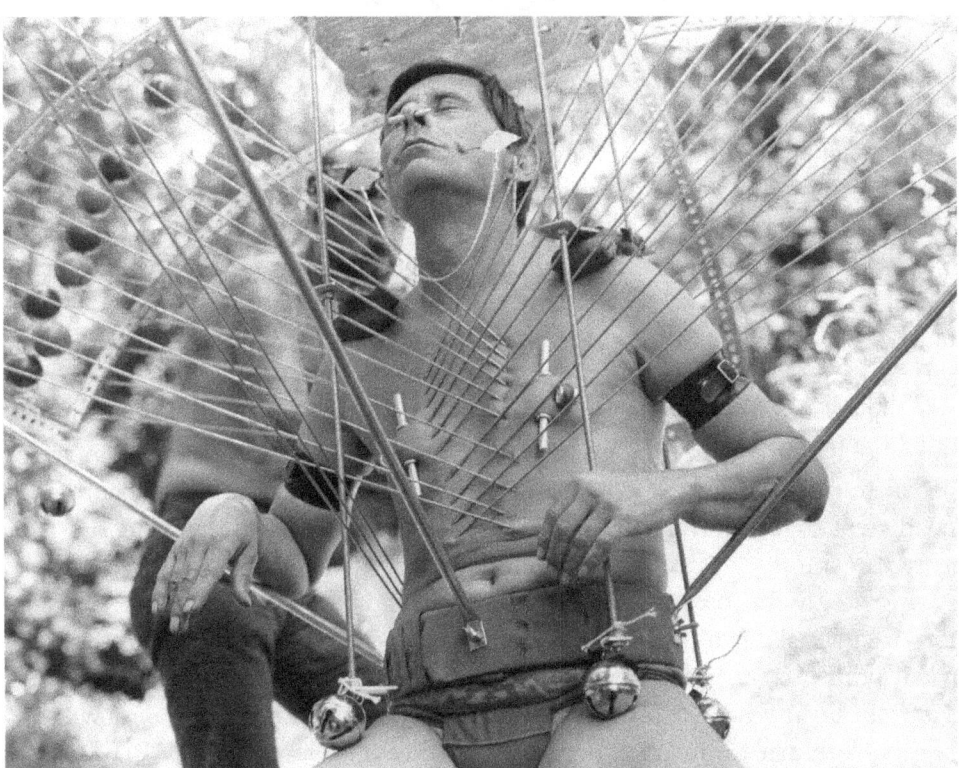

Rigging Fakir into the cage-like Kavandi for a ritual, Valhalla Ranch, California, 1983

and the film crew moved their equipment into position. Charles kept circling, documenting everything with still photos, many of which appeared in *PFIQ* issue #16. By noon, everything was in place, but the sun had yet to make an appearance. There's something incongruous about having a Sun Dance with no sun. But Fakir was undeterred. After donning our ceremonial garb, he headed for a nearby bluff, and I followed. We were going to attempt to make the sun shine.

This was an entirely new experience for me. I'd never participated in anything quite like it before, but with a little direction from Fakir I began making a wide circle, stopping at each of the four quarters to call upon the elements, the spirits, the deities of the place, and the sun itself to favor us with its presence. Thus began my connection with the Pagan path. After about half an hour, the clouds parted, and we were bathed in solar radiance. With thanks in our hearts, we returned to the site to begin the first ritual.

We spread a blanket on the ground

and took turns piercing each other's chest, inserting a metal pin. The ropes we had earlier strung to a nearby tree were then attached, and we were ready to begin. Cautiously and gingerly at first, we began to pull against the piercings, gradually becoming more insistent as the hours passed. Few people realize just how tough skin really is.

By late afternoon, there was no sign that we were going to break free any time soon, and we still had the second Sun Dance to perform. The filmmakers had been shooting almost continuously, and their stock of film was starting to run low. Left to run its course, who knew how much longer it would take for our skin to finally give way, and this was something the Jurys definitely wanted to capture.

Fakir and I took a break. We realized that the only way we could be certain to tear free soon was to intervene. Fakir took a razor blade and carefully cut the skin on both our chests, weakening it so that when we returned to our dancing, a few good tugs against the piercings and we were free.

The sun was nearing the Western horizon when we finally began the second dance. Fakir had prepared the tree earlier, throwing a rope over a limb and attaching it a foot or so above our heads to the ends of a short piece of branch. From this were suspended the metal hooks from which he would hang. From one end of the branch was attached a cord. Once he had inserted the hooks into his chest piercings, I took hold of the dangling cord and began to circle. As the rope above his head twisted, Fakir was slowly lifted from the ground. Once airborne he swung gently for 10 or 15 minutes before finally asking to be lowered. We gave thanks to the spirits and beings that had been with us, and gradually began to return to awareness of the world around us. The rites were over.

We packed up everything and headed back to what passes for civilization in this part of the country: a hotel, a warm shower, and food—not very good unfortunately, but food nonetheless—with a glass of expensive wine provided by the Jury brothers.

Over dinner that night, the subject of a film title came up. I suggested that it would be nice to somehow reflect the contrasts in the material that ran the gamut from the raucous raunchiness of nudist camps, S/M parties, and Mardi Gras to the subdued reverence of our Sun Dances. What immediately came to me was the title of a famous piece of music by Debussy for harp and strings called *Danses Sacrée et Profane* (*Dances Sacred and Profane*). Mark got what I was suggesting and liked the name. It stuck, at least for the film's initial release. When Mark started editing the film he even considered using that particular music as background before settling on something better tailored to the film and without the licensing issues.

Unfortunately *Dances*, has led at best half a life. It took several years for Mark to get financing in order and complete the editing of the film. It debuted at the Brussels Film Festival in the summer of 1985. Fakir and I attended the U.S. premiere at the Roxie Theater in San Francisco on May 30, 1986. Though it played in a number of cities, it quickly disappeared. *The New York Times* gave it a lukewarm review and dismissed it by saying, "It should appeal to people who like seeing a man twisting slowly in the wind." Gorgon Video, known for "extreme horror and 'dark documentaries,'" released the film on video in 1987 with the title *Bizarre Rituals*.

In 2005, after being out of contact for many years, I received an unexpected phone call from Mark Jury. He was once again in control of the film and with his son was re-releasing it on DVD under its original title. Mark sent me a copy, and I heard nothing further. When I attempted to contact him via email, the address was no longer valid. In 2010 Fakir sent me an email that he had purchased and was selling the last 400 copies of the DVD. When they're gone, will that be the end? Only time will tell.

After the original release of the film, Fakir got some flak from Native American groups who thought we were usurping their rituals. This seems like so many sour grapes to me. We never claimed that what we were doing was authentic. We had no sweat lodge and only minimal fasting in preparation. No matter how much study was done beforehand, there was no way we could reenact these rituals the way they were traditionally done. They are not part of our culture. I'm not entirely sure many Native Americans, particularly in 1982, could have done them the way their ancestors had either. Our rites were in the spirit of the originals, and we would never pretend that they were anything else. Interestingly, in the last decade or so the phenomenon of suspension or hanging from flesh hooks is being followed by a dedicated group of devotees all over the world. If any of them have been criticized for infringement of someone's spiritual tradition, I'm not aware of it.

I've been asked if I had any kind of altered state from doing the Sun Dance, and in all honesty I had to say no. I don't regret doing it, and felt that it established a special bond between Fakir and myself. It felt like a testing of my mettle. I had faced the challenge and emerged somehow transformed, though in what way, it would be difficult to say. I did come away from the experience with a sense of not being quite fulfilled. As time passed my interest in doing these types of rituals began to wane, though at first I didn't quite realize it.

In the fall of 1988 Fakir and I and eight others converged on Valhalla Ranch in Northern California for a weekend of what he described as "group body rites, blood rituals, and ecstasy through piercing." A professional photographer/friend from San Francisco named Michael Rosen documented everything on film, and photos subsequently appeared in *PFIQ* issue #32. Fakir and a friend who called himself Brad did the "ripping flesh" type of Sun Dance. Fakir and a woman named Sharon took turns in the Kavandi, a metal framework through which sharp, thin spears are inserted about a quarter inch into the skin. They then danced and whirled down the hill while a group of us chanted and played drums and other instruments, every movement making the spears pierce deeper and triggering out-of-body experiences. The largest group ritual—the only one in which I was a participant—was a ball dance in which balls and apples were sewn to the chest and back of participants who then danced in much the same way as the Kavandi bearers had done previously. Through all of this, Fakir and I took turns doing the many piercings.

This was the last large-scale ritual during which I was pierced myself. Those who were involved wrote short descriptions of their experiences that weekend for *PFIQ*. At the end of mine I wrote, "I've yet to have an out-of-body experience. The kind of ecstasy others report and describe has somehow eluded me. But I have tested my mettle and come to know and understand myself on a deeper level." Though I didn't realize it at the time, my spiritual journey was ready to take me in another direction.

Perhaps it was the experience of standing that morning on a Wyoming bluff invoking the Sun or the turmoil brewing around me over the next few years, but something inside me seemed to be shifting. I became disgusted with Christianity: all the talk of love by some of the most hateful people imaginable. Televangelists discovered it was highly profitable to demonize gays and lesbians, and politicians used the same scare tactic to frighten people into voting for them. People like Jerry Falwell had the audacity to claim, "AIDS is not just God's punishment for homosexuals; it is God's punishment for the society that tolerates homosexuals." In the wake of the epidemic, it wasn't uncommon for Christian parents to abandon their dying gay sons, but they could hardly wait to lay claim to the estate that often by rights should have gone to a surviving partner.

The religion's obsession with torture, blood, and suffering are sickening. There is a hymn I remember from my childhood that opens with these lines: "There is a fountain filled with blood drawn from Emmanuel's veins; And sinners plunged beneath that flood lose all their guilty stains..." Yuck!

By 1985 I could no longer stomach the grotesque charade that is the Christian religion. This set me on my journey down the Pagan path. Early one morning in that twilight state between awake and asleep, the words "I want to be a witch" sprang into my consciousness. I've no idea where the prompting came from, but I felt strongly compelled to pursue it.

At the time there was a metaphysical shop in Hollywood called the House of Hermetic. A visit there proved quite worthwhile. Though the clerk was a bit pretentious, he at least steered me toward a couple of well-written, informative books that presented the Wiccan religion in a sensible, non-sensational light. I also noticed and purchased a copy of *Circle Network News*, a newspaper for Pagans, and through the classified ads subsequently made contact with a local coven calling themselves Mooncircle. In 1986 I was initiated into the coven, and over two decades later several of the women are still as close as family.

By the late Eighties I was coming into my own. Gauntlet was growing and I was developing a following. I was coming up from L.A. on a fairly regular basis to do piercing clinics in the Bay Area. On occasion there would be piercing rituals held in the apartment of San Francisco photographer Mark Chester. We would create a sacred space, and Fakir and I would pierce people in a ceremonial way with the nurturing and support of the group. Frequently 25 or more people would show up.

Back in Gauntlet's early days, when I was somewhat paranoid about government interference with my fledgling business, someone suggested I look into starting a church. Because of the U.S. Constitution, authorities tend to be reluctant to meddle with any sincere religious organization that meets at least certain minimal standards. The notorious Universal Life Church (ULC) had established its legitimacy and fought and won the legal battle over its right not only to call itself a church, but also to offer ordination to anyone who applied. For a while I contemplated a "church of piercing" where that would be our central rite. What would it take to make it a real, legitimate organization? As one step in the process I applied for and received my ULC ordination.

The church of piercing[2] came to naught, but I still have my ministerial credential and have actually used it once—to marry Fakir and his girlfriend Carla, a.k.a. Cleo. In mid-August 1990, many mutual friends gathered at Orr Hot Springs near Ukiah in Northern California for their wedding. On August 18, in a large, Pagan circle at nearby Montgomery Woods, they became husband and wife, myself officiating.

Once I relocated to the Bay Area my relationship with Fakir became increasingly strained, and by 1993, we had gone our separate ways. Part of me expired when that happened. While I personally take full responsibility for Gauntlet's demise, it was the end of my friendship with Fakir that set in motion the actions on my part that ultimately lead to the business's undoing. I felt so angry, hurt, and betrayed at the time that I didn't fully realize just how much the friendship had meant to me. As a result, I simply withdrew. It was as if something inside closed down and died. If Fakir's behavior was any reflection of his spirituality, I wanted no part of it. I was repulsed by the very thought of participating in piercing rituals and body play as I'd once done with Fakir. My business and spiritual lives became more separate, and for a number of years my interaction with other Pagans was minimal. Fakir had accused me of being in business only for the money. Was he right? Though I certainly enjoyed the income, it never felt like that was my motivation. Ultimately it didn't matter anyway, for within a few short years Gauntlet would be history.

Back in the late 1960s, I had developed a fascination with the western mystery tradition[3] but was unable to pursue it at the time. In 2001 that dream finally became a reality when the opportunity presented itself to join a local Golden Dawn Lodge.[4] That affiliation has provided a source of spiritual satisfaction that very much resonates with my heart.

Fakir and I have reestablished communication, exchanging the occasional email. Relations have been cordial and respectful, and he has graciously given his blessing to inclusion of some of his photos in this book. We've discussed the possibility of having lunch together sometime. What the future holds remains to be seen.

I've had a lot of time to contemplate what I call "the path of the body," the form of spirituality followed by Fakir and many others for whom body modification is a way of life. For the sake of argument one needs to begin from the assumption that every spiritual way is equally valid; however, in my opinion the path of the body has one large and treacherous pitfall: ego. So many people have fallen victim. "I have more piercings than anyone I know." "I set a record hanging from flesh hooks." "I've invented this new piercing that will revolutionize the industry and make me famous." It never ends. Needlesticks are perhaps the greatest occupational hazard to people in the industry. I would place ego second,

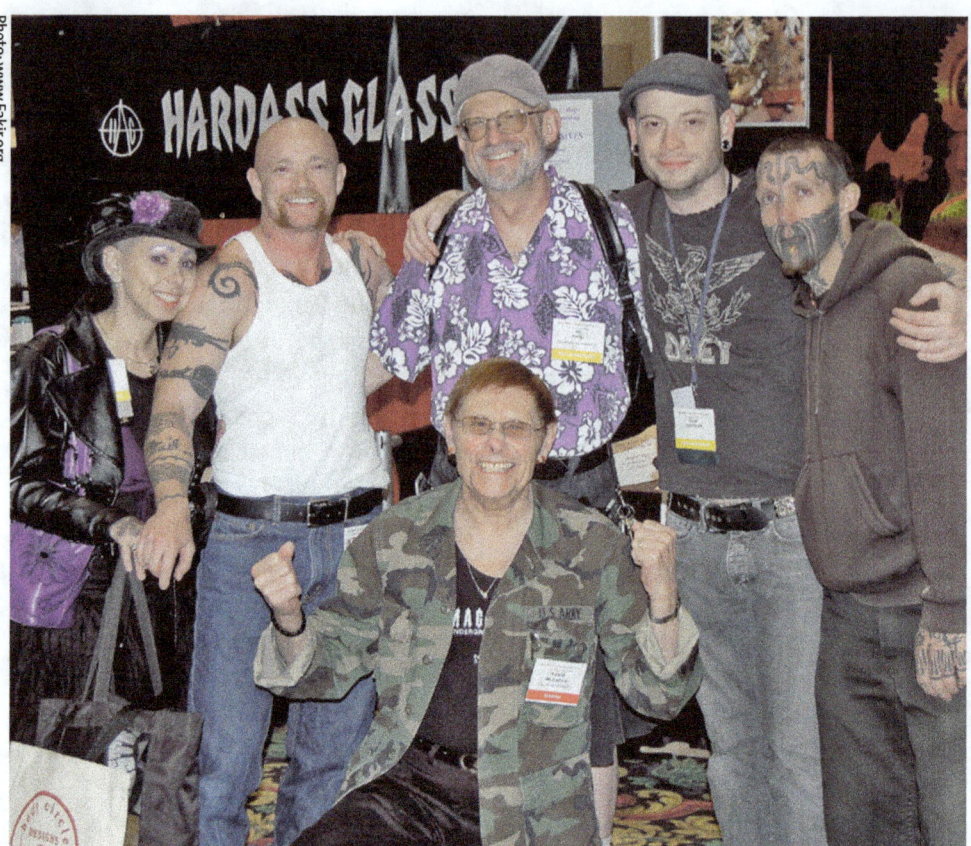

Reunion at the APP conference in 2008. *Back row, left to right*, Elayne Angel, Buck Angel, me, Sean Christian, Kristian White. *Kneeling*, Fakir Musafar.

the greatest trap for anyone on this particular road to realization.

A word of advice: don't take yourself too seriously. Also, every once in a while spend a few hours in a cemetery. Look at the headstones, especially those dating back 50 years or longer. Ask yourself how many of these people are remembered by anyone alive today. How likely are you to be remembered half a century after you're dead?

Andy Warhol once quipped, "In the future, everyone will be world-famous for 15 minutes." I've been fortunate to have enjoyed more time in the limelight than that, but despite my accomplishments, a hundred years hence I'll be lucky to be more than a footnote in a book or a handful of bytes in some obscure computer archive.

---

[1]If you want to know more, get a copy of the book *Modern Primitives* or see *Fakir Musafar: Spirit + Flesh* co-authored with Mark Thompson, or see *Body Play* magazine (http://www.bodyplay.com/bodyplay/index.htm).

[2]There is now a Church of Body Modification (http://uscobm.com/).

[3]Sam Webster, who founded the Lodge to which I belong (http://osogd.org) says, "The western magickal [or mystery] tradition was created by Christians appropriating the spiritual technology, both practical and evolutionary, of the pre-Christian Classical cultures. It had to be given a cover for respectability or simply hidden because the practices were those of the forbidden religions, and punishable by death. Now those same technologies are being reappropriated by those who have abandoned Christianity and redeployed for both practical purposes and for spiritual development. These people are generally called Pagan."

[4]Sam Webster defines the Golden Dawn, which originated in Britain in the late 1800s, as "Freemasonry with women and Qabalah," a westernized form of the Jewish mystical tradition. In our Lodge, we have stripped away the Judeo-Christian veneer from the original Golden Dawn system, exposing its Pagan underpinnings, and have incorporated elements of Tibetan Buddhism and Aleister Crowley's Thelema.

CHAPTER 12

Once I'd made the decision to move to San Francisco to be with Drew, I faced the dilemma of what to do about the L.A. store. The most obvious solution was to hire and train a manager. One of the applicants was a man named Tom. I must confess I was particularly taken with him for a very stupid reason: he reminded me of me. Somehow it felt as if I would be cloning myself, but it turned out we were similar only superficially. His hair was reddish rather than brown, but he could easily have passed as my brother. Not only did we look much alike, but also our speech patterns were similar, and we moved and gestured much the same. I know I can be a bit of a cranky curmudgeon and saw that mirrored in Tom, but I underestimated how much rage seethed just below the surface. The man had serious anger issues.

Tom's term of employment began before I left for San Francisco and ended soon after. To prepare for the job, he was given an intensive course of piercer training. He appeared to already possess most of the management skills. Once I relocated to the Bay Area I would travel down to L.A. frequently to check on things and see how he was doing—unfortunately, not as well as I had hoped. "Princess Tom the Hysterical," as Drew took to calling him, had a very short fuse, and when something ticked him off, he would stomp out of the store in a rage. After this had happened one time too many, I refused to let him return.

Crystal Cross,[1] a young lesbian who worked in our manufacturing department replaced Tom. She persuaded me to let her assume the managerial duties. Unfortunately, this was not a happy match either. At the time, Crystal had her own anger issues and seemed to have a perpetual chip on her shoulder. Diplomacy and tact, so nec-

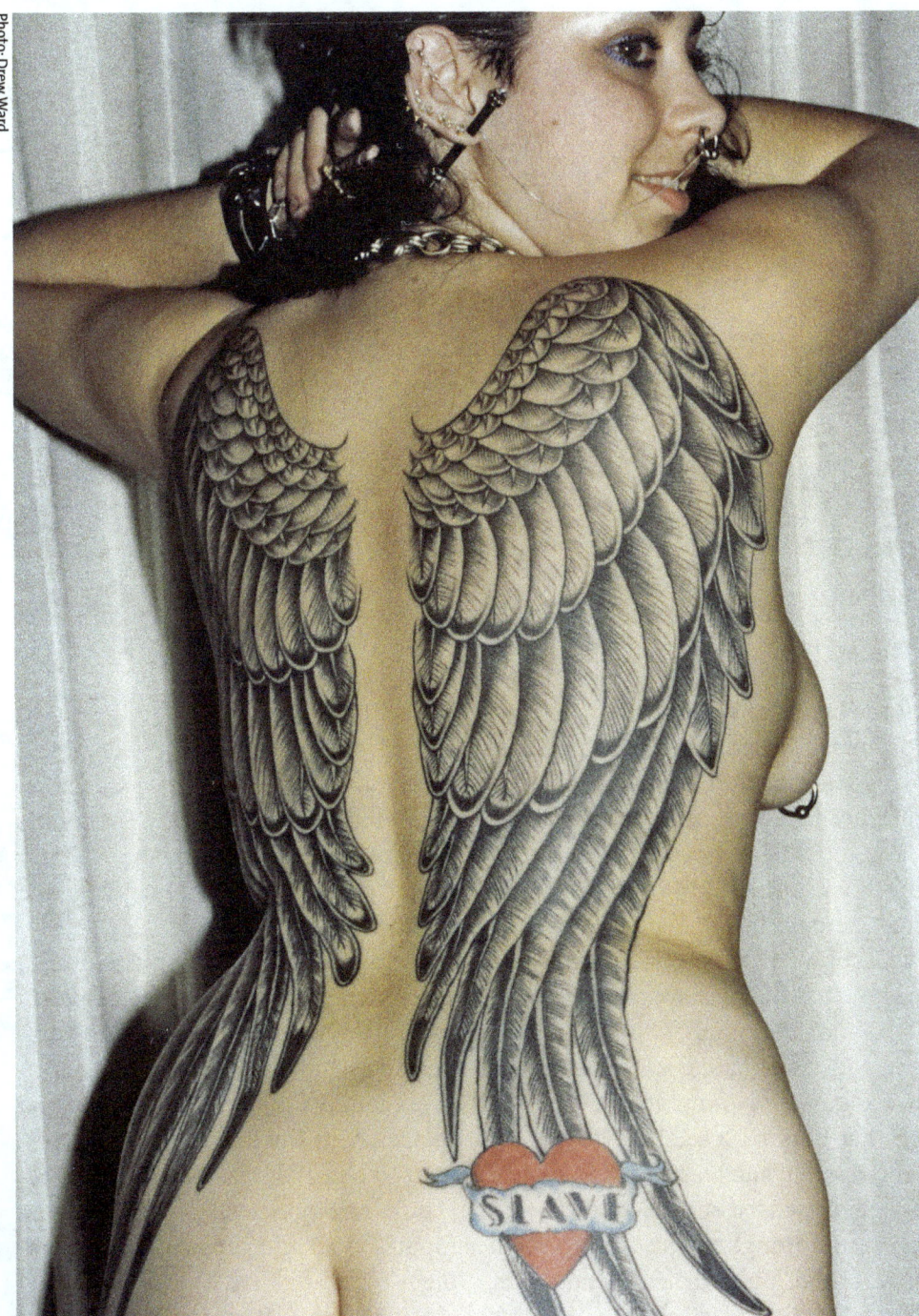

Photo: Drew Ward

Elayne Angel

essary in a managerial position and in dealing with customers, were not her strong points. It became clear that this arrangement wasn't working. What to do? By this time, I was desperate. I either had to find the right person or close the shop and move manufacturing and mail order to San Francisco.

One of my regular clients was a young woman whose name at the time was Elayne Steinberg. She has

gone through several name changes. In the mid 1980s she married porn director Ira Levine in a white leather gown of her own design, made for her by Trashy Lingerie in West Hollywood. As the centerpiece of their S/M wedding, I pierced her septum. She was married briefly to British tattooist Alex Binnie who went on to open the London studio Into You. She is now well-known in the piercing communi-

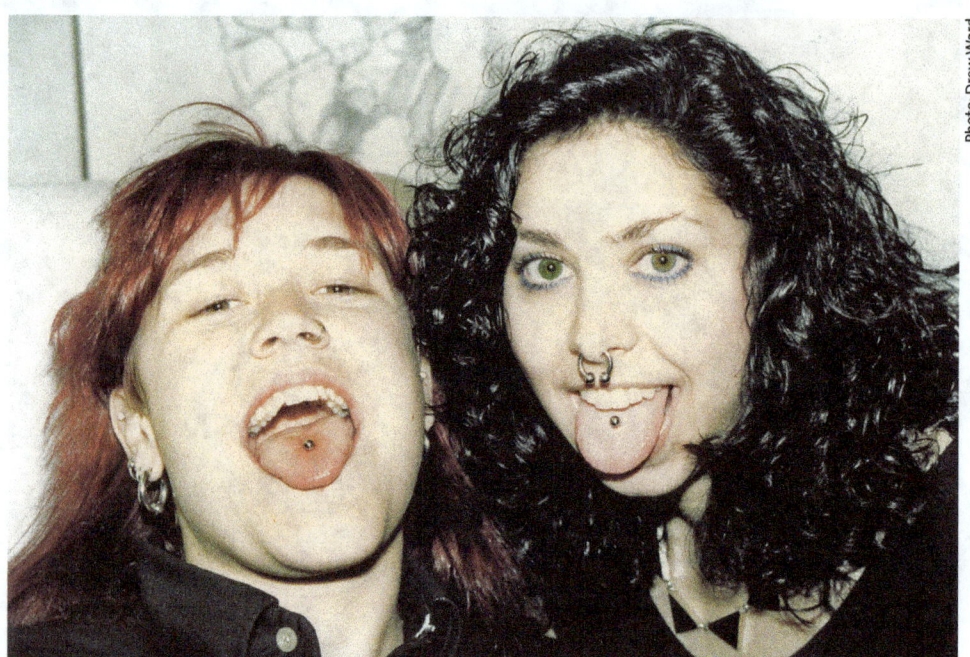

Two of my first tongue piercings: Crystal Cross and Elayne Angel

ty as Elayne Angel, a name she chose for herself because of the large angel wings tattooed on her back. Husband number three, whom she married in 2003, took the Angel surname becoming Buck Angel. Having transitioned from female to male, he has become well-known in the porn industry and beyond as "the man with a pussy."

Elayne's obsession with piercing began early when at age five she started to badger her parents into letting her get her ears pierced. They finally relented when she was seven. In 1972 at age 12, she added second holes in each ear and throughout junior high and high school pierced her friends' ears. Though it didn't last, she did a surface piercing on her own wrist in 1975.

While working as a sign language interpreter at the Southern California Renaissance Faire in the spring of 1981 she met a deaf couple whose nipples were pierced. Instantly fascinated, she rushed home to pierce her own, inserting a small, gold hoop earring. The piercing was shallow and crooked so she removed it. Knowing she had to have these piercings, she asked her new friends where they had gotten theirs. This lead her to Gauntlet, where she

got her nipples pierced by my assistant George. Those piercings were her introduction to a long and happy association with erotic pain and BDSM. Passionate and persuasive, she brought in every friend, acquaintance, and stranger she could talk into getting pierced.

On one of her visits to Gauntlet, I suggested she might be interested in a lecture and play piercing demonstration I was going to be doing at the Society of Janus. She went to the demo and that's where she first saw a photo of a pierced clitoris. She said, "Oh my god! I could never do that!" At the time her nipples were still stinging, rather happily, she remembers.

Six months later, she was back in the hot seat, and I pierced her tiny little clitoris, which she has since stretched up to 6-gauge. It isn't small any more.

Elayne and I had mutual friends, a lesbian couple named Elaine and Susie. On one of my visits to L.A. they threw a piercing party. Their friend Lauren, who wanted a clitoris piercing, ended up with something like an early triangle instead. Elaine and Susie got tragus piercings. Another girlfriend, Martha (now Mike), got her nipple pierced. Not wanting to be odd woman out, Elayne had me pierce

her tongue, one of my first and possibly one of the first in the U.S.

Soon after the party, Elaine and Susie came to the shop, and regarding the manager position asked, "Would you consider hiring a woman?" Although I hadn't actually thought about it one way or the other, I couldn't see why gender would even be an issue. Yes, in the beginning most of my clientele were gay men who might not want a female piercer, but by this time my customers were so diverse it no longer mattered. If someone insisted on being pierced by a man, Pete Morrison, my head jeweler, was well versed in doing the common male piercings. He just didn't want to be store manager or a full-time piercer. When Elaine told me the person she had in mind was Elayne, I couldn't think of anyone better suited for the position.

At the time, Elayne had just finished an intensive marketing and management course at the Fashion Institute of Design and Merchandising (FIDM). At her interview, I looked over her résumé and asked a few mundane questions. Only after I'd agreed to give her a trial did it occur to me to ask, "By the way, how are your piercing skills?" She replied, "Better than most," though none of her experience had been in a professional capacity. Fortunately, since her father was a doctor, she had some medical background and understanding of cross-contamination control. I've never had an employee who was more personable, passionate, and energetic. As a bonus, she had a natural aptitude and quickly developed her piercing skills to a professional level.

To be honest I didn't do a very good job of introducing Elayne into the store's work environment. Crystal was not pleased, and became a hostile and uncooperative employee. Not long afterward she quit and opened her own piercing establishments: Red Devil Piercing Studio and later Primeval Body.

Within six months of becoming manager, Elayne generated sufficient income to capitalize a San Francisco operation, but it took about a year from the time I left L.A. until I was able to open a studio there.

My first year in San Francisco was not just one long honeymoon. I continued doing regular piercing clinics at Mr. S Leather, Image Leather, and piercing rituals with Fakir at Mark Chester's Folsom Street apartment. Through regular classified ads in the *Bay Area Reporter* (*BAR*), the local gay newspaper, I was also doing occasional piercings out of our apartment.

Drew and I were living in a third floor flat on Landers Street in the Castro, the city's gay ghetto. We had a doorbell, but no way to buzz visitors in. To save running up and down stairs, when someone rang the bell, I would open an upstairs window over the street and lower a key on a string.

Although Elayne was generating most of the income, I was far from idle. The time afforded me an opportunity to network and make connections in the local gay and leather communities. I was also keeping an eye open for a shop location.

About this time Vaughn and Esther Saldana came to me with a proposal to join forces and open a piercing business together. I declined, and they subsequently opened Body Manipulations, which was Gauntlet's primary competitor for many years. In addition to piercing, they offered tattooing, branding, and cutting, services that Gauntlet did not.

In the fall, my classified ad was answered by an attractive and well-mannered Latino named Hector. As we chatted while I took care of his piercing needs, I learned that he owned The Café, a restaurant and nightspot on the top floor of a building he also owned at Castro and Market Streets. I fur-

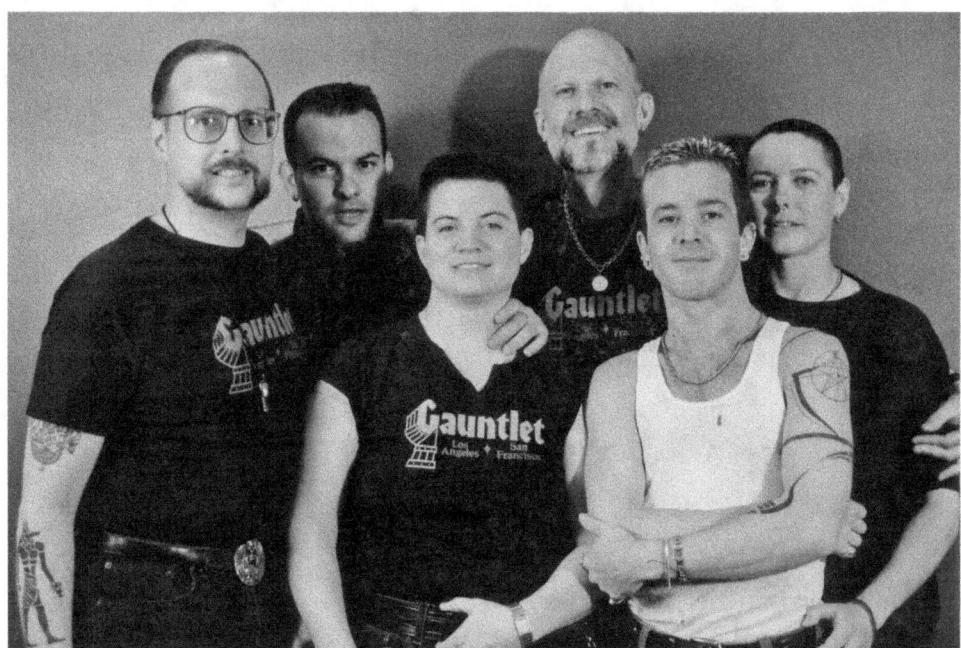

San Francisco Gauntlet staff, May, 1991: *left to right*, Drew, Scott Shatsky, Lou Duff, me, Mark Seitchik, and Karen Hurt

ther learned that he had a boy-toy for whom he'd bankrolled an upscale gift shop on the building's second floor, 2377 Market Street. The inventory and equipment suggested that there also might have been trade in some dubious substances going on. Aside from being a poor location for this type of retail operation, the young man had no head for business. He kept irregular hours that were determined by how late he'd been out partying the night before. Walking by one day, Drew and I had actually noticed a hand-scrawled sign on the front door that read, "Fuck off! I'm on my break."

Hector had run out of patience and rather than continuing to put good money after bad, had decided to sell the stock, close the business, and lease the 1100 square feet space. Since he hadn't made his intentions public or even listed a vacancy yet, no one knew that it was coming available. This gave us first dibs. The location seemed ideal for San Francisco Gauntlet. Drew and I checked out the space, loved it, and negotiated a reasonable rent with Hector. We also made arrangements to purchase the display cases

and some of the other furnishings.

Once the lease was signed, a flurry of activity began in order to prepare the space for business. A sign was designed, fabricated, and installed over the front entrance. A local leatherman who was a carpenter built partitions creating two cubicles for piercing. Walls and ceiling received a fresh coat of paint. Since these were the days before health department regulations, and we didn't know any better, we kept the gray carpeting, even in the piercing rooms. The color scheme throughout was gray, black, and, of course, our signature purple. All the areas needed to be furnished and outfitted. Plans for the grand opening had to be made, invitations sent out, a caterer hired. Somehow we managed to pull it all together. The grand opening party was held on December 15, 1989. Elayne attended, as did my old friend and first bookkeeper, Alayne.

In addition to all the other preparations, additional staff had to be hired. One of the first was Karen Hurt, who was with us for many years. She is now co-owner of a body piercing jewelry manufacturing business in San Francisco called Future Primitives.

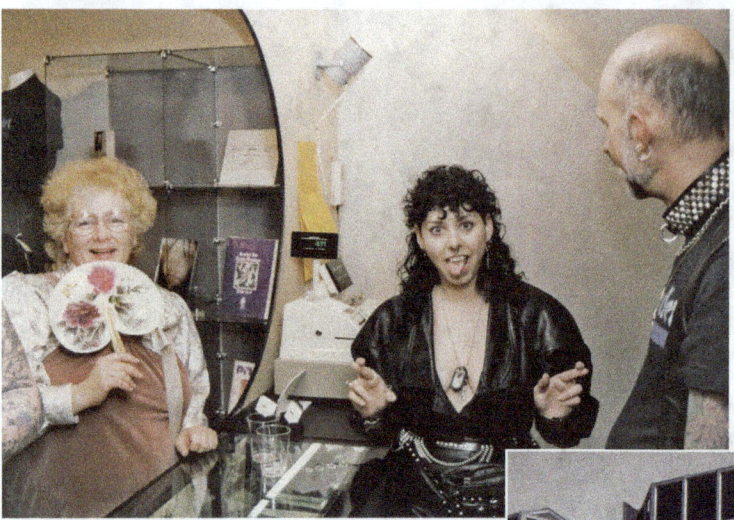

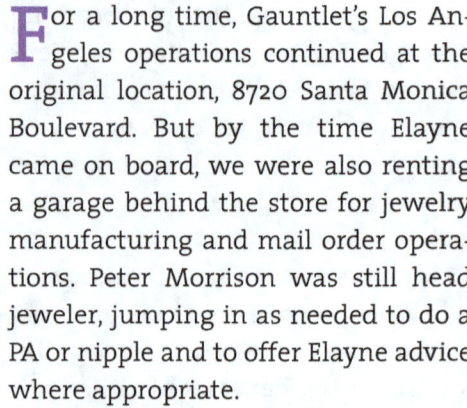

Gauntlet San Francisco, *top to bottom*, our bookkeeper Alayne (with fan) and Elayne chat with me at the studio's grand opening; the entrance; the jewelry display case; the grand opening just getting underway. Two piercing rooms are visible on the right. Photos by Drew Ward.

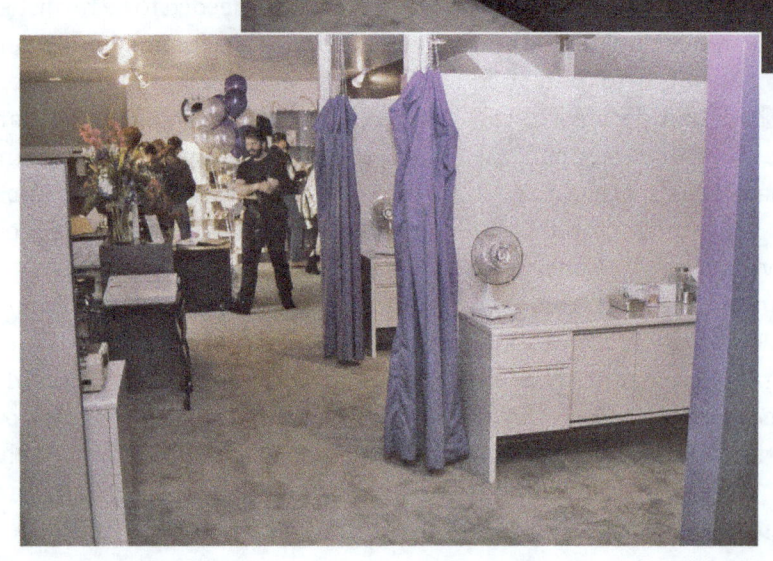

For a long time, Gauntlet's Los Angeles operations continued at the original location, 8720 Santa Monica Boulevard. But by the time Elayne came on board, we were also renting a garage behind the store for jewelry manufacturing and mail order operations. Peter Morrison was still head jeweler, jumping in as needed to do a PA or nipple and to offer Elayne advice where appropriate.

Elayne quickly gained a reputation for her signature piercing: the tongue. Tattoo Samy from Frankfurt had the first I'd ever seen. They may be common now, but this was not the case in the early 1990s, before body piercing was so much in the public eye. Elayne's was the second I'd ever done; I remember performing only one other at a piercing clinic in New York on a young woman named Jen Dunham, who eventually became a Gauntlet L.A. employee. For a Society of Janus demonstration soon after her own tongue piercing, Elayne gleefully assisted me in doing one on a truck driver named Dennis. From then on she managed to convince a constant stream of clients to allow her to outfit them with a tongue stud.

Elayne often told people (shall we say tongue in cheek?) that this piercing was a type of acupuncture intended for weight control, diminishing her appetite, satisfying her palate, and preventing her from eating quickly or thoughtlessly. People believed her, and instead of asking, "Didn't that hurt?" asked instead, "Does it work?" Maybe it does, especially if you believe it will.

Elayne rapidly became the friendly, female face of piercing. The press loved her, and she was interviewed on CNN, Inside Report, Afterhours, MTV, Much-Music, French TV, Japanese TV, and other networks and TV shows, bringing publicity for Gauntlet in all of them. She and I jointly appeared on a pilot episode for the Mother Love TV talk show, shocking the hostess with a copy of *PFIQ*. Unfortunately, the press had a tendency to sensationalize everything. In May of 1990, Elayne appeared, with tongue piercing, in *The National Enquirer* in an article with the headline, "Bizarre New Fashion Fad Turns Folks Into Human Pincushions." There truly is no such thing as bad publicity. It didn't matter what they said; piercing just kept surging in popularity.

Elayne became a regular guest piercer at Gauntlet S.F. Her ambition was to pierce San Francisco's tongues, a goal toward which she made significant strides. There was a time when it seemed more people there had them than didn't!

During her years at Gauntlet, sometimes working alone, sometimes with clients or other piercers, Elayne helped name or innovate several piercings. First was the lorum. Located at the natural fold that divides the penis shaft from the scrotal sack, the name was coined in the late 1980s as Elayne was performing a genital piercing on the late Dan Kopka, her former coworker at Gauntlet L.A. He wanted a frenum, he said, only lower. "Not a frenum, a lower-um," Dan declared, pinching the tissue at the

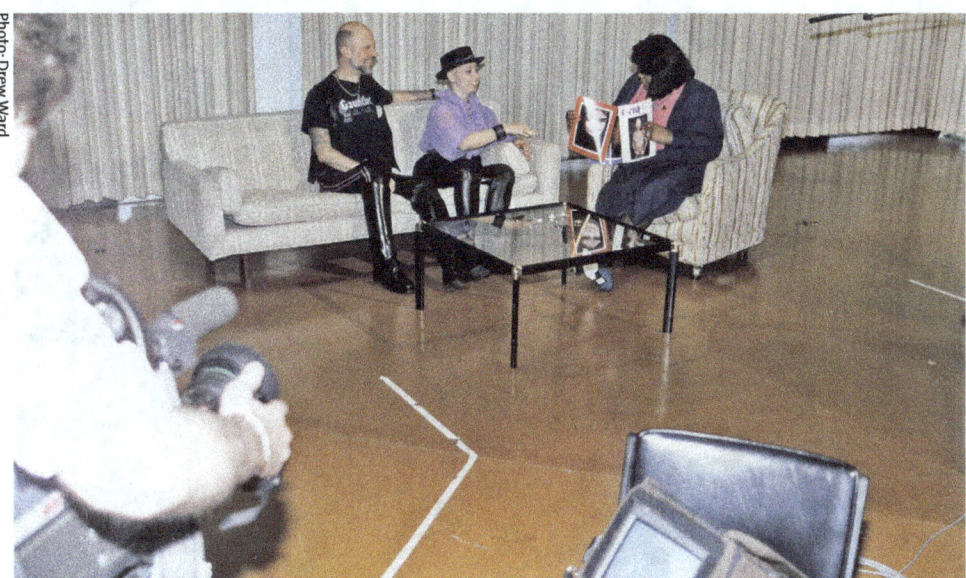

Photo: Drew Ward

Elayne and I discuss piercing on the Mother Love TV talk show (early 1990s) while the host examines a copy of *PFIQ* issue #19

desired spot. "Oh, that would be a good spot. Yeah, a 'lorum,'" was her reply, and the name stuck.

The fourchette piercing was another of Elayne's innovations dating from the 1990s. It is located at the back edge of the vaginal opening. Elayne got the piercing done on herself three separate times, each in a slightly different spot to help identify the optimal placement. Her investigation, while enjoyable, revealed that the best place for a fourchette is on a woman who has a defined flap or fold of tissue in the region. She unfortunately did not. The research was worthwhile, however, because many of the women who wear them find that the fourchette piercing produces unique and enjoyable sensations. Hers did too, while they lasted.

Though championed by Elayne, the third piercing was the innovation (1991) of San Francisco Gauntlet piercer Lou Duff: the triangle. The name derives from the space in which it is placed, a tetrahedron shaped area behind the clitoral shaft. Few women are anatomically suited for it, as it requires room to "accommodate a 12-gauge ring without causing distortion or pressure against any of the surrounding anatomy," according to the "Pierce with a

Pro" article in *PFIQ* issue #49.

In addition to multiple tongue piercings, Elayne's list of firsts—at least as far as anyone knows—includes conceptualizing and getting the first horizontal eyebrow piercing, the first ear head (a.k.a. Helix Root) piercing, the first enlarged conch piercing, and performing the first philtrum (center upper lip) piercing.

Elayne established the practice of keeping statistics on the number of piercings and their placements that were done each month. This helped to track trends and business levels and she instituted other protocols to improve the functioning of the business.

Elayne trained and mentored a whole new generation of young piercers: Dan Kopka, Jacqueline, Brian Murphy, Jen Dunham, Lilia Judd (Beast) who became administrator when Elayne moved on, Bobby Ferris, Lauren Pine (though she didn't apprentice to pierce), Steffan Santoro (Elayne's acupuncturist), and, briefly, Kristian White.

By the early '90s, piercing shops were sprouting up like toadstools after a spring rain. When Doug was still alive, the two of us made regular visits to New York for piercing parties.

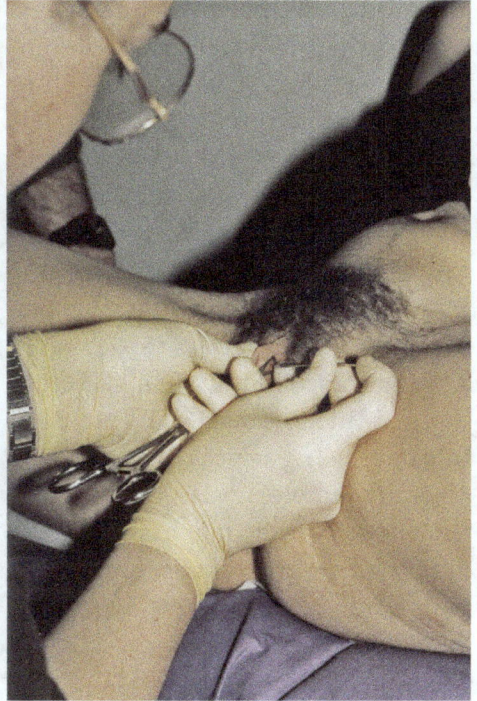

Lou Duff performing her signature piercing, the triangle

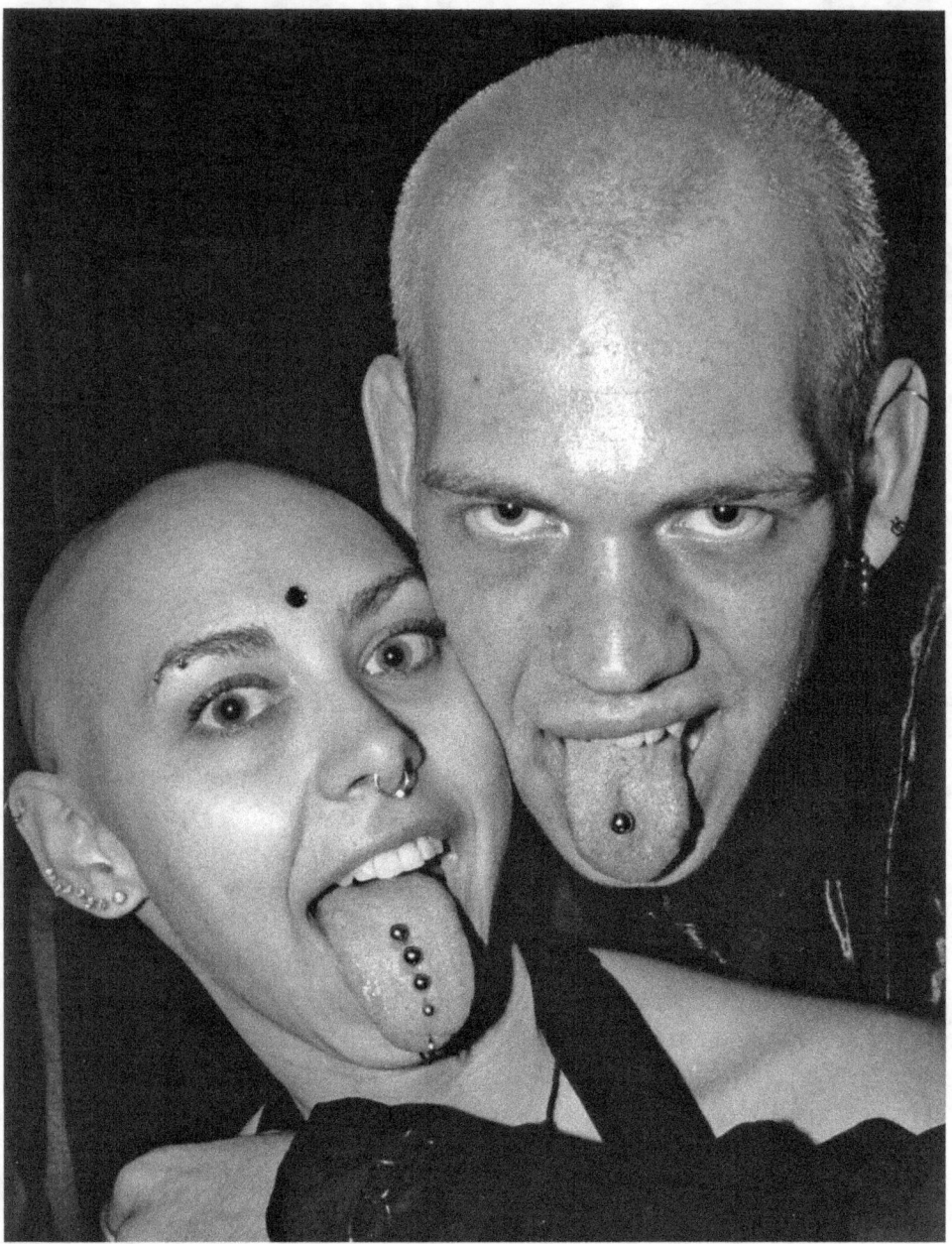
Elayne with Dan Kopka. Photo by Efrain Gonzalez

I had been making regular trips to the Big Apple to hold piercing clinics, frequently at The Noose, a leather/fetish wear shop in the Chelsea district. On every visit, I would be asked repeatedly, "When are you going to open a Gauntlet in New York?" It was clear that if we didn't open a branch there soon, someone else would steal our dominant position in the market. Considering all the responsibilities I was already juggling, and that San Francisco had opened less than two years previously, it was foolhardy. The logistics were monumental. Oversee-ing the operation from the West Coast would mean trusting whomever I put in charge of the location. It would be so easy for them to rob me blind, and I'd be none the wiser.

Ignoring the little inner voice that told me this was premature if not outright insane, I flew to New York and met with Dennis, the brother of an old friend, who was a lawyer and real estate broker. He put together a number of listings, and we began pounding the streets checking them out. New York's East Village had become trendy. Spaces were small and rents inordinately ex-pensive. I decided to pass on it. Christopher Street was still the gay ghetto, and though by this time Gauntlet's business had expanded beyond the limits of the gay community, it was natural for me to gravitate in that direction. In fact, the first locations we scouted were in the West Village, but the spaces were too small, too shabby, too expensive, or all of the above. I had forgotten how old Manhattan is. Every building, unless it's one of the rare new ones, has been painted so many times the surfaces look like they've been spread with cake frosting instead of paint. Security demands barred windows and multiple locks on the doors. Smells are everywhere, many of them pervasive and unpleasant.

Since piercing, at least in those days, did not rely on having a visible, street-level location, I was willing to consider lofts again. One space Dennis had scouted was a second-floor space in the Chelsea area of the city at 144 Fifth Avenue near 19th Street. I fell in love with it. It was a terrific address in a great neighborhood. The floors were hardwood. It was huge and with minimal work could easily meet our requirements. The entrance led into a sizable, single-story area that could serve our retail needs with lots of counter space and a comfortable waiting area. Behind this and down a few steps was room for a couple of piercing cubicles. Still further back was an enormous, spectacular room at least two stories high. Around the ceiling was an elaborate pressed-tin molding. I could envision this once being a speakeasy or even a Masonic temple. I wasn't sure at the time how to use so much space, but it didn't matter. Eventually, I reasoned, we would grow into it. I met with the landlord, signed the lease, and began preparing for business.

For years I had attended an international, gay S/M event held in Michigan and organized by the Chicago Hellfire Club. I had become well acquainted with a number of the CHC members from New York. One of them, a hot little bottom named Stevie who I'd pierced many times, was a contractor. He was only too happy to undertake whatever construction needed to be done and had connections with painters, electricians, and floor refinishers. Drew flew out and together we shopped for all the fixtures, furnishings, and equipment. Somehow it all came together. Elayne (Binnie at the time) arrived from L.A. to help train piercing staff. On her recommendation I hired one of her protégés, Dan Kopka, to be the store manager.

For the New York grand opening (November 1, 1991) over two hundred piercing fans and well-wishers, among them retired porn star Annie Sprinkle and photographer Efrain Gonzalez, showed up for the festive occasion. Balloons of black, silver, and purple hovered lazily over the crowd as the guests enjoyed wine and hors d'oeuvres, and each other's conversation.

Dan was never one of my favorite employees. He was a skilled piercer and, as far as I know, a capable manager. The store did well, and his staff and clients respected and spoke well of him. Personally, I thought he was a bit of a cold fish. He had an icy, penetrating gaze that looked as if he was always sizing people up. I never completely trusted him. Perhaps it was with good reason. As it turned out ,Dan had a secret of his own.

He was visiting Southern California and staying with Elayne. She arose early one morning to discover him on her deck shooting up heroin. It ended his career with Gauntlet. He returned to New York and soon after set up his own piercing business. I've sometimes wondered if he might have taken money to feed his habit, but Elayne doesn't believe it, and if he did, he covered his tracks very well.

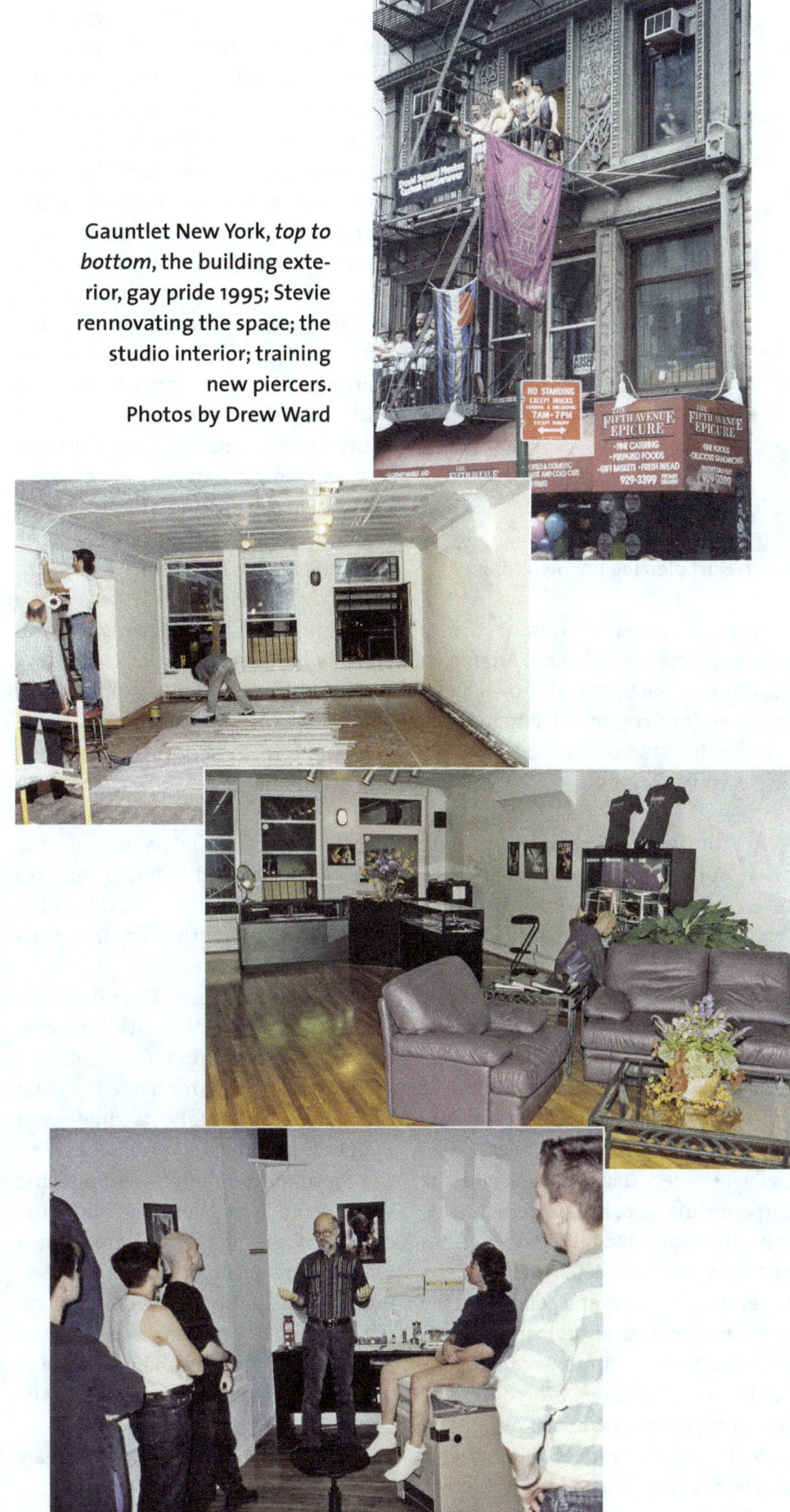

Gauntlet New York, *top to bottom*, the building exterior, gay pride 1995; Stevie rennovating the space; the studio interior; training new piercers.
Photos by Drew Ward

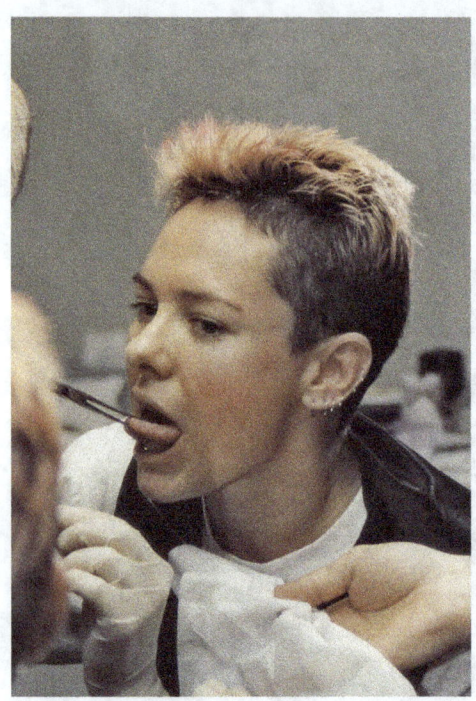

Karen Hurt piercing her own tongue

Purportedly, Dan went into recovery and overcame his addiction. After leaving Gauntlet, he persued his own piercing career, and continued to train piercers for other studios. He died suddenly on December 8, 2005.

With the San Francisco and New York locations, Gauntlet now had seven departments or divisions: three retail shops, mail order, manufacturing, *PFIQ*, and a fairly new corporate entity (1992) that was attempting to oversee it all. This was a lot to keep track of, especially in terms of money. Every bookkeeper up to this time had problems with it. Communication difficulties and financial frustration developed, especially between Gauntlet L.A. and the corporate division. In an attempt to resolve the issues we initiated meetings of managers and department heads. We even held a weekend getaway at the Russian River in an effort to iron out differences. Some matters were resolved, but as so often happens, there were always new ones to take their place.

Following the death of a close friend, Elayne decided to travel the U.S., scout a location, and open her own piercing studio somewhere far away from any of the Gauntlet branches so as not to compete. With her following, she could very easily have been a formidable competitor, especially if she had stayed in L.A. Most people in her position would have had no qualms about doing so, but Elayne has more integrity than that, something I admire and for which I have the utmost respect. She settled in New Orleans, where she opened Rings of Desire. Following her marriage and post-Katrina, she and Buck moved to Merida, Mexico. For many years Elayne has been a driving force within the Association of Professional Piercers, dealing primarily with medical issues. In 2009 her book *The Piercing Bible—The Definitive Guide to Safe Body Piercing* was released.

Gauntlet had begun giving titles to piercers based on to their level of expertise. They started as Apprentices, and as their skills advanced, they graduated to Piercer, Senior Piercer, and eventually to Master Piercer. Even though Elayne had given her notice, I wanted to acknowledge not just the level of skill she had acquired, but also her years of dedication. On December 21, 1992 I issued her the very first Master Piercer certificate.

In the early years of Gauntlet's certification program that title meant a lot and was something our employees respected and were motivated to work toward. Unfortunately, as time went by it ceased to mean very much. With the overnight proliferation of piercing studios, suddenly everyone who hung out a shingle was a self-proclaimed Master Piercer. The practice became so widespread that we considered abandoning the certification altogether, but decided to retain it as an internal measure of our piercers' accomplishments.

Another of our noteworthy female staff was Karen Hurt. She was the first employee hired for the San Francisco studio. About her years with us she wrote:

My journey to Gauntlet began in the winter of 1988. For several years I had been very intrigued by an ad in *On Our Backs*, a lesbian erotica magazine. The ad was for piercing services by Raelyn Gallina[2] of Oakland, California and contained a sensual photo of an inner labia piercing. I knew that one day I must have this piercing. Living in Atlanta, Georgia, piercings were not available, and none of my friends seemed at all interested.

In 1988, on a trip to San Francisco with a new girlfriend, we excitedly and with some trepidation phoned Raelyn. As we both nervously listened to the phone receiver, Raelyn described the process. She said she was available that night if we were interested. We momentarily hesitated, then said yes, let's go for it! At the last minute my girlfriend and I both decided to get both of our nipples pierced. Wow, what a rush! It was winter in San Francisco and very windy that night. As we walked the streets of the Castro, our nipples were in a state of maximum aliveness. We were ecstatic.

Raelyn told us about Gauntlet in Los Angeles and *PFIQ* magazine. These were the only available resources for all things piercing related. For years I had been a fan and avid reader of *Drummer*, a men's leather magazine. I was especially interested in the straight barbells I saw the pierced leathermen wearing in their nipples.

I requested a catalog from Gauntlet. I ordered my straight barbells in white gold and also some play piercing needles to threaten and entertain my friends, wanting all of them to have the experience of having and wearing piercing jewelry. They were skeptical at best. While I anxiously awaited the arrival of my shipment of jewelry, I decided to move from Atlanta to San Francisco.

I phoned Jim at Gauntlet in Los Angeles and asked that he hold my jewelry and supplies telling him I would come L.A. to meet him and get my jewelry. Arriving in Los Angeles, I learned that Jim had relocated to San Francisco. This was most exciting news. When I finally met with Jim to get my jewelry, he said he was opening a piercing studio in San Francisco. He asked if I might be interested in working in the new piercing shop. I could not believe my good fortune. Could it be true...working with Jim and learning to pierce?

In November 1989 I was hired to work part-time when the store opened the following month. Scott Shatsky and I were the first two employees, both working part-time. In the early days, we had no idea how the public would respond to a piercing studio. Within two months, business was growing, and Scott and I were full-time piercers.

I was fortunate to be one the first apprentices and learn directly from Jim everything he had to offer. He had a calm and reassuring style and made learning methodical, fun, and exciting. In the early days, when we were not busy, we practiced marking piercing placements on each other and we regularly pierced each other. For many of us, piercing ourselves was the ultimate thrill and learning experience.

We were doing something totally new. Customers were visiting a piercing studio for the first time. Body piercings had never been available to the general public. It was thrilling and exciting for us as piercers and for the clients. Recently pierced clients came to the studio often just to hang out and visit, always thinking of what to get pierced next. A strong personal bond was created; every piercing was special for us as piercers and also for the clients. These regular visits also gave us the opportunity to closely observe piercing healing times and adapt and evolve piercing placement criteria.

In the summer of 1991, Fakir Musa-

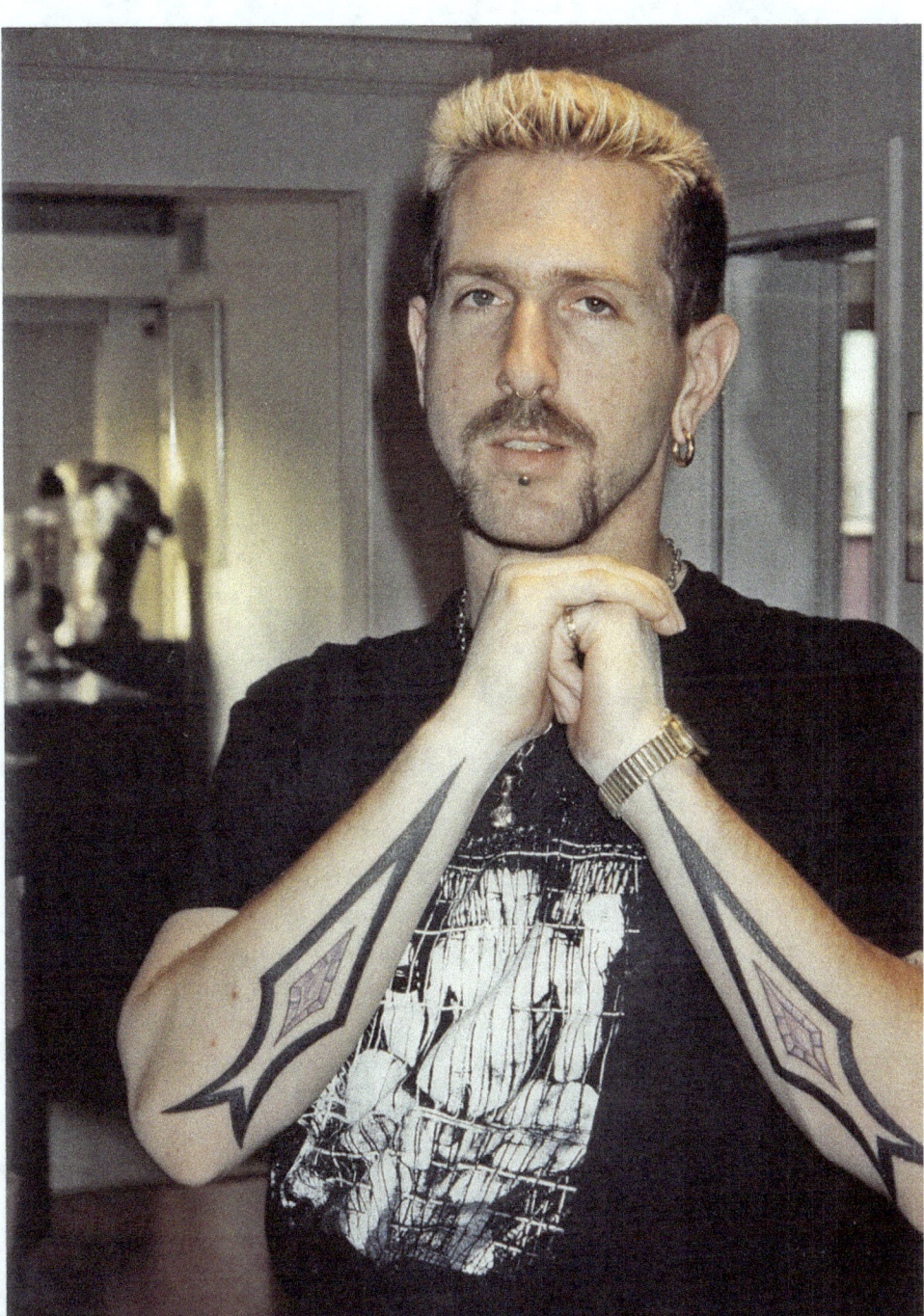

Photo: Drew Ward

Paul King

far worked part-time as a piercer. I was very excited to observe and work with Fakir. He had a different style and set of experiences. I was happy to absorb any new information and enjoyed my time with him.

Paul King has been a professional body piercer since 1991 and an enthusiast before that. He was Gauntlet-trained, serving an apprenticeship under Elayne Angel for a year and a half. He worked

in all three Gauntlet locations, Los Angeles, New York, and San Francisco, and was store manager of L.A. and N.Y.C. In 1996 he was awarded the title of Master Piercer. He apprenticed many piercers for Gauntlet as well as co-taught Gauntlet's Piercer Training Seminars.

Paul explains how he became involved in piercing:

As a kid I felt bored with life and largely uninspired by the usual kid offerings of sports, school, and the opposite sex. As a high school freshman in 1980, there were three punk rock kids in my school. Like a moth to a flame, I was compulsively drawn to them. Shoving safety pins through my ears and nostrils soon followed.

In 1981 I worked at a summer camp in the Midwest. As a 14-year-old showing off, I demonstrated to another worker how we West Coast punks cut ourselves. He wanted me to cut him too. We ended up having sex that night. The association of male bonding coupled with pain/blood/sexual arousal imprinted on my psyche.

In 1983, I remember a friend coming to school one day with an ear stud through the right side of her lower lip. Honestly, while it was healing, we all thought it looked gross. Without proper aftercare or jewelry, she soon abandoned the experiment. But I'll never forget my visual shock and her bravery.

In 1986, I discovered Anne Rice's book, *The Claiming of Sleeping Beauty*. The Beauty series uses the children's story as a stepping off point for a sado-masochistic fantasy. At the point in the plot when male characters were being enslaved by men and women, something clicked; I got it! These books showed the fantasy world of power exchange; the complete offering of oneself or controlling of another. This launched a conscious exploration of my S/M desires. In 1988, I flipped through a copy of *Drummer* and saw an ad featuring a hot man with his nipples pierced. I reacted with a surprised, "WOW!" From time to time the image would cross my mind, making me smile.

In 1989, I visited a friend in San Francisco. She wanted to get her nipple repierced. We went to Body Manipulations, which had just opened. It was the tiniest shop, then on Fillmore Street. Though the opportunity was presented, that day I wasn't ready. However, witnessing the process watered the seed of desire. Soon after, I had a dream

about having pierced nipples! That was the sign I could no longer ignore.

Back in L.A., I told a friend I wanted to have my nipples pierced but had no knowledge of a professional shop. That month she found Gauntlet. As a Christmas present to myself, I made an appointment for early January 1990.

I walked into Gauntlet and remember seeing two women. One was Elayne Angel. Both excitedly showed off their tongue piercings. I freaked (in a good way) having never seen one before. Dan Kopka pierced my nipples. Yes, mine hurt like fuck! Dan's bedside demeanor seemed a bit detached. After the piercing he left the room without any closure or aftercare. After about 10 minutes, I figured out he wasn't returning, got dressed, and left.

Coincidentally it turned out a high school mate worked in Gauntlet's gold manufacturing department. We started hanging out again which eventually led to Dan and me dating for a quick moment. As it turned out, Dan and I made much better friends. I remember for my birthday Dan offered me a Prince Albert piercing, but he and Elayne somehow talked me into an ampallang. As Dan and I hung out more, Elayne and I became better friends. Business was booming at the L.A. store, and Elayne decided she needed a bookkeeper to take the accounting load off her plate. I had experience in accounting but hated working at a corporate job. I made an agreement that if they taught me to pierce, I would do the books.

I had just gotten clean and sober again. Elayne had been repeatedly burned by alcoholics and addicts in the workplace and told me I had to have one year of sobriety under my belt before she would hire me. This delayed my job interview until 1991. To impress that I would take this job seriously and not exploit our friendship, I showed up to the interview in a suit

and tie with my résumé in hand.

Those early days at Gauntlet were a blast! Piercing performances were hot in the underground with S/M/industrial dance clubs like FUCK! The media pounded down our door daily. With the exploding popularity of piercing came exponential growth for the company. This presented an amazing opportunity to pierce and train piercers all over the U.S. and Europe.

Customers were extremely diverse including punks, grandparents, superstars, hookers, Masters (and Mistresses) and slaves, and of course, perverts. I'll never forget the lesson taught when a stripper went to tip me, and I modestly declined. She said, 'Honey, rule number one, ALWAYS TAKE the MONEY!' I've never turned down a tip since.

Masturbatory phone calls were so prevalent we included specific protocol training for new hires. For the few folks that physically 'got off' on piercing, (habitually getting pierced), we had to ban them from the shop for periods of time.

The staff was constantly playing with new ideas for procedures and placements. Jim Ward hated the old method of septum piercings. They're difficult to consistently pierce straight. So Jim invented septum forceps. Since I was the only employee without a septum piercing—I never liked them—I was the company guinea pig. Elayne pierced me perfectly straight, and out of sentiment I've never taken it out.

Elayne warned me that being a piercer was a 24/7 job and that I was expected to always be professional and courteous with the public. I may have brought my strong work ethic to the job, but Elayne taught me how to apply this quality to customer service, bedside manner, and impeccable piercing standards. Today, Elayne is one of my dearest friends, and I will always remain grateful for her professional guidance.

In 1999 Paul partnered to create Cold Steel America, tattooing and piercing services in San Francisco.[3] He is an active member of the Association of Professional Piercers. Recently, he successfully completed a three-year elected position as a board member for the APP. In 2007 he received the APP's President's Award for contributions to the piercing industry. Currently he is the board-appointed treasurer for the APP.

Paul got an early start talking before audiences in high schools as a teenage peer health counselor. Currently, he lectures at universities and conferences on various aspects of body modification. His lecture credits include San Francisco State University, San Francisco Academy of Art, Skyline Community College, Association of Professional Piercers (Las Vegas, USA and Amsterdam, Netherlands,), BMX Conference (Essen, Germany,), Oslo SusCon (Oslo, Norway,), and APTPI Conference (Milan, Italy.)

He is an avid traveler, collector, and layman anthropologist and has published articles on piercing history and traditional practices as well as information on his documentary, *Rituals of Life: The Phuket Vegetarian Festival* in *The Point*, the newsletter of the APP.[4]

Paul has done a great deal to popularize piercing. According to BMEzine. com, "The release—and subsequent winning of MTV's "1994 Best Music Video of the Year" award—of Aerosmith's *Cryin'* is widely regarded as the moment when body piercing became mainstream." Directed by Marty Callner and starring Alicia Silverstone with young Paul as her piercer, "it was the first time body piercing was presented in a mainstream medium in a relatively positive context, and it was the first time many people had really seen body piercing up close." Actually, the close-ups hid the fact that a stand-in for Silverstone was the one who actually got pierced. As a result of see-ing this video, millions of people went out and got navel piercings. They were suddenly cool. Today Paul is very blasé about the whole experience—he was in his early 20s when the video was made—and claims he only did it for the money.

Over the years, Gauntlet was blessed to have had any number of gifted employees, among them Michaela Grey. Even before I met her she was obsessed with piercing. As a student at Sarah Lawrence, she was doing what she describes as "wretched for-pay piercing" out of her dorm room. She and her girlfriend of the time were piercing each other.

We met at a piercing clinic I was doing at the loft of my friend David Menkes, a New York maker of leather wear and fetish fashion. Though barely of legal age, she wanted a clitoris piercing, but I felt she wasn't anatomically suited for it, so she settled instead for a second clit hood piercing.

Somehow I made an impression on her, sufficiently so that she realized she had no business doing any more piercing until she could learn properly. This was a primary incentive for her to move to San Francisco and seek an apprenticeship at Gauntlet. It took a while, but she eventually succeeded. She was hired as a summer counter person in May 1991. Lou Duff departed, affording Michaela an opportunity to advance into an apprenticeship position under Scott Shatsky and Karen Hurt.

By 1993 the mass proliferation of body piercing studios staffed with inadequately trained piercers was causing grave concern with health departments and legislators. In some places there was talk of outlawing body piercing altogether. We at Gauntlet had tried repeatedly to get others in the industry to police and regulate themselves, but with minimal success. It became apparent that unless we banded together and became proactive, we could very well find ourselves out of business. We knew that if body piercing were made illegal, the only piercers continuing to operate would be doing so clandestinely, and piercing clients would be no better off than they already were.

Any Gauntlet Senior Piercer who wanted to get their Master Piercer certification was required to undertake a special project. Michaela was ready to make this advancement, and her special project, the magnitude of which we didn't realize at the time, was to attempt to create a network of responsible studios willing to work together with healthcare professionals and legislators to set reasonable standards for the industry and regulate rather than outlaw it. This became so time consuming that friction developed between Michaela and her coworkers. The store manager wanted to fire her.

During Michaela's early days at Gauntlet the "corporate office" was in the back of the San Francisco store. There was an area containing my desk and a huge drawing board for laying out *PFIQ*. Drew had come on staff as my assistant, and had a desk, as did our bookkeeper. Things were so crowded it quickly became clear that we needed to move the corporate operations into their own location. We located a second floor office space at 537 Castro Street, a block and a half from the store.

Despite her rough edges, it was apparent to me that Michaela had too many things going for her to simply turn her out in the street. So rather than abandon her I made the decision to mentor her and take her on at corporate as my assistant. This gave her the time and freedom to work on a number of projects, including what eventually became the Association of Professional Piercers (APP). One of the benefits of working with other piercers and people in the health department and the legislature was that she began to

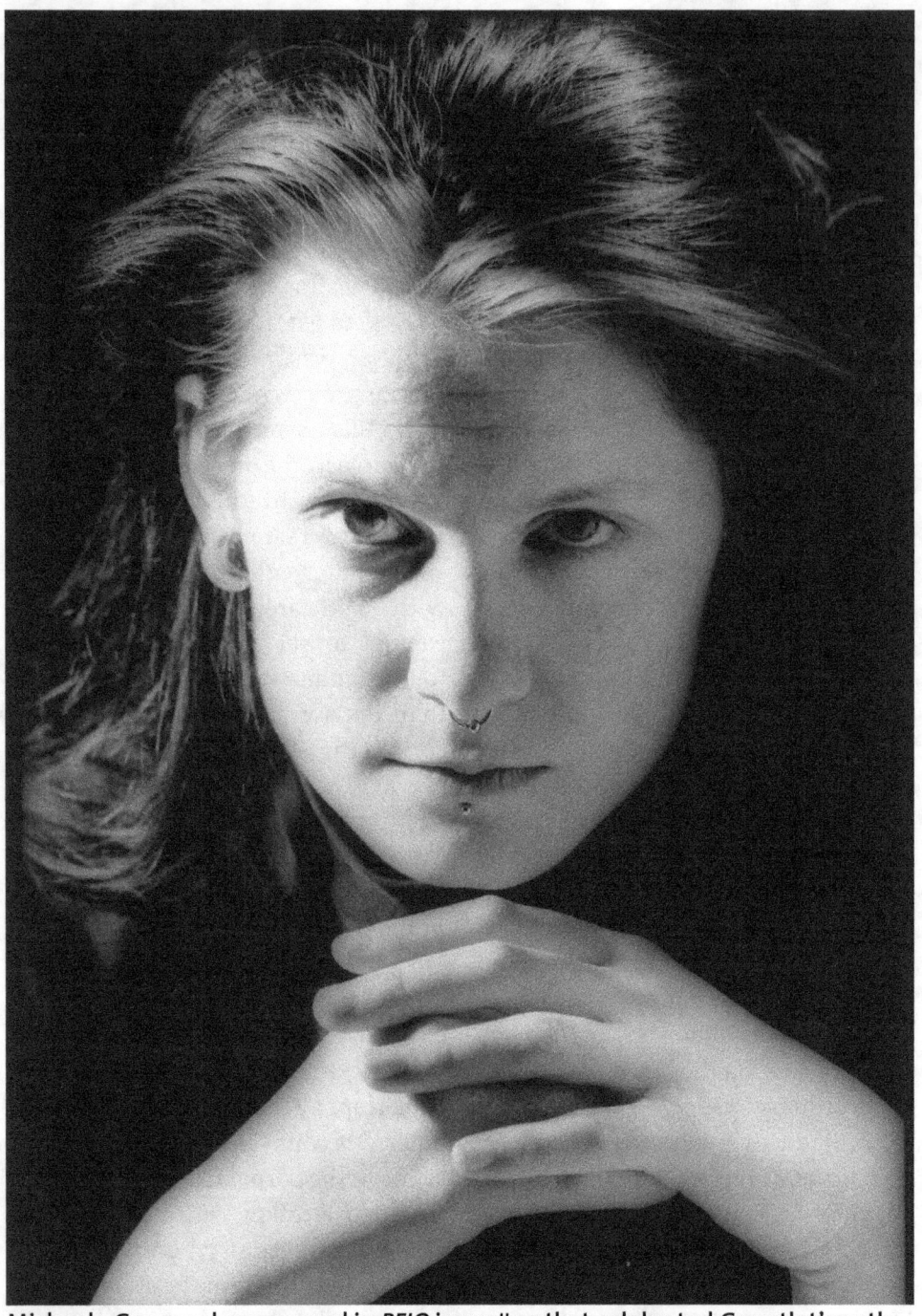

Michaela Grey as she appeared in *PFIQ* issue #45 that celebrated Gauntlet's 20th Anniversary, 1995. Photo by Michael Adrianne.

ings for the bill. She also did a number of television interviews. The bill ultimately failed thanks to lobbying by the ear-piercing gun manufacturers. However, this did not end the threats to the industry, and the need for a professional organization to deal with them.

Future meetings were held after hours at the Market Street store. From these the APP came into being. Not surprisingly, there was much wrangling, many heated discussions, and some friction. Some of those who attended left in a huff never to return or to come back many years later. Blake Perlingieri helped Michaela with registering the organization for nonprofit status, opening a joint bank account for the funds, and starting its newsletter *The Point*. With the assistance of Ghadi Elias from Mastodon in San Diego, APP moved forward and organized its first board.

I was deeply troubled when Fakir began offering piercing seminars. It wasn't so much the fact that he was doing so that bothered me, but I considered some of his early policies not only unsafe but also unethical. Our conflicting perspectives eventually severed our relationship. So once APP was beginning to stand on its own, I enlisted Michaela's aid to help develop Gauntlet's own piercer training seminars. During the summer of 1993, she and I worked together to develop a curriculum and write a manual. One of the wonderful discoveries that we made was that her writing style and my own were so much alike that our work was often indistinguishable. Michaela went on to become the director and primary instructor for Gauntlet's seminars with other piercers, mostly from the San Francisco store, co-teaching.

If there's one word to describe Michaela, it is driven. In addition to all her other duties, she also assumed the position of co-editor for *PFIQ* and helped it become less male/leather oriented

develop much-needed tact and diplomacy. In the process, she matured and blossomed into a woman.

In 1994 the State of California was poised to pass legislation (Assembly Bill 3787) that would regulate body piercing, tattooing, and permanent cosmetics. A handful of piercers from several studios began to network and strategize how best to assure that these forms of body modification were not outlawed. Those

who met at the Gauntlet corporate office for those early meetings included Raelyn Gallina, several representatives from Body Manipulations, Nomad, and Primeval Body in L.A. Along with some of his students, including Idexa, Fakir also attended. The office was full. As the pending legislation grew closer to passing, a group got together and drove to Sacramento. Michaela spoke on behalf of the industry during one of the hear-

and more female-friendly. Each of the later issues was built around a theme. She and I would brainstorm an idea, and she took it upon herself to gather, edit, and organize the material, passing it on to me for layout and design. Not infrequently she wrote articles. It was a wonderful collaboration, one that I enjoyed immensely.

In 1997 at the Orlando APP conference, Michaela stepped down from the board. The drama that had gone on within the APP over the years, encouraged by Shannon Larratt at BMEzine.com, lead to Michaela becoming stamped with the same "conservative" label as Gauntlet because we opposed the use of dermal punches, anesthetics, scalpels, and implants, among other things. In my opinion, there are good reasons for this opposition because unless you're a licensed medical professional, they are illegal. These were the very types of things that placed piercing under the scrutiny of government agencies in the first place, necessitating the formation of an organization like APP. I can't understand why so many young people doing body modification fail to realize that ignoring the law, no matter how absurd it might seem to them, could very well endanger the livelihood of everyone in the industry.

Michaela is human. Unfortunately, she made some errors in judgment which still haunt her and for which she has never been forgiven. In her zeal, she sometimes made statements that were inaccurate or inflammatory and she repeated as facts rumors which were later discovered to be untrue. Thus, she undermined her credibility in some quarters and made enemies in others.

As a result of the abuse heaped upon her, Michaela became understandably disenchanted with the body piercing community and finally broke with it. She went on to pursue a 10-year career in graphic design and production art,

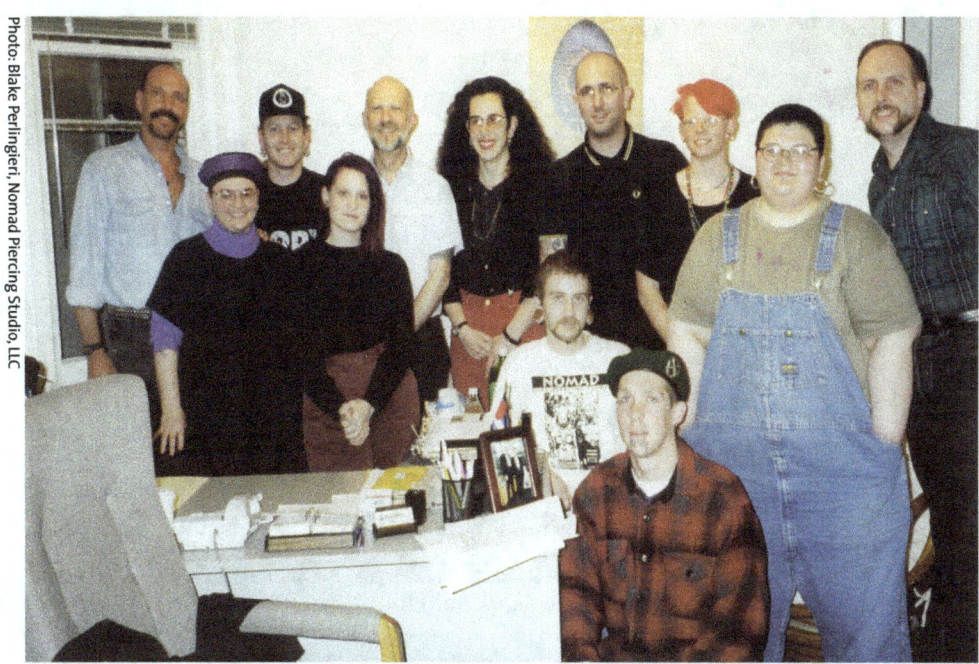

APP Founding members, *left to right*, Irwin Kane (Gauntlet), Raelyn Gallina, Vaughn (Body Manipulations), Michaela Grey (Gauntlet), Jim Ward (Gauntlet), Melisa Kaye (Body Manipulations), Richard Carter (Primeval Body), JoAnn Wyman (Body Manipulations), Elizabeth Brassil (Body Manipulations), Drew Ward (Gauntlet); *kneeling*, Blake Perlingieri (Nomad), Kristian White (Nomad)

after which she went back to school to follow another of her passions: costume design. She is a graduate of the Fashion Institute of Design and Merchandising (FIDM) in L.A. and happily married to her wife of many years.

Michaela and I have remained close friends. She looks up to me as a surrogate father and appreciates that I was willing to take her under my wing and help her grow up. I feel that I have acquired a daughter of whom I am justly proud.

Another of Gauntlet's Master Piercers was Scott Shatsky. He had this to say about his experience:

I'll never forget the first time I walked into Gauntlet as an eager punk fag and met Jim Ward as he was drying his freshly washed hands on a paper towel. For me, Jim was warm and calm, offering a fresh perspective on what it meant to be alternative. The gold and purple peacock wallpaper enticed me; I knew I was in the right place and in great hands. Even then, I looked upon Jim as a role model.

He was one of the first gay men with whom I felt hopeful. One summer, I returned to L.A. from attending college in S.F. Crystal Cross was working with Jim at Gauntlet and we got to talking about a summer job. As far as my memory serves me, I did not have aspirations to become a Master Piercer, I really just wanted to be accepted by other alternative people.

As luck would have it, Jim decided to open Gauntlet S.F., which is when I recall a piercing god-shot; an overwhelming calling that I could be a body piercer. Initially, this world opened my mind and heart. Being trained as a body piercer felt important, culturally significant, personally gratifying. I embraced the responsibility and was honored by the trust of the clients. In retrospect, working towards Master Piercer status derailed the passionate journey I was on. At Gauntlet, there evolved a sense of competition, which I participated in willingly. Today, I see that being a body piercer was enough. I had the unique opportunity to help

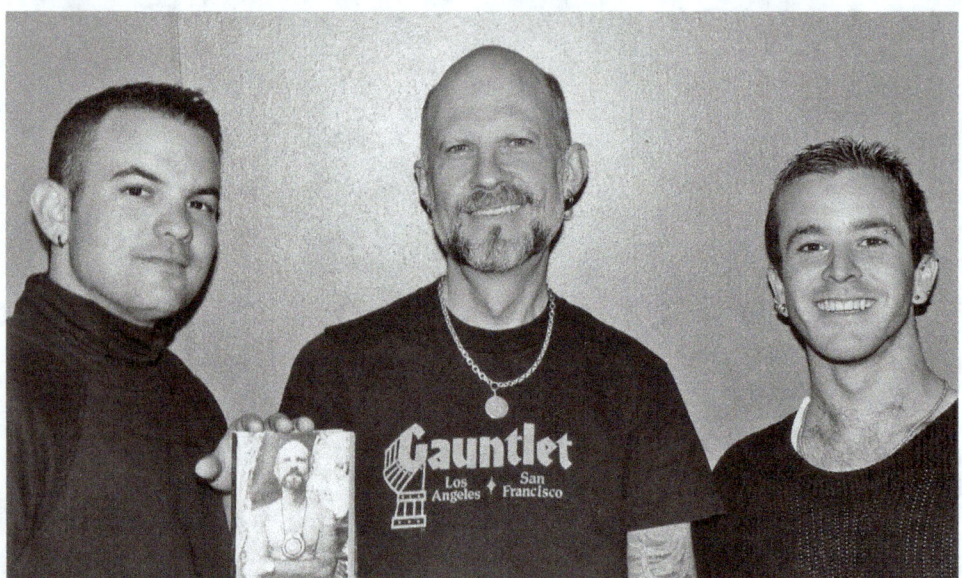

Left to right, Scott Shatsky, myself, and Mark Seitchik

people claim their identity (if even for a moment) and to connect with clients on the physical, psychological, spiritual, and psychosexual nature of body piercing. For me, other titles, including manager and Master Piercer, came without much support and created disharmony and deceit between me and the company I once identified with.

I've often thought of writing *Confessions of a Body Piercer*, but it's not mine to write; this belongs to Jim. On a personal level it's not about the "modern primitive culture," it's about working alongside people like Jim Ward and Karen Hurt. And, about nurturing those that came to Gauntlet to be pierced and healed at the same time.

During his career as a piercer, Scott appeared on *The Arsenio Hall Show*, where he pierced a navel during the opening monologue. He also flashed his pierced cock at the audience.

One of Scott's fellow Master Piercers was Mark Seitchik. He shared with me some of his own experiences:

I started out with Gauntlet as an apprentice body piercer in 1989, at the San Francisco shop at Market and Castro streets. I remember my first day and my shift with just Fakir Musafar and me. I was surely a bit intimidated

as I was very new to the whole world of body piercing, and, of course, Fakir was a legend. Jim was always around as well with his calmer-than-calm presence, working on jewelry at the bench in the back, and dispensing his expertise to us. I felt and knew that I was in a special place at a special time with great people.

A few years later in 1992, I got the opportunity to move to the Big Apple, the newest Gauntlet to open. Dan Kopka was the manager. At the time there was surprisingly little body piercing being done professionally in New York, so when we opened up, it was a big deal. There was a lot of media attention, and we quickly got a lot of exposure. Dan put together a great staff, and again it felt like a special place to be. As a Senior, and then Master Piercer, I was given the opportunity to be included with Dan, or on my own, in much of the media events. Talk shows, MTV, panels at galleries, radio, etc. It was an exciting time, and as far as I remember we ran a great shop. There were some staffing changes here and there, and I eventually took on the title of Manager. At one point, it was decided that we would also have an administrative manager. The person was hired, and things got computerized.

We always played nice music in the studio in order to help clients relax. We also played it over the telephone system when someone was put on hold. One particular morning before we were open for business, our admin manager was playing the newest Madonna album for the umpteenth time that week, and let's just say it was driving me a bit crazy.

In any case, I was frustrated about something that morning and having just one of those New York bad mood days. I was in the middle of some really messed up paperwork from the previous day's totals. The phone was ringing; I was busy, and no one was picking it up in the front. I picked up the phone, and the woman on the other end immediately goes right into asking if we had a number of different nostril screws, in various types of metals with a variety of gemstones. This was way more then I had hoped to handle when I picked up the phone, but there you go. I asked the woman to hold as I went out front to see if the nostril screws she wanted were in stock. When I picked the phone back up she immediately says, "I love that you're playing the new Madonna album!"

I said, "Yeah, a guy here likes it, to be honest, it's driving me crazy. So here's what I have for nostril screws...."

Let me just say this was all very "New York," She was demanding, and I was frustrated, but we "got each other," and we were good.

She then says that she will send a courier to pick them up, and how much will they all cost. I explained that nostril screws needed to be shaped just right for the person wearing them, that measurements were taken and refitting done a time or two, so sending a courier would not work, She would have to come in herself to be measured and fitted. "Well!" she said really snooty. "That is just not possible. I'll send the courier. Just bend them. It'll be fine."

"I'm sorry, but we really do know how this works, and I'm quite sure that you'll just end up having to come to have them fitted."

Her: "No, won't happen."

Me: "Why not?"

Her: "Well, they're not for me, they're for Madonna, and she's not coming in."

Me, trying to sound like I was not impressed: "Why, did she break her leg?"

Her: "Very funny!" then shouting to someone in the background: "Hey, they said you have to come in; they need to measure your nostril so they can bend them for you."

Madonna, shouting back: "Tell him to call the guy who did it; he'll remember."

I'm thinking: "Thank god! That's a great idea; I'm sure Scott will remember. How the hell am I going to get out of this?" To this day I will always remember that the thickness of Madonna's nostril measures 5/16".

One of my most vivid memories of a piercing was at a convention. A few of us were out in Chicago working at the International Mister Leather convention. Jim, Drew, and Irwin were down on the convention floor at the Gauntlet booth, and Scott Chance, I believe, and I were up in the hotel room performing the piercings. It was a typical hotel room with two beds and a clock radio on the table between them. Back at the studios, we of course had nice relaxing music on all the time in order to create a calm atmosphere. Well, we neglected to bring our own music source, so the clock radio was our only source of music. There was nothing relaxing available, so we had it tuned to something decent, but it still had obnoxious DJs.

On this day, we had a very rare clitoral piercing scheduled. As you may know, these are very rare for several reasons, the first being that most women's clits are simply too small. The second reason is that even if the clit is large enough, when you go over placement with her, she will often say, "Oh my god! I didn't mean I want it to actually go through the clit, just around it." Not only is this piercing rare, but also it's pretty intense. That being said, we still had one scheduled that day.

The woman and her boyfriend show up at the hotel room, and we explain everything, determine that we are indeed going to proceed, and all is set. She has been anticipating getting the piercing for months, ever since she learned that Gauntlet was going to be in her area for the convention. She brought her boyfriend, and he was going to be her support.

In the studio we use a gynecological table with stirrups for genital piercings, but lacking one suggested she lean back against her boyfriend while he supports her, holds her, and breaths with her—very Lamaze technique. After the area is cleaned and marked, we all get into a few nice deep breaths as I apply the forceps, tight enough to hold and not slip, but not so tight that they would be overly intense. A few more deep breaths while I place the needle, and you can feel the air in the room getting very charged, and then whooooosh! The needle quickly passes through with a deep exhale, and all in the room feel a healthy dose of endorphins. The forceps are removed, and there's a big sigh of relief. As I prepare to insert the ring by pressing the end against the hollow back end of the needle, a small drop of blood trickles from the piercing, and just as the music ends the DJ says, "This is WWXX, where we have our finger on the pulse. Where's your finger?"

Not being able to hold back, I say out loud, "Well, right now it's on a bloody clit." Our silent room broke into stupidly ridiculous laughter. I'll never forget that afternoon.

Fast forward to 2010, I am presently living in Costa Rica with my partner of twelve years and our dog. I teach yoga at the beach while we build our home and retreat spa in the rainforest on the border of Manuel Antonio National Park. We have both been massage therapists for many years, and I have to say that as much as I enjoyed the hell out of my piercings, I do not have any metal in my body anymore. I guess now that I think about it, it was one of my wholesale changes, sort of like a snake shedding its skin. Perhaps the further removed I was physically from professional piercing, the more distant the whole scene seemed. I was very comfortable with having them, but I'm equally at home without.

---

[1]Crystal has since transitioned from female to male and has taken the name Clayton. Crystal may have had her anger issues, but Clayton seems like a pretty mellow guy.

[2]I met Raelyn in San Francisco when Fakir and I were doing a piercing presentation for the Society of Janus. She approached us afterward, very serious about wanting to learn how to become a professional piercer. I shamefully have to admit that I brushed her off. With Fakir's guidance she achieved her ambition and has gained a following particularly in the women's community. A one-woman operation, she makes her own jewelry as well as does the piercing. She is also one of the pioneers in scarification.

[3]1783 Haight Street, San Francisco, CA 94117, (415) 933-SAFE, www.coldsteelpiercing.com

[4]See www.safepiercing.org

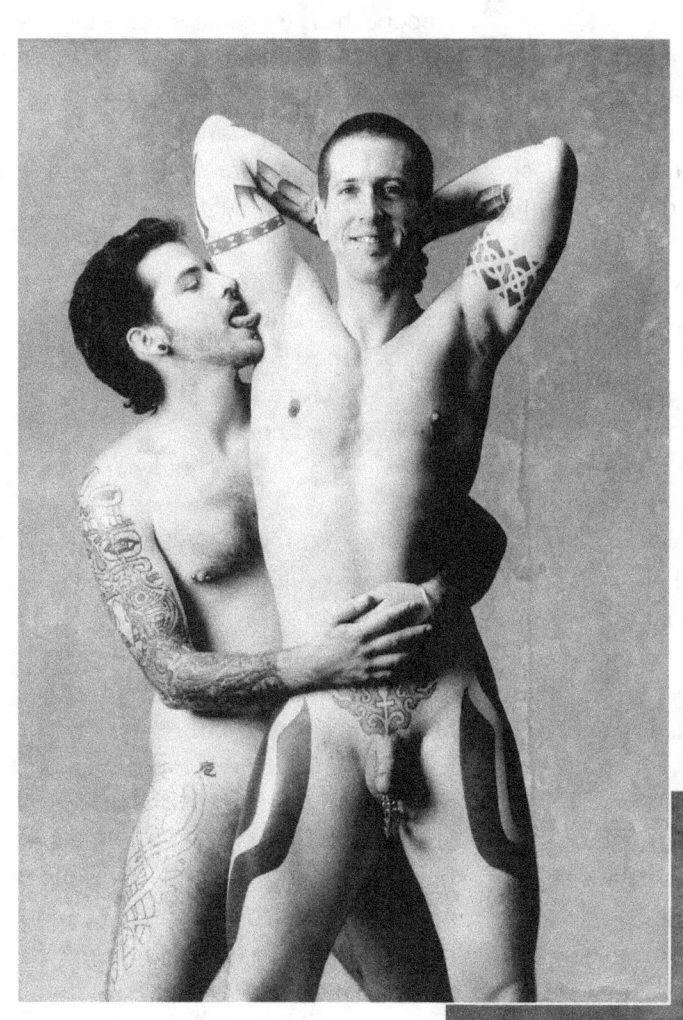

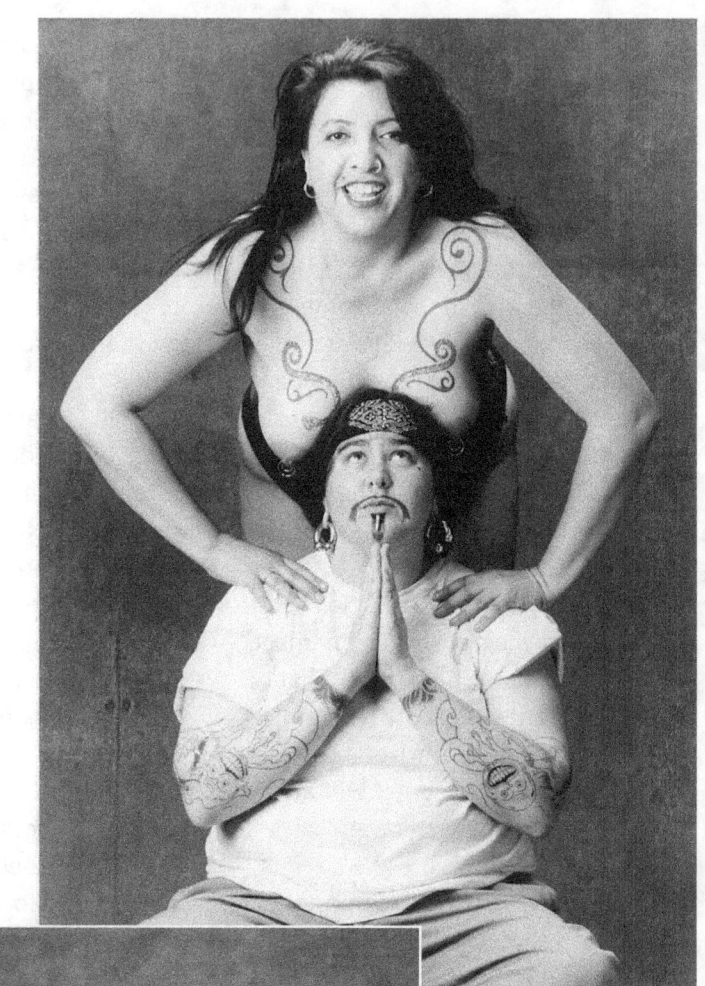

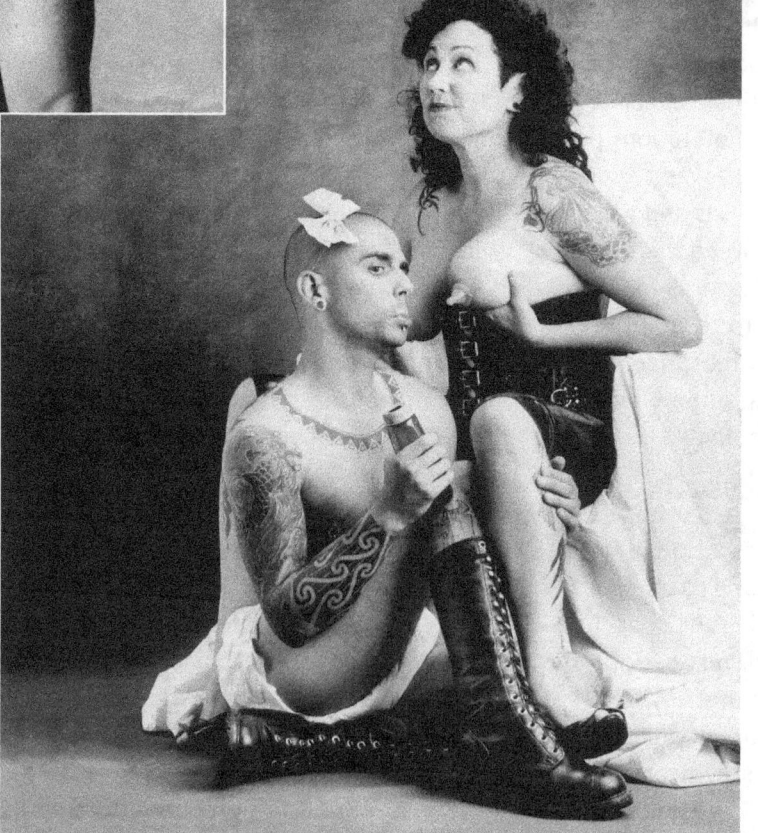

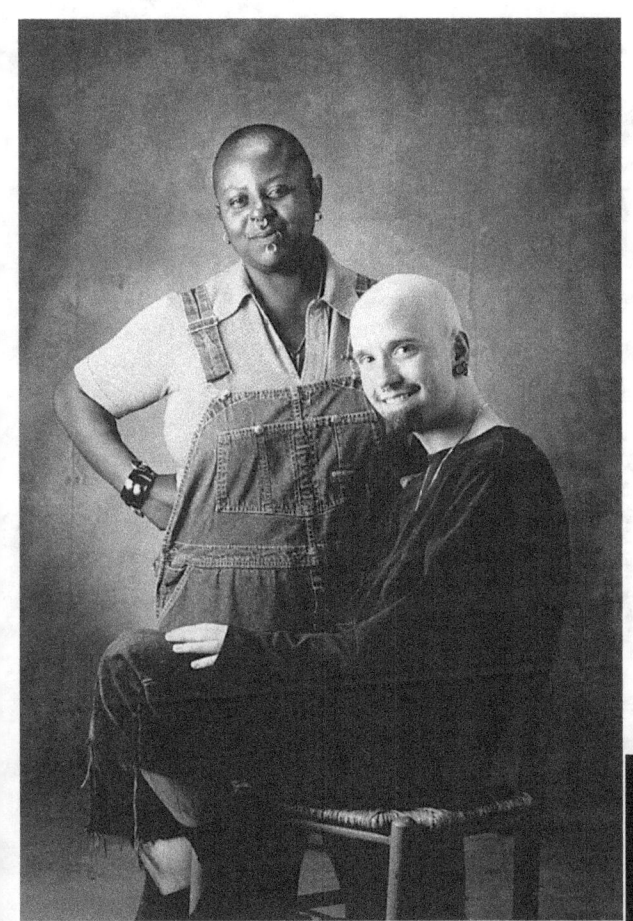

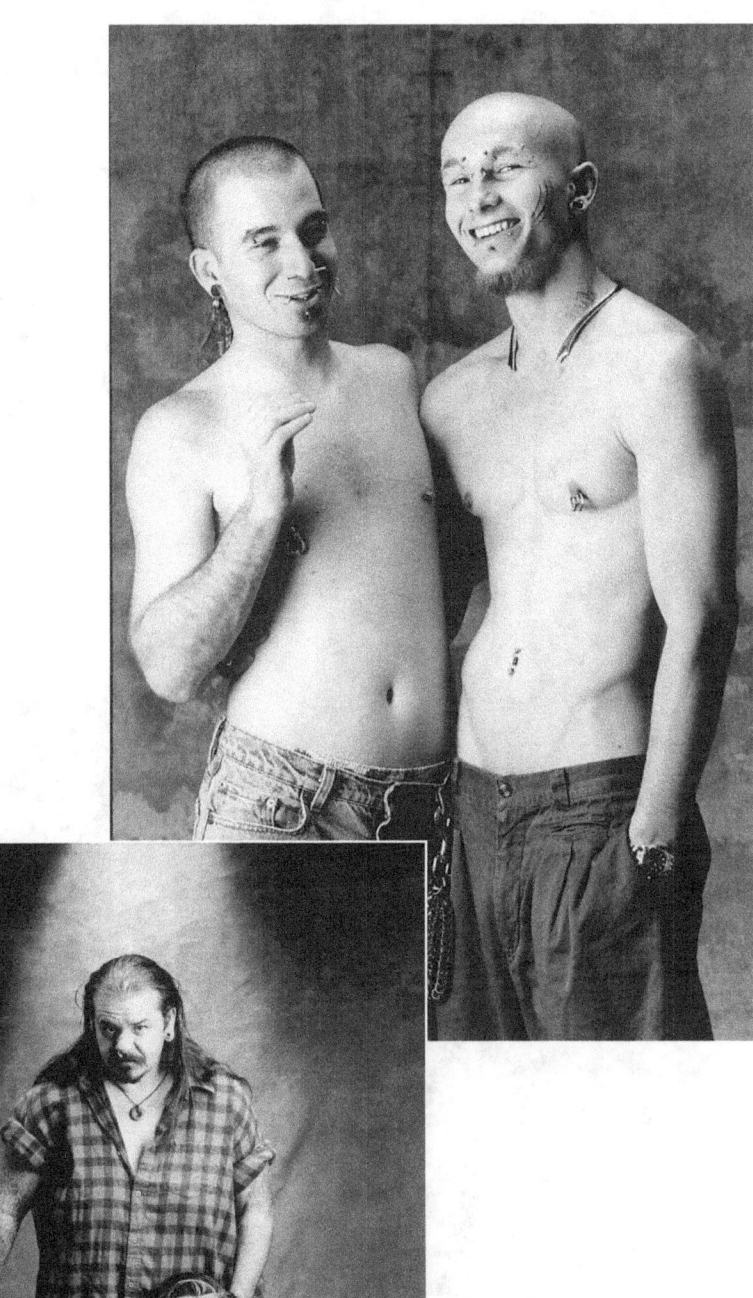

I love this series of employee photos taken by Michael Adrianne for *PFIQ* #45 celebrating Gauntlet's 20th Anniversary. *Opposite page, left to right*, John Stryker and Paul King; Brian Murphy and Debra Miller; Ruth Villaseñor and "Paco" (Taj Treva); *this page, left to right*, Crystal Mason and Jhan Dean Egg; Sky Renfro and Scott Chance; Mic Rawls and Jon Cobb.

MANY FACES OF GAUNTLET

The individuals are identified by number on page 120.

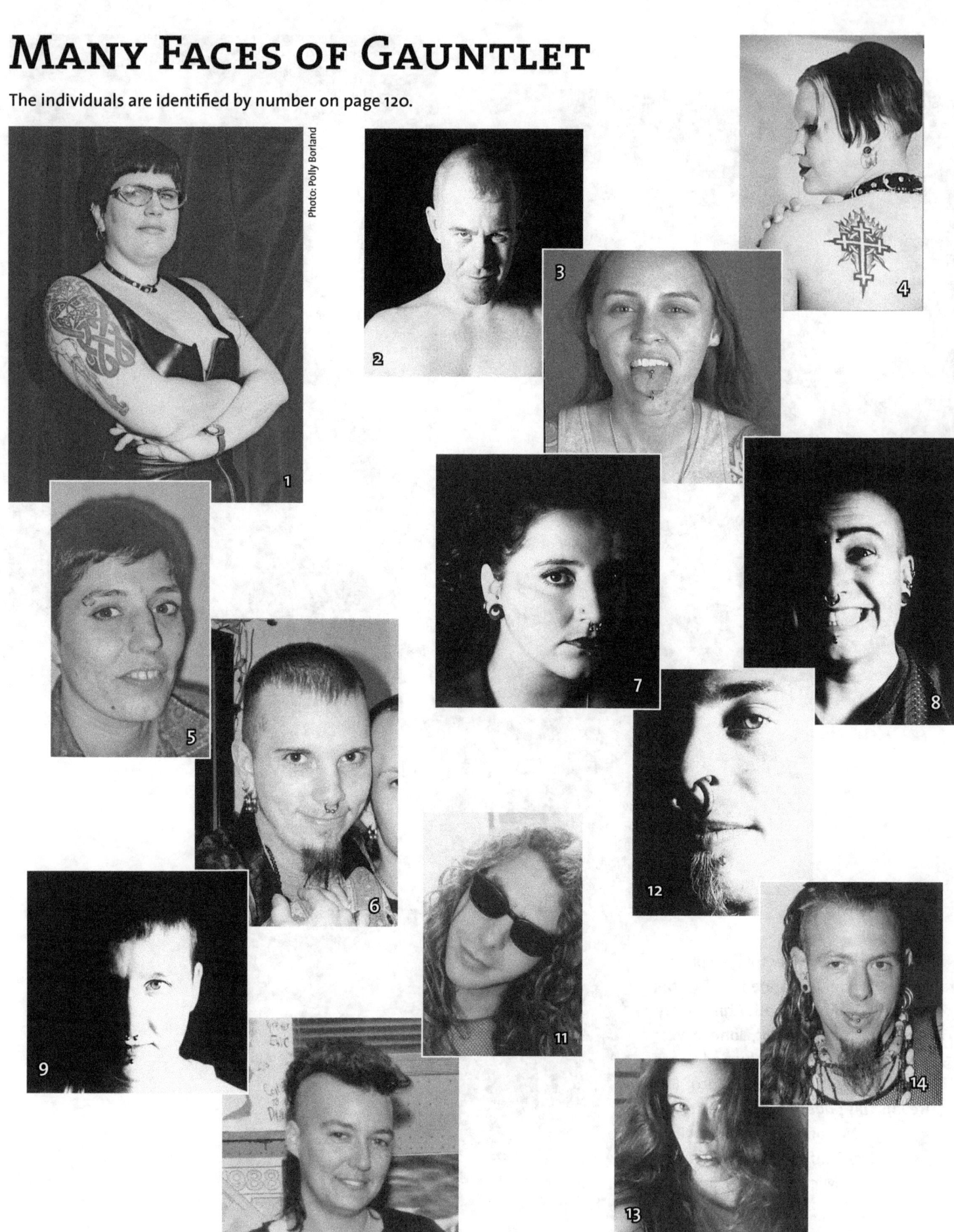

Photo: Polly Borland

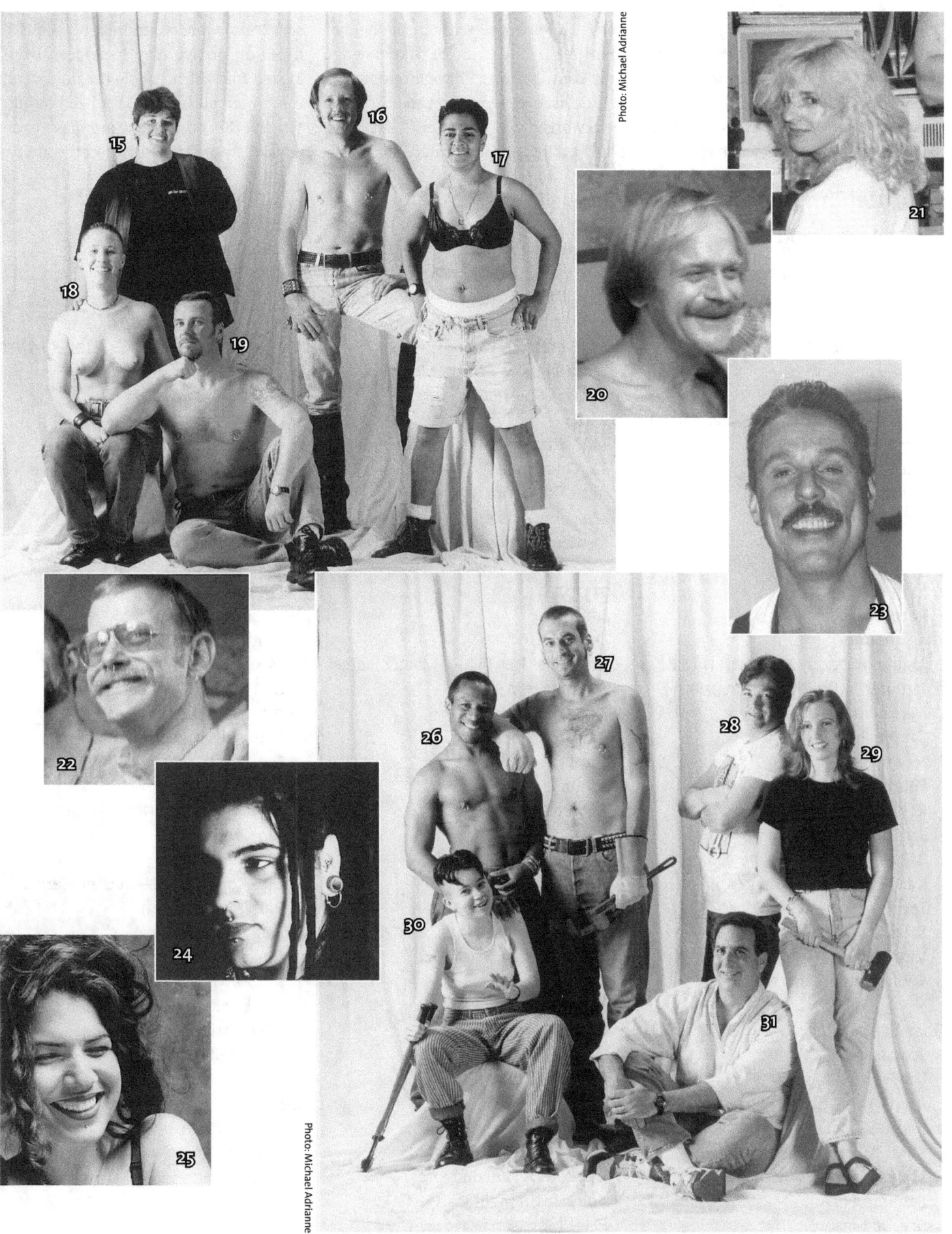

Photo: Michael Adrianne

Photo: Michael Adrianne

I wish I remembered everyone who worked for Gauntlet and that I could include all their stories. Unfortunately, I've only been able to write about a few, those I was most involved with day-to-day. Gauntlet would never have prospered quite so well without the help of them all. In an effort to acknowledge their contributions, I have attempted to at least list everyone, good and bad, who ever worked for Gauntlet. Most were hardworking and dedicated, some less so; several were scoundrels. It's possible a person or two may have been overlooked for which I apologize. In several cases their surnames have been forgotten. In others the last names have been consiously omitted to protect the guilty.

Gauntlet Employees, 1975–1998

West Hollywood

Elayne Angel—Master Piercer
Skip Arnold
Tasha Berg (#7)
Manny Betancourt
Boomer
Brad Bradley
Crystal Cross (now Clayton, also mfg.)
Tim Davis
Eric Drummond
Jen Dunham
Bob Flanagan
Rebecca Jarvis
Lilia "Beast" Judd (#3)
Jenne King (#1)
Rebecca Lewis
Jacqueline
Jaguar (formerly Bill Blitz, also S.F.)
Jennifer "Jeffy" Middleton (#8)
Michael Mulcahy
Lauren Pine (N.Y.)
Joe Powers (#22)
Sharon Rose (#24)
Robbie Heinz (#6)
Steffan Santoro (#11)
Bobby Ferris (a.k.a. Bobby Sun) (#14)
Karin "Kitten" Swinney (#9)
Tom
Kristian White
Vince Weiner (#12)
Robin Ziemer (also N.Y.)

San Francisco

Scott Chance
Lou Duff
Jhan Dean Egg
Kenny Fraser
Karen Hurt—Master Piercer
Melisa Kaye
Paul King (L.A.)—Master Piercer
Crystal Mason

Debra Miller
Michael Mulcahy
Brian Murphy (L.A.)—Master Piercer
Fakir Musafar
Sky Renfro (L.A.)
Scott Shatsky—Master Piercer
Tamara Sherman
Terri
John Stryker—Master Piercer
Taj Treva (nee Waggaman)
Ruth Villaseñor (L.A.)
Malcolm Wilson
Debbie Wortheim

Corporate

Jim Ward
Drew Ward
Michaela Grey (S.F.)—Master Piercer
Alayne Stern
Alavan
Richard Winchester
Gloria Morales
Irwin
Robert
Rik

Manufacturing

Chuck Atmore
Margie Atmore
Tomas Barnes III (#26)
Cirus Bass
Katie Childe
Donna[30]
Diane Farrison
James Green (#31)
Guido
John Henderson
Mary Helen Hinson (#39)
Mark "Mo" Huisman (#27)
Bob Martin (#28)
Peter Morrison (#23)

Erik Niles
Greg Patton
Alison Ridgway

Customer Service & Mail Order

Val Altamirano (#17)
Bear
Gordon Finch
George Forthman (L.A.) (#20)
Liz Henderson (#21)
Michele Hunt (#15)
Linck (#16)
Tiffany Magnolia
Vayena Moon (now Kai T. Rogue) (#10)
Robert O'Locksley
Susie Quon
Leigh Ann Sargent (#18)
Mike Warren
Marcus-Jay Wonacott (#19)

New York City

Keith Alexander
Lee Anderson
Autumn Asbury
Denise Gianetta (#25)
Jon Cobb (S.F.)
Liz Getschal (#4)
Dan Kopka (L.A.)—Master Piercer
Rain Murphy (#13)
Dug McDowell (#2)
Jonathan Palmer
Mic Rawls (S.F.)
Mark Seitchik—Master Piercer
Nikki Strippolli (#5)
Jason Teitel

Seattle

Meredith Lee
Krysteen Lomonaco
Al D. Sowers

Celebrities were a part of Gauntlet's clientele at least from the early Eighties, possibly before. In those days, prior to body modification becoming so common and widely acceptable, unless they were already public about it we tried to keep their names confidential. Nowadays, almost no one is scandalized to hear that one of their idols has a body piercing, and most celebrities couldn't care less, so I have no qualms about revealing the identities of and experiences with some of our more famous clients.

The first I personally recall piercing was punk rocker Wendy O. Williams of the Plasmatics. When she came into the store, there was nothing out of the ordinary about her, and I had no clue who she was until my office assistant Liz, an aspiring rocker herself, practically swooned that I'd pierced someone so famous.

David Carradine I remember well. He was one of the stranger people who passed through Gauntlet's door, and I was hardly surprised reading about the circumstances surrounding his bizarre death. He came into the L.A. store one afternoon for a penis piercing and though his conversation was definitely weird, there was no indication that he was drunk or stoned. While he was on the table he told me how he and his girlfriend enjoyed piercing each other and how she had pierced one of his hemorrhoids. That isn't something one hears every day.

Carradine was also pierced by others including Michael Mulcahy. On one occasion Elayne declined to pierce him because he was drunk.

Over the years, practically every Gauntlet piercer had a celebrity client or two. Elayne has enjoyed a long-running relationship with Lenny Kravitz. She first met him at Gauntlet L.A., and then ran into him again in New Orleans after she'd settled there. They became fast friends, frequently socializ-

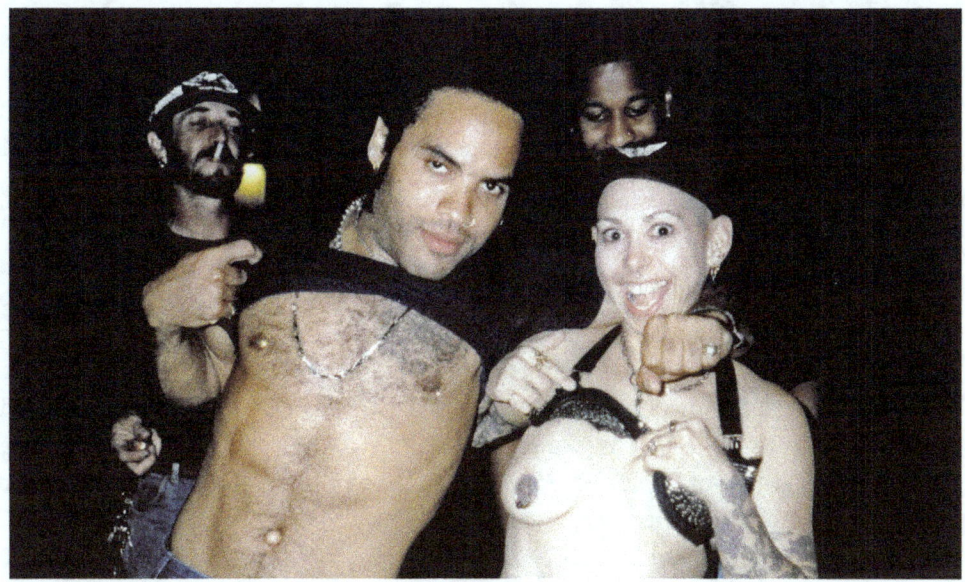

Lenny Kravitz with his official piercer, Elayne

ing whenever he was in town. She describes him as a down-to-earth, lovely person, wildly enthusiastic about piercing. I had pierced his nostril. He later had Elayne do a second nostril piercing to match, as well as pubic and nipple piercings. When his nipples were pierced Lenny remarked, "I love it! I wish I had ten nipples so you could pierce all of them!"

Lenny was always encouraging his friends and associates and brought many of them in to get pierced. On one of his tours, Elayne traveled with the band for about 10 days and pierced all its members and entourage, from his personal assistant to his bus driver's daughter.

Some of Elayne's other clients included Wendy Melvoin of Prince and the Revolution and her twin sister Susana, as well as guitarist Steve Vai.

In MTV's 2003 documentary *The Social History of Piercing*, Perry Ferrell of the band Jane's Addiction called Gauntlet "the ace place to get pierced," and it was where he got his first piercing. As a farewell tour for his band in 1991, Perry conceived of and created the music festival Lollapalooza. Thanks to this huge event, piercing hit the mainstream in a big way. "Originally

there was [sic] body piercing tents at Lollapalooza because I wanted to be pierced and I brought 'em along with me....I looked at piercing like passing a joint. It wasn't that important, but it was pretty good, and if you want some, here you go."

As a business move it would probably have been quite profitable for Gauntlet to have been present at Lollapalooza, but I rejected the idea. Gauntlet always prided itself on promoting safe, responsible piercing, something I felt the venue couldn't guarantee. Drug use would likely be rampant, it would be difficult if not impossible to maintain an environment for doing the piercing that was sufficiently sanitary, and the risk of contaminating or doing damage to the new piercing was too high. It's no wonder that Gauntlet and I got the reputation for being conservative, and unfortunately my attitude accomplished little other than make us appear smug and snobbish. In retrospect, it was also probably hypocritical considering that for many years, Gauntlet had a piercing booth at the Folsom Street Fair in San Francisco, a venue that carried all the same risks though on a smaller scale.

Many other famous people were pierced at Gauntlet.

Celebrities Pierced at Gauntlet

★ Marc Almond: Keith (nostril)

★ Cher: Scott went to her home and pierced her navel. John Stryker went to her house, stole a Tampon from the bathroom. We hung it in ours.

★ Iman: Elayne, Jen

★ Madonna: Scott pierced her on several occasions and went to the set to change her jewelry. On one occasion Jeff was sent to her studio to help with jewelry.

★ Ogre of Skinny Puppy: Steffan, Beast

★ Seal: Jeffy (nipples), Paul King, and Dan Kopka

★ Watty, lead singer of Exploited: Paul

★ Joey Arias: Paul and Brian

★ Clive Barker: Jaguar, Bobby Sun

★ Rosanne Barr: Scott pierced her fiancé. She wanted to see his pierced penis and shrieked when he showed it to her.

★ Justine Bateman: Kitten

★ Justin Bond of Kiki and Herb: Paul, Brian, and Kenny

★ Lisa Bonet : Elayne (declined to do her navel because it was too flat), and Kitten Swinney (ear cartilage)

★ David Bowie: Scott pierced his ears. Stryker

★ Terry Bozzio, drummer for Missing Persons and Frank Zappa: Crystal (nipples)

★ David Carradine: Jim, Michael Mulcahy, Vince (Elayne had to ask him to leave on one occasion when he came in drunk)

★ Margaret Cho: Jeffy

★ John Cusack: Elayne (ear cartilage)

★ Rebecca DeMornay: Elayne (ears)

★ Johnny Depp: Beast

★ Farrah Fawcett: came in with a girlfriend and wanted something unique. She showed Scott her gall bladder scar from surgery and decided to have a piercing with a small ring just under the scar. Jeffy (Jennifer Middleton)

★ Perry Ferrell: nameless piercer

★ Althea Flynt, wife of *Hustler* publisher Larry Flynt: Jim

★ Reeves Gabrels, guitarist for David Bowie: Stryker

★ Jean Paul Gautier: Mark (multiple ear)

★ Corey Haim: Kitten Swinney (nostril)

★ Kurt Hammett: Paul King, Brian Murphy

★ Joan Jett, rock star: Denise

★ Matt Johnson, lead singer of The The: Denise

★ Steve Jones of the Sex Pistols: Paul

★ Lenny Kravitz: Jim (one nostril), Elayne

★ Tommy Lee: Kitten Swinney (nipples), Beast once on Dennis Rodman's MTV show (eyebrow), Michael Mulcahy, Jeffy

★ Lisa "Left Eye" Lopes of TLC: Kitten Swinney

★ Jim Marcus, singer for a group called Die Warzau: pierced by Shatsky

★ Armisted Maupin: Jhan Dean Egg

★ Wendy and Susanna Melvoin: Elayne

★ Kate Moss: Beast, ear cartilage

★ Thierry Mugler, fashion designer: Liz, Mark

★ Dave Navarro of Jane's Addiction and Red Hot Chili Peppers: Sharon

★ Todd Oldham, fashion designer: Kenny

★ Joan Osborne: nameless piercer

★ Beverly Peele, supermodel: Kenny

★ Lynda Perry: Elayne, Michaela (navel), Mark (eyebrow)

★ Dana Plato, actress from *Diff'rent Strokes*

★ Suzanne Pleshette: nameless piercer

★ Genesis P-Orridge of Psychic TV: (Paul did work, but not pierce, on him)

★ Susan Powter: Jeffy (Jennifer Middleton)

★ Dennis Rodman: Scott. Elayne thinks she pierced him in N.Y. also Jeffy (Jennifer Middleton) (for world tour on MTV), Bill (L.A.)

★ Tim Roth: nameless piercer

★ Louis Rove (a.k.a. Indy), adoptive father of Karl Rove: Jim

★ Craig Scheffer, actor from One Life to Live and Clive Barker movies *Nightbreed* and *Hellraiser Inferno*: Elayne (septum and stretched his ears)

★ Gina Shock (drummer for the GoGo's): Beast (nostril)

★ Nikki Sixx: nameless piercer

★ Dee Snider of Twisted Sister: Keith

★ Wesley Snipes: (Paul did work, Robin pierced him)

★ Lars Ulrich of Metalica: Mic Rawls, maybe Sharon

★ Steve Vai: Elayne, Jeffy did insertions

★ Erl Van Aken: Jim (Septum, PA, Erl), Dan (nape of the neck), Elayne (axillaries)

★ Wendy O. Williams: Jim, Elayne

★ B.D. Wong: Elayne

Gauntlet staff also pierced lots of porn stars, provided actor Dwight Yoakam with a fake pierced nipple for the movie *Sling Blade*, and Paul King play pierced Udo Kier for a Greg Gorman photo shoot. We also lent or sold jewelry to several film projects and offered advice to them when they had pierced characters or piercers in the movie. For instance, the buyer for *Pulp Fiction* came in for jewelry and advice on how to make Rosanna Arquette's character look pierced. Greg Araki sent us a script for *Nowhere* and then borrowed (and returned) a number of items for the film. MTV filmed an episode of *The Rodman World Tour* in one of our piercing rooms at Gauntlet L.A.

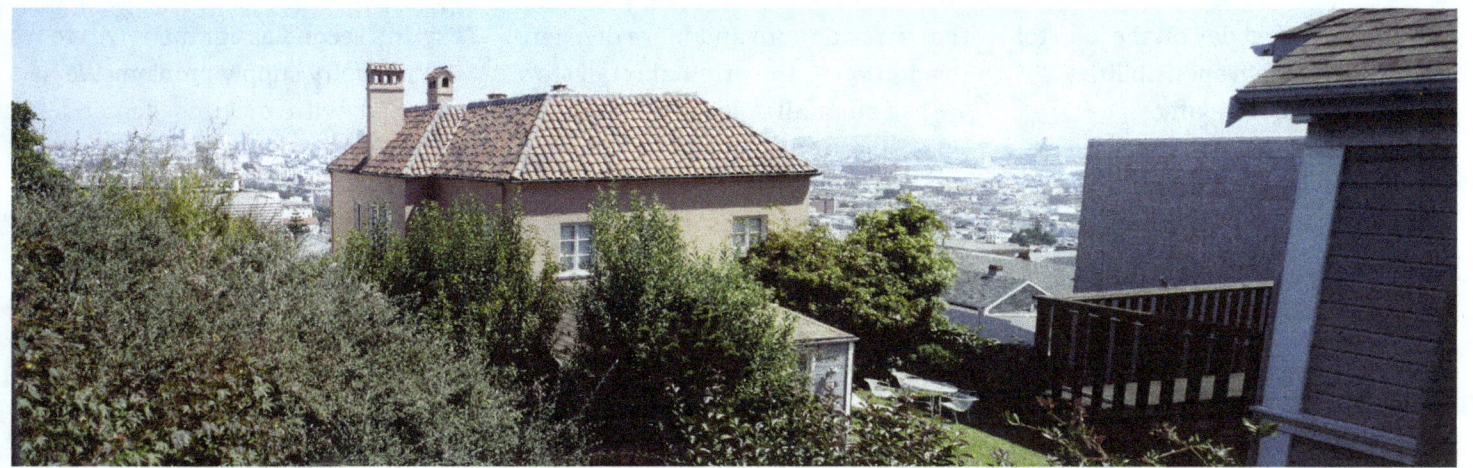

The view from the bedroom of our 21st street dream house. The dream was short-lived and soon followed by the nightmare.

CHAPTER 13

I certainly don't blame Fakir for what ultimately transpired, but as I see it, the end of our relationship in 1992 marked the beginning of Gauntlet's decline for which I hold myself fully responsible. Though not really aware of the fact, I was beginning to experience burnout, and for some time it was clear that the business had grown beyond my ability to manage. True to the *Peter Principle*, I had, in fact, risen to my level of incompetence. And, frankly, I lacked the head and passion for business. I was also quite addicted to the computer. Once I got a taste of designing and producing *PFIQ* without a drawing board, T-square, glue, and all the other old-fashioned tools of the trade, I was hooked. It also provided the ideal refuge in which to escape from the anger and grief of my breakup with Fakir. All together, these factors led me to take the actions that ultimately destroyed the company, though at the time I actually believed they would benefit it and simultaneously help relieve a lot of the pressure that I had been under.

In 1993 I decided to hire a general manager to run the business and free me to spend more time working on the magazine and other projects that were out of the public eye. It wasn't a bad idea and had the potential to succeed; I just hired the wrong person.

Drew and I had become good friends with Elaine and Susie, the S/M lesbian couple who had suggested Elayne as manager of the L.A. store. By this time Elaine held an executive office with a company in Palo Alto, and because of her experience, I asked her for guidance to help me select the right candidate for the general manager position. Just how much help she was able to impart in such a short time is questionable, and as a student of business management, I was sadly lacking in aptitude.

About eight or ten people applied for the job, and although I was in way over my head, I interviewed them all and tried to apply what I'd learned from Elaine. It wasn't particularly hard eliminating those applicants who were clearly unsuited for the position. The difficulty was with the ones who at least seemed to be qualified. These I agonized over. In my mind the ideal candidate would have not only business experience and savvy but also have piercings or at very least a clue what Gauntlet was about. Only one appeared to have it all: Irwin.

I had met, pierced, and had a one-night stand with Irwin and his then lover many years before, when Doug and I had done a piercing clinic in New York. Irwin was what a friend of mine once described as an "FU," a "fascinating ugly." He had bad teeth and was far from handsome, but he exuded animal magnetism and irresistible sex appeal. He was great with people, charming and charismatic, and a spellbinding conversationalist. Though I didn't know it at the time, he and his lover were both junkies.

By the time Irwin resurfaced in San Francisco many years later, his lover was long dead from AIDS, he had gotten his teeth fixed, kicked drugs, and was working as a rehab counselor for one of the local agencies, mostly with gay men. At the interview, I was completely taken in and ignored what, in retrospect, should have been red flags. Irwin had worked for many years with his father who owned a big carpet business in New York. He made it seem charming and funny that Dad had been a "gonif," the Yiddish word for a thief or scoundrel, and was a master at gouging the customer to maximize profits and fill his pockets with cash. I was too much of an altruistic liberal at the time to even consider there might be truth in the old adage that "the fruit doesn't fall far from the tree." After all, Irwin had managed to get off drugs and make something of himself. He had firsthand business experience and was pierced and a member of the local leather community. I was convinced I had found the perfect manager.

Not that it would have made any difference, but I wish I had put on paper the verbal list of job duties and goals I gave Irwin his first day on the job. I told him he had three responsibilities.

1. Prosper the company.
2. Fix the jewelry supply problem.
3. Relieve me of stress.

Irwin was such a superb con man that it wasn't until much later—and too late—that I realized just how abysmally he had failed at all three.

Gauntlet was already prospering, but I envisioned it continuing to grow and become even more profitable, to become to piercing what Starbucks had become to coffee. The stores and all of the divisions were doing well, so it was difficult to gauge if Irwin was having any significant impact on the bottom line. Thanks to years of tireless promotion, the business had acquired enough momentum that even if Irwin did nothing it would be some time before it became evident. In its peak year, Gauntlet's gross income was a little over $3 million.

My partner Drew claims to be a math atheist. If your eyes glaze over when someone starts talking about bookkeeping or accounting, you're probably right there with him. It tends to be not a very interesting subject for most of us. I mention it because, as the song says, "Money makes the world go 'round." Keeping track of it is essential to the well being of a business.

In the beginning, Gauntlet's bookkeeping was pretty simple. I actually took care of the day-to-day record keeping and my friend Alayne took care of making sure everything was in order and filing forms and tax returns. It was a job she was able to handle on a part-time basis while maintaining a regular 9-to-5. But the time came when her primary job demanded so much of her that she was no longer able to handle Gauntlet's books.

After Alayne's departure Gauntlet had started having accounting problems. These stemmed from the fact that we had more and more divisions. In addition to the original retail store, we had our mail order department, the magazine, and then added all the additional locations. I never fully understood the difficulties, but a string of incompetent bookkeepers struggled to deal with them. It's impossible to remember the number of times I had to hire someone only to eventually go to their home to regain possession of the books.

Alayne and I had remained friends over the years, and soon after the San Francisco store opened, I learned that her job in L.A. was coming to an end. She had always been conscientious in keeping the books, so I offered her a full-time position and was willing to move her to the Bay Area to take it. She was looking for a change and accepted.

Things went well for a while. A friend and client of mine, a leatherman named Steve who was our accountant, helped keep Alayne on track. Steve was also responsible for setting up our first computerized bookkeeping system and trying to teach Alayne how to use it. This proved to be only partially successful. Alayne was never able to get up to speed working on the computer and continually fell behind.

Steve was a great accountant, and one reason he was so good at his job was that he was obsessively detail oriented. I remember his once taking two hours to track down 23 cents. Working for him must have been maddening, so it came as no surprise when I learned that his chief assistant, a man named Robert, was looking to strike out on his own.

It was obvious that Alayne needed help. Robert knew the bookkeeping software inside and out, so we offered him a position as Alayne's assistant, and he accepted. For the first time we had someone for whom our unique bookkeeping problems were little more than interesting challenges.

Irwin's second assignment was to fix our jewelry supply problem. We had struggled with meeting demand for years. Even our own manufacturing department wasn't able to keep up. I hired Elaine's partner Susie to work on the matter, but nothing came of it.

I brainstormed with Irwin on numerous occasions and at length tossing back and forth various possibilities. Although I had some ethical misgivings about having our jewelry manufactured out of the country, it was something we considered and set aside as too impractical in terms of oversight. Gauntlet now had competition, and we needed to get product that was up to our standards but could be sold at a competitive price.

Matters came to a head after January 1, 1994 when President Bill Clinton signed the North American Free Trade Agreement (NAFTA) the purpose of which was to eliminate barriers to free trade between the U.S., Canada, and Mexico. Very quickly small businesses called *maquiladoras* were springing up just south of the border where cheap Mexican labor was turning American raw materials into goods for tariff-free import back into the U.S. Irwin convincingly pitched this as the perfect solution to our problem.

I've no idea what rock he found them under, but Irwin had located a Mexican couple who owned a maquiladora in Tijuana I'll call ASW. We took them to dinner and they pitched a scheme that they assured me would solve our problem. Gauntlet would hire an American engineer who would be on our payroll and oversee the operation. ASW would find and equip the factory and hire the workers with our manager's approval. We would be billed for the equipment and receive regular invoices for the Mexican payroll. Irwin went for this in a big way, and with no in-depth financial evaluation and no clear picture of how long it would take to get the plant up and running, he and Robert persuaded me to obtain a line of credit to finance the endeavor. In a recent email, Michele Hunt, the woman who at the time managed our mail order department wrote, "What comes first to mind is all of us in mail order and manufacturing trying to figure out why Irwin and Robert were so gung ho about it [the Mexican operation]. They were telling us one thing and our own research had a different take."

We found and hired an engineer named Art who lived in San Diego and who was willing to make the daily commute to Tijuana. ASW located an appropriate industrial space, equipped it, and began interviewing potential workers. The bills started rolling in, and months went by before we began to receive jewelry prototypes. More time passed until a trickle of product began to arrive, the quality of which fell short of our standards.

In the interim and in desperation we turned to competitors like Good Art and Anatometal to keep us supplied with the common sizes of stainless steel jewelry. We had moved our own manufacturing facility from Los Angeles to a warehouse on Natoma Street in San Francisco. At this location our gold, silver, and niobium jewelry was being made as well as the custom, one-of-a-kind stainless steel pieces.

For a long time I was under the impression that we never quite got the Mexican manufacturing operation up to production before everything fell apart. Looking through my files recently, I came across a document claiming Mexico was producing so much jewelry we weren't able to sell it fast enough. If such was the case, why were we turning to Good Art and Anatometal to fill our needs?

It seems evident now that Mexico was Gauntlet's downfall and testament not only of Irwin's incompetence, but also my enormous error

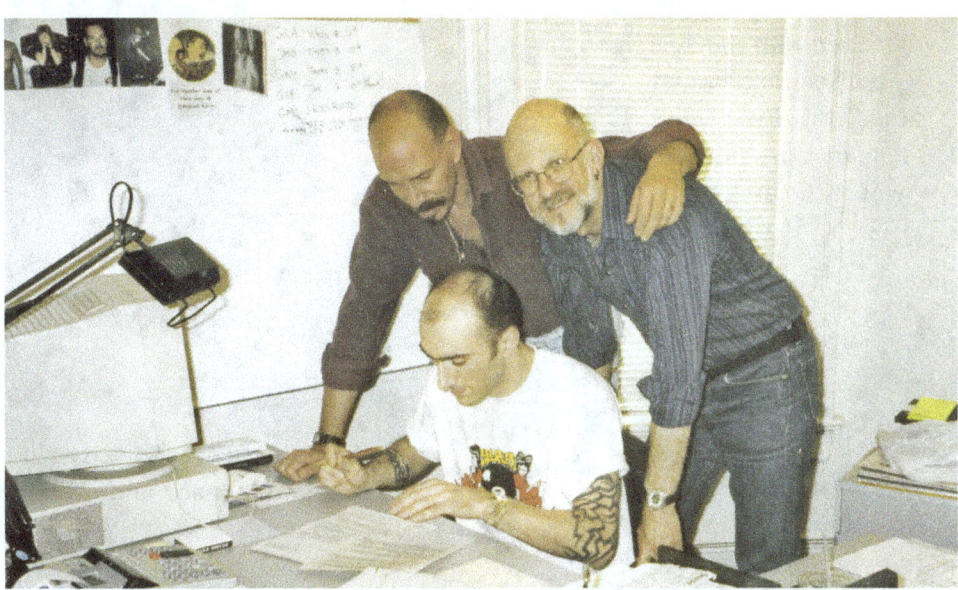

Dominique Minchelli (seated) signs the contract to open a Paris franchise. Irwin and I observe.

in judgment in hiring him and my abysmal failure to see his shortcomings while giving him so much power. It was a division that consumed hundreds of thousands of dollars with very little return. Add the financial burden of opening the New York and Seattle studios, and even though they generated some income, all the divisions combined could not carry the Mexican facility. Looking back, it becomes crystal clear how the business was fatally overextended and why.

To all appearances our jewelry supply problem would soon be a thing of the past. Using this as leverage, Irwin and Robert both came into my office one day and demanded sizable raises. I should have said their request was premature and insisted that they wait until there was a steady flow of high-quality product. Instead, I asked Robert if the company could afford such large increases in salary and was assured that it could. What was I afraid would happen if I said no? Irwin might leave, and the full responsibility of running the company would once again fall on my shoulders. Robert controlled the finances. Replacing him would have been difficult. It's hard to admit that even though I knew I was being used,

I caved in. Irwin's and Robert's salaries both ended up jumping by many thousands of dollars. When I stop and think what a spineless fool I was, I cringe with shame. Several employees had warned me that Irwin was intent on taking over the company, but I dismissed the rumors. In retrospect it's so clear he had me where he wanted me.

Irwin and Robert became thick as thieves and determined to drive a wedge between my friend Alayne and me. It was true that she wasn't carrying her weight as far as the bookkeeping was concerned, but she was reliable and honest and looked out for my interests. Had they not persuaded me to lay her off, I wonder how much grief I might have been spared. Of course, it ended our friendship. As she departed she warned me that Irwin and Robert could not be trusted. That much was borne out. She also accused Drew of being a gold-digger, something he proved untrue.[1]

In November of 1994 Gauntlet Paris (France), our first and only franchise studio and one of the first piercing shops in Europe, had its grand opening. I envisioned having more, but they never became a reality. Owner Domin-

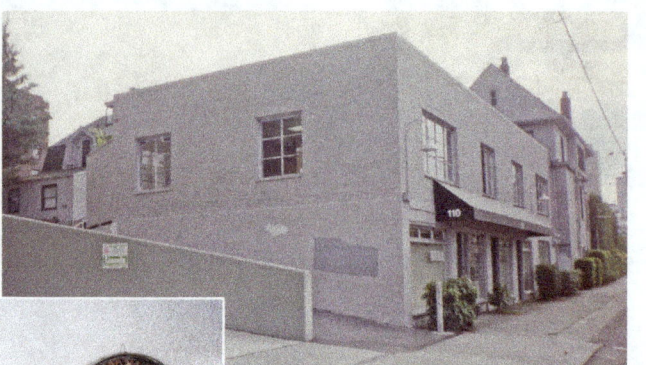

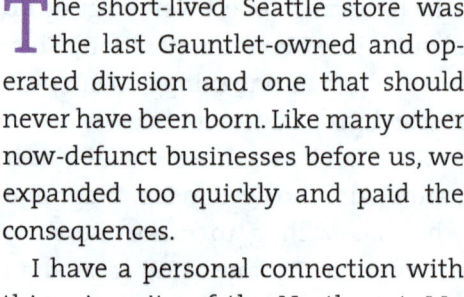

Left, The staff: Al D. Sowers, Kristeen Lomonaco, and Meredith Lee

Above, One of the guests at the grand opening on Halloween night. *Left*, Michaela Grey and I chatting during the party.

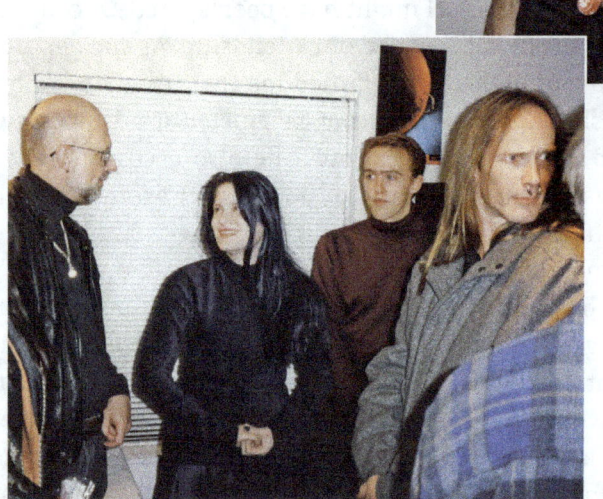

ique Minchelli approached us with the idea, and after some negotiations, an agreement was reached and a contract signed. Over a period of months, several of our Master Piercers took turns working in the studio and training Dominique. The studio flourished.

The short-lived Seattle store was the last Gauntlet-owned and operated division and one that should never have been born. Like many other now-defunct businesses before us, we expanded too quickly and paid the consequences.

I have a personal connection with this rainy city of the Northwest. My brother settled there after he graduated from college and has remained ever since. For many years I would visit and began doing piercing clinics on a regular basis. One frequent venue was The Crypt, a sex shop on Capitol Hill, Seattle's gay neighborhood, although there were other locations including the Lake Union houseboat of my brother and his wife, a few public spaces, and the homes of friends in the leather community.

One of those friends was Al D. Sowers. I have never known a more active, outgoing person. I'm still amazed that one man could be involved in so many causes and organizations and still have a life. His two main passions were probably body piercing and the leather community. He had attended Gauntlet's beginning and intermediate/advanced Piercer Training Seminars as well as Fakir's Basic Pro Piercing Seminar, and was passionately concerned about issues of health and safety. For some time, he was an APP board member. Over the years, Al garnered a number of leather titles including Mr. Washington State Drummer (1990) and Mr. Northwest Drummer (1994). Issue #50 of *PFIQ* (1997) described how Al and fellow piercer Krysteen Lomonaco planted and nurtured the seeds for Gauntlet Seattle:

While attending the APP general meeting held in Las Vegas last May, the concept of Gauntlet Seattle was born. Seattle piercers Al D. and Krysteen began a friendly conversation with Gauntlet staff members Michaela Grey and Sky Renfro. The question arose from all: why not open a Gauntlet store in Seattle?

What followed were several months of phone calls, email messages, six rewrites of Al and Krysteen's proposal, endless number-crunching, demographic plotting, and a whole lot of sweat. In the meantime Al wasn't feeling well and underwent major surgery, leaving poor Krysteen to run their current business all by herself. After many delays the proposal was finally finished and presented to Gauntlet's general manager Irwin Kane.

Krysteen and Al flew to San Francisco in late August to meet with Irwin and Gauntlet owner Jim Ward. Now the task at hand was for Kysteen and Al to find a good location—easier said than done! Irwin made two trips to Seattle to help. Despite a few leads and setbacks, an excellent space finally presented itself.

The new location at 112 Boylston Ave. E. is spacious, with six parking spaces and a view of the Olympic mountains on clear days. It's a little off Broadway, the Capitol Hill district's main drag. Well known as Seattle's gay/lesbian/alternative neighborhood, it is easily accessible by foot, public transportation, and main thoroughfares and highways.

Krysteen, Al, and their assistant Meredith, as well as visiting Gauntleteers Chance and Sky, had their work cut out for them in renovating the space. Fortunately they had a lot of much-needed assistance from their friends Jaime Barber, Tanith Kim-Sing, Jon Littrell, Rick Rollins, and Tim Bootz. After a month of sawing, painting, tile-laying, furniture and fixture-ordering and setup, the store was ready for its grand opening.

The store made its debut on Halloween [1997] at a private and very popular party."

Quite frankly, I was disappointed with the location and didn't think that Irwin, who had been entrusted with the job of helping find it, had done a satisfactory job. Although it was right off the main drag and readily accessible, it was also pretty invisible. The store was never profitable, and when finances became tight, Seattle got the ax.

Gauntlet's first piercing seminars were conducted at various local hotels. Though not bad venues, they were expensive, and there was the inconvenience of having to transport and set up each time. With the lease on the Castro Street office coming to an end, Irwin, Drew, and I consulted with Michaela (who was seminars director) and Robert (who was now our controller) and came to the conclusion that, all things considered, it would be more economical to find a location where we could accommodate not only the corporate offices but also the seminars and the mail order department, which at the time was in Menlo Park. A commercial real estate broker who was a customer and member of the leather community found us a spacious second floor location at Folsom and Seventh Streets. It was ideal. We signed the lease and with minor construction, paint, royal purple carpet that Irwin ordered through his father at who knows what rip-off price, and some essential furniture, we were ready to move in and re-commence operations.

One of our seminar students was an enthusiastic young woman from Japan named Demi. Her ambition was to open a piercing studio in her home country and become a distributor there of Gauntlet jewelry. In due course she was able to make these happen.

For the first year or so after I moved in with Drew, we shared the apartment on Landers Street. It took almost a year, but my house in Van Nuys finally sold, providing the equity to purchase a home in S.F.. Our first house (1991) was a tiny cottage on Elsie Street on the west side of Bernal Heights. We spent a lot of money improving the property, but with nowhere to add a much-needed second bathroom, we decided to sell the house and buy a larger one.

By this time I thought I had it made. Between us, Drew and I enjoyed a very comfortable six-figure income. Yet before giving us such generous salaries, I conferred with Robert asking him if the company could afford it. He said yes, and I then reminded him that his job included monitoring Gauntlet's financial health and that he was to alert me if it was ever in jeopardy. He never fulfilled that part of his responsibility.

The property that our brokers found for us was a dream house, a multi-storied Edwardian home, circa 1909, on 21st Street between Church and Dolores streets. It was completely detached, something of a rarity in San Francisco. The upstairs master bedroom had a panoramic view of the city; the downstairs dining room looked out on a peaceful Japanese-style garden complete with koi pond and gazebo. A spacious entryway included a semicircular bay with windows looking out onto the street. It was an ideal place to display my harp. The price seemed reasonable, though the mortgage payments strained our budget and didn't allow us to immediately afford all of the upgrades and repairs the place needed. We worked on house and property little by little as the money was available.

Drew and I were on top of the world. It appeared that we had arrived and that the gravy train would never end. Little did we realize that the curtain

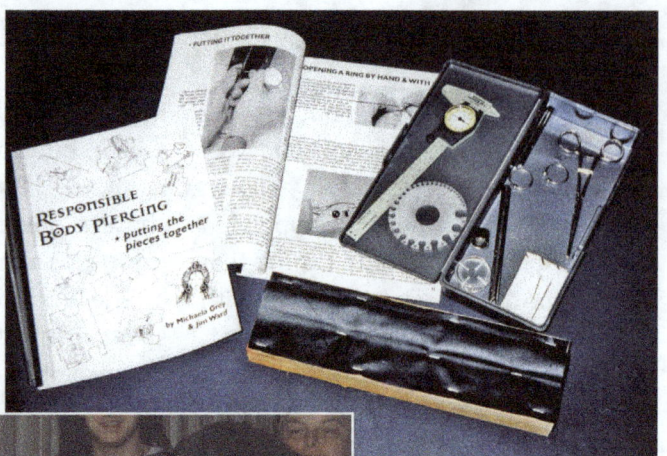

Right, Every student received a training kit containing a manual, a box of piercing implements, a few pieces of jewelry, and a piercing practice board.

Above, Michaela Grey (left) oversees aspiring piercer, Kevin McKinley.

Right and below, Gauntlet piercer Chance (in red) supervises seminar students' hands-on training.

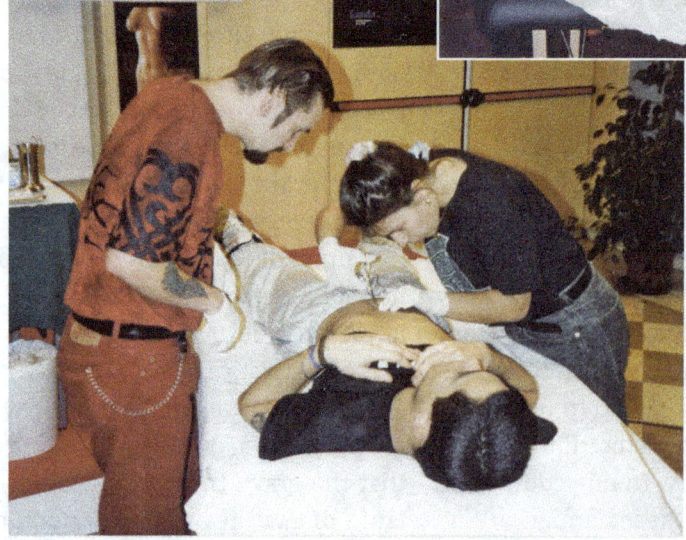

was going up on Gauntlet's last act.

About a year after acquiring the property Drew and I decided it was time to buy some quality furniture for it. One sunny morning we drove to an upscale home furnishing store and spent several hours picking out half a dozen pieces, choosing the finishes and the fabrics. The bill totaled about $10,000. Thankfully, everything had to be special ordered.

We had scarcely arrived back at the office when Irwin came to my door with a somber expression on his face. My heart sank; I knew something was wrong. The business, he told us, was in serious financial straits. We needed to brainstorm ways to assure its survival. I excused myself for a few minutes, called the furniture store, and cancelled the order.

One of the ways Drew, Irwin, and I agreed to help with the cash flow was to reduce our salaries. Drew and I agreed to 40% pay cuts as did Irwin, except he conveniently neglected to inform our payroll person of his agreement and, without my knowledge, continued drawing his full salary.

In the sequence of events that marked Gauntlet's decline, one of the most bizarre involved our bookkeeper Robert. One Monday morning in December of 1996, he simply didn't show up for work. We called his home; no answer. After several worrisome days he turned up. The story relayed to me was that he had gone on an alcoholic binge and ended up in a psych ward. Irwin facilitated a leave of absence, and Robert supposedly went to stay with a brother in San Diego. He virtually disappeared and to the best of my knowledge hasn't been heard from since.

Whatever actually happened will probably remain forever a mystery. After he left, we discovered that the bookkeeping office was a shambles. Records had been misfiled or disappeared entirely. It was impossible to know what was going on. Richard, Robert's assistant, attempted to step in temporarily, but it was hopeless, and Irwin took steps to keep Richard in the dark about the real state of affairs. We limped along month after month from one crisis to another. I have sometimes wondered if Irwin himself created the bookkeeping chaos to cover his tracks. We'll never know.

The third of Irwin's job duties, given to him the day he started work, was to reduce my stress. There is no way to adequately express how abysmally he failed. It seems likely, in fact, that his intention was to create as much stress as possible in order to weaken and undermine my morale and mental and physical health to better facilitate the company takeover. In the wild, predators take down the weak and the sick. By the time Irwin introduced Rik as our salvation, I was easy prey.

To put things in their proper chronology, in June of 1997 I finally bit the bullet and laid Irwin off in order to cut back on expenses. This didn't go well at all. He left in a fury, making ugly threats, and telling me it was the worst choice I could have made—that proved only half correct. He took with him a number of boxes that likely contained, in addition to personal belongings, documents that would have incriminated him of mismanagement if not actual criminal wrongdoing.

Not to be done out of his handsome salary, Irwin orchestrated a scheme whereby he could return to an executive position and his neighbor, a wealthy local businessmen, would help get the company back on its feet. Subsequently, he introduced me to Rik.

From the moment I met him, I disliked him. He is frequently abrasive, verbally abusive, and rude, and made it clear from the beginning that his only interest in Gauntlet was as a way to make money for himself. In the time that I knew and had dealings with him, my dislike escalated to unadulterated hate. I have never despised another human being as much as I loathed Rik, and he is the only one I ever actually contemplated murdering. At our first meeting, my little voice of intuition sounded a deafening alarm, but I was so weighed down with emotional pain and distressed about the state of my health that I put up no fight.

According to Irwin, Rik was willing to get Gauntlet back on its financial feet. Unfortunately, the price was steep. I had given Drew stock in the company. This was to be transferred back to me, and Drew was to seek employment elsewhere. Per the terms of an initial temporary contract all stock was then to be divided: 33.5% to Rik and the same to me, 23% to Irwin, and 10% to then L.A. store manager Sky Renfro.

Before the final contract was signed, a number of curious things came to light. Invoices from ASW, the Mexican maquiladora, indicated that we were being double-billed for merchandise and charged exorbitant amounts for everything from a $100 birthday cake to $26,000 air conditioners. Irwin was unwilling to do anything about it, claiming that we had to honor our contract with ASW. This was highly suspicious, and in retrospect makes me wonder if he was getting kickbacks from the overcharges. Regardless, while I was away in Tijuana getting medical treatments, Rik, with my agreement, fired Irwin.

By this time Rik, had made it clear that he wasn't going to get involved in Gauntlet for less than controlling interest. Reluctantly I acquiesced. The final contract dated June 19, 1997 gave him 51% of the shares; I had 29% and Sky 20%. On paper, even though I gave up control of the business, the terms looked like the answer to my prayers. I received the title Honorary President, and according to clause (h) of the contract:

"Jim Ward shall be entitled to lifetime employment by the Corporation at a rate of pay commensurate with his percentage ownership of the shares in relation to the net income of the corporation, which rate is currently approximately $2000 per week. The Corporation shall also advance the cost of Ward's prescribed medical treatments not covered by the Corporation's health insurance policy, up to a maximum of $30,000 per year, which shall be credited to the Corporation as a portion of the payment Ward is entitled to based on his percentage of shares in relation to net income.

"The duties of the Honorary President shall include providing input into the long-term strategic planning of the business of the Corporation, assistance with graphic design, and development of PFIQ for publication on the Internet, but shall not include responsibility for or involvement in the daily operations of the business. As such, Ward shall have lifetime access to Gauntlet archived material and photos, but publication decisions shall be subject to the approval of the Chief Executive Officer. The Honorary President shall not be required to devote his full time to the business." The remainder outlined my authority, which was nonexistent.

Two attorneys reviewed the contract before I signed it. One thought I was getting a sweet deal. The other indicated misgivings, but whatever they were I either did not understand or was incapable of hearing. I learned the truth much too late. The way the contract was written, as soon as Gauntlet went into bankruptcy, which was inevitable, my contract became null and void.

There are two common types of bankruptcy: Chapter 11 and Chapter 7. The first provides a company with relief from creditors and an opportunity to reorganize and get back on its feet. Many large, well-known corporations have been through it and are still in business today. A significant feature of this type is that the company must provide the bankruptcy court with a reorganization plan. Under Chapter 7 the business and its assets are seized by the court and liquidated to help pay off creditors. The company ceases to exist.

Rik filed for Chapter 11 on February 27, 1998. About the same time, Sky Renfro resigned. Drew and I had sold our dream house in San Francisco, which we could no longer afford, and purchased a modest townhouse in Berkeley. He found work at a health professions college.

More than once I cringed when I observed the way Rik treated employees. He could be verbally abusive, and a number of good people, including Michaela Grey, quit rather than tolerate it. He attempted to instate employee contracts and piercing quotas, but the San Francisco store staff rebelled and, as a result voted to unionize in January of 1998.[2] To help economize, Rik decided to move the corporate offices from Seventh Street to the second floor of a building he owned in which he had another business.

At some point Rik took issue concerning our agreements with Gauntlet Paris and our Japanese distributor. The situation turned ugly, and when the dust settled, Dominique Minchelli, owner of the French franchise, had severed affiliation and renamed his business 23 Keller; we no longer had a European outlet. We were out of the Japanese market as well, replaced by one of our primary competitors.

I was undergoing chemotherapy and needed expensive medications to survive. Even though my contract was meaningless—something I still didn't realize—I was attempting to fulfill my duties in order to remain covered by Gauntlet's health insurance. Suffering from the side effects of the chemo and unable to tolerate Rik any longer, I asked for a medical leave of absence that he subsequently claimed was a resignation. After some wrangling, thankfully I was able to retain my health insurance through COBRA.

The time passed for Rik to file a reorganization plan with the bankruptcy court. Instead, he offered to buy the company's assets for $10,000. The court found this unacceptable, and according to one of the court documents stated, "The case should be converted to a chapter 7 on the grounds that debtor has no intention of reorganizing and has failed to file a plan within a time fixed by the court." After a hearing with the major creditors, that is precisely what was done.

When Gauntlet went into Chapter 7 bankruptcy December 4, 1998, the bankruptcy court theoretically seized everything, to be sold to satisfy creditors. But the court trustee took no steps I am aware of to protect the property. No sooner had the business been declared dead than anyone with a key, alarm code, and/or safe combination was free to prey upon it like vultures on carrion, and some did.

There was nothing I could do, and, as painful as it was, I had to accept that everything I had built was gone. My greatest fear was that the intellectual property—the name, logo, magazine and video copyrights—would end up in the hands of someone who would desecrate them.

The court broke the estate into two parts. Good Art, a competing body jewelry company in Los Angeles, purchased what remained of the inventory and equipment. The name and intellectual property went unsold, perhaps because the court trustee set her financial expectations too high. The estate languished for nearly six years.

In June of 2004, the trustee finally took steps to dispose of the property and put it up for auction on eBay. On June 26 Barry Blanchard, the owner of Anatometal, a body piercing jewelry manufacturer in Santa Cruz, California, stepped forward and placed the winning bid of $6,623.32 in the last five seconds of the auction.

In an email to friends prior to the auction, he had this to say: "It brings a tear to my eye every time I think about what has happened over the years. Jim has done so much for me and others that words could never be put forth in this format.... Now it's time to give him something."

On July 20th Barry took possession of the estate from the court trustee in San Francisco. He drove it to our home in Berkeley, California and sold it to re:Ward, Inc., the small corporation Drew had started several years earlier, for the sum of $1.00. I am still touched by Barry's generosity.

The financial nightmare that we endured in Gauntlet's final months and for several years afterward took their toll particularly on Drew. He has developed something resembling post-traumatic stress disorder that plagues him to this day. Any financial surprise, no matter how small, triggers an anxiety attack and drives his blood pressure to alarming levels. Just attempting to reconcile a bank statement causes him incredible stress.

Our personal bankruptcy came as no surprise; we had seen the handwriting on the wall. The process was painful, and when it was over, our savings were gone.

One particular incident that really threw us came out of nowhere in 2003, when we applied to refinance our home. Everything appeared to be going smoothly when the process came to an abrupt halt because there was an outstanding lien of nearly $40,000 against the property for Gauntlet's unpaid N.Y. sales taxes. Even if we'd known about them, our bankruptcy would not have discharged them. It's a miracle neither of us had a heart attack. Thankfully, the N.Y. tax agency granted us amnesty that eliminated penalties and interest, but we were still left owing over $26,000. Fortunately, we were able to persuade the mortgage company to use a portion of our equity to pay off the lien and finalize our refinance.

In the years immediately following the end of Gauntlet, I felt like an utter failure. When I voiced that feeling to a friend in the industry, he emphatically refuted it. I had, he said, provided a profession for thousands of people, many of whom might otherwise be unemployable.

There are times when I find it extremely difficult not to be bitter. Considering I poured over 20 years of my life into Gauntlet and created an industry that profits many, I have very little to show for it. There are no royalties and no residuals. Drew and I have food on the table and a roof over our heads. Our townhouse is comfortable, if a little shabby, and our combined income leaves room for few luxuries. Yet somehow we manage to survive.

After Irwin was fired he attempted briefly to start his own piercing jewelry business. He worked for Mr. S Leather for a short while before pulling up stakes and moving back to New York with his lover Mark. There he joined forces with a fellow leatherman and Chicago Hellfire Club member named Fred to open a fetish clothing, sex toys, and body piercing business called DV8. The partnership was short-lived. At some point Irwin had started using again. Fred told me that he showed up for work one morning so high that he wasn't even aware that he'd shit his pants.

Irwin's relationship also hit the skids, and Mark left him to return to San Francisco. Tragically, Mark had

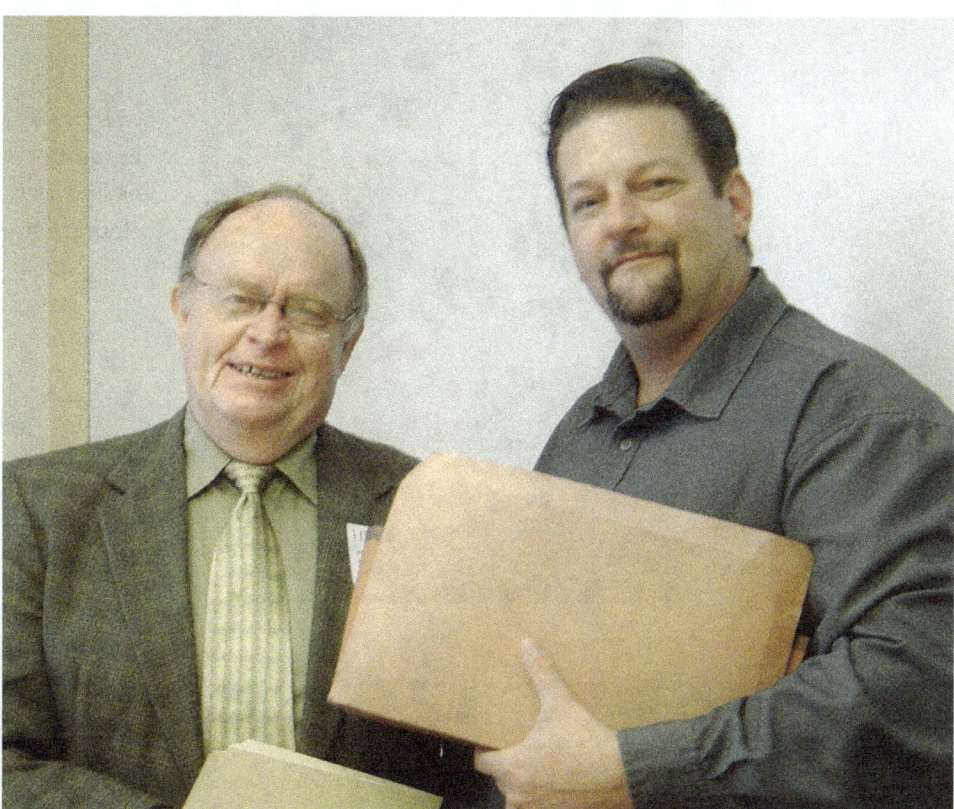

Jim Seeman (left), administrative manager to the U.S. bankruptcy trustee, turning over the Gauntlet intellectual property to Barry Blanchard, owner of Anatometal.

some serious mental issues and in March 2009 put a plastic bag over his head and ended his life. He was a sweet soul with a delightful, impish twist. I photographed him a number of times and used some of the images for advertising. One of my favorite photos of all time (taken by Michael Adrianne and based on a concept of my own) is the cover of *PFIQ* issue #48. It shows Mark with the high heel of a lipstick-red shoe through his tongue piercing.

The drug abuse finally caught up with Irwin. His trashed liver succumbed to cancer, and he died August 23, 2010 after a prolonged illness.

I can't remember how or when my views took shape regarding modern allopathic medicine which seems more focused on relieving symptoms than on finding and attempting to remove the cause of disease. Though my perspective has changed somewhat since the late 1990s, I am still convinced that the medical establishment is all too often more concerned with profit than with patient well-being.

Early in the AIDS epidemic, I became convinced by the work of UC Berkeley professor of molecular and cell biology Dr. Peter Duesberg that HIV is not the cause of AIDS, a position he maintains to this day. Consequently, I refused to take AZT and to my doctor's chagrin began to explore alternative therapies.

Around 1993, despite all my best efforts, my health had begun to noticeably deteriorate. Eventually, I could ignore the obvious no longer. My left ear, which I'd scraped badly on the car door, developed ugly red patches just like some on my nose, that by then had spread onto my upper lip. My doctor insisted on doing a biopsy. Not surprisingly, the test confirmed Kaposi's sarcoma (KS), one of the serious, usually fatal, diseases associated with AIDS.

By this time, thanks to a number of new, effective drugs, fewer people were dying of AIDS. My doctor tried to

Celebration

September 25, 2004, a group of past Gauntlet employees and well-wishers met at our home in Berkeley to celebrate the return of Gauntlet's intellectual property.

Right, Elayne Angel holding a photo of deceased and dearly loved Gauntlet jeweler Pete Morrison

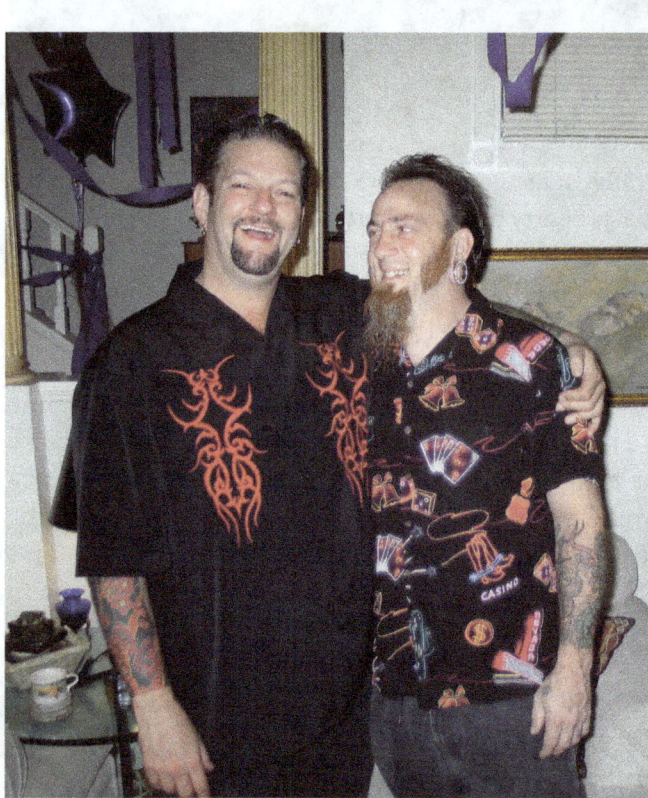

Above, Barry Blanchard and Brian Gilliam of Anatometal

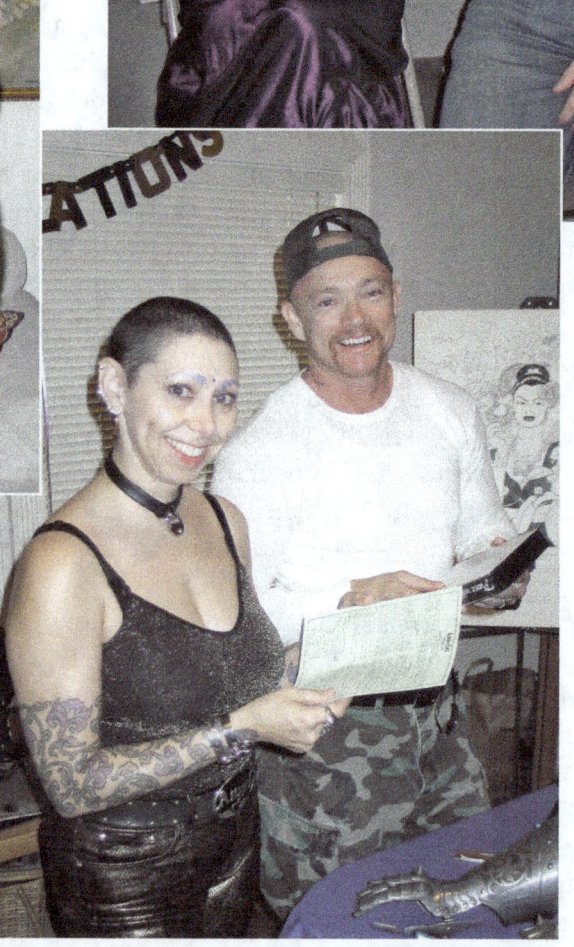

Above, Michaela Grey, Barry Blanchard, and Paul King. *Left*, the Angels, Elayne and Buck, examining old Gauntlet memorabilia

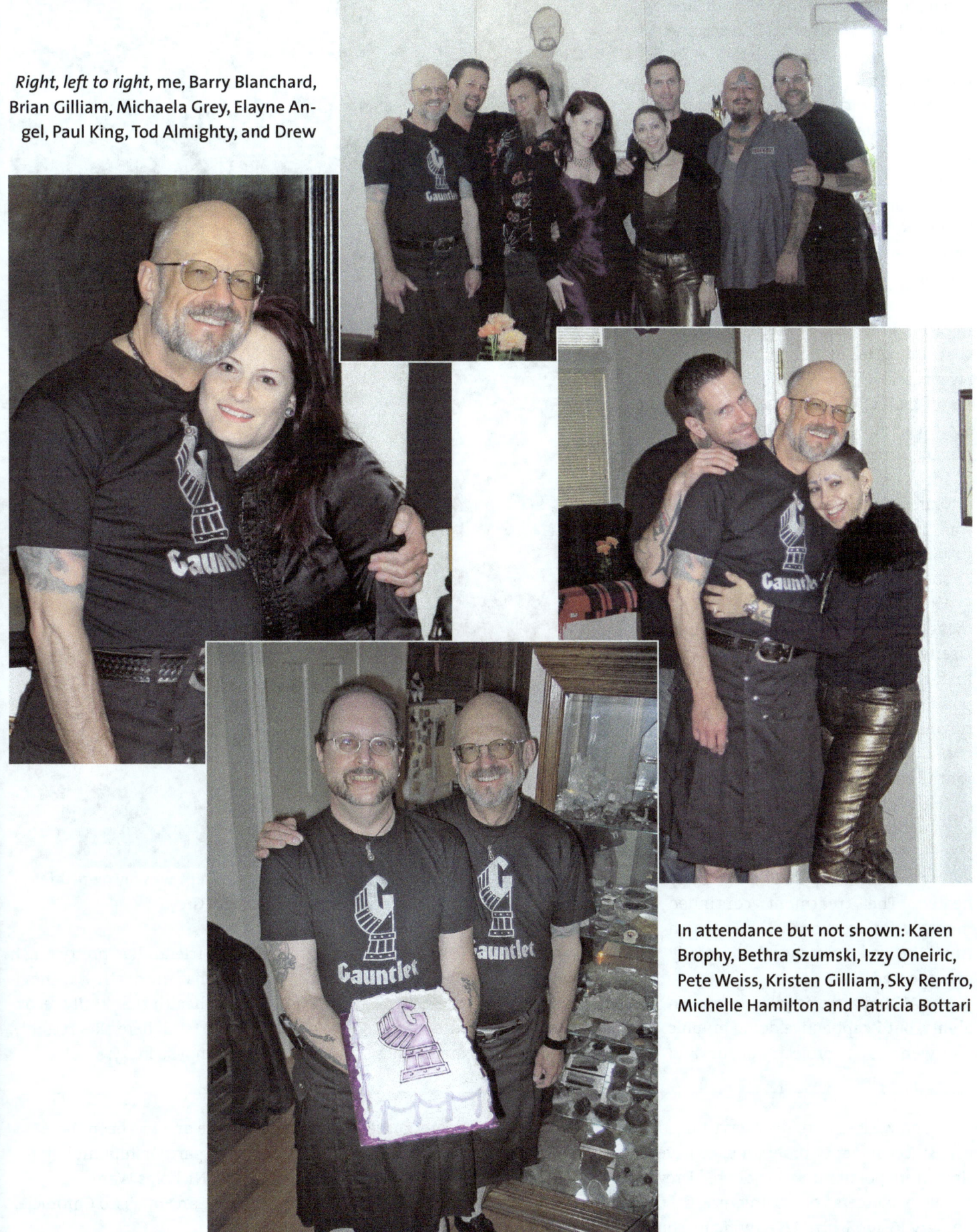

Right, left to right, me, Barry Blanchard, Brian Gilliam, Michaela Grey, Elayne Angel, Paul King, Tod Almighty, and Drew

In attendance but not shown: Karen Brophy, Bethra Szumski, Izzy Oneiric, Pete Weiss, Kristen Gilliam, Sky Renfro, Michelle Hamilton and Patricia Bottari persuade me to go on the "cocktail," the combination of drugs that had become the accepted treatment, but I stubbornly refused, clinging desperately to the belief that there was something out there, something I hadn't found yet, that would heal me.

My nutritionist Scott, with whom I'd worked for a number of years, no doubt could see the way things were going and began distancing himself from me. He was of the opinion that I should have my mercury amalgam fillings replaced; this I did...with gold. He thought I should go to a clinic in Lustmühle, Switzerland. I went...and returned poorer but no better off than when I left. As a last resort Scott recommended a clinic in Tijuana run by an Arizona M.D. The doctor, a quack as it turned out, assured him the cytokine therapy they administered was "100% effective against KS"—like gasoline is 100% effective against fire, he should have added.

After two depressing weeks of treatment I returned home, and not long afterward it became alarmingly clear that, thanks to the cytokines, the Kaposi's sarcoma was out of control. I had run out of options.

My doctor wrote out prescriptions for the cocktail and referred me to an oncologist to treat the KS. Only a few days after receiving chemotherapy, the lesions began to dry up. Within a few weeks they had completely healed. The treatment continued monthly for six months, after which time the red splotches had totally disappeared.

My AIDS diagnosis put me on disability, but I kept active doing graphic and web design projects for fun and

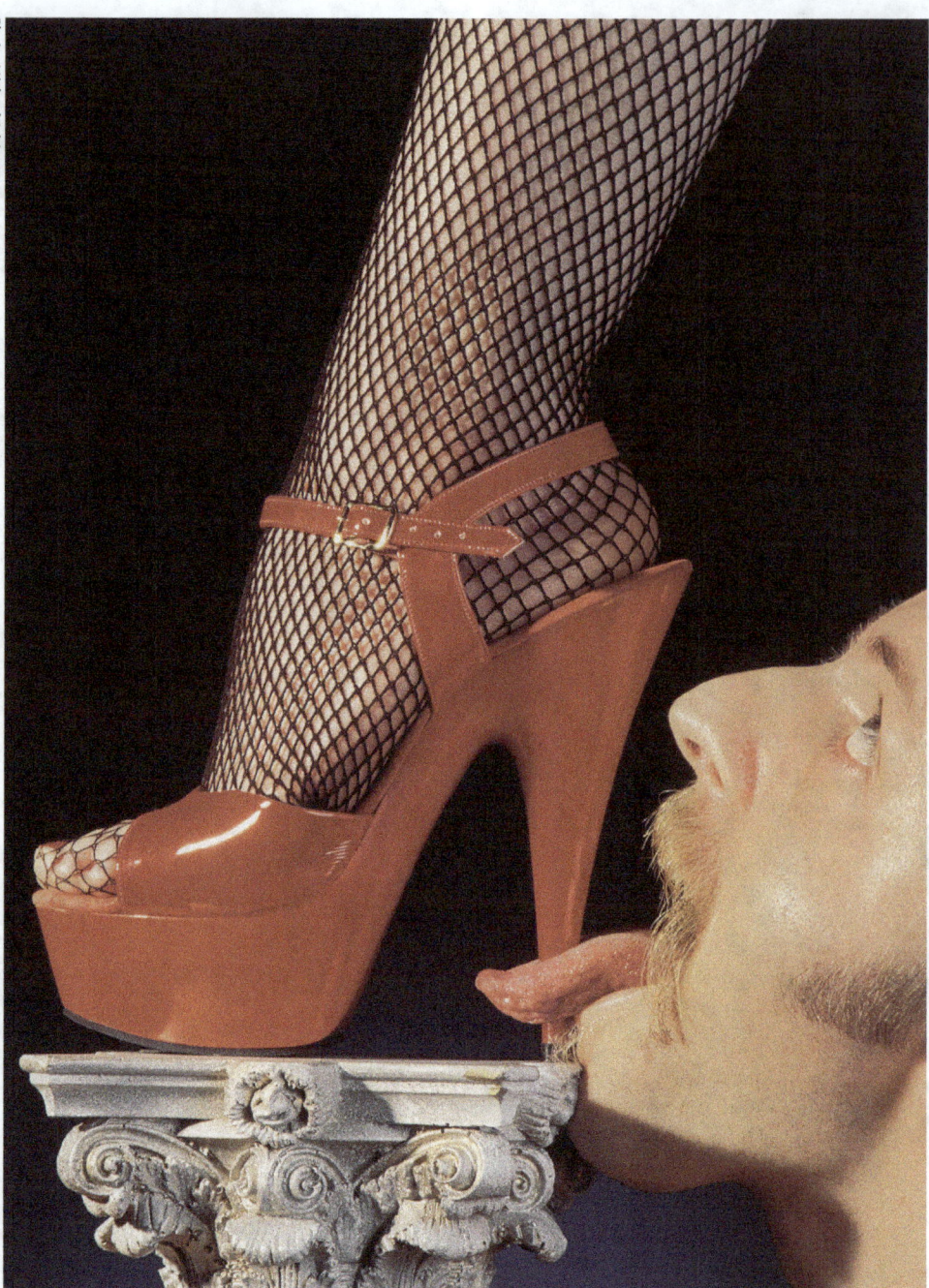

Photo: Michael Adrianne

The cover of *PFIQ* issue #48, one of my favorites. The concept was my own. It featured Irwin's lover Mark, and the shapely leg of Michaela Grey.

working on this book. Though pretty thoroughly retired from piercing, I have occasionally acquiesced to the request of someone I know to pierce them or one of their acquaintances.

Family and friends had pretty much accepted that my death was inevitable, but my health thankfully recovered, and I'm still here. Regrettably, Gauntlet was not so lucky.

---

[1]When we lost virtually everything and my health was rapidly deteriorating, Drew stood by me and has been there ever since. In fact, in order for us to have a legally recognized relationship—long before domestic partnerships and marriage were possibilities—I adopted Drew in 1992, and at that time he changed his name to Drew Nicholas Ward.

[2]"Body piercers vote to unionize: Castro District salon workers don't like hole-making quotas," San Francisco Chronicle, January 16, 1998. http://www.sfgate.com/cgi-bin/article.cgi?f=/e/a/1998/01/16/NEWS7252.dtl

CHAPTER 14

For over 20 years Gauntlet reigned as the undisputed leader of the body piercing industry. But even before its demise, there was already a younger generation asserting itself, writing its own rules, and seeking to gain dominance. In the eyes of these young rebels, Gauntlet represented the old establishment that needed to be swept aside and replaced by something newer and more cutting-edge (pun intended). While doing just that, piercing itself seems to have been abducted into a polygamous marriage with every imaginable form of adornment—branding, scarification, tongue splitting, and implantation, to name a few—and in the process becoming more extreme itself.

Of those pushing the boundaries, at the forefront was probably Steve Haworth, listed in *The Guinness Book of World Records* as the "Most Advanced Body Modification Artist," 1999 to present. If it can be done to the body, Steve has probably managed it.

Perhaps the most strident voice of the new wave has been that of Shannon Larratt, the founder in 1994 of the online body mod community, BMEzine. com, and originator of ModCon which began in 1999 and is described as "a heavy body modification convention... an invite-only party for those actively involved in making significant changes to their own body or to the bodies of others."[1] The permanent alterations included, but were not limited to, those listed above plus castration and penectomy (removal of the penis), subincision (opening up the male urethra), penis splitting, genital implants, and amputation. Activities included hook hanging (suspension) and saline infusion, primarily of the scrotum.

Aside from the fact that he is essentially a body-mod anarchist, is it any wonder that Shannon considered Gauntlet conservative? The most ad-

Right, Steve Haworth considered by many to be the father of extreme body modification.

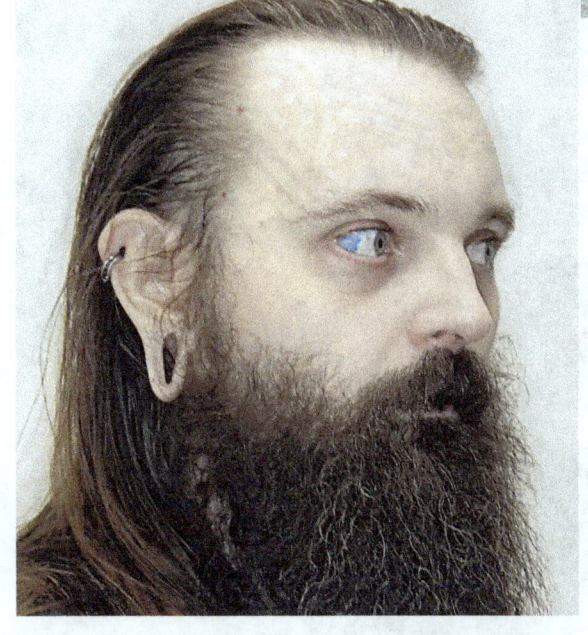

Left, Shannon Larratt, the voice of the extreme body mod movement. His forehead work is a white ink tattoo (done by Shane Faulkner) that continues down onto his cheeks as scarification (by Lukas Zpira). The eyeball tattooing was done by Howie/Lunacobra using a procedure of Shannon's invention.

vanced piercings that we did—ampallangs, apadravyas, and the occasional clitoris—pale by comparison. Being so focused on the most extreme modifications conceivable, how could he be anything other than jaded?

The average piercer does not make a living doing any of these over-the-top alterations, and I think attempting to compare them with the bread and butter of the ordinary studio is unfair and unrealistic. On this point James Weber of Infinite Body Piercing in Philadel-

phia, who is an officer of the Association of Professional Piercers, has made some pertinent though slightly different observations:

"True, the AVERAGE piercer can't make a living doing heavy modifications only, but there are quite a few who started as piercers (or still call themselves that), whose main income is heavy modification. In addition to Steve Haworth, there is Lukas Zpira (http://www.body-art.net/), Brian Decker in New York (http://purebodyarts.com/),

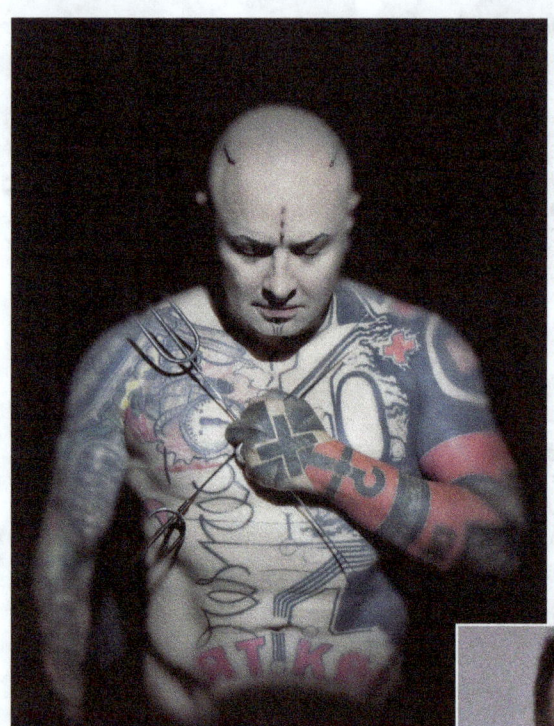

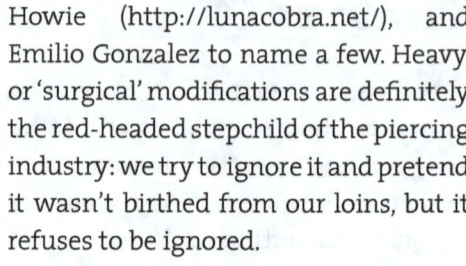

Howie (http://lunacobra.net/), and Emilio Gonzalez to name a few. Heavy, or 'surgical' modifications are definitely the red-headed stepchild of the piercing industry: we try to ignore it and pretend it wasn't birthed from our loins, but it refuses to be ignored.

Top to bottom, four pioneers of extreme body modification: Lukas Zpira, Howie (Lunacobra), Emilio Gonzalez, and Brian Decker

"I often think the heavy mod movement is a natural extension of piercing. We spent a lot of time—as piercers—convincing our clients that their bodies were their own, and that they should be free to do with them what they wanted. (Taking our cues from the gay rights and pro-BDSM and pro-sex feminists.) Once people were ready to challenge traditional wisdom—and traditional medicine too—it was only so long before they started to take 'medicine' (i.e. plastic surgery) into their own hands, and try to beautify themselves in ways that were contrary to traditional beauty standards. I thought it was an amazing movement to see the start of, and to be involved with in at least a small way."

When I began examining some of the things considered new and innovative today, I realized that I or another Gauntlet piercer had actually attempted quite a few of them, often decades ago. For various reasons, they didn't seem worth pursuing, at least at the time. What needs to be remembered is that the industry was still in its infancy, and in many cases there just weren't enough people interested in a particular piercing to provide an incentive or opportunity to refine the technique and perfect the appropriate jewelry. Of the many new and unusual ideas that have popped up in the last decade or two, you might be surprised at how many were at least attempted by someone on my payroll.

Take for instance the various piercings of the lips and around the mouth. These have a long history and have appeared in a myriad of cultures and eras. Especially if you live in any large

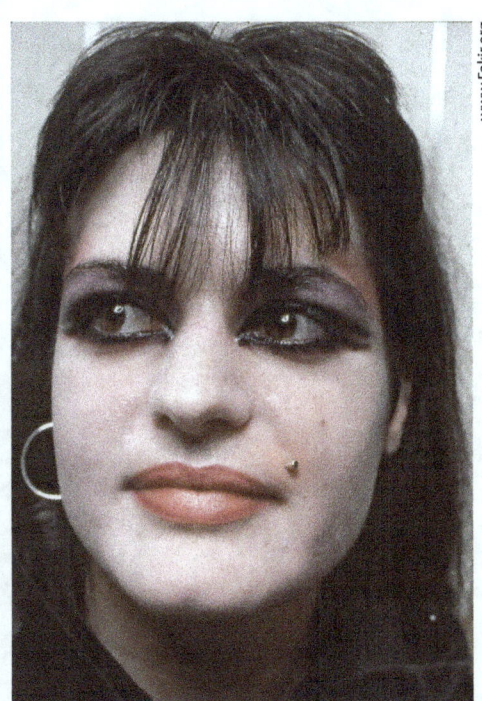

The labret was first featured in *PFIQ* issue #24 (1985) with a "Pierce with a Pro" article in issue #29 (1987).

metropolitan area, you're likely to see one or more of them. Although I did my first in 1986—what is now called a Monroe or sometimes Madonna piercing—and documented the procedure in *PFIQ* #29—I had no sense of the best placement, and it took a while for jewelry to be developed that was comfortable and minimized the risk of damage to teeth or gums. One of the first innovations was the fishtail labret conceived by Raelyn Gallina, but it is practical only for a lower labret centered at the gum line. Since there are a number of other possible placements, much experimentation by many different piercers had to be done to perfect the best designs for them.

The hand-web, another radical piercing that periodically resurfaces, goes through the thin tissue between two fingers, most commonly the thumb and forefinger. This was the subject of a "Pierce with a Pro" article in *PFIQ* issue #23 (1984), and Doug claimed to have seen a Las Vegas card dealer with one, wearing a diamond stud in it. As many piercers who have attempted it

will attest, the odds of success are low. To get it to actually heal requires the sedentary existence of a Chinese princess. It's difficult to keep the piercing from being exposed to pathogens and prevent it from becoming inflamed by the constant movement of the fingers.

Then there was Earl van Aken II, a.k.a. Erl van Douglas, a character actor and all-around interesting guy who was a regular client in the late 1980s and who has lent his name to the piercing vocabulary. In 1997 he was slated to be the featured personality in *PFIQ* issue #51, which, sadly, was never published. Here, belatedly, is the article that didn't appear:

My name is Erl—to some in the modeling field it is Just Erl. For convenience and singularity, I shortened my given name of Earl Douglas van Aken II.

Even at an early age I never quite "fit in." There always seemed to be some problem with my appearance, attitude, or apparel. I have long since become aware of the fact that it is not generally me, but most people's limited view of what is going on around them. It seems to me rather arrogant of someone who does not know me to assume or dictate what they feel is appropriate behavior for my journey on this path of life...my life! We are all different and endowed with the ability to make choices and decisions. In making those choices and decisions, I try to do what I say and not infringe on others. I have many times from an early age to the present been condescendingly urged to make my appearance more suitable—to what, I ask? Your vision? As ever, I refuse to yield. I always try to enhance others' views about individual choice.

In the mid '60s I quit doing work for NASA, JPL, and Bell Labs, etc. because I chose not to conform to a "no beard, no long hair" policy imposed from somewhere up the corporate ladder. The next day, I started out as a multi-

media artist—some older readers may remember the Mind Shaft Co. In time I became quite successful and eventually was unable to supply my demand.

Without going into a lot of detail, many of my earlier years were fraught with addiction to many substances. I went through three marriages, non-criminal jail terms, numerous heart attacks, seizures, convulsions, two flat-lines, and a twice-broken neck. There were also serious suicide attempts, though fortunately people always seemed to find me in time.

There was a long period of recovery. It began after the second flatline. I experienced what I would call a divine intervention. I saw the light! My psyche was dramatically changed, my behavior altered, and a whole new path in life was set before me. I set foot on this path with the élan and zest of someone just born. That experience was in July of 1981. My life now is so far removed from that past mode I find it hard to believe I lived and survived it all.

After a period of recovery—AA, de-

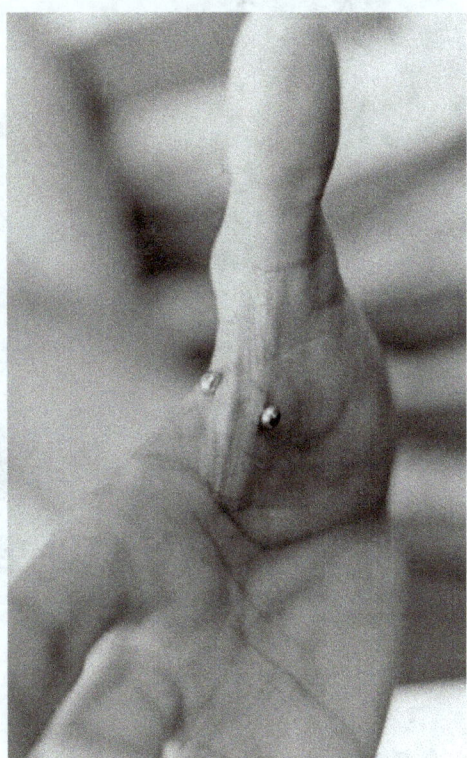

The hand-web piercing was featured in *PFIQ* issue #23 (1984).

137

Photos: Ward Boult

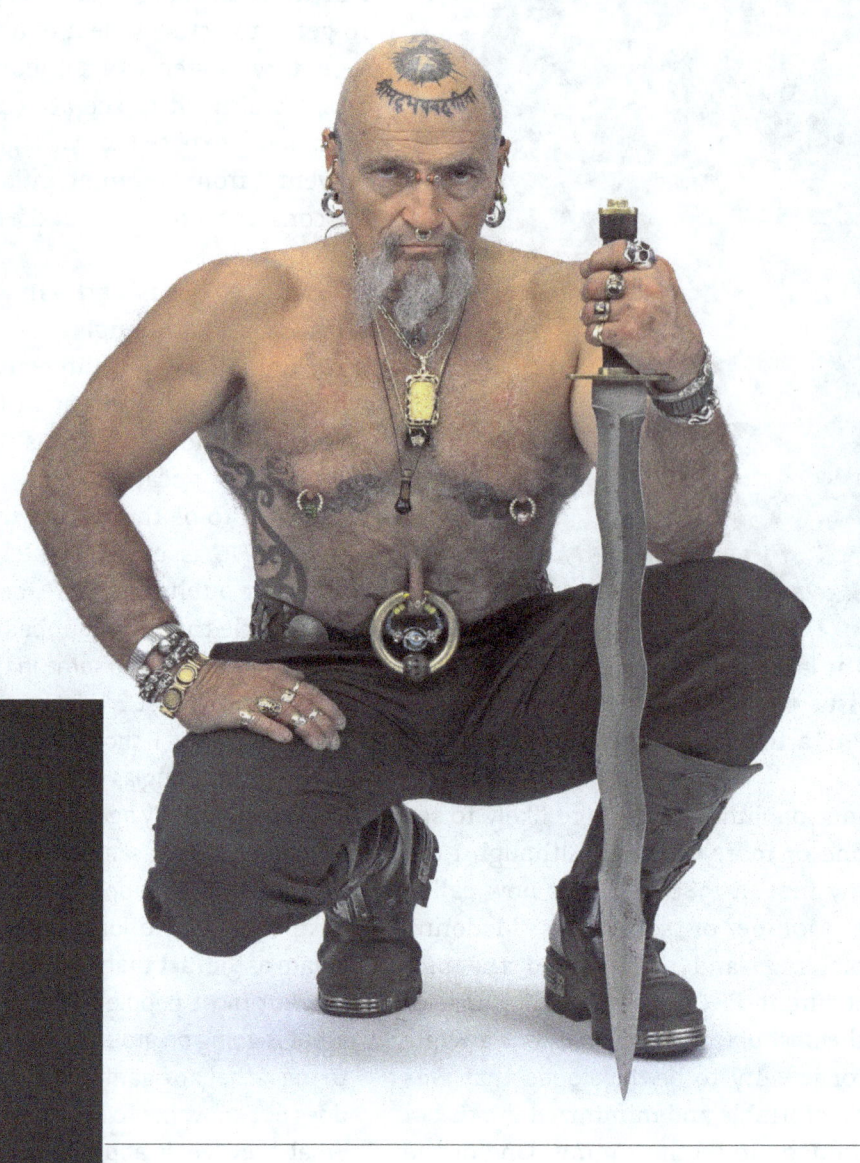

Earl Douglas van Aken II, a.k.a. Erl. He was slated to be the featured personality in the unpublished *PFIQ* issue #51 (1997). These photos would have appeared in that article.

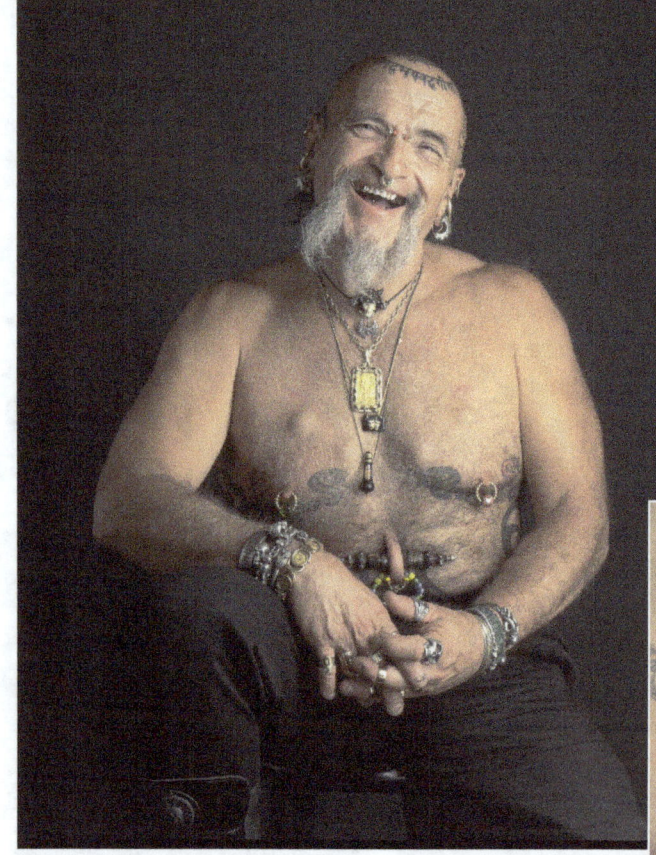

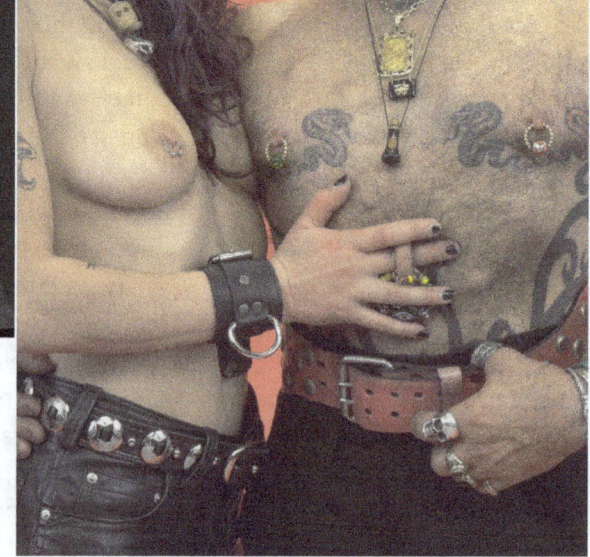

tox, dietary shift, exercise, and spiritual alignment—I found I had a renewed vigor and passion for the arts. I was an art and science major through much of school and also had a "lab" of my own at home. So, starting with the pierced ears I'd had since the mid '60s, I added more ear piercings, all done by myself.

As ear piercing became more popular, I decided to enlarge the holes by cutting and stretching them to $3/8$". It took only three months to accomplish this via a rather speedy method. Using an X-ACTO blade, I would make many small cuts on the inside upper periphery of each hole. I would then insert a plug large enough to stretch the cuts open until they healed. The process was repeated until the desired final size was reached. Numerous additional holes were added. Using a dermal punch, four holes were cut into the conch and upper ear flap. These were very painful!

In time other piercings were added, most done at Gauntlet in L.A. by Jim Ward and Angel Binnie [Elayne Angel], my personal favorite piercer.

Jim did my septum, first with a needle, then later with a $5/16$" dermal punch. My eventual goal is to stretch that piercing to accommodate a $3/8$" spool that I am saving. I believe Jim also did my PA and areola piercings. My ampallang was also done at Gauntlet, but I don't recall by whom.

As for the "Erl" piercing [the bridge of the nose], it was also done by Jim, who was at first reluctant since it had never been done. After some discussion and consideration, it was indeed accomplished. I was looking for a new piercing to open up another area of facial adornment. This was followed by multiple Erl eyebrows, forehead, and upper cheek piercings.

The back of my neck was also done at Gauntlet [by Dan Kopka] with a 10-gauge needle. Everyone stopped what they were doing to watch another first, as far

as we all knew. It was a difficult piercing since the tissue there is quite tough. I don't know who was sweating most, myself or the piercer! It took two very hard pushes to get the needle through. This piercing was difficult to heal.

Angel did splendidly accurate piercings at anterior and posterior of each armpit. As I lead a rather active, sweaty lifestyle, these would not heal. I was quite disappointed to lose them, and I may try again later.

I also have two barbells in the center of my tongue and one ring on the left side which nests inside the space left by three missing upper teeth. Although the side ring took several months to heal, it is now quite comfortable. My newest piercing is through the web of my top inner lip; it was done by Steve Haworth.

The "abdominal handle" was done surgically with a cauterizing laser and some stitches. This was accomplished, per my design, by Dr. Nicole, a world-class plastic surgeon in Long Beach.

Tattooing is an ongoing project that will run for many years. I have been tattooed exclusively by Jeff Kincaid for about three years now. He has also taught me much of what I know about this art; I have tattooed myself and several others. I did all the color work on my upper legs and the Celtic braid myself. I also have extensive genital tattoo work, which so far has taken over two and a half years. It has been an extreme experience! The time between my mindset and function increases with each sitting. The penis shaft and glans are red, green, black, and gold tribal. My testicles are as yet unfinished, but will be covered with various geometric patterns.

My other body artwork is dental: my front teeth were all filed to points to the maximum degree that tooth structure would allow. The front two teeth were inset with triangular opals, quite pleasing especially in

sunlight. The next two teeth were inset with 14K gold lightning bolts, based on a personal inner spiritual experience. Lastly, the next two teeth were capped with dental alloy made from a cut up Krugerrand, part of a penny, some scrap silver yield, and nice rose gold. I hand carried caps to my lapidary jeweler and had them set with dark green tourmalines in white gold bezels. Then back to the dentist for placement. I am very pleased with the results, all performed by Dr. Wood in Cypress, California.

My current project is subdermal implants of various sized glass marbles. I want to bring dimension into tattooing. Dr. Nicole has implanted marbles in my lower abdomen. Steve Haworth has done work on my inner forearms and chest, more of which is planned. My goal is a synergy between tattoos and elevated areas. Selective electrolysis will also add to the effect. I would also like to use other shaped objects: stars, rings, crescents, etc.

As for cyber modifications, I guess my future plans for subdermal LEDs and fiber optics would fit that niche. I am also considering micro motors, subdermal of course, to create movement effects. I think it would be really wild to have tattoos, piercings, or implants that were affected by any of these means.

What I do I simply call body art, a collective terminology. I consider what I do a fine art. I research, seeking out people and materials, preparing the body through the mind to receive these modifications. I'm no longer concerned with the response of others, although an understanding, intelligent response is always appreciated. Neither is there any sexual aspect to what I do. I have been celibate some sixteen years now. I quite enjoy the spiritual freedom and energy I receive from this state of being and have no plan to alter this grand state of being.

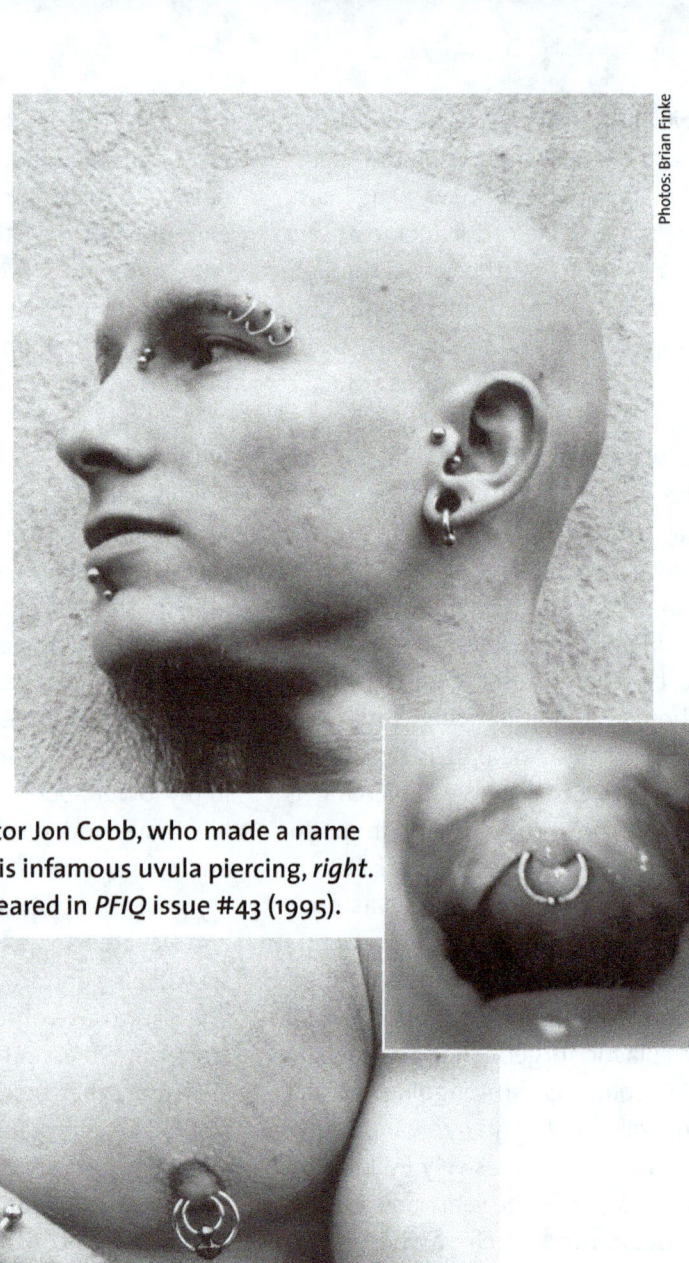

I enjoy my pursuit of body art and will no doubt continue in some fashion for many years to come. I neither lead nor follow but go where no one has gone and leave a trail.

As well as being an artist and model, I'm also an active member of the Screen Actors Guild. While writing this I'm sitting in my trailer at New Line Cinemas production lot. If I don't end up on the cutting room floor, I will be seen as perhaps the first pierced and tattooed vampire in film in *Blade* starring Wesley Snipes, Stephen Dorff, and N'aushe Wright, directed by Stephen Norrington.

May the blessing be. As always, your friend Erl.

Body mod innovator Jon Cobb, who made a name for himself with his infamous uvula piercing, *right*. These photos appeared in *PFIQ* issue #43 (1995).

Another of the more venturesome young body modifiers was Jon Cobb. He has taken credit for popularizing surface piercings, particularly the nape of the neck, as well as innovating the transscrotal, the creation of a hole through the scrotum from front to back between the testicles. Not to discredit him, but I attempted the latter back in Gauntlet's very early days at the request of one of the T&P Group members. I thought it was a bad idea, but he insisted, and I was such a novice that I finally gave in. Not surprisingly, it refused to heal. Under the circumstances it's virtually impossible for the body to form a channel. Several years later another of my clients succeeded where I had failed by having a kinky doctor friend clamp the front and back of the scrotum together, cut a hole with a dermal punch, and suture the edges together.

Of course, Gauntlet can't claim responsibility for every new innovation, and in some cases I'm just as glad we haven't. Around 1995 Jon became notorious for dreaming up the uvula piercing. Paul King performed it and then went on to get one himself. His comment? "It was a VERY stupid piercing."

Regardless, those young piercers out to push beyond current limitations were in awe and embraced Jon as a visionary and trendsetter, while the older among us shuddered, concerned what the consequences might be. Thankfully, despite its shock value, there has been no stampede to either acquire or to perform this particular modification.

Jon was interviewed in *PFIQ* issue #43 (1995). He worked at Gauntlet for a while before eventually striking out on his own.

I find the advancements that have made surface piercings more viable are truly amazing. From the attempts made in Gauntlet's time, we concluded that success was often iffy. At some point, it was common for the piercings to simply migrate and reject. With improvements in the actual piercing technique and the invention of special surface bars, the success rate has improved. I must confess that some of the placements, such as the nape of the neck, still alarm me, but I have yet to hear of anyone suffering serious damage from them. Who can argue with success?

Stretched piercings are certainly nothing new; in fact Fakir wrote an article on the subject for *PFIQ* #2 (1978). It's just that during Gauntlet's heyday they were almost all below the neck and not visible. Nowadays enlarged earlobe piercings have become so popular that most studios carry huge displays of jewelry for them in every conceivable design, size, and material. They also usually stock tapers in corresponding sizes to facilitate stretching and insertion.

Piercing World Magazine, a British publication from the late 1980s, brought our attention to what, at the time, we regarded as two truly horrific female piercings, the Isabella and the Princess Albertina. Most piercers I know agree to this assessment as far as the Isabella is concerned since it actually passes through the clitoral

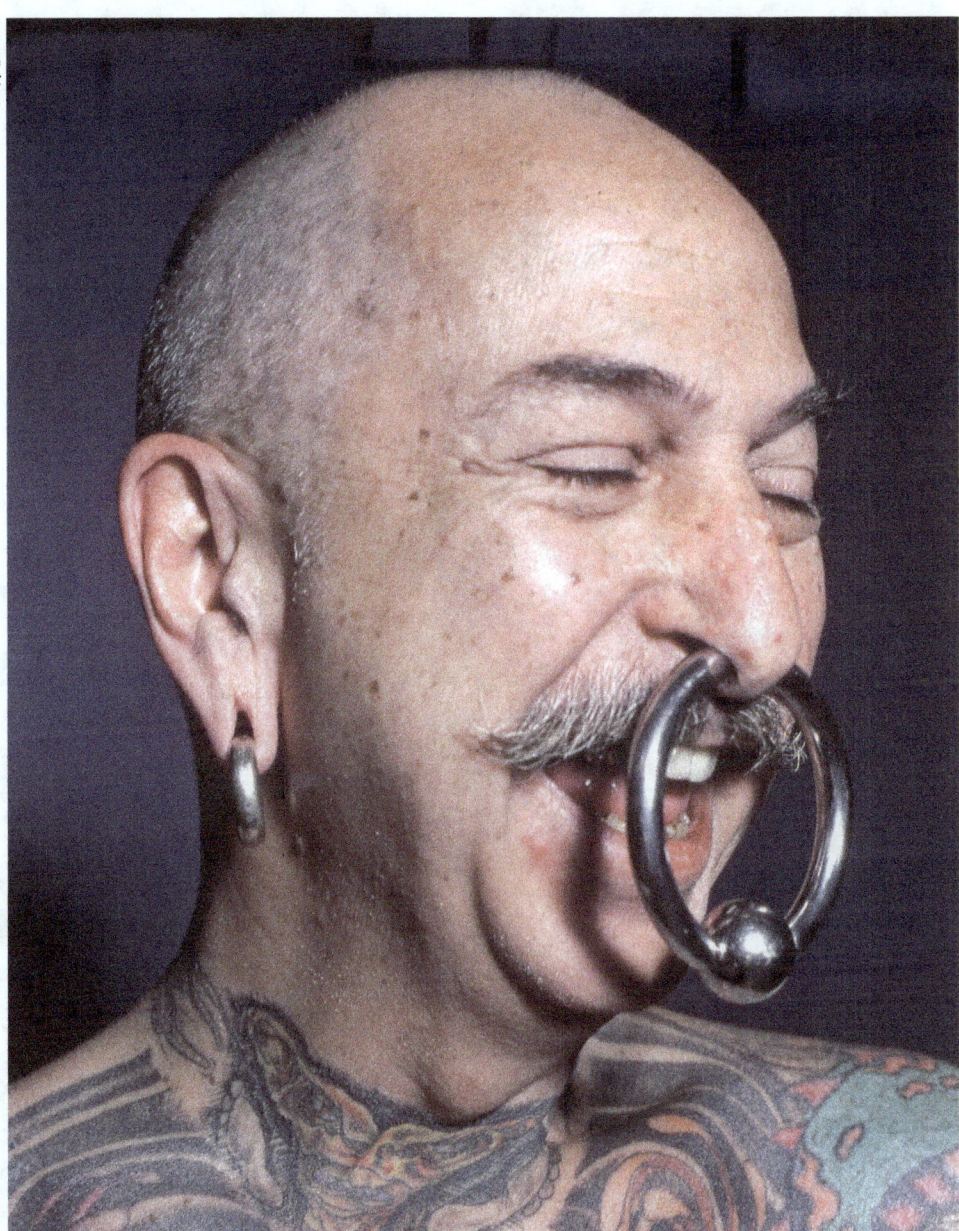

Hans of Denmark appeared with his stretched piercings, above and below the neck, in *PFIQ* #19 (1983).

shaft, risking nerve damage. There has been more debate over the Princess Albertina, the female equivalent of the Prince Albert. Michaela Grey, speaking on behalf of Gauntlet, was vehemently against it. Not everyone, especially in recent times, agrees. Some women who enjoy urethral play have endorsed it enthusiastically. James Weber tells me that if a woman is contemplating this piercing, she needs to discuss the risks with her piercer and be particularly diligent with the aftercare.

Bay Area piercer Erik Dakota made a reputation for himself by developing what he called the "Industrial" and "Orbital" ear projects, multiple piercings connected by a single piece of jewelry. Ideally these are best healed individually before connecting them, though some people don't bother. They are pretty straightforward, though they sometimes require the use of special equipment. Erik's contributions also include the Daith and Rook.

Currently on the cutting edge of popularity are the surface or dermal

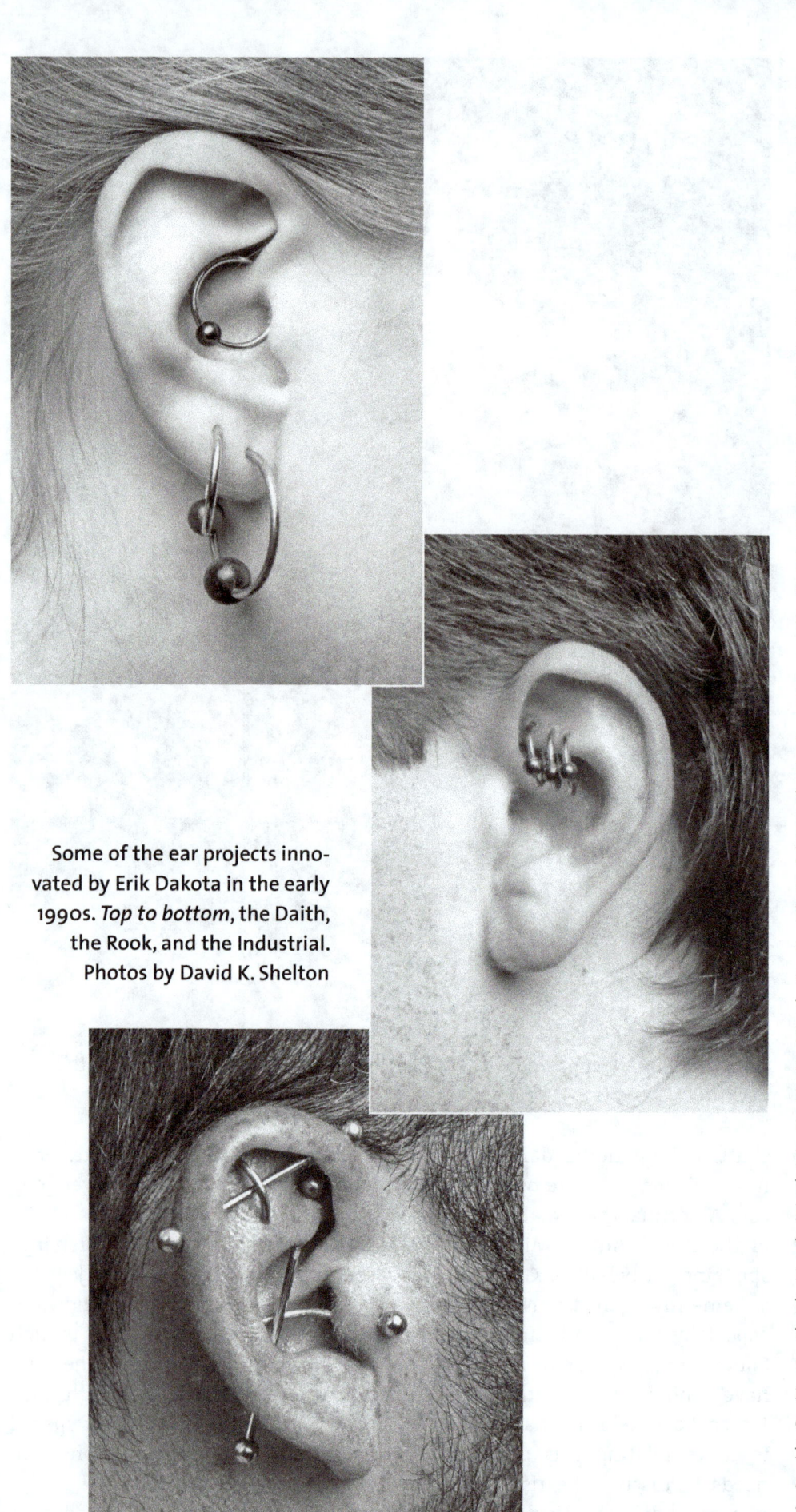

Some of the ear projects innovated by Erik Dakota in the early 1990s. *Top to bottom*, the Daith, the Rook, and the Industrial. Photos by David K. Shelton

anchors. Also known as microdermals, it seems debatable to me whether these are technically even piercings since there is only an entrance and no exit. A pocket is created in the skin, into which is inserted a very short post with a small foot on one end and an ornament on the other. According to *The Piercing Bible*, "Single-point piercing (yet another name used for the process) is a relatively new and experimental modification, so there is no data on long-term successes or complications. However, this apparently promising alternative may be superior to surface piercings. Surface anchors are more like ordinary piercings, much less invasive to insert, and certainly not as risky as most of the advanced body art forms...."

On the technical side, freehand piercing, which has been part of every piercer's skill set since the beginning, has become a huge movement. It would be almost impossible to do such piercings as Prince Alberts and clit hoods or the more exotic ear projects any other way, but some piercers have become snobbish about the technique and turned it into a cult, using it for all piercings and belittling those who work with tools. Some even argue that if you do so, you're not a good piercer, and that a piercing needle alone is more convenient than having to buy and utilize an autoclave and other expensive equipment. Personally, I find this attitude smacks of ego, and I have little patience with it. In my opinion, the primary impetus for this whole movement has probably been the rationale of people unwilling or too poor to invest in professional equipment. Can you imagine going into a restaurant and having the chef tell you, "I use only a paring knife to prepare all the food. Other chefs who use other tools are no good"? Using nothing but a piercing needle makes about as much sense. A good, competent piercer uses every available means to assure that all piercings are done properly and are as safe and comfortable as possible for both their clients and themselves.

Freehand technique has one serious downside. It is much more dangerous because it increases the risk to the piercer of accidental needlesticks. In *The Piercing Bible*, author Elayne Angel notes, "The U.S. Occupational Safety and Health Administration (OSHA) has issued the following statement, which calls the technique into question: 'The practice of 'freehand' piercing without the use of forceps or other available engineering and work practice controls to prevent contact with the used end of the piercing needle violates 29 CFr 1910.1030(d)(2)(i), an important provision of the bloodborne pathogens standard that requires that engineering and work practice controls shall be used to eliminate or minimize employee exposure.'[2]

"The method, however, is not prohibited if some type of engineering or work practice control is used, such as a device to cover the tip of the needle, or to protect the fingers."

Another significant, fairly recent advancement is the use of vacuum flash-cycle sterilizers such as the Statim. Unlike traditional autoclaves that typically take 45 minutes to process a batch of instruments, they only take five. Everything gets sterilized immediately before the procedure, and the piercer can work right from the cassette. My guess is that we'll see more and more piercers using them.

There is currently a debate raging within the piercing community regarding the use of dermal punches. Despite the furor, there's nothing new about them. I experimented with them briefly back in the early 80s, and articles on septum and tongue piercings done with them appeared in *PFIQ* issues #18 and 19 in 1983. The newer ones are disposable, sharper, and easier to use, but in some states to do so is technically illegal unless you're a member of the medical profession. For the piercings that we were doing at the time, they didn't seem to provide enough of an advantage to make it worthwhile to break the law.

The one job where dermal punches excel is large ear cartilage piercings, or more accurately, "punchings." If someone is prepared to spend the rest of their life with a significant hole in their ear, the punch is decidedly superior to the needle;[3] for everything else that can more easily be stretched, I fail to see much of an advantage. The final verdict in the debate has yet to be rendered. Many of the more extreme body art forms involve the use of scalpels, which are also used by some to create very large ear loops. Like dermal punches, they are illegal to use unless you are a medical professional.

Certainly dermal punches and scalpels can be dangerous in the wrong hands, but should their use be restricted? My personal opinion is no. What does concern me, as well as many others who do piercing for a living, is that if people insist on using them, and especially if they post videos of the procedure on the Internet, they could be jeopardizing their entire industry, at least within their own state. If you can get the same results with a piercing needle and an insertion taper, I can't help asking, is it worth the risk?

What new innovations lay around the corner, no one knows. No crystal ball can predict what the future holds for the industry. Despite poor and questionable decisions by some in the business, I can't imagine it ever going away.

In the 20th anniversary issue of *PFIQ* (1995,) I wrote, "Growing a business must have certain similarities to raising a child. Both are conceived, carried for a time, and finally brought into the world after an often painful labor. They keep you awake at night, demand copious amounts of your time, money, and energy, and eventually take on a distinct personality, very likely at odds with your own. As they grow older, you find yourself perpetually torn between emotions of self-satisfaction that you could produce something so wonderful and the depressing conviction that your offspring should have been strangled in its crib."

There's no question that the industry has taken on a personality of its own and is much more conjoined with other forms of body modification. I feel a little wistful sometimes that the erotic aspect of piercing that was my inspiration for starting it has been so overshadowed by the aesthetic, but realistically I have to admit it would probably never have become such a worldwide phenomenon otherwise. Gauntlet was gone before its 25th anniversary. But the industry it spawned, the dream that began with only a handful of hardcore fetishists, now provides a livelihood for thousands and has enriched the lives of millions.

In keeping with its name, Gauntlet faced the challenge and endured the ordeal. Sadly, it did not survive. I'm still here, bloody and bruised metaphorically speaking. Through the experience I've learned a lot and hopefully emerged a stronger and wiser man.

"My life has been a tapestry of rich and royal hue," or so begins a song by Carole King. Though my own life, especially the Gauntlet period, has certainly had its colorful moments, there have also been plenty that were drab and somber. Toward the end, I watched in horror as my own tapestry unraveled around me, and although I lost almost everything, there was one thing that could never be taken away. Despite everything, I can say with pride that I accomplished something rare that very few people are ever able to achieve: turn a personal fetish into a huge industry and a profession that never existed before, one that now employs and supports countless men and women all around the world. Every day, those same people continue to share my legacy, and the circle just keeps widening. It does my heart good knowing that long after I'm gone, what I started in 1975 will continue to enrich innumerable lives for generations to come.

I recently received an email from former Gauntlet employee, Master Piercer Paul King, that touched me. In it he said, "Lots of people worked for the Gauntlet, and shared lots of ideas. This was the 'secret' to its early success and rapid advances in technique during a time when there was no competition or sharing of ideas within an industry that hadn't developed yet. What few piercers there were almost never shared information between shops. Gauntlet was always an exception. The spirit or secret of Gauntlet's success was one piercer sharing their knowledge with another. That has now become the credo of the greater industry. In every country in which piercing is established, fellowships and associations are growing, with conferences found in Mexico, Germany, Italy, etc. This, I think, is Gauntlet's greatest gift."

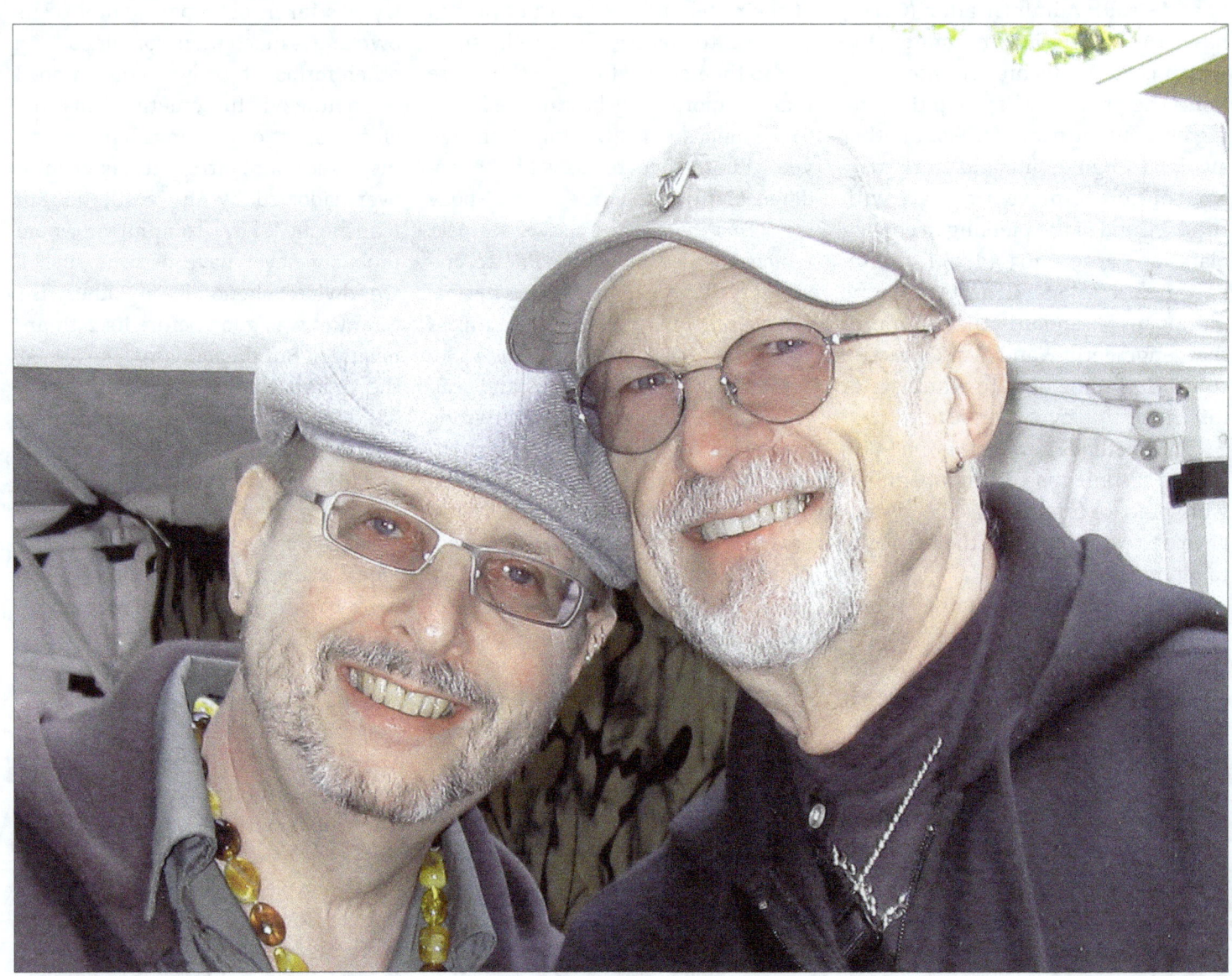

[1]Shannon produced a book covering the first three conventions. As I write this it is available only as a free PDF, but that status is subject to change. For current information visit http://www.zentastic.com/blog/modcon/

[2]U.S. Department of Labor Occupational Safety & Health Administration Standard Interpretations, "December 8, 2005, 'Freehand' Piercing without the Use of Forceps or Other Engineering Controls Violates the Bloodborne Pathogens Standards," www.osha.gov/pls/oshaweb/owadisp.show_document?p_table=INTERPRETATIONS&p_id=25338

[3]I remember back in the early 1980s having a client who wanted me to punch large holes through his ear cartilage. He brought me a leather punch specifically for the job. I autoclaved it and did the perforations, inserting clear plastic plugs that he had made himself. He was way ahead of his time.

MAGNIFICENT GAUNTLET STORIES

In the quarter-century during which Gauntlet provided body piercing services, there were many "eye-rolling" moments. The below treasured collection of anecdotes represents just a small sampling.

The late Gauntlet San Francisco piercer Jhan Dean Egg collected these anecdotes. Josh Warner, who purchased the furnishings and equipment from the bankrupt estate, discovered them in a little notebook and sent it to me.

These have been grouped by subject of comment.

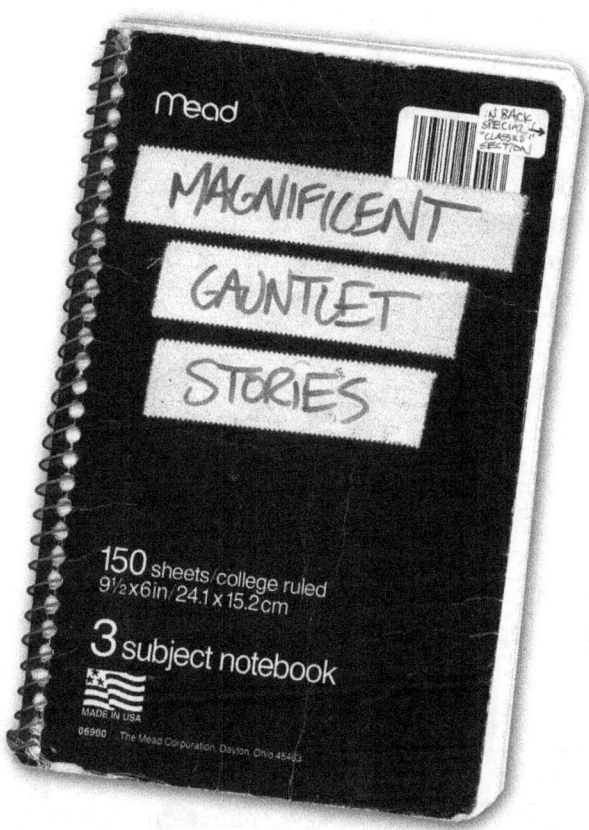

Nipples

Chance to girl getting nipple piercing: "Go ahead and lay down on the table now."
Customer: "Should I lie down on my back?"

Customer comes in playing with fresh nipple piercing and starts handling it.
Jon Cobb: "You don't want to handle that; it contaminates the piercing."
Customer: "No way! I washed it this morning!"

I was playing with the nipple clamps—they were clamped on my fingers, and a customer asked "Are your fingers pierced?" (Finger web piercings have been attempted.)

Customer: "My friend told me right after he got his nipple pierced the estrogen kicked in. He was horny for about an hour and a half." (While he must have meant "endorphin," that natural rush had a number of pleasant effects for customers, regardless of which piercing was received.)

"If I get my nipple pierced, will the milk squirt out weird?" (Women who anticipated a future pregnancy often had nursing-related questions.)

Customer shortly after nipple piercing: "When does the pain start?"

Customer: "I heard that you should avoid getting your nipple pierced on Thursday because it really hurts after about three or four days." Me: "Well, I don't think that happens . . . but is there a reason you don't want your nipple to hurt on Sunday or Monday?" Customer: "No . . . that's just what I heard."

I clean and mark for a woman's nipple piercings and ask her to look in the mirror. She's confused—she thought I had just pierced her and was looking for the rings. (Our techniques were always state of the art, and being literally painless was not something we achieved.)

Ears

Customer requests for us to put solution on his recently stretched earlobe piercing so it will stop feeling sore.

In L.A.: A customer wants me to change her earlobe jewelry—Me: "How old is the piercing?" Her: "One month." Me: "That's too soon to change." Her: "Oh, it's two months."

Enlarged Ears

"Does that go all the way through?"
"Is that holding your piercing open?"
"Is that jewelry in your ear or is it a process?"
"Is that stretching your piercing?"
"Is that a magnifying glass?"
"Is that a mirror?"
"Doesn't that hurt?"
"Is your ear around that whole thing?"
"That's neat. Your earring makes it look like there's a hole that big all the way through!"
"What about 30 years from now when you want to take that out? What will you tell your grandchildren?"

Facial

Me: Your eyebrow piercing can grow out because of stress.
Her: Why—because of all the frowning?

I make two dots as a marking for a woman's eyebrow piercing and show them to her. She tells me she wants the top one. (An explanation of the function of the marks no doubt followed.)

Nose

Customer on phone asks if getting her nose pierced and wearing a ring would affect her doing aerobics.

A customer's nostril piercing is bleeding. I hand her a tissue; she immediately spits on it before putting it on her nose. (Yes, I stopped her.)

Customer on phone: "Do y'all pierce noses?" (He had a heavy southern drawl.)
"Yes!"
"'Cause I want three nose piercings on each nostril and a big ring through the center. Do you think I'll have any problems? Have y'all done that before? Have y'all seen that before?"
Yikes!

Customer complained that a competitor pierced her nostril too close to her nostril. A conversation followed to help the Gauntlet staffer determine more specifically what she wanted done.

Customer asked: "Are you more susceptible to a brain infection with a septum piercing than any other piercing?" (This was actually an often-repeated urban myth.)

Young woman getting a nostril piercing wanted to know: A) "Can I still breathe?" My answer, "No." B) "Can I still eat? My answer, "Well, if you can't breathe . . . "

Customer on the phone: Got nostril pierced 20 minutes ago, and was thinking of taking it out, but decided she should leave it in in case it's infected. (She was advised to follow aftercare instructions, and to come back if she was worried about the progress of healing.)

A woman on the phone asks the price of a nostril piercing. I tell her. She says she's heard she can get it done for $10—do I know anywhere that she can do that? I tell her that if she goes to a place like that, she could get a serious infection,

possibly leading to brain damage. She says "OK, what's the phone number?" (While we were always extremely careful about hygiene and safety, not all of our customers considered that more important than price.)

Female Genital

Customer is setting up for a genital piercing asking all sorts of questions—Does it hurt? Can I have sex? Does it feel good during sex? etc. Then she leans close and whispers "I have to go to the ladies' room."

Karen does a very intense clit piercing. The woman screams out; Karen soothes her, and she relaxes. Karen offers her a mirror. A long, pregnant, pause . . . "That's not what I wanted." (Karen—like other Gauntlet staffers, was always careful to make sure she understood the customer's requests before proceeding.)

Male Genital

Customer on the phone to Jhan: "I don't perceive penises as having a 'lip'." (It's a mystery which piercing the customer wanted.)

Chance on the phone: "The urethra is an amazing thing. You can do anything with it."

My boyfriend has a PA and whenever I give him head I get a sore throat. Is it because I'm allergic to nickel? (This called for a particularly sensitive response from the Gauntlet staffer.)

Customer asks "Can an ampallang be done in one sitting?" (I don't think we ever had a customer request a drawn-out multi-stage process for that—or any other—piercing!)

Customer who clearly expected a much more radical piercing than he got asked "When you get a guiche piercing, do you pierce the prostate?"

Muscle queen asks me if he can go in the bathroom and put in his PA jewelry. "Well, no, we can do it for you. We like to keep things really clean." "I am really clean." (Storms out.)

In speaking with Customer asked: "Where's Brian?" Taj: "He's in New York." Customer: "What about Debra?" Taj: "She took a leave—she's trying other things." Customer: "Paul?" Taj: "He's not here any more either, he took a leave as well." Customer: "You see, that's what I'm talking about, it's just like when I was four." Taj: "What happened when you were four?" Customer: "That thing with Mr. Penis." (Not sure how that relates to particular piercers being unavailable.)

Customer: "My piercer always asks me to have an erection when I get my piercings." Gauntlet: "Maybe he just wants to make sure his markings are OK when you're erect." Customer: "It was for a guiche." (Not all piercers had our professional and ethical standards.)

Navel

Customer asks "I'm a singer. If I get my navel pierced, is breathing OK?" (We preferred that our customers continued to breathe.)

(Sometimes it took a bit of coaxing to get information out of a reluctant customer):
Would you like to make an appointment?
Yes.
What kind of piercing are you getting?
I can't say.
Is it a genital piercing?
No.
Is it above the neck?
No.
Nipple?
No.
Navel?
No.
That's all the piercings there are . . .
OK, it's my belly button.

Customer thought it would not be good to use a circular barbell in his new navel piercing because we'd "have to push the ball all the way through."

Woman on the phone with Taj: "Hi, I had a couple of questions. I wanted to get my stomach pierced and I want to know how much is it for the earring?" I reply appropriately and she has one more question: "Ah, yeah, can I come in drunk?" (Hopefully, she still came in after being told that she had to be sober.)

Customer suggests if you have a navel piercing and want to sleep on your stomach, put a bagel around your navel. (Interesting, though not very practical.)

Tongue

If you get your tongue pierced, can you still drink soda? (Perhaps the bubbles would tickle more than in the past?)

"I've been reluctant to get my tongue pierced because of that floating bone in your tongue." (Customers' knowledge of anatomy was not always based in fact.)

Someone just got a tongue piercing downsized. Their friend asks "Did they downsize it on the top or the bottom?"

Customer called and said, "I got my tongue pierced and swallowed the ball." so I got ready for the routine "Did you get it pierced here?—Well you could come in and buy another one." She replied, "I luckily have a spare, I just wanted to share that with you." (Thanks for sharing?)

Healing

Customer: "Can I just use alcohol?"
Gauntlet: "Alcohol will burn the skin out of your piercing."
Customer: "Is that good or bad?"

Customer concerned about aftereffects asked "Should I avoid drinking coffee after getting my ear pierced?"

Sometimes customers wanted to use whatever they had on hand for after care—one asked "For cleaning new ear piercing, can I use bleach?"

Man on the phone: "Karen did my nipple piercing. I'm having problems with it. I've been cleaning it with hydrogen peroxide. And Karen gave me a mambadreevil" (Hint: mambadreevil means apadravya. New names for piercings were adopted over the years, though this one was not included.)

Unconventional Requests

Customer: "Do you do fangs?" (While some Gauntlet stores leased space to tattoo artists, dental work was not one of our services.)

Customer request: Jewelry for teeth (also for fingernails, dog's ears, and for scars.)

"Do you do pinky nails?"

Customer request: to cut the web under his tongue. (While we turned down many such exotic requests, it would be interesting to know a) does the customer know the function of that web, and b) what benefit the customer expected from having it severed.)

Generally Noteworthy

Customer on phone (comment): "It's fun to come into the store and see all the people that look like Hellraiser."

Customer on phone: "So say I wanted to get there on the bus, what bus would I take?"
Taj: "Where are you coming from?"
Customer: "San Francisco" (Duh! Customer called San Francisco Gauntlet store.)

Customer on phone: "When I take the jewelry out of my piercing overnight, it closes. I think my piercing is defective."

Customer: "Can I get the I-slept-with-Paul-King discount?" (Honest, Paul, it happened.)
Jhan: "Only if you were good."

Customer: "Do you have to make a hole to put this ring in?"

Jhan on phone: "Be sure to have some food before you come in."
Customer: "Why? Do you want me to puke?"

Me: "You need to get some food before we do your piercing."
Her: "Could I just smoke this cigarette instead?"

Conversation between customers: "I don't think I want to change the bead. I'm not a bead kind of person." "You could become a bead kind of person."

Customer is looking for the smallest earring possible. Points at a place on the display—there's nothing there.

Paul—tooth questions: #1 "Is your tooth pierced?" #2 "Is your tooth tattooed?"

Customer quote: "You guys got a bar here?" (No, not only did we not serve alcohol, our policy was to refuse service to anyone who appeared to be under the influence of anything.)
Customer sees bleach on piercing table—"Is that pee?"

(April 25, 1998) Malcolm and I are sitting at the front desk. A man walks in and says "Excuse me, I'm from the City of Chicago" (Shows us a badge in his wallet.) "Can I use your washroom?" (We allowed just regular folks to use the facilities—maybe things are different in Chicago.)

Customer (very, very young-looking 19-year-old queer boy): "How long have you been piercing?"
Me: "Five years."
Customer: "They had piercings five years ago?" (Would he be impressed to know that piercings existed when his grandfather was his age?)

Nervousness sometimes led to odd questions. Customer asks what the staples on the display are for. (To hold jewelry on the display).

Guy walks in and hands me his I.D. and G.A. (General Assistance = welfare) check and asks me to cash it. (Yet another request for a service we did not provide.)

(A frighteningly repeated classic—) I make the markings for a piercing, then ask them to look at the markings—confused squinting, and they say they can't see it. I say, "Do you wear glasses?" "Yes." "Could you put them on?" They put their glasses on and look. "Oh yes, that's fine."

"Do I have to buy the jewelry now if I want to get pierced?" (If healing was instantaneous, getting the jewelry later might work.)

Me: "When you swim, other people's germs in the water can irritate your piercing." Them: "Oh, so I should take it out when I go swimming."

In the room, after cleaning and marking, the customer asks "So, who's going to be doing the piercing?" (Gauntlet staffers did not specialize to that degree. Maybe the customer wanted the piercing to be a group effort.)

Conversation on the phone: Taj: "Hello, Gauntlet, can I help you?" Customer: "Yea, do you pierce assholes?" Taj: "No, that wouldn't be very professional." Customer: "Yeah, but if you did, would you pierce an asshole?" Taj: "No, a piercing needs to stay clean, or it will not heal—if you pierce the anus, fecal matter will get in it . . ."etc. Customer: "Yeah, but what if you pierced an asshole, and it farted?" Taj: "I have to go now!"

APPENDIX

An Interview with Doug Malloy

This interview appeared in the first issue of PFIQ (1977) and was reprinted in issue #42 (1994).

PFIQ: To start our interview off perhaps you would tell our readers what you believe to be the causes for the current revival of interest in piercing?

DM: I don't know that you would be justified in calling it a revival. I doubt that the interest in piercing has ever really ceased to the point that it needed to be revived. People have been doing it for thousands of years. I do think that there are a couple of reasons why piercing is becoming more visible. One reason, of course, would be the relaxation in the social structures we've been living under from our Puritan and Victorian past. People are much more open about their sexual desires now. The other reason, believe it or not, is the new availability of jewelry made especially for piercing. During the years when it was an underground phenomenon, it was virtually impossible to find suitable insertables. What little was available was often of very shoddy workmanship. All that has changed now.

I firmly believe that in the future we are going to see a lot of both piercing and tattooing. We are now in the Age of Aquarius. It began the moment our astronauts set foot on the Moon. During the Aquarian Age man's natural inclination toward self-adornment will flourish. Tattooing and piercing will be very popular. They will be a part of a universal desire for people to express their individuality and "do their own thing."

Since we are basically talking about the reasons people desire to be pierced, I would like to make one last point. In primitive societies when a child, usually a boy, reaches puberty, he undergoes some form of rite of passage whereby he becomes a man. These rites usually involve some form of pain. The boy expects it and suffers it gladly. As we so-called "civilized" people have no such rites of passage, I believe many individuals find a void in their lives, which the piercing experience often fills.

PFIQ: This leads to my next question. On several occasions you have expressed the opinion that the desire to be pierced is a subconscious holdover from a previous incarnation. Would you mind elaborating on that?

DM: How else would you explain its occurrence?

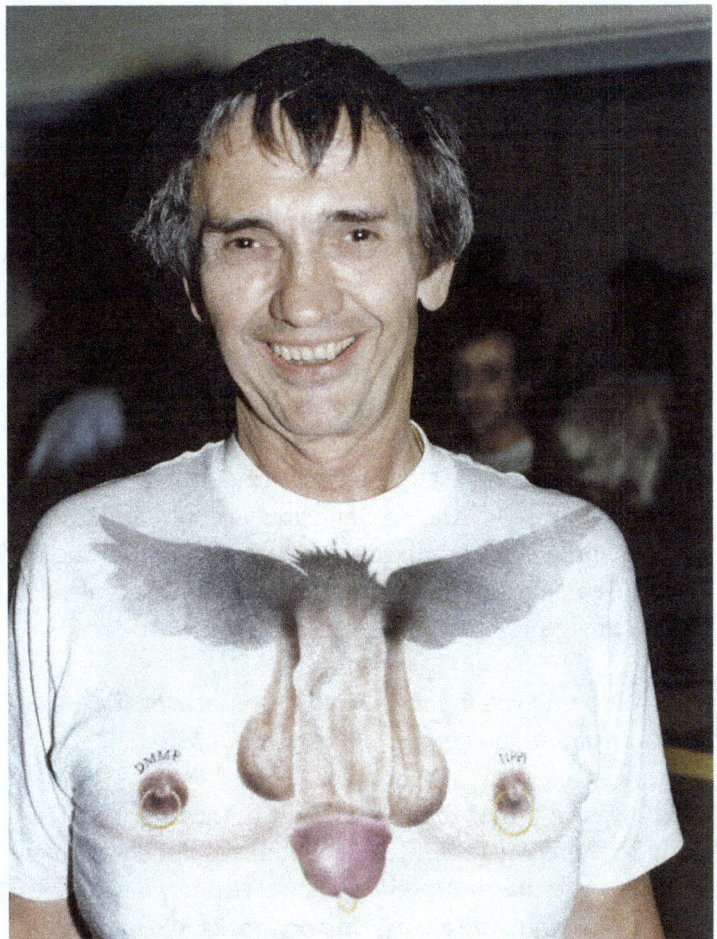

Doug wearing a hand airbrushed T-shirt made as a gift for him by tattooist Cliff Raven. The letters DMMP over the right nipple stand for Doug Malloy, Master Piercer. IIPPI over the left nipple is an acronym for one of Doug's favorite sayings, "If it protrudes, pierce it." He sometimes added, "If it doesn't, tattoo it."

PFIQ: Doubtless the psychologists and psychiatrists could go wild coming up with all kinds of reasons—for example, injections in childhood evolving into a fascination with needles.

DM: This was never my case. In fact, my mother avoided any form of injection for me. She didn't even want me to be vaccinated. I never had any contact with a needle. Reincarnation is the only way you can rationalize people's predisposition to certain things. We carry so much back. I know this is true for many men and women. It doesn't all start in this period of time. Look at child prodigies. Though few realize it, their talent goes back to a previous incarnation. With me I still have rather vivid flashes of a previous time—too vivid to be just casual suggestion. You see, I was very highly placed in the ancient Egyptian court of Akhenaten. The wearing of jewelry was a very significant and important part of that culture. It was a status symbol. I seem to have carried that desire for self-adornment over into the present incarnation.

PFIQ: Your involvement with piercing goes back many years. Can you tell us at what age you first became fascinated with or, shall we say, aware of the concept of piercing?

DM: I could hardly have been older than two because we were still living in Chicago. We moved to Seattle when I was about three. Anyway, a lady friend of my mother came to visit and she had diamond ear studs. I couldn't keep my eyes off them. It was a mystery how they could stay there. Were they glued on or what? The earrings my mother wore had little loops with screws in the back. When I asked the lady to put them on me mother shushed me up and said, "Keep quiet." Of course, once shushed up with a thing like that it keeps churning over and over and you've got to find the answer. At some point I noticed that there was something behind the ear, and then I realized the mechanics involved. It was an intriguing method of attaching some little bauble.

PFIQ: When did you first turn on to, or conceive of, the idea of body and genital piercing as opposed to ear piercing?

DM: I was in junior high—I would say thirteen, fourteen, along in there. My father had an extensive library with everybody's favorite source, the *National Geographic* and other books like that, the natural history books. We had a lot of those. In some of those books there were pictures of natives in India who were hooking things to their skin for festivals. They would get into a form of ecstasy by doing this. There were also pictures of the Penitentes of New Mexico and the Southwest, who hang from poles with skewers in their backs. Of course, these were only temporary, but they fired the imagination on to other things.

There was one issue of the *Geographic* about the Sea Dayaks of Borneo, which showed some of their piercings, largely male. While they didn't show the genital piercings, something in the text implied there was more than met the eye. I also found a great deal of information at the local university library. The anthropological texts revealed a lot, as did the medical books, not with pictures as much as with drawings.

PFIQ: When did you get your first piercing?

DM: Toward the end of my freshman year in college. I was destined to have piercings. That's all there is to it. The opportunities just fell into my lap.

I was studying marine biology at the state university. Because my professor liked me and because I was a good swimmer, he arranged for me to work with a team of shallow-water divers during the summer vacation. Our job was to examine the harbor dock pilings for marine worms. Anyway, when you're spending a lot of time underwater like that it seems as if you always need to piss, which if you do, of course, you get the inside of your suit messed up and it takes days to dry out. I was in something of a quandary over what to do until one of the fellow divers, a Swede named Kurt, showed me how he had solved the problem by attaching the hose of a rubber urinal to a ring in the head of his cock. It was what we now call a Prince Albert piercing, and apparently done by many Swedish divers for just this purpose. Needless to say I too, had to have one, and couldn't have been more pleased to have a legitimate excuse for getting it.

PFIQ: Would you mind telling us about some of your later piercings?

DM: Not at all. I got my dydoes during my junior year in college. My roommate Jake introduced me into a group of predominantly Jewish fellows who called themselves the Cyprian Society. They would probably have been considered religious renegades as they strongly objected to the indiscriminate circumcision of males at birth. They felt they had been robbed of much of the sensitivity provided by the foreskin. To compensate for its loss they advocated piercing of the sides of the glans of the penis and installing small studs. How could I pass up an opportunity like that? It's a pity that the Cyprian Society got lost in the shuffle of World War II.

After college I spent some time in Hawaii. I was beach bumming around and the navel piercing was considered part of the required image. I made friends with a guy named Moki who took me to a Chinese jewelry shop on River Street in Honolulu where I had it done.

I was fortunate to have the guiche piercing done in Tahiti where it is part of the culture. I was there after the war compiling anthropological material collected in Borneo and New Guinea. I met an Australian chap named Reggie Jones who had jumped ship in Tahiti many years before. He had married a native girl and sired seven sons. Having been there some time he knew much about the local sex lore, and when he told me about the guiche—well I had to have one and he did the honors.

Over the years I've had just about every kind of piercing that's worth having and some not worth having. My Prince Albert was extended into an apadravya, which hasn't given me much pleasure, but the frenum piercing is another story. It's great and so are my nipples. I only had them done a couple of years ago. Boy, was I missing out. My last piercing was a hafada, but I had to abandon it because it never healed properly. Anyway, that's my inventory.

PFIQ: *Exactly which piercings would you consider functional and worth having?*

DM: Nipples, Prince Albert, frenum, guiche, dydoes—pretty much in that order.

PFIQ: *Is there any advice you would give to someone who is considering piercings, but hasn't done it yet?*

DM: Placement is very important especially with the guiche and cock piercings. Both hygiene and the proper jewelry for the job are equally important. For these reasons I advise the individual who wants to be pierced to find someone who knows what he is doing rather than attempt to do the job himself. Also, people into the S/M thing are best advised not to attempt permanent piercings within the context of a scene. If you take the time to do the piercings properly, you disrupt the pace of the scene.

PFIQ: *You are leaving soon on a trip around the world and will be spending almost a month in India. Do you anticipate finding much material on piercing while you are there?*

DM: I certainly hope so.

PFIQ: *Would you write an article about your trip for one of the future issues of the* Quarterly?

DM: I'd be glad to.

PFIQ: *We will be looking forward to it. Best of luck on your trip, and thank you for talking with us.*

(Doug's trip proved unproductive. No article was ever forthcoming.)

The Adventures of a Piercing Freak

Doug Malloy wrote this "autobiography" about 1975. At the time he and I had not met, and Gauntlet was still in the future. The story was sold to a fetish publication and appeared in soft-cover booklet form under the somewhat deceptive title The Art of Pierced Penises and Decorative Tattoos. *Money from the sale was used to bring English piercer and tattooist Mr. Sebastian (Alan Oversby) to America for a visit. Many of the piercing photos in the book were of him. It was his and Doug's first meeting.*

Pierced Penises *appeared briefly and quickly disappeared from print. If the current piercing mania has brought about its reissue, we are unaware of it.*

What makes me a piercing freak? Hell, I was born one. There's always been something in my genes making me turn on to piercings. This is the story of my adventures. All of my piercings are for a purpose. They enhance my sexual equipment or, at least, call attention to my sexual desires. Some people get pierced for different reasons—vanity, bravado, symbols. Not me, and none of my piercings have been stretched as some piercing freaks do. My holes are what they call "sleeper size" which serves my purposes just fine.

These are permissive times. Wear an earring (or two or three) if you feel like it. To hell with convention! This is the Aquarian Age. Recently there has been lots of evidence that piercing freaks do exist and plenty of them. Maybe this article will turn more of you on.

When I was about three years old I first noticed that some people had unusual ornaments in their earlobes. I was so

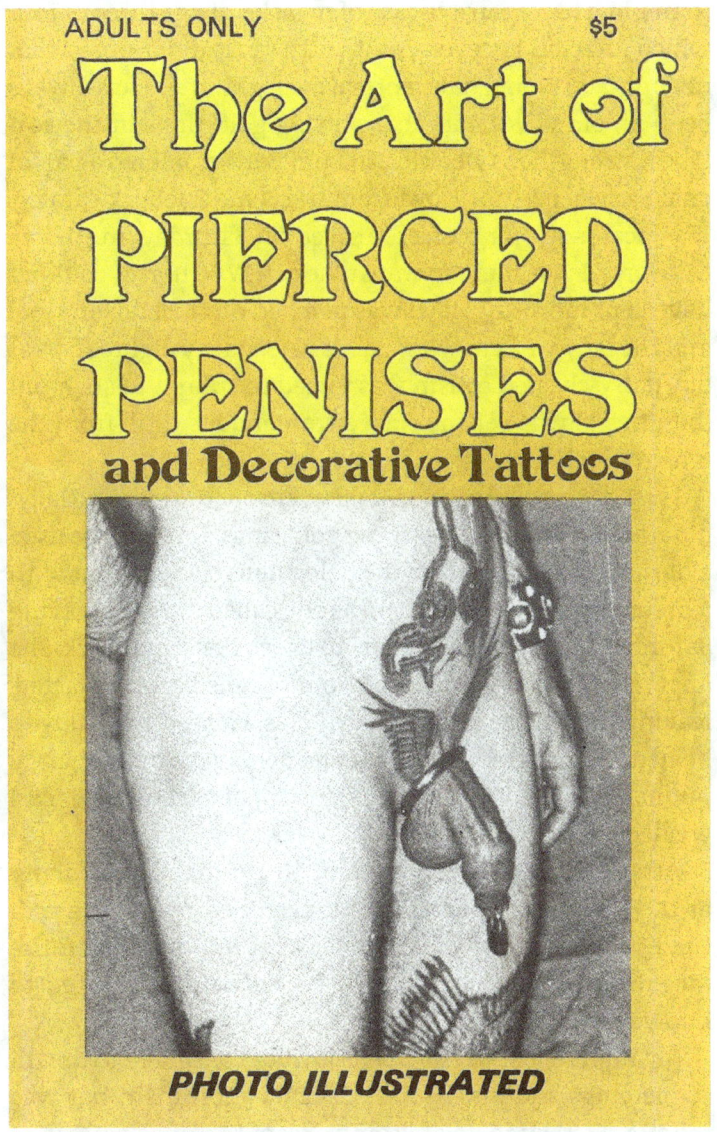

ADULTS ONLY $5

The Art of PIERCED PENISES and Decorative Tattoos

PHOTO ILLUSTRATED

fascinated that I asked a lady visiting our house to remove her earrings and put them on me. My mother was horrified and told me to keep my mouth shut and never think, much less say, such awful things again.

In my pre-adolescent days I spent many evenings at the local library looking through old volumes of National Geographic to find examples of native piercings. I carried around a little notebook for quick access to my favorite piercing styles. Of course all natives were draped for the photographer, but in my fantasies I mentally undressed them.

About that time I found a glass-headed corsage pin that I stuck through the skin of my balls. Wow, that was a thrill, and it really didn't hurt much. Besides, it looked good on my skin. Saturday night was bath night, and my corsage pin got the same workout I did. My mother couldn't understand why it took me so long to take a bath.

When I was twelve years old we moved to a very small town. We lived next door to my mother's older sister, a dominant, strong-willed woman. Her son, Lloyd, six years older than I, had had a terrible case of measles at age three or four which affected his eyes. Aunt Bertha was determined that her only son would have normal eyesight. There has always been an old wives' tale that putting gold rings in the earlobes "strengthens weak eyes." Aunt Bertha ordered a pair of gold ear sleepers for Lloyd from the Sears Roebuck catalog. The local lady "ear piercer" arrived on Saturday afternoon. Of course, I was there to watch the act. Wild horses couldn't have kept me away. Lloyd was perched on the kitchen stool and the lady went to work on his ears. As my eighteen-year old, hairy-chested cousin was forced to submit to such "indignities," I was getting such a tremendous thrill from the whole experience that I shot my little wad.

I was disappointed that Mrs. Stevenson (the piercing lady) did not immediately insert the gold rings. Instead she used a darning needle to make the hole, then followed that with a broom-straw "as a retainer," as she called it. The following Saturday Mrs. Stevenson came to check her handiwork. She apparently was satisfied, so the retainers were extracted, leaving little holes in Lloyd's earlobes. Pleased with Lloyd's healed ear piercings, the gold sleepers were permanently put in the holes. What a thrill I got out of that experience. I wished I had been the one with weak eyes.

After Lloyd's experience I got in the habit of looking at the earlobes of people I met, even before looking into their faces. Usually the earlobes told me more than the face. If the lobes had been tampered with, I wanted to know them better.

My high school days passed slowly. I continued to dream of piercings and other forms of body adornment but was too timid or shy to do anything except to fantasize. One of my high school classmates went to the city and got a tattoo. I'd have had one also, but there were no tattoo artists operating in my small town.

My world suddenly expanded when I went away to the state university with the intention of becoming a marine biologist. Being a good student, I got along well in the dorm and with other roommates. I was physically big, muscular and strong, even rugged, and had been a championship swimmer in my high school days. At the end of my freshman year, one of the professors who liked me, arranged for me to be on his team of shallow-water divers for the three summer months. We were to examine harbor pilings for marine worms, which were eating the docks. We were also supposedly planting seed oysters shipped from Japan to start new oyster beds.

I was assigned to an area to be surveyed where regular divers were working, and they issued my diving gear: woolen underwear, rubberized canvas, dry-diving suit and helmet. I was to learn much before that summer was out.

The pay was a fabulous $2.50 per hour "down time" which means when you are actually under water. "Up time" doesn't count. I was a reasonably good diver, but I didn't realize that the gurgling of the water around my suit would make me want to piss constantly. Maybe it was psychological, but the first week I was up more than I was down. In that old style dry-suit diving, it's a terrible thing to foul your diving suit. You have to flush it out and it takes a couple of days to dry it, so any error would cost you money.

One of the regular divers, Kurt, only a few years older than I, helped me out. He told me to send to the city for a man's rubber urinal, which holds the cock and balls and attaches to a rubber tube down your leg to a bladder strapped to the calf of your leg. It came and it also worked. I was able to stay down for longer periods and enjoyed my work for the first week. However, the thing irritated my cock and balls so much they became a bloody mess. I used all the Vaseline I could find, but the oil base dissolved the rubber sheath that encloses the whole genital area. I became very discouraged. My world seemed to collapse. It had seemed like such a good job, not to mention the fantastic pay.

It finally dawned on me that the other divers must have had the same problem, thus there must be a solution. Fortunately I found it, the hard way. I told Kurt about my problem, and he assured me there was a solution if I was willing to submit to a small operation. He called me into his bedroom in the bunkhouse, undressed, and showed me the gold ring he wore through the underside of the head of his cock. It went through the urethra and angled back toward the frenulum. It was a thick ring about ⅝" in diameter. The regular divers didn't use the typical rubber male genital bag requiring straps and buckles. Instead, they pierced their cocks with the gold ring and attached a very small rubber nipple over the tip of the cock, with the ring inside. The nipple was internally secured to the gold ring. The nipple cup fit snugly and was attached to the rubber tube making it urine-proof. The entire scrotum and cock were kept free and ventilated without constant chafing.

Kurt told me all about the piercing procedure used by so many of the sea-divers of Scandinavian parentage. His father also wore a gold ring, and Kurt got his piercing when he was only sixteen years old.

The piercing is from the inside through the piss-hole and down, where at the base of the glans there is a natural place for the hole, thick tissue, not very sensitive, and able to take considerable abuse before tearing. They use a small curved sail needle, typical of the salt-water sailors.

My head was in a whirl. I was groggy with delight. To be pierced for a useful purpose was too good to be true. My fondest dream seemed to be coming true. I asked Kurt if he would do the piercing for me. He said he would, but he would prefer to have me ask Ole, and older Swede who had more experience. He was sort of the elder statesman of the group, and Kurt felt it would be politic if I asked him.

Ole was away from our base of operation on another assignment but was due back in four or five days. Those four or five days seemed like a month as I anticipated the thrilling prospect of my first piercing.

The afternoon Ole came home, I popped the question to him. "Ya, I'd pierce your cock," he said in his thick Swedish accent, "tonight, if you want it." I said, "Ya, tonight, I'm sure I'll be a better man for it."

During dinner in the mess hall I hardly ate. Ole puffed on his pipe, one pipe full after another. How could I stand it any longer? Finally he stood up, knocked out the ashes from his pipe and said, "Come on, kid," and I followed him to his room.

In my enthusiasm I had not realized that Ole had been drinking all day. Ole motioned for me to sit on the only chair, and he sat on the bed. I took my cock out for him to look over. I've always been big for my age (then nineteen). I was reasonably well-hung and circumcised at birth. Most of the Swedes went uncut with their ring keeping their foreskins retracted.

Kurt wandered in and saw Ole examining me, and they discussed the placement and procedure. I wasn't afraid of the pain of the piercing, but Ole's breath about knocked me out anyway without any anesthesia. Each time he exhaled I had to hold my breath.

After considerable deliberation and discussion Ole went to his dresser and brought out a tin tobacco box. Out came a medium-sized, curved sail needle threaded with heavy black thread. Kurt held my cock while Ole went at it. I was on cloud nine and shot my wad before Ole actually touched me. I had to excuse myself and get cleaned up before continuing.

The next few minutes were sheer disaster. Ole's hand had the shakes and his vision was blurry. The first point of contact with the needle was a long way from target. There were several misdirected jabs, and I got less and less enthusiastic about the whole idea. Finally Kurt stepped in and offered Ole a beer. Ole gladly accepted and stood aside while Kurt went about the business of piercing my cock. With Kurt's steady hand and expertise, the whole project was neatly finished within a few minutes. There was no great pain, just a steady pressure from inside, and soon the point of the needle was visible, at the perfect place for it. Pushing a little more, the whole needle came through, and Kurt "rattled" it (worked it back and forth) to stretch the newly pierced hole.

After the "rattling" process the needle slipped through easily and brought with it the doubled thread. Kurt made a large loop and knotted the ends. He told me to move the thread from end to end several times a day. The only discomfort was a slight sting when I pissed. It was amazing how quickly the piercing healed. It seemed like it was less than a week.

About ten days after the piercing, and the next chance we had to get into town and visit the jeweler, Kurt went with me and bought the gold ring to fit me. It was a little ring that I wore for many years. It really became a part of me. Since then I've replaced it with a new ring, but there will always be a ring of some sort down there.

In the meantime Kurt modified my rubber urinal. He cut it down to use just the very end of it, just enough to cover the end of my cock. From the inside of the rubber cup he attached a rubber band to hold the head of the cock in the cup with a small hook inside my newly installed ring. It was all very, very, clever and a delightful sensation.

There was no further discomfort. It was a perfect solution to the problem. There is also another happy side to this encounter. I like to fuck as well as the next guy, and on Saturday evenings when we went into town, the girls were very anxious to meet us. The divers had a reputation for being great sex, we fellows with gold rings that tickled. I'd get laid three times a Saturday night without half trying. That gold ring was wild!

Later I learned that such a piercing was called a "Prince Albert" — named after the husband of Queen Victoria. The historians say that Albert wore one to retract his foreskin to keep it from becoming "foul-smelling" when he visited the Queen. True or otherwise, it makes an interesting story.

Before I knew it, it was Labor Day and time to start back to school. My sophomore year was uneventful but academically productive. At college the gold ring was a sensation even though I don't usually show it off. Somehow or other the word got around, and literally dozens of fellows asked me to see it; and I'm sure they were envious. Several asked me for instruction on how to do it, and there must have been some who tried the same thing.

The following summer I got an even better paying diving job. By now I was more experienced, and on Saturday nights I was capable of a least five girls now. The same gold ring was still working wonders.

Around Labor Day I was offered a full scholarship to one of the most prestigious eastern universities. It was the time for a change, and I was ready for a new adventure. My professor, who had gotten me the diving job, suggested that I would be happier as an anthropologist than a marine biologist, and he arranged for the transfer at the eastern university. It's a big jump from a small state university to one of the most sophisticated American universities of the east. Somehow I bridged the gap and was soon accepted.

My roommate, Jake, was a senior, and I was a junior. He kept me from making any big social mistakes, and we got along fine. Sometime during the first semester Jake mentioned a meeting that was going to be held in one of the frat houses with a representative from the Cyprian Society. I agreed to go with Jake who, I should add, was Jewish.

There were about thirty who attended this meeting. The speaker outlined the objectives of the Cyprian Society. It was formed right after World War I to offset the indiscriminate circumcision of male babies who didn't have a choice or a chance to fight back. I hadn't realized there were such strong feelings on this subject, especially among the Jews. They bitterly resented that they had been ceremoniously circumcised, and they were out to change the prevailing attitudes about it. "Okay," I thought, "I'll buy that, but it is too late for me also. If I have sons, I'll give them a choice."

Then the speaker dropped a bombshell. He advocated piercing the sides of the glans of the head of the cock to put in special little studs. These studs would heighten the sexual pleasure by increasing the friction during intercourse and offset the thickened and less sensitive skin of the cockhead, which came with the loss of the foreskin. Was I hearing right? I broke out in a sweat. Could it be real? Yes, it was true, and of the thirty attending, none of them walked out on the suggestion. Me, I'd have unbuttoned my fly on the spot. Later that evening Doctor Rosenthal (a very young M.D., and the representative who spoke) privately showed me his glans piercing and, not to be outdone, I showed him my own piercing. That was a switch! The young doctor creamed his jeans, and I took it in good stride. After all, I had had some previous experience in

such matters, more than he realized.

There were several more meetings. Some guys stopped attending, and some new ones joined. About thirty of us were still signed up. I was the leader, naturally, and first one to sign up for the piercing. Jake signed up also, and we were given an appointment for ten p.m. the following night. Jake was sorry he had ever suggested going to the first meeting, but I wouldn't let him forget it. It was his idea at the start, and I wouldn't let him back down. I was thrilled beyond words. Jake was worried, so I calmed his fears and told him that I'd go first.

The piercing wasn't as painful as some may think. It might be, if it's done slowly, exerting a steady pressure. The "operator" who worked on me was a medical student I had never seen before or after. He was an expert and knew what he was doing and went right ahead with it. The most important part of such a piercing is the placement. To achieve the maximum sensation, the wearer (me, in this case) holds his cock in his hand and rotates it ninety degrees to the right exposing the left side of the shaft. The piercings are done with hollow needles, which have a flattened side like a hypodermic needle without the syringe attachment. The operator selects the exact center of the side of the shaft, then pierces it through the glans edge, at exactly ninety degrees to the edge of the glans, with the needle entering from the bottom groove. The needle is pressured from the surface of the shaft until the needle emerges on the top side. It requires several minutes for it to travel through the spongy material of the glans. Both the left and right side of the glans are done together with the needles forced through at exactly parallel lines of travel so the piercings on each side are at exactly the same angle. Both piercings then result in a matched pair.

Within a few minutes both penetrations were accomplished, and I was none the worse for the wear. I had exactly parallel surgical needles sticking through the sides of my cock, somewhat like a man-size pickle fork.

Jake took it all in and said not one word, probably expecting me to make some outcry, but it was not forthcoming. I thought Jake would be a problem, but he wasn't, and I really didn't give him an alternative. I suggested to the "operator" that we do Jake's next and keep my needles in place before the retainers were installed, but Jake would have none of that. He wanted to see the finished product before any needles touched his skin.

Tiny fourteen-carat wire retainer rings were fitted down inside the hollow needles, and withdrawing the needles pulled the retainers into the piercings. The withdrawal procedure sometimes brings a flow of blood. The operator shakes some alum powder on the holes to stem the flow. Usually the bleeding is of very short duration.

The operator bathed my cock and dusted it with some antiseptic powder and put several layers of gauze around the cock. I put my pants on and watched Jake get his turn. He took it like a man, maybe because I had set a good example. Me, I'd have had it done every day if I'd had the chance because I'm a piercing freak, and I admit it. Total time, for both of us, was about forty minutes.

The piercing usually takes three to four weeks to fully heal. After six to eight days it forms a hard spot around each penetration and becomes somewhat thicker than normal but never particularly painful.

The operator said, "After the piercing, forget it for a month. However be sure to bathe it daily and dust it with antiseptic powder."

Within three to four weeks the lumps slowly dissolved, and when the area of the glans was normal again it was time to think about some kind of studs. Doctor Rosenthal had some gold studs with solid screw ends, available in various lengths to fit the individuals. Both ends were the same diameter and really very handsome. At this writing it's years since this happened, and I still treasure those little gold Dydoes (as they are called by aficionados of the art of piercing.) I've removed them many times but always put them back where they belong. As someone once said of them, they are my "constant companions, and always give that added sensation, a little something extra in my sex life, that delicious little something for the man who had everything." A pair of Dydoes will heighten the sensation and increase your pleasure.

During my senior year in college there were several meetings of the Cyprian Society. I was very involved and did some of the lecture meetings. Also I developed a skillful hand for the little operation, of which I performed quite a few.

I graduated just before the outbreak of World War II, and our age group was one of the first to be called up. The Cyprian Society got lost in the shuffle. It was too difficult to maintain contact. Several years after the end of the war I tried to track down Dr. Horowitz of New York City who was the major spokesman of the Society. I discovered he had died of a heart attack a year before. I met the widow and she gave me a box of old meeting records and correspondence, which made fascinating reading. Maybe we should rejuvenate the Cyprian Society and start it functioning again. It served a good purpose, especially for me.

For my graduation present my aunt gave me a gift of cash. I went to Hawaii as a beach bum. In those days, just before Pearl Harbor, we beach bums wore knit wool swim trunks, rather tight-fitting. If you rub your palms down your hips, the knit swim trunks roll up and, with one motion, expose as much of your body as you wish to display — your navel or further, depending on what you had in mind. One of my beach bum friends, Moki, was the first person I'd ever seen with a navel piercing. Wow, that was a whole new dimension in the scheme of sexual attractions.

My two previous piercing encounters were for useful purposes, but this one was strictly advertising. It let the opposite sex know you were interested and man, how it worked! Rolling down your trunks was like pulling down her panties! Many beach bums wore these navel piercings. Tattooing was also part of the required image to be accepted socially, even with the girls.

When I had a little cash windfall I went into a tattoo parlor and asked the prices at the best-known establishment in Honolulu. I was shocked at how much it cost for a modest size design, too rich for my blood. One of my beach bum friends had a mail-order tattooing machine. It was in constant use, but the quality of work was awful. If I got a tattoo, at least it would be artistically acceptable. I couldn't see getting one of those tattoos, and I couldn't afford the good ones. Unfortunately I never had gotten one. Moki did take me to a Chinese jewelry shop on River Street where they got their navel piercings, however.

A navel piercing is quick and easy if your navel is formed that way, so you can get behind, at, or into the opening. Some people cannot be pierced there because there is no real opening. After a little Chinese negotiation we agreed on a complete navel piercing job for $2.50, and I laid the cash on the counter. I looked around for a "back room with a curtain", but there was none, so I stood there at the end of the counter. The little Chinese merchant squatted down on a small stool and with a very dull, old-fashioned straight razor, scraped off the hairs from my belly, without benefit of shaving cream or lather. He then took a length of straight gold wire and filed it to a fine point. He put his left little finger up into my navel opening and found the center spot and slowly pushed the pointed wire through the fleshy overhang. Soon he felt the point touching his finger. With a pair of fine jewelers' pliers he fashioned a nice little gold ring just the right scale for my belly button. It was all done in about ten to fifteen minutes and at very little cost. It was sore for a few days, but the salt water was a natural cleansing agent.

That was my third piercing encounter, not as thrilling to me as the earlier ones, and not nearly as sexually stimulating. The navel piercing is not really related to the sex equipment, just sort of window dressing for other things to happen, sort of a prelude to the big act. I got good mileage from my navel piercing and, there in Hawaii, it was one of the sex symbols, sort of an unspoken indication of your intentions without having to blurt it out loud.

After V-E Day, I went back into anthropology to work at a

Ph.D. The subject I selected (naturally) was "male initiation rites in Borneo" which gave me a wonderful opportunity for further study of piercings. In those parts of the world I saw some amazing and somewhat terrifying "mutilations." Even I had to have a strong stomach for some of it.

On my return from Borneo and New Guinea, I stopped off in Tahiti to compile the data I had collected. It was there that I met Reggie Jones, a delightful soul who greatly enriched my life. Reggie, an Australian, was a seaman on tramp steamers in the copra trade when he was young. Reggie had jumped ship and stayed in Tahiti. He married a native girl, and they had seven sons. When I knew him he was sixty, and I was thirty. Reggie taught me about Tahitian sex lore. The natives wear a pareo, a square of cotton fabric draped around their hips and never in such a way to bind or constrict the genital area. They wear no cloth between the legs since it would prevent the cooling breezes needed for comfort.

Many males at the age of twelve to fourteen pierce the thin web of skin behind the balls and halfway between the legs, sort of an equidistant triangle seen from the floor looking up. The hole is usually large enough for a pencil, and the purpose is to hang a leather thong through it. Hanging on the thong is a shell or rock, or anything heavy enough to dangle from a three or four-inch thong. Even a lead sinker did very well in a pinch. The French colonists called this unique piercing a Guiche (pronounced "geesh") meaning "opening in something."

When Reggie told me this, I started panting. Here we go again! Reggie showed me his adornment. I had to have one to "keep up with the Joneses." The following day after our night of fishing, we went into the Chinese general store, and Reggie bought a ring for me. That afternoon Reggie looked me over and was amazed at my other piercings.

Then he showed me where the guiche would be most practical for my purpose. I slipped off my pareo, leaned over, hands on thighs, and Reggie, from the rear, did the honors. He placed the ring in its proper placement and just squeezed it gently but firmly. So quick and easy, no aftercare, no real preparation for its installation.

Today my guiche piercing is permanently placed and the bangle removed if not being used. It's not pencil size but a modest ⅝" interlocking ring. I never remove my guiche ring because it never interferes with tight underwear. One of the real pleasures of life is a guiche if you're able to wear the tropical clothing for which it is intended. Walking the bangle bangs against my balls and legs and gives me an added delight, a constant reminder that I'm a fully developed, sexually adequate man.

In the course of the years I've been involved in some exciting experiments. Once in Florida we decided to extend my

original through-the-end "Prince Albert" to connect it at the same angle to a hole coming out the top of the cockhead. The trans-piercing was no problem and healed soon, but it was never a pleasure to wear a stud or a ring through it. There was a constant irritation so the piercing was abandoned. However, it is still "on call" if wanted for later action.

Early in the game I had my nipples pierced, but the chap who did it was inexperienced and nervous. His work was sloppy, one ring slanted to the left, ant the other cocked to the right. The following day when I looked in the mirror I removed them and never had them re-pierced. I admire these men with big round, fully developed nipples, but mine were such little pimples that I really had little to work with. Some men want their piercings at the base, the surface next to the nipple shield, while others want it at the center, midway between the tip and the shield. To each his own, I've seen them both ways, including top to bottom variations. Usually a piercing buff wants his nipples pierced as a starter, right after his left ear is pierced, but most beginners are inexperienced, and today I see the bad result of many impulsive piercings.

It seems so simple and easy to poke a hole in the side of the scrotum, but to what purpose? Yes, you can hang an earring there, but what will that gain you? The hole will spread and heal eventually, but it will be no real pleasure sexually. Scrotum piercing can be done by real experts who know their trade. But be sure that's what you really want.

In closing, once a piercing freak, always a piercing freak. I pity the poor lonesome sonofabitch who locks himself in his closet. He is missing so much. Piercing can be a real joy to do and have done by another who appreciates it. The loners are short-changing themselves. Under the right conditions, piercing is one of the greatest of the indoor sports.

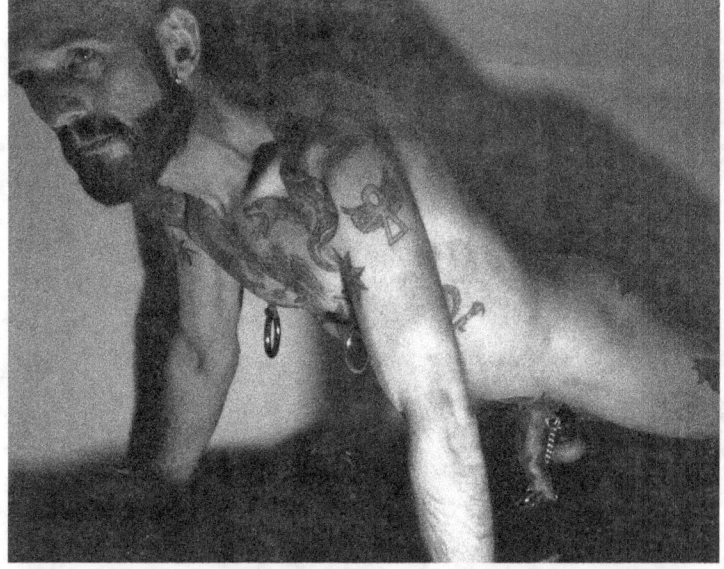

Many of the images in *Pierced Penises* were of Alan Oversby better known as Mr. Sebastian. This one is typical.

The Versatile & Sensual Prince Albert

This article originally appeared in PFIQ issue #6 dating from early 1979, several months prior to Doug's death, and was reprinted in issue #42 (1994). No evidence has ever been presented to substantiate any of Doug's claims, but the piece is filled with the colorful storytelling so characteristic of the man.

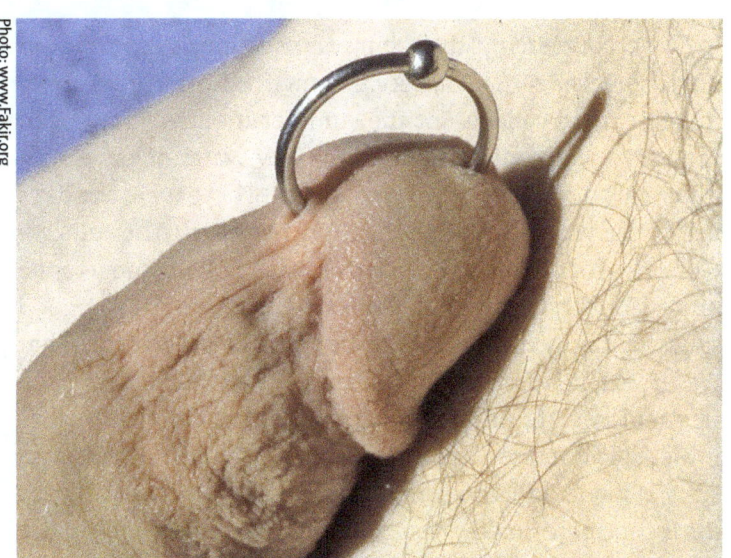

The most functional penile attachment was named after Queen Victoria's consort, Albert. Known for his manliness and concern for his queen, he was an ambitious man, handsome and fecund, who would do anything for his monarch.

Born in 1819, he wooed Victoria and married her in 1840 when he was 21 years old. They produced eight children, most of whom became attached to the royal houses of Europe. Albert was literally a maker of kings. The marriage of Victoria and Albert endured until his death in 1861.

From all indications, Albert was greatly influenced and was a great admirer of Beau Brummell, a gay, effete bachelor of the previous generation. They were not contemporaries and there is no evidence the two ever met, yet Brummell appears to have been the instigator of the piercing which bears Albert's name. Between approximately 1815 and 1820, Beau Brummell reigned supreme in style-conscious circles. Though a man without visible funds, he circulated through the social world of his day displaying the wares of and dropping the name of his probable patron and benefactor, Jonathan Barlow, one of London's leading haberdashers.

Fashion of the period dictated very tight trousers for men. They were usually buff-colored, crotch binding, and often had straps that went under the instep to keep them taut and foldless. Propriety allowed only a vague outline of the manly endowments to be displayed. To achieve this diminution, a dress accessory called a haberdasher's or dressing ring was worn in a piercing through the underside of the urethra, just behind the penis head. Using this ring the penis could be held securely against the upper leg, left or right, depending on the gentleman's preference. Trousers were fitted accordingly and were made without pockets and usually opened on the side. Needless to say, urination presented something of a problem, all for the sake of vanity.

While no concrete evidence exists to substantiate the rumor, Prince Albert is reputed to have bowed to the dictates of fashion embodied by Beau Brummell by having a dressing ring installed. This was probably done c. 1842-3 when he was 25 years old. Soon, of course, the social grapevine was buzzing with the news. Some of the gossip magazines of the day proclaimed Albert's acquisition, and soon London's haberdashers were urging their customers to follow suit. The young dandies and social climbers seem to have lost little time in

doing so. It was an era of extremes in styles for both men and women. Tight, constricting clothes were all the rage. The even tighter peg-top style trousers came into favor. Before long these fashions reached New York, complete with dressing ring, and remained popular until the outbreak of the Civil War. In time the tight-fitting trousers gave way to looser styles and the need for the dressing ring ceased.

But life is cyclic, and something as functional as the Prince Albert rarely dies out completely. In time, it may assume other functions, thus enjoying a revival. Until fairly recently within the Soviet Union, it was not acceptable for a male ballet dancer to display his genitals by even so much as a slight bulge in his tights. The male performer was considered sexless or at most androgynous. I have it on good authority that for perhaps the last 25-30 years male ballet dancers, in much the same way as our Victorian predecessors did, used the equivalent of a Prince Albert to bind the penis to the leg so as to render it invisible. Study the pictures of Nijinsky and you will note no visible evidence of genitalia. A Prince Albert held them securely in place, but it did not inhibit his fantastic leaps.

Dancers have found other interesting uses for the versatile Prince Albert. During the days of vaudeville there was a scandalous nude revue that shocked Paris and every town it played in America. It was originally called "Elysian Fields" (the name was later changed) and toured many burlesque houses throughout the States. Each town where it appeared imposed its own variety of censorship, often forcing the dancers to perform behind a scrim. The ballerinas wore angel wings, the men only fig leaves held firmly in place despite vigorous dancing, leaps and jetés by a Prince Albert. At the climax of the piece, a clever disconnect mechanism allowed the leaves to fall, revealing the "Greek gods," emancipated and free, as the curtain fell on a classic pose.

The versatile Prince Albert was my own point of entry into

the world of piercing, though it was used for a very different purpose. I was nineteen, between my freshman and sophomore years of college. For the summer months, I had been chosen to work with a team of shallow water divers examining harbor pilings for marine worms. These were the days before the wet suits used by scuba divers today. The suits we wore were of rubber and rubberized canvas. Being new to the profession, I had some problems to solve. I was paid a good salary, but only for the time I was actually underwater. That was fine, but I discovered that being underwater produces a frequent need to urinate. If I got out of the water to relieve myself, I lost money, and one didn't dare foul those old-style suits. What to do? I tried one of those rubber urinals designed for incontinent male invalids, but it chafed terribly. Finally, in desperation I asked one of the regular divers (they were all Swedes) what their secret was. They, too, used the male urinal, but with a difference. Instead of holding the device in place by means of straps, it was attached to a small ring worn in a piercing on the underside of the cock head. Not wanting to be left out, I was most anxious to acquire one of these rings. I soon discovered that not only was it functional for my diving work, but that it provided a wonderful sensation as well. It was several years later when I was a graduate student that I finally discovered the name of this delightful genital attachment: the Prince Albert.

Shortly after World War II I discovered another interesting use for this versatile piercing. A doctor friend who was an orthopedist working within the athletic world made the revelation. It is well-known that many body builders have been tragically under endowed in the cock department and often pose wearing a codpiece to give the illusion of abundant genital development. Try as they might, no amount of physical training could fully compensate for their lack. One bodybuilder and Mr. Universe titlist decided to do something about his own inadequacy in this department.

The tissue through which the Prince Albert passes is rather insensitive. While this tissue is also tough, piercing it is usually a fairly simple process, especially with proper equipment, and not especially painful. After healing, the piercing itself can sustain pulling a weight without pain or tearing. Under constant moderate tension, some types of tissue will lengthen in an effort to relieve that pressure. This is seen most dramatically in the neck elongation, ear lobe and lip stretching of certain primitive cultures. The same principle can be and has been used to lengthen the penis. Our Mr. Universe started with a Prince Albert. An elastic band similar to a garter was attached at one end to the ring in the piercing and at the other to his upper leg, exerting constant tension on the penis. Over a period of time, there was a permanent increase in the length of this organ. I have personally seen examples where under-endowed men have gained 1½" of length in this manner.

In India, some of the mendicant fakirs, using a slightly different method, have successfully stretched the penis to lengths of two and three feet, though at this extreme the organ becomes very thin and ceases to be functional. These individuals wind the cock around their waists and will display themselves in an effort to solicit alms. Be that as it may, moderate stretching can provide not only greater endowment, but greater confidence as well. Kept within moderation, the procedure will not affect the man's ability to achieve erection.

This is one therapeutic application of the Prince Albert; there are others. Some years ago, while visiting the Mediterranean, I was pleased to discover my old friend the Prince Albert being worn by the fishermen of southern Italy. An Italian friend who is a medical doctor informed me that in fact it is not uncommon among this group. The reason for this device, he told me, is an almost universal delight among Italian males in the fondling of one's penis, from which practice they seem to derive assurance and confidence. While no evidence exists that the Italian dictator Benito Mussolini had a Prince Albert, newsreel footage exists showing Il Duce fondling his cock through a hole in his pants pocket, a practice he indulged in to gain confidence, particularly when the need to make a decision arose.

Other therapeutic uses for the Prince Albert are still in the experimental stage. It has been suggested and some initial research indicates that this ring can be used as a point of mental focus, alone or with hypnosis, to overcome obesity. Attached by means of a chain or string to the pants pocket, the Prince Albert can be tugged or fondled at times when the obese individual craves food. In this way his mind can be diverted away from his hunger. While my research in this area is still scant, I hope in the future to extend it.

Ultimately, of course, the Prince Albert is for sex. It doesn't matter which kind, hetero or homo; the mechanical stimulation it provides can be greatly rewarding to both partners. Those who have never tried this particular device might do well to consider it. Unlike a tattoo, a piercing need not be with you always. The ring can be removed for a period of time, then later reinserted. Also, men who suffer from impotence or lack of penis sensitivity often report an improvement in sexual function after the installation of a Prince Albert.

In conclusion, I encourage my readers to ponder this delightful invention. If you lack a Prince Albert, consider one. If you have one already, try fondling it the next time you have to make a difficult decision or if you are trying to lose weight and need to divert you attention from food. Regardless of how you use it, enjoy it. If you let it, it can give you a lifetime of pleasure.

Body Piercing in Brief

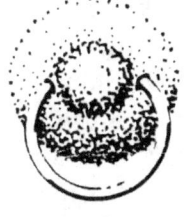
Nipple

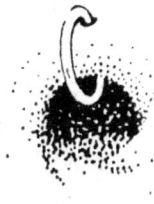
Navel

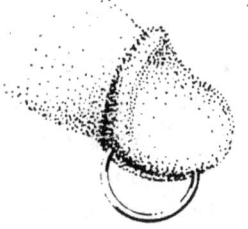
Prince Albert

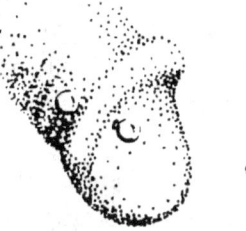
Dydoe

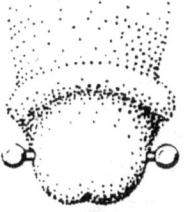
Ampallang

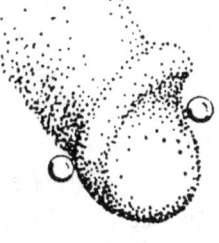
Apadravya

The following is the complete text of the original "Piercing Brief" (1976) with minor edits. By the early '90s the document was clearly out-of-date and was subsequently revised to reflect what we had learned after more than a decade of experience. The revision also mentioned several newer piercings including the clit hood, tongue, eyebrow, and labret.

The set of illustrations I created for the first version were too crude for my taste and replaced by those used here.

Piercing of the body, for a variety of reasons, is an ancient, if not always venerable, art. For many years an underground phenomenon, it is at last emerging into the light.

Piercing of the nipples is not really new. The proud Roman Centurions, Caesar's bodyguard, wore nipple rings as a sign of their virility and courage, and as a dress accessory for holding their short capes. The practice was also quite common among society girls of the Victorian era to enhance the size and shape of the nipples. Today, the lure of piercing is primarily a sexual one. It provides a mechanical "titillation" achieved by no other means. For many, especially the men and women into the bondage and discipline, and S & M scenes, there is a tremendous psychological turn-on. Where possible, piercing should be professionally done as placement determines the nipple's development, shape, and aesthetic effect. While difficult to obtain unless one knows a sympathetic doctor, anesthetics are available for the faint-of-heart. Healing normally takes six to eight weeks and is quickest where a retainer with straight post is used.

Navel piercing, a sign of royalty to the ancient Egyptians, was something denied commoners. Hence, a deep navel was highly prized. But times change. Today this piercing is becoming increasingly popular especially with young swingers of the "in" set, male and female. Possible only to those with a well-shaped navel, the piercing is usually done through the little flap of skin above the opening and retained with a ring during healing, usually four to six weeks. Later the ring may be replaced by a decorative stud or bangle selected to suit the wearer's fancy. While not a sexually functional piercing, the visual effect is sensual and directs the viewer's attention to the pelvic area.

The Prince Albert, called a "dressing ring" by Victorian haberdashers, was originally used to firmly secure the male genitalia in either the left or right pant leg during that era's craze tor extremely tight, crotch-binding trousers, thus minimizing a man's natural endowment. Legend has it that Prince Albert wore such a ring to retract his foreskin and thus keep his member sweet-smelling so as not to offend the Queen. Today its function is strictly erotic, providing the ultimate in sexual pleasure to men of both persuasions. Piercing is through the urethra at the base of the penis head. The procedure is quick; the pain, minimal; the healing, rapid; and the pleasure, lifelong.

The use of dydoes seems to be of fairly recent origin. As they return much of the sensation lost with the foreskin, their emergence corresponds with the widespread practice of circumcision. Nor does the man alone benefit. During intercourse his dydoes provide delightful vaginal stimulation for his consort. The flagging sexual interest in many relationships has been revived with the use of these devices. Piercing is done through both sides of the upper edge of the glans. As proper placement is imperative, piercing should be done professionally. Small barbell studs, rings, "D" rings, or clamps may be inserted according to the wearer's preference. While healing usually takes four to six weeks, abstinence during this period is not necessary.

The ampallang, relatively unknown to the Western world but gaining foothold, is indigenous to the areas surrounding the Indian Ocean. Though sometimes done in childhood, the piercing is usually done as part of a puberty rite, the service being performed by an old woman who places the ampallang horizontally through the center of the head of the penis above the urethra. A metal bar retained with metal discs may be used or studs of bone, ivory, or even gold, if the man is well-to-do. This sexual device greatly enhances the sensual pleasure of both partners. Many women may deny intercourse to a man not so pierced, or specify the size ampallang he should wear if he is.

As described in the Kama Sutra, the ancient classic Hindu treatise on love and social conduct, the apadravya is any one of a number of devices (antique "French ticklers" and/or dildoes, if you will) used during intercourse to excite the woman. Among the Dravidian people of southern India, the word also refers to the device worn through the pierced male member. The piercing is generally vertical through the penis shaft behind the head, but sometimes in the head itself. It should be noted that this piercing is neither common nor widespread.

Piercing of the frenum, the loose piece of flesh beneath the penis head, is of European origin, having served, strange to say, the extremes of both chastity and sexual stimulation. A padlock through the frenum will prevent copulation. A special chastity device called a Franey cage, secured at one end through the frenum and at the other through a second piercing at the base of the penis, prevents even masturbation. By contrast, a ring which passes through the piercing and encircles the head, fitting snuggly but comfortably in the groove around the glans when the penis is flaccid, can be extremely erotic, acting to increase erection, much like a cock ring. Many men find it calming to sleep with the ring flipped down over the middle finger. Ring size is important, measurement being readily obtained using a draftsman's circle template. Piercing is quick and simple, and healing rapidly.

It is a proud day in the life of an Arab youth when he achieves manhood. A stag party "rite of passage" is arranged by his male relatives and friends, and one of his gifts will be a silver stud or perhaps a ring or clasp. At a ceremonial piercing, this will be inserted through the left side of the scrotum between the testicle and the base of the penis. Believed to prevent the testes from ever returning to the groin from whence they descended in childhood, the hafada, as it is called, gives visual evidence that the youth is now and forever a man. Wealthy Arabs eventually install hafadas set with precious stones, the most highly prized (at least in the Persian Gulf area) being the Kuwait pearl. French Foreign Legionnaires have returned from North Africa wearing this genital adornment, usually only on the left side, but occasionally on both. Piercing is quick and not particularly painful, although the healing period is somewhat prolonged. While not the most erotic of piercings, it does provide some stimulation when stroked.

Even today the guiche (pronounced "geesh") is very common among the male natives of the South Pacific. The piercing is done, usually at puberty, through the raphe perinei, the ridge of skin between the scrotum and the anus, at what would be the inseam. A knife point is used to make the hole, more accurately a tiny slit, and a rawhide thong is place in it. Less primitive individuals who have adopted this highly sensual device use more conventional piercing tools with ring or stud retainers. Either way, when healing is complete (usually six to eight weeks), a bangle is attached which enhances sensation and provides a convenient grip. The guiche is one of the more erotic piercings and Westerners can benefit from its adoption. Light pressure applied to the piercing greatly increases arousal and gentle tugging on the bangle at climax prolongs and intensifies orgasm. Anyone desiring this piercing is advised to consult an experienced piercer as placement is of great importance.

While piercing is primarily done for erotic reasons, it has often been used to prohibit sexual indulgence—though to those of the bondage and discipline persuasion, even such restraint is doubtless erotic. When used for purposes of chastity it is commonly called infibulation, and both men and women have been its victims. Ancient Roman male slaves were often subjected to the practice, some form of device being locked through the perforated foreskin. With women the device was inserted through the labia. Though both piercings are not uncommon today, they less often imply chastity. In Europe the genital ring is vying with the finger ring as the symbol of betrothal. The man has his fiancée's labia pierced and ringed; and she, his frenum, usually at the same appointment. Through their mutual pain a more intense commitment has been made. It should be mentioned in passing that piercing of the clitoris, while rarely seen, is also being done by some women who are very much into the scene. Though not particularly functional in a sexual sense, it is an eye-catching place to display ornaments. As with most piercings, those considering any such "needlework" are advised to consult an experienced piercer.

Mr. Malloy is a piercing master with many years experience. He is the author of many articles and a book on the subject, and is currently working on a comprehensive study of his consuming passion.

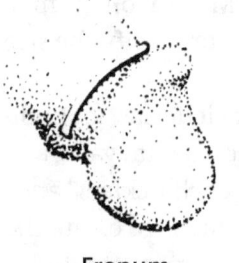

Frenum

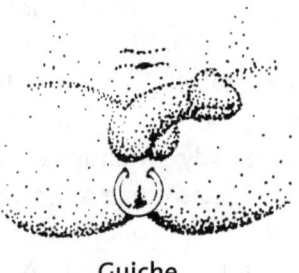

Hafada

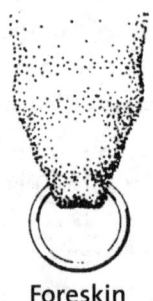

Guiche

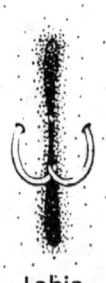

Foreskin

Labia

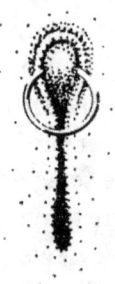

Clitoris

INDEX